The Gillingham Manual

Remedial Training for Students
with Specific Disability in
Reading, Spelling, and Penmanship

Anna Gillingham
Bessie W. Stillman

EDUCATORS PUBLISHING SERVICE
Cambridge and Toronto

PRINTING HISTORY OF THE MANUAL

1936 Light brown
1940 Light brown, 3rd edition
1946 Blue, 4th edition (in two parts)
1956 Red, 5th edition
1960 Green, 6th and 7th editions
1997 Green, 8th edition

Eighth Edition, Revised

Printed in Westford, MA, in August 2015
ISBN 978-0-8388-0200-7

18 19 RRD 16 15

Contents

Preface to This Edition

As in the 1960 revision, this edition was undertaken to bring the manual into agreement with a current dictionary; in this case, the tenth edition of *Merriam-Webster's Collegiate Dictionary*. However, as work progressed it became apparent that Anna Gillingham and Bessie Stillman's work should be updated and brought into the upcoming twenty-first century.

It is no longer possible for the remedial student to "do no reading or spelling except with the remedial teacher" (seventh edition, page 42). Teachers must devise new ways to keep students from falling farther and farther behind in learning content while they are being tutored to reach their potential. Time and research have resulted in more up-to-date ways of meeting the needs of specific-language-disabled students. Computers are now one of our greatest assets; we must be open to their usefulness.

We have made various changes in the order of presentation. While the original Gillingham Manual used male pronouns to refer to students and female pronouns to refer to teachers, this revised 1997 edition uses both pronouns for students and teachers. Some key words have been changed to make them more concrete and make the initial sounds easier to produce in isolation. After many requests, we have added pictures to the phonics drill cards, though we have retained the originals for use with older students and adults. In some cases, we have changed the book's original language to make the content easier to understand. New formatting emphasizes specific information and makes the text more readable. A Chapter Overview outlines each chapter. The expanded Appendix includes sample lessons, activity sheets, and letter-formation charts.

In addition, there are many supplementary materials that teachers have found useful. Since a list of such materials in this book would soon be outdated, we have prepared a separate flier that can be ordered from Educators Publishing Service, Inc. It lists books, workbooks, games, and computer software for use in teaching concepts such as word attack, reading, spelling, dictionary skills, and handwriting. Though most of the materials are published by Educators Publishing Service, other publishers are represented as well. To order the list, call or write EPS at the number or address listed on the copyright page, and ask for the Gillingham Supplementary Materials List.

We stress that in *no* way have any basic principles, philosophies, or techniques been changed. It is still the same multisensory, alphabetic, structured approach to language that we have always used. For more than fifty years, language-disabled students have found that they can learn to read, spell, and write using this approach. Why would we change it?

We have been helped in many ways by many people—Charlotte Chamberlain, Jean Foss, Alice Garside, Eleanor Thurston Hall, Alice Koontz, Marcia Mann, Phyllis Meisel, Carol Murray, Margaret Rawson, Dorothy Whitehead, and Angela Wilkins—to name only a few. Special thanks go to Diana Hanbury King for her assistance with the history of language section and the handwriting chapter. Everyone's advice, support, and openness to change have contributed not only to the revision of this manual, but also to the continuation of Samuel Orton, Anna Gillingham, and Bessie Stillman's work. And finally, Robert Hall saw to it that this book remained actively in use. A man who spent much of his life helping and giving to others, his inspiration, vision, leadership, and humor touched many lives. The revision of this book is dedicated to his memory, and to the memory of Samuel Orton, Anna Gillingham, and Bessie Stillman.

Melany Appelle
Vanessa Banyas
Kay Goranson

Preface

My two years as Research Associate in the study of the Language Function with the late Samuel T. Orton, M.D. have become one of the outstanding experiences of my life. Contact with his thorough knowledge of neurology, always checked by scientific caution, set a criterion for evaluation of my own procedures never to be forgotten.

His charge to me to organize remedial techniques consistent with his working hypothesis has steadily enlarged in scope until it has become the consummation of my lifelong service to children.

The few pages of my first contribution, enlarged and revised five times, have grown into this Manual.

I was soon joined in this work by my friend, Bessie W. Stillman. A classroom teacher and devoted lover of children, she had spent hours of patient effort in attempting to help those with apparently insuperable difficulty in reading and spelling, only to realize sadly the futility of her ineffectual labor.

Dr. Orton's exposition came to her as a revelation. She soon far outstripped me in recognizing topics to be presented and in methods of presentation, so that by the time the 1946 edition was ready, a large part of the text was hers. Her thoroughness and scholarly research have called forth from many qualified persons the statement that my carrying on of our work since her death in 1947 is in the nature of a memorial to her. Her devotion to accuracy never flagged even when her failing strength limited her work to a few brief hours each day. Chapters IV through IX of the 1946 and 1956 editions are largely hers and in such respect do I hold them that I should feel incapable of making any essential changes.

In all my work since she left me, I have felt sadly the need of her help. However, as the years have passed, other helpers have appeared—teachers using the procedures described in this Manual. Among them one is outstanding for her experience, her skill, and her grasp of essential principles. When it becomes necessary for me to lay down the work which for many years has meant so much to me it is my earnest hope that it will be carried on by Sally B. Childs.

No less helpful than the practical suggestions of these teachers have been their many assurances of the happiness they felt on finding themselves able to change the attitude of frustrated and discouraged children to one of self-confident success by the application of the techniques developed in this volume. It is to such children as these that the Sixth Edition was in spirit dedicated.

I wish here to express my thanks to my neighbor, Suzanne K. Orr, for her unique assistance. Her tireless zeal for perfection carried her through innumerable hours of manuscript preparation and proof reading.

The Sixth Edition was undertaken solely to bring the Manual into conformity with the new system of pronunciation symbols employed in the 1956 edition of *Webster's Elementary Dictionary* and the 1959 edition of *Webster's New Secondary School Dictionary*, both copyrighted by G. & C. Merriam Co.

However, as the revision proceeded, certain other alterations seemed advisable, the most conspicuous being the introduction of a new chapter dealing with Remedial Procedures for Older Pupils. Simple as these alterations appear, their completion proved an arduous task. This could not have been accomplished without the patient labor of my friend, the late Paul Dozier, M.D. Closely as he had followed my work since we were Research Associates together under Dr. Orton, he understood the changes necessary at this time as no one else could have understood them. It is fitting that I here express my sincere appreciation and gratitude for his unfailing help.

Bronxville, New York   Anna Gillingham
            1960

Preliminary Considerations

CHAPTER OVERVIEW

This chapter contains case histories of children who have various specific language differences that make the acquisition of written language more difficult. Also included is an informative and concise outline of the historical development of written language.

Throughout this book, /slash marks/ are used to indicate the sound of a letter or group of letters.

Supplementary Materials

- Additional sources on the history of language (see Appendix for a list)
- World map

THE CHALLENGE

Many children and adults have difficulty learning to read and spell. Research indicates that children with lower intellectual ability tend to be poor readers, and too often, people assume that any poor reader has a relatively low mentality. When it is discovered that a child of average or high intelligence is not reading, the first reaction is usually reproach—of the child for lack of effort, of the preceding teacher for inefficiency. Thus, the college blames the high school for its poor readers, the high school the grammar school, and at last, reproach falls back on the unfortunate primary teacher or parent.

Increasingly, conscientious and discerning teachers and anxious parents are realizing that there are intelligent nonreaders who try very hard, and that such children present a challenge that conventional training does not enable the teacher to meet.

The following student profiles exemplify the types of challenges that educators encounter as they work to meet the educational needs of their students. No attempt will be made to present them uniformly as in clinical case studies. They are, rather, chapters out of children's lives, all with special points of their own.

Most of the following case histories were compiled prior to 1945. Increasing awareness of students' needs has led to better diagnostic tools and programs to provide the appropriate support and remediation. We are now aware that a great many intelligent and accomplished people struggle in school. We also know that as adults, they may excel in fields such as architecture, mathematics, engineering, science, medicine, entertainment, and even writing. As we help students to improve their reading and writing skills, we must also encourage them to continue improving and succeeding in the areas in which they already show talent. We all come into the world with our own unique gifts.

Robert

Robert was a pleasant and well-mannered ten-year-old boy who became hesitant and evasive when reading was mentioned.

He began his education in a school where students attempted reading early in the first grade. Although outstanding in his grasp of situations and management of class affairs, he had not advanced in reading, either in the first or second year. In the third grade, his mother had been asked to help, but the task was so baffling that she confessed she had lost patience and scolded the boy for his carelessness. During the year he was placed in a small school for children with behavioral difficulties. His new teacher had had exceptional training, especially in the area of reading difficulties. She believed in extensive use of phonics and had given Robert the sounds of most of the letters. But he had no clear visual image of the individual letters, and he seldom remembered which sounds belonged with which letter. He memorized a few primers, but the teacher was wise and honest enough to realize after several months that under her guidance he was not learning to read. She asked that he be taken to a specialist for in-depth testing.

Tests showed that his IQ was 125. Although he preferred his right hand, he could write very well with the left. Also, he frequently made letters in mirrored form quite unconsciously. His expression when asked to read was so strained that the examiner was convinced that there was some deep-seated emotional cause. Since after considerable investigation she was unable to discover any, she suggested consulting an ophthalmologist: "He reads words from the wrong end, and perhaps he sees them wrong."

The ophthalmologist, who was particularly interested in reading difficulties, sent the child to a reading specialist with the diagnosis: "Vision normal. Muscle balance normal. Emotional condition almost certainly augmented if not caused by the failure and discouragement resulting from his reading difficulty." He reported a history of mirror-writing and ambidexterity on both sides of the family.

Robert could not score at all on an oral reading test. He was much too slow and made too many errors. He read *saw* as *was* and several times started to read a sentence at the wrong end. He could not recognize little words such as *an, at, or, did, may, out, son*, etc. Asked to read *wolf*, he read *flow*; asked to read *forget*, he read *tegrof*; asked to read *careful*, he read *fulcare*.

Long daily remedial lessons transformed Robert's attitude, and his progress was delightful to watch. However, at the end of about half a year, his mother decided that, since there was nothing abnormal about him and he could learn so well, he might after all better apply himself to work in a regular class and save her the expense. The hours of what one remedial teacher calls "passive sitting" began again, and when last heard from, he was hopelessly watching the stream of bewildering events drift past him.

In this case, neither Robert nor his mother fully understood what the remedial lessons were providing for him. Nor did they understand that he was not lazy or unmotivated, given his superior intellectual ability. Rather, his learning difference stemmed from a neurological dysfunction.

When the appropriate teaching method was provided, Robert was given a structure for learning, and he began to succeed. However, when this teaching was removed, his handicapping condition returned because he had not been given ample time to internalize and apply these techniques on his own.

Today, as students are integrated into the mainstream, they are better equipped to meet the academic challenges while they are still supported by appropriate modifications and accommodations. In addition, many regular classroom teachers and special educators work together as a team to meet the ever-changing needs of *all* their students.

Sarah

When Sarah entered school, she still used "baby talk" and was left-handed. She did not demonstrate typical errors of poorly formed letters and reversals when she wrote. Yet after three years of hard work, Sarah, whose IQ was 116, was nearly a complete nonreader. Her attempts to express her ideas often yielded mispronunciations so extreme that she was sent for a hearing exam. This exam revealed no deafness in any range. Nevertheless, she could not distinguish or reproduce many speech sounds.

> For example:
> - In trying to echo words she gave back \b\, \p\, \d\, \t\ interchangeably.
> - Plurals and other \s\ sounds were completely absent from her speech.

For a long time after training began she could not initiate the vowel sounds when she looked at a word; for example, looking at *big* she knew that it meant *large*, but was uncertain whether to say *beg* or *big*. Later, four- and five-letter words caused great confusion. For example, by studying *lamp* carefully she could learn to spell it, l-a-m-p, but when asked to pronounce it she might say *plam* or *malp* and then spell it so, or even with other letters inserted if the word were dictated. Acquisition of vocabulary from listening to speech around her was slow, and her misapplication of common words truly astonishing. One day, after she was reading well enough to understand a fair amount from seventh grade social studies, she read a statement about conditions as they were "formerly." She thought this meant "formally," a place where it was not required to dress up much!

A large part of Sarah's training consisted of careful repetition of sounds made by the teacher, and forming associations between seen symbols and their sounds, between heard symbolic sounds and their appearance in print, and between heard symbolic sounds and the sensation in her hand as she wrote the corresponding letters. She had technical remedial training for four years, and her English lessons were conducted largely individually for several years thereafter. She went on to graduate from high school and college.

The next two cases show interesting reversals in material other than words, and can in no sense be regarded as tragedies. The casual reader may even find them amusing. Each boy had had difficulties, but none greater than he could overcome with the satisfaction of hard work rewarded. However, the drawings reproduced below caused the teachers some annoyance, the boys considerable embarrassment, and both teachers and boys complete amazement.

Miguel

Background information about Miguel's family revealed an interesting pattern. His sister had such extreme difficulty with reading that she had to leave school and be tutored. His father could barely write a legible line because the letters went backwards or proceeded in no reliable order. His extensive correspondence and the papers he occasionally read before business organizations were all dictated to his secretary. He was almost perfectly ambidextrous. There were several left-handed relatives, including Miguel's academically successful brother.

Miguel, right-handed, IQ 111, had some early difficulty with reading and was a poor speller. At the time of this incident he was in high school, and was being tutored in French and Latin. While always a weak student, he ultimately graduated and went to college.

One day in science class the teacher demonstrated with apparatus arranged somewhat like this:

The class was to draw the apparatus from memory and explain the process. Miguel's exposition was one of the clearest in the class, but his drawing showed:

Steve

Steve, left-handed, had some trouble in beginning reading. He was given individual training for a few months in the third grade. He responded quickly and became a fair reader and a passable speller. He passed from grade to grade doing average work in a school of high standards. In the eighth grade, when his attention was too closely occupied with content to observe what his hand was doing, he produced the following freehand map from memory for a social studies test.

Adam

Adam's parents were intrigued by their son's early ability to construct intricate structures with blocks, milk cartons, and other materials. He was artistically talented as well as very verbal. They were convinced that they had a gifted child, whose joyful disposition brought them much pleasure.

When Adam entered school, he did not progress as rapidly as his peers. He had significant difficulty with letter recognition and handwriting. Eventually, with much effort, he did learn to read, but his ability to recognize sight words was weak. His written communication was labored and sentences were illegible at times, either because of bizarre spelling errors or poor handwriting. He moved on through the remaining grades with a very insecure feeling about himself as a learner. He knew that he was good at mathematics and was the first one chosen in gym when it came to team sports. He also knew that his teachers were always after him about messy papers, missed assignments, and unorganized notebooks. He frequently participated in class discussions and surprised teachers with his insightful comments and his ability to retain information. However, he continued to fail written examinations and did not complete assignments; consequently, Adam was failing many of his classes.

Finally, it became clear to Adam, his parents, and his teachers that he was very unhappy about his lack of academic progress. At a parent-teacher conference, they decided to have Adam evaluated.

The results supported his parents' earlier perceptions that Adam was indeed a gifted boy. Psychological testing revealed that he had a superior IQ of 130. By reviewing the wide discrepancies between his strengths and weaknesses, the psychologist was able to explain why Adam struggled with some academic tasks, yet excelled at others. The psychologist thought this information would help alleviate the frustration everyone felt about Adam's academic difficulties. He also hoped that Adam would begin to perceive himself as a capable person, despite being challenged by certain tasks. The boy was told that appropriate techniques could help address the skills with which he had trouble.

An educational plan was developed to try to meet his academic needs, which included daily remedial training sessions in handwriting, spelling, and organizational skills for written work (using a computer).

ANSWERING THE CHALLENGE

The Teacher

The remedial teacher works in an area of specialty. It requires specific training, a willingness to acknowledge and accept children's strengths and weaknesses, and the ability to be an encouraging, supportive advocate at all times.

The ideal candidate for training in the Orton-Gillingham-Stillman (OGS) remedial technique is preferably one who has been well trained in the traditional methods of teaching reading and spelling, and has teaching experience. She or he will know how to teach grammar, punctuation, and comprehension skills. Teachers must also be astute enough to realize that there are a few children in every class for whom the traditional methods do not work. The teacher must be flexible, structured, consistent, and patient, and have the ability to recognize that even small steps indicate progress. A person who eagerly welcomes the opportunity to learn and practice the technique, which more and more teachers are finding effective, will be a successful remedial teacher.

Whether or not the teacher has employed phonics in the past, she or he will discover that the OGS phonetic approach is different. In some cases teachers may have to change their methods. Challenging as it may be to master this approach, the effectiveness of these principles in teaching students to read makes the time needed for training worthwhile.

Preparation

Many excellent teachers are not aware of the evolution of the function of language; this technique depends on this understanding. To use the OGS technique, it is important to learn not only the methods described within this book, but also the reasons why they work, and why certain intelligent children (and adults) are unable to acquire reading skills as their peers do.

A list of books and articles that may be of interest to those wishing to read the research of Dr. Orton, his associates, and other neurologists can be found in the Appendix.

EVOLUTION OF THE LANGUAGE FUNCTION

Language is the outstanding characteristic that distinguishes higher animals from lower. Human language appears to be the most highly developed. Yet when evolution produced speech, no new structure seems to have been created for its control. Instead it was placed in the charge of one hemisphere of the brain. Each hemisphere is dominant in certain functions. The left hemisphere controls language, speech, and arithmetic in most right-handed people. In left-handers, the brain's organization varies.

Some of the opponents of Dr. Samuel T. Orton's explanation of Specific Language Disability seem to assume that he was somehow the inventor of hemispheric dominance; actually, he did not even discover it. It was first recognized during the nineteenth century. Paul Broca, writing in France in 1861, formulated his classic statement that language is controlled by the hemisphere of the brain opposite the more skilled hand. Brain surgeons have accepted this premise for years, using it to help predict whether a brain injury will cause impairment of language.

Dr. Orton was, however, the first neurologist to apply this knowledge to a special field of education and to connect it with Specific Language Disability. The practical value of his contribution is becoming more and more widely accepted as the evidence of experience accumulates.

In their study of ancient artifacts, anthropologists have long recognized that motor laterality (a tendency to prefer one hand for skilled acts) was manifested among very primitive people, probably beginning at about the same time that language was being developed.

By prolonged investigation, Dr. Orton established the fact that handedness is not always clearly right or clearly left, but that many people manifest varying degrees of ambidexterity: for example, a man may prefer his right hand in all activities except dealing cards; or a woman who writes and eats with her right hand may pour water out of a pitcher with her left.

Since complete motor laterality (a consistent preference for one side) is not a universal phenomenon, Dr. Orton questioned whether or not the hemisphere opposite the supposedly more skilled hand would always be in consistent control of language.

He believed that records are always present on the side of the brain that is not usually in control of language. These records are usually ignored, but may sometimes assert themselves. Records made on the two hemispheres, according to Dr. Orton, are in reverse pattern, and so the intrusion of one from the wrong side would account for the "reversals"; the collision of two from opposite sides would produce complete confusion.

Both reversals and confusions are familiar to teachers. In the visual field, for example, the word *go* may be read *og*; *was* may be called *saw*. A well-educated woman glanced at *eat* and read it *tea*. In the auditory field one may hear *loop* called *pool*. As a five-year-old passed by a pasture in which black-and-white cattle grazed, he remarked, "Those are Steinhols." Tired of a prolonged ordeal, a little boy asked querulously, "How last will it long, Daddy?" In the kinesthetic field the same cause probably underlies the much-discussed mirror-writing.

In other words, the evolution of the language function is not yet complete, and, being a late achievement, it is still subject to variation.

The degree to which the language function of an individual is controlled by one hemisphere determines the degree of language skills or disability in that individual. In only a very few people is there the complete unilaterality of language function that Broca assumed. Very few, indeed, learn to read at two and a half or three years, and fewer still cannot remember ever misspelling a word. Most people, who learned to read by ordinary methods at school age, occasionally misspell a word or embarrass themselves and amuse their friends with Spoonerisms (such as the transposed question, "May I sew you to your sheet?") or mirror-writing. Approximately ten percent or more of the school population experience sufficient difficulty in reading and spelling to be seriously impeded in their school progress, while an additional five to ten percent are on the borderline, falling in reading and spelling skill far below their ability to comprehend the content.

We are not considering here students with low mentality or sensory defects. This discussion has to do solely with confusion in language function. That is the reason for saying that they have a "specific language disability."

We are often asked whether or not a reading difficulty is inherited. It is believed that over fifty percent of dyslexics may have inherited the genetic pattern from one or both of their parents. Just as we inherit hair and eye color, so may we derive from our parents the unique neurological makeup that defines our learning style and the learning challenges that result. Recent research supports Dr. Orton's theory that dyslexia is a neurologically-based learning disorder, and not related to laziness, low intelligence, economic status, or poor teaching.

Since the evolution of the language function has been the same throughout human development, the general proportion of children with difficulty in reading should be the same in all countries. "Oddly enough we are also frequently told, again without adequate evidence, that dyslexia is less common among the Japanese and Chinese because these languages are not phonetic at all. Obviously, we need data on the real occurrence of dyslexia in different population groups, since information of this type will undoubtedly lead to a deepening of our understanding of the causes of the condition and help in future attempts to remedy or prevent it." (Geschwind, Norman, M.D., *Why Orton Was Right*. The Reprint Series, No. 98. Baltimore: The Orton Dyslexia Society, 1982, pages 19–20.)

People with specific reading difficulties, in whatever country they live, probably cannot learn to read successfully by "sight-word" methods, even when these are later reinforced by "functional," "incidental," or "analytical" phonics, based on 150–200 learned words, or by tracing procedures. (Fernald, Grace M., *Remedial Techniques in Basic School Subjects*. New York: McGraw-Hill, 1943.) The technique in this book is based on the constant association of all of the following:

- how a letter or word looks
- how it sounds
- how the speech organs or the hand feels when producing the letter or sound in writing

THE SYMPATHETIC ATTITUDE
OF A REMEDIAL TEACHER

Not only must remedial teachers fully comprehend why they are designing lessons and teaching the program as described in this manual, but they must also be fully sympathetic to the needs and disabilities of the individual students with whom they work.

With a blind, deaf, or physically challenged person, the disability or handicap is quite evident. It may be easier for some to feel sympathy toward those with obvious disabilities. In contrast, a learning disability is often referred to as "the hidden handicap." For children or adults, this learning difference is often the cause of much frustration and despair, as they struggle with their teachers and parents to understand why they have not learned to read. When a "bright" person is not achieving his or her full potential, some teachers or parents may become judgmental and reproachful toward that person. A blind, deaf, or physically handicapped person is usually conscious of a helpful, loving, and sympathetic attitude on the part of family, friends, or even strangers. The learning-disabled person does not exhibit a visible disorder that might prompt others to view this person more compassionately. Therefore, the child or adult who struggles with a learning disability may lose a sense of self, as he struggles to overcome his invisible disability. Nonreaders are for the most part "normal" physically, have good thinking minds, are often creative, and can remember specific details of a given story, yet they cannot read.

The following is a typical case of a young boy with Specific Language Disability:

This boy started school with eager anticipation. In his family and neighborhood he had been regarded as a smart little kid. However, by the end of the first grade, he had not learned to read. The teacher said he was inattentive.

After a happy summer, in which he helped his older brother to keep the accounts for his paper route, his experience in the second grade amounted to another failure.

In the third grade an intelligence test was administered, and that settled the matter—his IQ was 118! "He's only lazy! Everybody knows that a child with an IQ of 118 could read if he tried!"

His whole world began to react violently:

- His teacher said he was very good in arithmetic, except for word problems, and with his IQ, he could do word problems if he only tried.
- His classmates called him a "dumbbell."
- His father promised him a bicycle if he could read by June.
- His mother stroked his hair and said she was sure that he was just as bright as the other little boys—if he would only try. It would make her so happy to have him read.

How he longed to silence those comments! But he wanted that bike and the approval of his parents and teacher. In short, he really wanted to try, but he didn't know how. He could not learn those groups of letters that the teacher called words.

This little boy, who didn't know how to try, was learning the most devastating lesson of all—*that his best effort might result in failure.*

So this boy went on year after year. Other children found mental stimulus and satisfaction in books—he did not. Those interests he did have, such as in science, had no chance for development because he could not read the books necessary for further knowledge.

Unfortunately, conflicting theories about the causes of reading disabilities compound the problem. One explanation, which has caused serious misconceptions, is that it is an emotional disturbance. Some educators, physicians, pediatricians, and psychiatrists have supported the notion that some emotional condition, due to a disrupted home life or lack of affection, is the cause of a reading disability.

Naturally, a child who has had such adverse experiences at home and school may have difficulty in overall school learning. However, the child with a specific reading and spelling disability, who has become frustrated and frightened by his failure, may develop an emotional or behavioral problem. To attribute his spelling and reading difficulty to an emotional cause is to put the cart before the horse.

The teacher's challenge is to teach the student to read in conformity with his inherited language pattern. Very often such children become excellent readers and can be helped considerably in spelling. After the student has become a successful reader and a passable speller, he may still occasionally read words with the letters turned around, even in adulthood. He might read *felt* for *left*, write hastily *og* for *go*, or reverse the numerals in telephone numbers.

Teachers should recognize that students with these tendencies will be far less likely to become emotional problems if they can feel the steadfast sympathy and *understanding* of their teachers and parents, and have the necessary individualized instruction.

THE STUDENT

The first question we must address is, "How can we identify the student with a learning difficulty?" He may be the student who has been in school one or two or even several years. He has been in the hands of teachers sufficiently skilled to teach the majority of the class to read and spell acceptably. He has at least a normal, and in many cases, a superior intelligence as measured on an individual psychometric scale. He has normal sensory acuity, both visual and auditory.

Yet, with all these average or superior attributes he has not acquired reading and spelling skills by ordinary school methods.

Many specialists in the field of education receive letters from anxious parents with desperate pleas to help "fix" their child.

- "My little girl is in the fourth grade, but her reading is only at a 2.3 grade level."
- "Dan is in the sixth grade, but his reading is only at a 3.6 grade level and spelling is at 2.5. He is so good in arithmetic that his teacher is sure that he could read if he only tried."

The concluding question is almost always, "Where should we go for examination and correct diagnosis? Will you help us?"

Standardized achievement tests have come to hold a recognized place in school routine and are useful in many ways, both in evaluating the progress of a class in comparison with other classes of the same grade, and in determining the relative standing of members of the same class. In our opinion these tests are not significant in the diagnosis of specific reading difficulty. These tests are standardized in different sections of the country. A child who attains a score of 5.3 on one test may score 6.5 on another test based on norms from another part of the country.

Life has already administered the pragmatic test. Everybody knows that the child in question does not derive information or pleasure from the printed page. The real question is, "What is to be done about it?" What the child sorely needs is a teacher expert in the appropriate techniques to train him in reading skills step by step, not one to hear him read for practice, or to break words up by means of "functional phonics," when he is unable to learn the words thus broken up.

EVALUATION/DIAGNOSIS

When a child of normal or superior intelligence and intact sensory perception has been instructed in reading by the whole-word/sight-word method by a competent teacher for months or years and has not acquired adequate reading skills, it is time for a radical change in approach. Anna Gillingham's approach to teaching students to read offers "solutions and not just sympathy."

SOME CHARACTERISTICS OF THE POTENTIAL POOR READER

As the teacher works with students such as those described in the case histories and as he observes them closely, he discovers that they share certain significant common characteristics:

Difficulty with Organization
- managing time
- completing assignments
- sequencing
- thinking (relating an isolated idea to a unifying concept)

Difficulty with Spoken or Written Language
- pronouncing words
- learning new vocabulary
- following directions
- discriminating among sounds
- reversing or omitting letters, words, or phrases
- reading comprehension
- writing stories and essays

Difficulty with Attention and Concentration
- daydreaming
- showing distractibility
- trouble completing tasks
- being restless

Difficulty with Memory
- learning the alphabet
- identifying letters
- spelling
- remembering names

Difficulty with Physical Coordination
- drawing
- manipulating small objects

Difficulty with Appropriate Social Behavior
- tolerating frustration (outbursts)
- interpreting nonverbal skills (body language)
- accepting changes in routine

Note: All children exhibit one or more of these behaviors from time to time. A consistent showing of a group of these behaviors indicates the need for an assessment from a qualified professional. (This adapted list comes from a general packet distributed by the National Center for Learning Disabilities, 381 Park Ave. South, Suite 1420, New York, NY 10016.)

If kindergarteners who share these common characteristics could be identified before they receive formal instruction in reading, and be given the appropriate individualized reading instruction they need (such as phonemic training), then they might be relieved of the fear that comes with failure. They will not have had ingrained in their unconscious minds that most devastating of all lessons—that failure can follow earnest effort.

REMEDIAL LESSONS

Ideally the remedial lessons should be offered daily to provide consistency and develop automaticity. The schedule of this instruction should not impede normal school activities, which might make the student feel inferior or less deserving than his peers. Furthermore, the instruction given to these students should not be viewed as a way of "curing" or "fixing." It is a kind of teaching appropriate to their unique way of learning. They are not broken, nor do they need fixing. As we have come to realize, they are the students who, like these well-known figures, may excel in science or invention (Thomas Edison), be highly endowed with artistic ability (Hans Christian Andersen), athletic ability (Magic Johnson, Bruce Jenner) or acting talent (Whoopi Goldberg).

In recent years we have come to believe that all children would benefit from the Alphabetic/Phonetic Approach. Instead of providing a systematic, highly structured, and multisensory approach to only a *select* group of students (constituting 10 to 20 percent of the population), the techniques in this program can benefit *all* beginning readers.

PARENTS

It is important that parents gain some understanding of the feelings and issues their children face, so they can be accepting and available to help when needed. It is also important for them to realize that dyslexia affects not just one's ability to read print, but many other areas as well. Dyslexic students have a tendency to read at a slower rate despite remediation. Figurative language can be difficult for them to understand. They may also have difficulty storing, organizing, and retrieving information, and trouble with verbal and written expression. Social behavior can also be affected, since a child with dyslexia may misinterpret language and often has difficulty understanding jokes. Parents should be aware of these tendencies, so that on a day-to-day basis their expectations will remain realistic and their attitude supportive. For example, in planning for their child's academic experience, they should realize that learning a foreign language may require tutorial assistance, be postponed until the junior year of high school, or eliminated altogether.

FOR THE STUDENT

Explaining Learning Differences and the History of Written Language

While it is important to help parents better understand and learn about their child's learning difference, it is imperative that the student receive an explanation as well.

For children and adults who have experienced failure and minimal progress year after year in trying to learn to read, self-esteem and attitude toward themselves as people, and school in general, will deteriorate. As they continue through the school years struggling as nonreaders, they may become young adults whose ambitions and desires are stifled or abandoned. This could, and does, contribute to dropout rates, truancy, and behavioral problems. Children who cannot read may know in their hearts that they are bright and capable in many ways. However, their inability to learn to read may cause them to perceive themselves as social outcasts. Former positive thoughts about themselves as people and learners, and encouragement and optimism expressed by their parents and teachers, will no longer be enough to support their self-esteem.

As Dr. Mel Levine states, "Struggling children comprise a very large and heterogeneous group. They differ from each other in their strengths as well as in the reasons for their learning difficulties. . . . However, they all share a deep desire to taste success and to feel good about themselves. Every one of them contains the seeds for mastery and gratification in life; none of them needs to fail." (Levine, Mel, M.D., *Educational Care: A System for Understanding and Helping Children with Learning Problems at Home and in School.* Cambridge, MA: Educators Publishing Service, Inc., 1994, pages 1–2.)

If they are given the information they need to understand themselves better as learners, along with encouragement, support, and remediation, students with learning differences can become empowered and successful learners. Until then, their misconceptions of themselves and of the world around them will only continue to add to their academic failures and rapidly diminishing self-esteem.

As part of the remedial process, it may be helpful to begin with an overview of the history of language. Through an understanding of its history, students will:

- get a historical background for language appreciation
- become engaged in the learning process
- better understand how many Anglo-Saxon words have been revised, with their original meanings lost or changed

The teacher should use his or her judgment and adapt such information to the maturity and comprehension level of the given student. However, everyone can grasp the overall sequence of events and development of language. It would be helpful to have a map nearby, so teachers and students can discuss the location of given areas.

HISTORY OF LANGUAGE *(sample script for the teacher)*

Written Language

Long, long ago, before there were written records, people talked to each other. They used spoken words to carry ideas from the lips of one to the ears of another.

This talking was very different from the noises and actions intelligent animals use to communicate. Animal noises and actions probably do not carry thoughts, merely feelings—fear or warning when danger is near, or distress, as when a mother cow calls her calf.

After many centuries, people began to realize how convenient it would be if they could get messages to someone not present. They drew pictures as messages.

Some of these pictures were drawn on pieces of bark or bone and have been lost. Many were drawn on the walls of caves and can still be seen. There are hundreds of such pictures in the caves of India and southern Europe.

Native Americans had a long recorded history before Europeans came. They drew pictures to serve as messages, or to be left as records. There are hundreds of such drawings all over North and South America.

Not all of their drawings were meant to convey messages. The people of long ago felt the same wish that many people today feel, to draw or paint the objects around them—to make something beautiful. So, many of the old drawings are just works of art.

Picture Writing

The pictures that we are considering were drawn with a practical purpose, that of getting thoughts across to other people. This is called picture writing. Many prehistoric people lived so long ago that we can only try to decipher what their pictures meant. The Native Americans who still live here have explained to modern scholars the meaning of some of their picture writing. Here are three pictures that I think will interest you.

[The student should have sufficient time to examine the following pictures, not to study them, but to help him see and remember how these people portrayed events.]

War episodes as depicted on a Blackfoot tepee cover*:

- **a.** Bear-chief, on foot, escapes from Assiniboin tribe members.
- **b.** Double-runner cuts loose from horses.
- **c.** He captures a Gros Ventre boy.
- **d.** He and a companion kill two Gros Ventre.
- **e.** He picks up a war bonnet dropped by a Gros Ventre, counting as a coup.
- **f.** He takes a gun from a Crow.
- **g.** He killed five Flathead.
- **h.** A Cree took shelter in some brush, but Big-nose went in for him.
- **i.** A Cree killed while running off Blackfoot horses.
- **j.** Double-runner, with medicine pipe, took a bow from a Gros Ventre and killed him.
- **k.** He took a shield and horse from a Crow and was pursued.
- **l.** (no "l" in the picture)
- **m.** He killed two Gros Ventre and took two guns.
- **n.** He captured a Gros Ventre woman and a boy.
- **o.** He took four mules.

---

* *Indians of the Plains* by Robert H. Lowie. New York: McGraw-Hill, 1954. Reproduced by permission of the publisher.

The capture of horses as recorded on a tepee cover, Blackfoot tribe.*

THE EXPEDITION OF MYEENGUN

In the second picture above, we see another Native American example, a painting made on a cliff near Lake Superior, Canada, which records an exploit of Chief Myeengun. This was an expedition in which five canoes took part. The number of men in the boats is shown by the lines running out of them—there were sixteen in the first, nine in the second, ten in the third, and eight in the fourth and fifth. The leading canoe was commanded by Kishkemunasee, whose totem sign (kingfisher) is above it. Three days were spent on the expedition. This is ingeniously shown by three suns under the vault of the sky. The man on horseback is the maker of magic who assisted the expedition; the land tortoise is the sign that they safely reached land; the eagle on the left symbolizes courage, and the fabulous creatures at the bottom were sought for their aid.**

---

* *Indians of the Plains* by Robert H. Lowie. New York: McGraw-Hill, 1954. Reproduced by permission of the publisher.

** *The Triumph of the Alphabet* by Alfred C. Moorhouse. Abelard-Schuman, Inc., 1953.

[When the student has grasped the idea of picture writing, the teacher should go on to develop the idea of using a picture to stand for a word.]

Script continues:

Most of the people of the world have passed or are passing through the same stages of writing, just as people today pass through certain stages in their play: as babies they shake rattles, later they play with larger toys. As young adults they may play baseball, tennis, field hockey, computer games, etc. Then they may enjoy golf, card games, chess, or other games.

The next stage in writing was that instead of drawing a whole scene to represent a story, people used a little picture to stand for a word.

Pictographs

[Be sure that the student has some idea of the location of China and Egypt.]

The ancient Egyptians wrote in this way, and their symbols are pictographs, which are usually called hieroglyphics or sacred carvings. Some of these pictures were drawn on a kind of paper called papyrus. Great numbers of them, however, were chiseled into stone, and so are called carvings. They were sacred because many of them had to do with religion and creation. Like many other early people, the Egyptians watched the stars very closely. They were astrologers, those who studied the stars for meaning long before the science of astronomy was known. Many of the hieroglyphs have something to do with the stars. Below are some of the pictographs that stood for words.

MEN

| Seated man | Man with hand to mouth | Man sitting on heel | Man with arms raised | Man receiving purification |

| Man sinking to ground from fatigue | Man steadying basket on head | Man holding oar | Man holding the sceptre | Soldier with bow and quiver |

WOMEN

Seated woman

Squatting woman

Woman seated on
chair with child
on lap

Queen wearing
diadem and
carrying flower

ANIMALS

Bull

Aggressive bull

Calf

Sacred cow

Calf suckling cow

Horse

Donkey

Goat

Ram

Pig

Cat

Greyhound

Sometimes they started with the symbol for a word and by adding lines gave it a slightly different meaning.

Below you will see how the pictures for "person," "man," "woman," "child," and others were made by adding to an original drawing.

man, person

child, young

woman

old man, old, lean upon

people

official, man in authority

Ideograms

In very ancient times the Chinese people communicated with pictographs. Perhaps three thousand years ago ingenious scholars began to invent simpler drawings, easier to make than pictures, but less closely resembling the thing for which they stood.

The examples below will show you some of these changes, from pictures to what are called ideograms.*

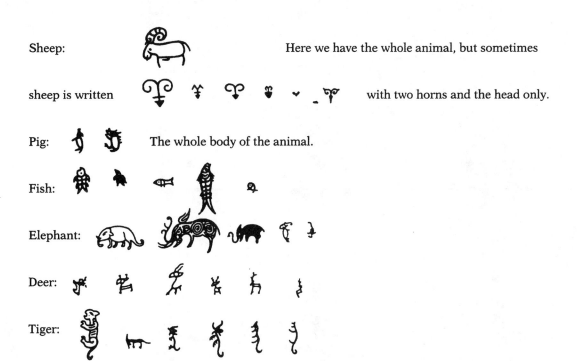

Sheep: Here we have the whole animal, but sometimes

sheep is written   with two horns and the head only.

Pig: The whole body of the animal.

Fish:

Elephant:

Deer:

Tiger:

Chinese Calligraphy, by Chiang Yee. London: Methuen & Co., Ltd. Reproduced by permission of the publisher.

These ideograms were improved and came to be used more and more often. The original pictures were forgotten even by well-educated scholars, who still write very often with the ideograms, even after they have been educated in America or Europe. Like most people, they prefer to write in their native language.

The ideograms below were made especially for this book.

牛	山	父	天
Cow	Mountain	Father	Sky
羊	水	母	地
Sheep	Water	Mother	Earth
雞	花	子	日
Chicken	Flower	Son	Sun
犬	草	女	月
Dog	Grass	Daughter	Moon

[Discuss the alphabet. See whether the student knows part or all of our alphabet. Then begin the explanation of its origin.]

Alphabetic Writing

Writing with ideograms or hieroglyphics was very slow, and it took a very long time to learn so many characters—twenty-two thousand for really well-educated Chinese people. The majority of the people in ancient countries were too poor to go to school, and there were no laws to make them go.

In addition, it was not always easy to write the correct ideogram. Two that looked alike might be confused with each other.

Three thousand or more years ago some people had a wonderful idea and started the world on the next stage of writing. There are a great many words in every language, but they are made up of only a few sounds. People developed the idea of making a symbol to stand for a sound.

Primitive people drew the objects around them. So when they wanted to select symbols for sounds they often drew little birds or animals or something to do with the stars. They didn't draw objects they were unfamiliar with.

They often chose an object that began with a certain sound to stand for that particular sound. For example, suppose you were making up an alphabet. You might let a boy   stand for the \b\ sound and an apple   for the \a\ sound

and a top   for the \t\ sound. Then the spoken word \bat\ would be written

On the following page are some early alphabets. While they look considerably different from each other, there are still some resemblances. The alphabet idea was probably first invented in the region at the eastern end of the Mediterranean Sea.

Some people think that there was just one original alphabet. "The fact that all true alphabets have an unmistakable family likeness if we trace them back far enough forces us to believe that mankind has only once taken this step. Other scholars believe that the alphabet idea came to people independently in several countries, and the various peoples learned from each other." (Bodmer, Frederick, *The Loom of Language*. W. W. Norton & Co., 1944.)

As people used such symbols more and more often in writing, many parts were left out; the symbols became simpler and simpler, until they looked like letters that we know today.

AFFILIATION OF EGYPTIAN AND SEMITIC ALPHABETS.

Values.	EGYPTIAN.			SEMITIC.	LATER EQUIVALENTS.			
	Hieroglyphic.		Hieratic.	Phœnician.	Greek.	Roman.	Hebrew.	
a	eagle				A	A	א	1
b	crane				B	B	ב	2
k (g)	throne				Γ	C	ג	3
t̤ (d)	hand				Δ	D	ד	4
h	mæander				E	E	ה	5
f	cerastes				Υ	F	ו	6
z	duck				Ⅰ	Z	ז	7
χ (kh)	sieve				H	H	ח	8
θ (th)	tongs				Θ	...	ט	9
i	parallels				I	I	י	10
k	bowl				K	K	כ	11
l	lioness				Λ	L	ל	12
m	owl				M	M	מ	13
n	water				N	N	נ	14
s	chairback				Ξ	X	ס	15
ȧ	....	....	....		O	O	ע	16
p	shutter				Π	P	פ	17
t' (ts)	snake				...	...	צ	18
q	angle				...	Q	ק	19
r	mouth				P	R	ר	20
š (sh)	inundated garden				Σ	S	ש	21
t	lasso				T	T	ת	22
	I.	II.	III.	IV.	V.	VI.	VII.	

Isaac Taylor, *The Alphabet, An Account of the Origin and Development of Letters, Vol. I*. London: Kegan Paul, Trench & Co., 1883.

However the letters were made, the alphabet was a helpful invention. If there were a row of letters, the reader had only to say each sound belonging to each letter, one after another—and he had pronounced a word. If he wanted to write, he just said the sounds and wrote down the corresponding letters one by one—and he had spelled a word. It was as easy as that.

Of course, the older practice of using a symbol for a word or idea has continued to the present day, but only to a very limited extent. We are all familiar with such symbols as

     &   %   ?   #   @

        +   =   ÷   ! $

Nevertheless, with certain variations that you will learn later, the alphabetic method has been used for reading and writing for thousands of years.

Of course, during that time not everybody learned to read. Many people were too poor to go to school and a free public education system had not yet been developed. There was no disgrace in not reading and writing. Indeed, scholars were looked upon as a class by themselves. Even a great many kings could not read or write their names. They signed state documents by pressing their signet rings into wax. However, the alphabet idea made it quite easy to learn to read for those who had the leisure and the resources.

Changing Times

About a hundred and thirty years ago two events took place that had a marked effect upon the lives of many people. These events had nothing to do with each other, but they took place at about the same time.

First, laws were passed in various states in our country and in Europe compelling parents to send their children to school up to a certain legal age, fifteen, sixteen, or perhaps seventeen.

The other event was an unexpected return to the old method of learning to read and write by ideograms. People began to say, "Why not have children learn to recognize the whole word without bothering about the individual letters?"

There are some people today, however, who have the same type of mind as those in ancient China who found the ideograms difficult.

The following words are not actually ideograms (as are the Chinese characters previously mentioned) because they are made up of letters, but if a child does not know the names or sounds of these letters, to him the whole word is the same as an ideogram.

mother   girl   nutmeg

father   boy   sandal

When trying to read these ideograms, some students may turn the word around: "Is this word *was* or *saw?*" "Is this *tea* or *eat?*" "Is this *stop* or *spot?*" Many children completely misread the ideogram, so that a boy's name *Jack* is read as *Tom*.

To children taught by the whole-word recognition, or "sight" method, words become just things, and a child has to try to remember what they are just by looking at them. One girl looked at the word *garden* and called it *basket*. She did that because both words had been in the same story she read the day before. Another child saw a picture of a bird with the word *robin* beside it. But when *robin* occurred in a story, he called it *bird*. Another boy, asked to write the word *addition*, wrote *arithmetic*.

You, like these children and like a great many intelligent people, some of them very famous, are one of those who do not learn ideograms easily. That is the reason that reading and spelling have been so hard for you.

Now I am going to begin to teach you in an entirely different way. We are going to use the Alphabetic Method. You are going to learn the sounds of the letters and then build them into words. You will find it fun and it will be good for you to attempt something which you can do.

There are many great people, more than you have any idea of, who have had the same kind of trouble that you have. Some of them have grown up to be famous men and women. They are scientists, artists, writers, entertainers, athletes, politicians, and others. Here are some of their names:

Thomas Edison	Henry Winkler
Hans Christian Andersen	Bruce Jenner
Agatha Christie	Magic Johnson
Leonardo da Vinci	Greg Louganis
Auguste Rodin	Tom Cruise
Cher	Winston Churchill
Whoopi Goldberg	Woodrow Wilson
Danny Glover	John F. Kennedy

Reading and Spelling with Phonetic Words

CHAPTER OVERVIEW

Chapter 2 provides the reader with an understanding of the Orton-Gillingham-Stillman multisensory approach. It describes how to present reading and spelling skills using multisensory techniques through the language triangle, the concept upon which the Association techniques are built. A broad overview of the general procedures for daily lessons, the specific content to be covered, and the order of presentation of the initial lessons is also included. After learning the basic structure and procedures, the teacher can then move around within the chapters to develop individualized lesson plans.

This chapter was designed to acquaint the teacher with the early sequences of instruction. The lesson format and details are designed for use with students in grades three through six. When this technique is used with beginning readers in the first or second grade, or with remedial students in the upper grades, teachers will need to make adaptations. Examples of suggested adaptations and modifications for use with younger or remedial students are provided within the context of the given lesson. The teacher may need to provide additional modifications as needed.

Materials Needed

- Phonics Drill Cards (with or without pictures)*
- Phonetic Word Cards (Jewel Case)*
- Little Stories (Groups I–IV)*—booklets of short phonetic stories, or use the stories provided in this book
- *Merriam-Webster's Elementary Dictionary*, Merriam-Webster, Inc.
- Rough surface (sandpaper, sand, screen, etc., for tracing and writing)

---

* Gillingham Supplementary Materials—call Educators Publishing Service, Inc. (1-800-225-5750) or write to the address on the copyright page for information.

It is best to have a pack of drill cards and a Jewel Case for each student with whom you are working. The "Jewel Case" is the name children affectionately gave to the box of phonetic word cards many years ago. As drill cards are introduced, Jewel Case cards provide samples of words to use for reading and spelling practice.

THE SEQUENCE FOR CHAPTER 2

Teachers should introduce the skills in *italics* as needed, with consideration for the student's maturity level and educational needs.

First Group of Letters	Jewel Case Card Numbers
a	1–20
t	
b	
h	
i	
j	
k	
m	
p	
f	

Second Group of Letters	Card Numbers
g	21–27
o	28–38
r	39–47
l	48–52
n	53–65
th	66–67
u	68–87
ch	88–95
e	96–110
s	111–120
sh	121–132
d	133–162
w	163–170
wh	171–176
y	177–180
v	181–183
z	184–187

Spelling Pattern 1	188–211
Blends	212–246

Spelling Pattern 2 (Doubling the Final Consonant—Monosyllables)

Please see Chapter 7 for Pattern introduction.

Spelling Pattern 3 (Doubling the Final Consonant—Disyllables and Polysyllables)

It is usually best to postpone teaching this pattern because it does not appear in the younger student's vocabulary. Please see Chapter 7 for introduction of the pattern.

Vowel-Consonant-E (v-c-e)	247–271
Spelling Pattern 4 (Silent e)	Chapter 7
Syllable Concept/Patterns 1 and 2	Chapter 2
Detached-Separated-Jumbled Syllables	272–283
Dividing Syllables for Syllable Patterns 1, 2, and 3	Chapter 2

ASSESSING THE STUDENT'S NEEDS

If the tutor or teacher has not received an assessment of the student's reading and spelling levels, she should test the student herself to evaluate his skills. The following tests may be used before intervention and again at the appropriate time, to measure progress.

Reading

Gray Oral Reading Test–1986 (Pro–Ed, Inc., Austin, TX)

Slosson Oral Reading Test–1981 (Slosson Educational Publication, Inc., East Aurora, NY)

Gilmore Oral Reading Tests–1967 (Harcourt Brace Jovanovich, San Antonio, TX)

Woodcock Reading Mastery Tests–1973 (American Guidance Service, Circle Pines, MN)

Wide Range Achievement Test–1984 (Western Psychological Services, Los Angeles, CA)

Spelling

Morrison–McCall Spelling Lists

Test of Written Spelling–1976 (Pro–Ed, Inc., Austin, TX)

Wide Range Achievement Test–1984 (Western Psychological Services, Los Angeles, CA)

Additional testing such as the *Wepman Auditory Discrimination Test* (Western Psychological Services, Los Angeles, CA) provides information about auditory processing, specifically auditory discrimination. If you find a student who has severe deficits in this area, more time must be spent in training the ear to hear the likenesses and differences between sounds (e.g., you can elongate and hold the individual sounds, so the student has more of an opportunity to process). For testing visual-motor skills, the *Bender Visual-Motor Gestalt* is useful (Western

Psychological Services, Los Angeles, CA). If the student's visual discrimination and memory skills are poor, the teacher/tutor will probably need to spend more than the usual amount of time teaching letter formations, being sure to give verbal support to mediate any visual confusion. The Gillingham approach uses the visual, auditory, and kinesthetic senses to reinforce learning.

Even though informal inventories are not standardized, they can produce a wealth of information. Two such inventories, one for spelling and one for reading, can be found in the Appendix.

PROGRAM OF DAILY LESSON

A daily lesson is between forty-five and sixty minutes.

For a more detailed understanding of the Association techniques that are used in the daily lessons refer to pages 30–32.

Daily Schedule

   I. Phonics Drill Cards (phonograms which have been taught thus far—Association I)
- Translating seen symbols into sounds.

 II. Spelling Cards (yellow phonics drill cards—Association II)
- Translating sounds into letter names.

III. Simultaneous Oral Spelling (S.O.S.) (Association III)
- Translating letter names into writing.

> Sometimes letters will be traced, sometimes written to dictation (sometimes with eyes averted), but always S.O.S., following this procedure:
>
> 1. Teacher says the word or phoneme.
> 2. Student repeats the word.
> 3. Student segments the sounds and spells the word aloud.
> 4. If correct, student writes the letters, saying each letter as he or she writes.
> 5. Student reads the word he or she has written.
>
> A more detailed explanation of S.O.S. begins on page 35.

 IV. Drill Words for Reading
- Jewel Case (Group I, Group II, and so on)
- Stories/Readers (Be sure to tell the students the unknown words before they attempt to read them.)

  V. Handwriting Practice
- Words containing previously learned letters are dictated letter by letter.

 VI. Dictation
- Various phrases or sentences

PHONICS TEACHING

In response to the present widespread controversy over a literature-based program versus a phonetic approach to teaching reading, one might be inclined to say, "No one way is the right way!" However, given the extent of research, and the educational philosophies and practices on which this manual is based, we remain confident that a strong foundation using a multisensory approach to reading is one that can be accomplished only through an alphabetic/phonetic approach.

The many remedial teachers now using the Orton-Gillingham-Stillman approach would probably agree with Orton's own conclusions after some twenty years of research and practice in this field:

> Whether or not our theory is right, I do not know, but I do know that the methods of retraining which we have derived from that viewpoint have worked. I do not claim them to be a panacea for reading troubles of all sorts but I do feel that we understand the blockade which occurs so frequently in children with good minds and which results in the characteristic reading of the *strephosymbolic* type in childhood. (1946)

Anna Gillingham's philosophy emphasizes the importance of individual student lessons and daily sessions. Phonics should not be perceived as the "grunt and groan" method. Lessons can be fun, alive, and activity-based, while helping children and adults learn the structure of language for reading and writing. For example, a teacher can ask his students to create a list of fruits or sports, and write the items in alphabetical order. Creating lists of "nonsense" words can also be a fun activity, as well as a helpful tool in detecting weaknesses in reading and spelling.

Occasionally we hear about a student whose reading is *spoiled* by knowing "too much" phonics. The student's reading may be halting or labored, or meaning may be ignored. His ability to blend sounds and spell words may also be hampered because he has not learned how to make sounds correctly. Teachers need to pay careful attention to the way in which they present sounds, carefully "clipping" the sound without adding an additional vowel sound, \t\ and not \tuh\.

Current Practices in Teaching Phonics

Many schools teach phonics, but only after the student has mastered one hundred to two hundred sight words. Once these words are mastered as "whole units," the words are broken down into individual letter sounds. However, this approach is problematic. Without a systematic and sequential approach to reading, the student has no firm foundation. He cannot read many words because their phonetic elements may not have been taught or reinforced frequently enough for automaticity to result.

Our Approach

In direct contrast to current practices, the Orton-Gillingham-Stillman approach starts with the individual sounds, and then uses these sounds to build words. This "word-building method" also builds a close association or link between what the student sees in print (visual), what the student hears (auditory), and what the student feels as he or she makes the sounds of the letters and writes (kinesthetic—large muscle movements, and tactile—sensations in the

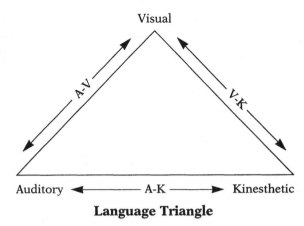

Language Triangle

mouth and on the fingertips). This technique is referred to as the "language triangle" or multisensory approach.

PHONETIC ASSOCIATIONS

Every phonogram (representation of a sound) is presented through each association (visual, auditory, and kinesthetic), and each association is linked and presented simultaneously. The individual pathway makes an imprint on the brain and thus strengthens the learning process.

For example:

- "If a student sees the letter <u>b</u> and responds by saying \ d \ , stop the student and ask him to trace the letter he sees. In most cases he will trace the letter correctly. Then, when asked the sound of the letter traced, he should reply with the correct sound. In effect, the student cannot see it to say it, but can see it to trace it, and can then say it correctly when it is traced. In short, we've used the kinesthetic mode to intervene in a perceptual misinterpretation." (Anderson, C. Wilson, Jr., *VAK Tasks Teacher's Manual*. Cambridge, MA: Educators Publishing Service, Inc., 1994.)

This is the process of translating *seen symbols* into *sounds*, which is the basis of oral reading.

ASSOCIATION I

This association emphasizes combined use of all three senses.

- **a.** Associating the symbol (visual) with the name of the letter
- **b.** Associating the symbol with the sound of the letter (auditory)
- **c.** Associating the symbol and the feel of the letter in the mouth as the student produces the name or sound of the letter (kinesthetic—the motion felt in the large arm muscles as he writes or traces)

The teacher presents the phonics drill cards using these procedures.

Step one (V-A):

When introducing a new association, the teacher shows the card (consonant phonograms will be on the white cards, and vowels on salmon-colored cards) and presents the name of the letter. The student repeats the name.

Step two (A-K):

The teacher then makes the sound of the letter, which the student repeats.

The key word is given as a cue to initiate the correct letter sound, *e.g., apple,* \a\; *boy,* \b\.

The teacher shows the student the card (phonogram) and prompts a response to the implied questions, *"What is the name of this letter?"; "What is the key word?"; "What sound does the letter stand for?"* The student should reply, "a, apple, \a\; t, top, \t\," and so on. Once the student has learned this sequence, the teacher can add a step and have the student write the letters, preferably on a rough surface to maximize the tactile sensations.

ASSOCIATION II

This association provides auditory training for oral spelling.

a. Associating auditory to auditory

Step one:

The teacher looks at the phonogram that is on the yellow card and makes the sound represented by the letter. The student does not see the face of the card.

Step two (A-A):

The teacher says, *"Tell me the name of the letter that has this sound."* The student should then be able to name the letter for the given sound:

<u>a</u>, apple, \a\
<u>b</u>, boy, \b\

ASSOCIATION III

This association is the basis of written spelling.

a. Associating the symbol (visual) with how it feels to make the letter as the student writes (kinesthetic)
b. Associating the feel of the letter (kinesthetic) with its symbol (visual)
c. Associating the sound of the letter (auditory) with the feel and letter form (kinesthetic)

The teacher should refer to the chapter on handwriting during this association. This is the procedure when a new symbol is introduced:

Step one:

The teacher models making the letter for the student, explaining letter form and orientation.

Step two (V-K):

The student then traces over the teacher's letter.

Step three (V-K):

The student copies the letter.

Step four (K-V):

The student writes the letter from memory.

To make this activity more strongly kinesthetic, the teacher should have the student write the letter on or in sand, roughboard, sugar, salt, or another rough surface.

Step five (K):

The student writes the letter while looking away from the paper.
(At this point the teacher watches closely.)

Step six (A-K):

The teacher makes the sound and says, *"Write the letter that has this sound."*
The student forms the cursive letter on the paper, or roughboard, or in the sand.

In each of the three associations, the goal is automaticity. The teacher holds up the card or says the sound, and the student produces the correct response without prompting.

Important Points

1. If a student's production of sound is faulty, additional practice and modeling of sounds are necessary. The teacher will produce the sound for the student to imitate. In some difficult cases, a speech professional may need to be involved.
2. Make sure that the student says the name of each letter as he writes it (except when tracing and copying).
3. If a student is not able to form a letter without looking at it as she writes, then automaticity has not been reached and fluency of expression will be affected. This includes starting at the correct point, and moving the pencil in the correct direction.
4. Since the core of this alphabetic approach is to establish the concept of words built out of phonetic units, the first essential step is to change the student's attitude toward words as ideograms *to be remembered as wholes*, and to eliminate all guessing.
5. Each phonogram is introduced by a key word that triggers the correct letter sound. For example, when the a̲ card is shown, the student's response is, "a̲, apple, \a\." The student should always give these key words when shown the phonogram.

6. The teacher should familiarize herself with the correct pronunciation of each sound before introducing a new letter, remembering to keep sounds "clipped" and "pure."

7. The student should be taught to recognize and to explain the difference between vowel sounds and consonant sounds. Vowel sounds are produced by the breath passing freely through the vocal cords and the mouth. Each can be prolonged indefinitely. When the consonant sounds are produced, the breath is obstructed by lips, tongue, or teeth. A few of the consonant sounds can be prolonged indefinitely, e.g., \f\, but the breath is obstructed slightly by placing the lower lip between the teeth.

8. To maximize kinesthetic and tactile reinforcement, the muscles in the upper arm need to be involved. The teacher should encourage the student to "bear down" while writing on the rough surface.

INITIAL LESSON PLANS

1. Phonics Drill Cards open each lesson. Consonants are found on white cards, and vowels on salmon cards.

Student says the letter, the key word, and the appropriate sound, while forming the letter in cursive on the rough surface or paper.

First Group of Letters

a	apple	\a\
t	top	\t\
b	boy	\b\
h	hat	\h\
i	itchy	\i\
j	jam	\j\
k	kite	\k\
m	man	\m\
p	pan	\p\
f	fish	\f\

There is no rigid order in which the letters should be taught. However, the early letters should start with unequivocal sounds and non-reversible forms. The number of phonograms to teach will depend on the needs and abilities of the student.

The following writing procedure must be applied to all new letters. As students learn the name of each letter, they should also learn to write it.

1. The teacher makes the letter.
2. The student traces the letter.
3. The student copies it.
4. The student writes it without model.
5. The student writes it with eyes averted.

2. Reading (blending):

A. After the ten letters in Group 1 are learned using all associations, blending them together into words begins. At this stage reading is only translating seen symbols into speech sounds. Drill cards from the group of learned letters are laid out on the table.

The student then

- gives the sounds of these letters in succession,
- repeats the series of sounds again and again while increasing speed and smoothness.

The student is helped to realize that he is actually saying a word. Encourage the student to pronounce the first two letters together, e.g., \ba\ \t\.

At first the student may need to produce each sound separately before he is able to blend the sounds. His goal is to look at the word and blend it without saying sounds orally or separately.

Too much time can be consumed if the teacher asks all the questions every time. The student should see the card and make an automatic response.

B. The teacher presents the yellow Jewel Case cards (numbers 1–20) and the student reads them as accurately as possible. Accuracy is more important than speed at this point. Responses can be recorded using a graph. (See Appendix.) During the early weeks students should perform this reading exercise almost daily. Later it can be twice a week.

3. Spelling:

A. After several days of practicing and blending successfully, students should begin to break down words into their component sounds.

- Teacher says: *"Please listen. I am going to say a word very slowly."*

  map \m\   \a\   \p\   (use elongated pronunciation)

  \m\ \a\ \p\ \m\ \a\ \p\   (decrease elongated pronunciation)

- *"What sound did you hear first?"*
- *"What letter says \m\?"*
- *"Find the **m** card and lay it on the table."*
- *"What is the second sound? Listen, \m\\a\\p\."* Repeat steps for each letter of the given word.
- When all cards for each letter are on the table, the student is able to see the word **map** as a whole unit.
- The student should now practice writing the word.

It is important that students spell with this precise, definite, and unvarying procedure; otherwise one association or another will be lost.

Research has demonstrated that phonemic awareness is very important for providing a foundation for learning to read and spell. Phonemic awareness is the ability to segment, manipulate, and blend sound segments (phonemes) of spoken language; it is also the awareness of these abilities and what they mean to language. There is a strong correlation between segmentation ability and the acquisition of skills in spelling, reading, and writing. Therefore, teachers should take great care to make sure that students whose segmentation ability is impaired have adequate training in these areas. Activities should include word play, rhyming, alliteration, segmentation, and blending.

For extended reading on phonemic awareness, available tests, and suggested activities, see the Appendix, which provides extremely helpful information for the teacher.

B. Four-Point Program or Simultaneous Oral Spelling (S.O.S.)

This is the naming of letters aloud as each is written, firmly establishing the visual-auditory-kinesthetic linkages or associations. Making connections is very important for the child who has integration, processing, and/or attention problems. These steps will provide the practice and remediation necessary to improve spelling and the retention of information. (In this revision, we have retained the traditional "Four-Point Program" name, though there are actually five steps, including the teacher saying the word.)

STEP 1:

- The teacher says the word. (These words are derived from the phonograms that have been learned thus far or taken from the Jewel Case.)
- The student hears his teacher's voice—auditory.

STEP 2:

- The student echoes the word. This allows the student to hear his own voice and feel his own speech organs—auditory-kinesthetic.
- The teacher can correct and check auditory processing.

STEP 3:

- The student segments the sounds and then names the letters. (The segmentation step can be dropped as soon as the student is ready.)
- This step gives the teacher an opportunity to correct any errors before writing. It is important to imprint the word correctly in the student's "mind's eye."

STEP 4:

- The student writes the letter, naming each letter as he forms it on the paper or rough surface.
- The student sees the letters and feels his hand form the letters—visual-kinesthetic.

STEP 5:

- The student reads what he has written.
- The student sees, hears, and feels (in his vocal cords) the word—visual-auditory-kinesthetic.
- This encourages the student to become his own proofreader.

Sometimes the student should write with eyes averted to focus attention on feeling the form his hand is following.

C. Handwriting:

Cursive writing is the preferred form. It helps to reduce the likelihood of letter reversals. Production is quicker and copying from the board is easier since each letter is linked to the next one.

Handwriting is a separate subject and should be taught as such. The student should not be concerned here with spelling, reading, or comprehension. The primary purpose of handwriting is to establish and reinforce automaticity of letter formation. The most difficult part of handwriting is learning the connectors between letters. The goal is legibility.

The teacher spells the word orally and the student writes each letter as it is dictated. This procedure will help the student maintain an appropriate rate of production.

In many instances the kinesthetic impression is the best, if not the only, means of securing the serviceable memory of a letter form. The student may look at the letter scores of times, but we have no assurance that when it is removed, she will not see it in her mind's eye in reversed pattern.

Schools that begin teaching manuscript and change to cursive in the second or third grades cause irreparable harm. Dr. Orton repeatedly asserted that impressions made on nerve tissue are never wholly eradicated. They are only whitewashed over. They linger on, confusing later impressions. This change in penmanship may often be seen in high school papers, where the manuscript form asserts itself in the middle of cursive words.

It is essential that the left-handed student be required to turn his paper to the position opposite that required of the right-handed student, so that with wrist straight, his arm is parallel with the edge of the paper (see Chapter 9).

The paper used should have double ruling so as to make clear the relative height of the letters. A great deal of harm is done by encouraging students to write smaller, with the implication that the smaller writing will make them appear older. Tiny, cramped letters do not make a distinct kinesthetic impression. Also, much poor spelling in the upper grades and high school is due to the fact that the student quite consciously makes his letters small and indistinct in the hope that the teacher will give him the benefit of the doubt and accept words misspelled. In our work any ambiguity is counted wrong.

See Chapter 9, "Handwriting," for further explanation, and Appendix for practice paper.

D. Dictation (for use when dictating individual letters, words, phrases, or sentences):

As introduced here, S.O.S. is a linkage of sound with letter form. In time we shall depend upon it more and more for impressing letter sequences in nonphonetic words. The natural speller can trust his visual memory of a word. The student with confused visual memory cannot. His greatest help in studying a difficult word is to associate the *names* of the letters in correct order with their kinesthetic records as his hand forms them and his voice speaks them one by one. It is essential that the teacher pronounce and the student repeat each sound distinctly, and that these sounds be instantly translated into letter names. The mistake is sometimes made of allowing the student to write the letters from the sound without naming them. The result will be correct in these simple phonetic words, but confusion will occur later. This is the period in which habits are to be fixed, and spelling must mean *naming* letters.

When the student names the letters as he writes them, he is establishing a useful habit, and the teacher is able to observe and correct his individual difficulties and confusions as they happen.

After the first days of initial practice in blending, it should be an invariable routine to have the student check his own errors. When he reads a word incorrectly, he should be asked to spell what he has just said, and match it against the original word. For example, suppose the word <u>tap</u> has been read \tep\.

"How do you spell \tep\?"
"t-e-p."
"Yes, but this is t-a-p."

Conversely, if a word such as <u>bit</u> is misspelled orally as b-i-p, the teacher may write the offered spelling and say,

"Read this."
"\bip\."
"Correct, but I dictated the word \bit\."

She may have him correct his own oral spelling directly from her repeated pronunciation. In all these initial exercises, the teacher should prevent the student from incorrectly writing the word if possible, and it *is* possible unless he writes a letter other than the one he named. Later, mistakes will occur when the teacher is not watching, perhaps when a sentence or paragraph is being written independently. The student spells orally as he writes to insure the S.O.S. habit, and he may both spell and write incorrectly. If so, he is then asked to find his mistakes by reading aloud.

Words are selected from the growing pack of available words. The Four-Point Program is followed. The teacher pronounces a word, the student repeats it, spells it orally, writes it S.O.S., and reads it as written.

The point is to see how many words a student can spell in this way correctly *in succession*. The omission of a single step or the misspelling of any words means a fresh start in the count. In the beginning four or five words constitute a satisfactory score. Later there may be fifteen, twenty-two, or even fifty correct words without a single break. In such a case, this exercise would not be given more often than once a week.

INITIAL LESSON

Day 1

- To begin, introduce the concept a, \a\.

1. The teacher presents the a drill card. The teacher names the letter and the student repeats the letter name. The key word apple is given, and the sound of the letter is given as a prompt. The student should say apple and the sound \a\.
2. The teacher holds the phonics drill card that represents the \a\ sound and says, *"Tell me the name of the letter that has this sound:* \a\." The student says a, apple, \a\.
3. The teacher models making the letter a, and a discussion of the letter formation begins. Work from the larger muscles to the smaller muscles to gain "muscle memory." For example, start by writing on the chalkboard, then large-lined paper, and finally regular size paper.

Use the following format to help the student form letters correctly:

- The teacher makes the letter.
- The student traces the letter.
- The student copies the letter.
- The student writes the letter without the copy.
- The student writes the letter with eyes averted.

Day 2

- Review the concept of a.
- Introduce t, \t\.

The specific phonograms and the number of them may be adjusted to suit the individual student.

1. The teacher shows the a and t drill cards. The student says the letter name a, apple, \a\; t, top, \t\.
2. The teacher refers to the yellow card and says, *"Tell me the name of the letter that makes the sound* \a\." (Student doesn't see the card. It is only to cue the teacher.) The student says, a, apple, \a\ while writing the letter in cursive on the rough surface.
3. The teacher presents a new phonogram. The teacher shows the t drill card. The teacher says the name of the letter t. The student repeats the letter name.
4. The teacher names the letter, and the student repeats the letter name. The key word is given, and the sound of the letter is given as a prompt. The student says top and the sound \t\. Remember to keep the sound "pure."
5. The teacher models making the letter. Follow the same procedure as used in Day 1 Lesson—Step 3.

Day 3

1. The teacher shows the drill cards <u>a</u> and <u>t</u>. The student says the letter names <u>a</u>, apple, \a\; <u>t</u>, top, \t\.

2. The teacher refers to the yellow card and says, *"Tell me the name of the letter that makes the sound* \a*."* The student says, <u>a</u>, apple, \a\ while writing the letter in cursive on a rough surface. *"Tell me the name of the letter that has the sound* \t*."* The student says <u>t</u>, top, \t\ while writing the letter in cursive on the rough surface.

Following this sequence will enable a student to read and spell a word (*at*) as soon as possible.

3. Introduce the next letter using all three associations.

After students learn the first vowel and several consonants (*a, h, t, m*), blending, reading, and spelling words can begin. Use the drill cards to assist in the blending activity and use S.O.S. procedure when spelling words:

- The teacher says the word.
- The student repeats the word.
- The student spells the word out loud.
- The student names each letter or sounds it while writing it.

COMPLETE LESSON

(Includes spelling, reading words, and nonsense syllables.)

1. **Drill card review** (*a, h, t, m* or other phonograms as needed)

   - While the teacher is showing the card to the student, the student gives the letter name, key word, and sound while writing the cursive letter on the rough surface or paper.

2. **Word lists to be read** (words made up of phonograms discussed)

hat	ham	mat	
at	am	*mam*	
tat	tam	*nam*	(*nonsense syllables*)

3. **Spelling drill** (the teacher holds the yellow card, but the face of the card is not shown)

   An early lesson example:

   - *"Tell me the name of the letter that makes the sound* \a*."*

   Eventually the teacher will just say the sound, and the student will automatically say the name.

   - The student says, <u>a</u>, apple, \a\ while writing the letter in cursive on the rough surface.
   - *"Tell me the name of the letter that has the sound* \t*."* The student says, <u>t</u>, top, \t\ while writing the letter in cursive on the rough surface, and so on.

4. **Spelling words** (Remember to use the S.O.S. procedure. Also, use words at this point that can only be spelled one way—e.g., "since" has many phonetic variations.)

hat	tat
at	mat
ham	tam
man	*nam* (*nonsense syllable*)
am	

5. **Handwriting practice**

Teacher dictates words containing previously learned letters to
   • increase fluidity in writing
   • reinforce motor memory of letter formation
   • improve legibility
   • learn and practice the connectors which tie the letters together

6. **Dictation** (remember to write sight words on a card for the student to copy)

Mat <u>the</u> man.
Tam <u>the</u> ham.

7. **Reading** (remember to underline the sight words)

<u>I</u> am Tat.
Tam <u>the</u> ham.

8. **Introduce new concept**

   • Concepts to be taught include letters, diphthongs, digraphs, blends, spelling patterns, silent <u>e</u> endings, compound words, spelling generalizations, silent letters, syllable types, rules for division, accent patterns, and affixes.

9. **Listening comprehension**

   • *Common Ground* by Priscilla Vail (Modern Learning Press, 1991) lists stories at individual grade levels that are good for oral reading. Jim Trelease's book, *The Read-Aloud Handbook*, (Penguin, 1995) lists many resources and stories that are especially suited for this type of reading activity.

Important General Points

   • Introduce new letters, not more than one or two a day, and sometimes not more than one in several days. Using the word list in the order presented in this book will assist the remedial teacher in lesson planning.
   • Shuffle the new phonemes into the pack of drill cards. The students' progress and automaticity with material should be presented visually to them by using a graph (see Appendix).

- Please refer to the Appendix for the letter sequence and key words (several of the letters have more than one sound, but at present only the one given here should be presented). See also page 42, Letters and Words.
- When preparing a selection for reading, the student reads it silently. If he has difficulty with a word, he must ask for help. The assistance will consist largely in helping him to sound out the word. When he says that he is "ready," he assumes a responsibility: he is to read the sentence perfectly and with inflection that "sounds like talking." The tutor and the student may also read a story aloud together. *The Read-Aloud Handbook*, as mentioned under Listening Comprehension, has stories that are suitable for this type of activity and are graded according to interest levels up to seventh grade. The student will remember some of these words from previous experience, and he will readily pronounce them. When possible it is best to review "unlearned words" before the student attempts to read them. Such words are underlined in the Gillingham Little Stories. Trying, but not guessing, should be encouraged. The student needs to be successful, so it is important that the lessons are geared toward success. Confidence in one's ability cannot be developed if trying brings failure too often. Success can breed success.
- The same stories that the student reads can also be used for dictation exercises.
- Words underscored in the controlled readers (see Little Stories—Groups I–IV), which the student has not yet learned, are to be written on a card or on paper and laid before him to be copied. (See Dictation, Chapter 6, for procedure.)
- The student must know that he is capable of spelling every word in the dictated paragraph. He needs to think—rather than guess—when he is challenged by a word.
- During dictation exercises the student is given several words or a sentence to write. As the dictation continues, the phrases or sentences should become longer. This will help to expand the student's auditory memory. This list should be read once, not dictated word by word. If a student forgets a word, the whole phrase must be repeated. (This procedure is outlined in Chapter 6.)
- The student should do syllable exercises three or four times a week. The exercises should be part of the lesson but must never constitute the main part of the lesson. This work on syllables should continue in successive steps, matching the maturity and skill level of the student.

Specific Points for Group I and Group II Letters

To avoid the classic mirror reversals of the letters <u>b</u>, <u>d</u> and <u>p</u>, <u>q</u> the OGS method teaches the writing of these letters in such a way that kinesthetically one does not suggest the other. Children should never be allowed to start a <u>d</u> or <u>b</u> with a vertical line and then lift their pencil to add a circle on one side or the other. This frequently results in a mirror image. Confusion can be avoided if <u>d</u> is started with a circle to the left as in making the letter <u>a</u>, the upstroke extended to the top and retraced downward. Below is the formation for the letter <u>b</u>.

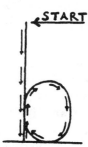

It was not an accident that <u>d</u> is introduced some distance from the letter <u>b</u> in the handwriting page (Chapter 9), and that <u>q</u> is separated from <u>p</u>. Under no conditions can this postponement do any harm. If a young student is being introduced to reading and spelling by this procedure as a preventive measure, the teacher may partially avoid trouble by firmly establishing one symbol before teaching the reversed form. If, however, a student has already used the two symbols interchangeably, this delay will be valueless. The picture of <u>d</u> imprinted upon his memory will be recalled sometimes as <u>d</u> and sometimes as <u>b</u>. The only help, besides the different kinesthetic implant, is to teach some arbitrary device to be remembered quickly when visual memory fails. In the room used for teaching, <u>b</u> and <u>p</u> should turn toward a picture of a plate of bread, <u>d</u> and <u>q</u> toward a picture of a quacking duck, or towards one's wristwatch or the door, or any other convenient object. These difficulties can also be avoided by teaching students to use cursive writing.

LETTERS AND WORDS
Several of these letters have more than one sound, but at present use only the one given here.

g <u>g</u>oat \g\. White drill card 5.

New Words: tag, bag, big, pig, jig, gap, jag

o <u>o</u>ctopus \ä\. Salmon card 4.

New Words: Tom, top, tog, hot, pot, jot, got, mop, hop, hog, jog

r <u>r</u>at \r\. White card 14.

Take care to avoid \ər\ as many teachers accept it. These false unit sounds cause serious difficulty with later spelling. A good method is to get the student to say \rat\, then start to say it again and stop: \r\.

New Words: ram, rap, rib, rip, rig, rim, rob, rot

<u>l</u> <u>lamp</u> \l\ not \əl\ as it is often mispronounced, leading to such spelling as u-l-a-m-p for <u>lamp</u>. Have the student say \lamp\, then start to say it again and stop: \l\. White card 9.

New Words: lap, lag, lip, lit, lot

<u>n</u> <u>nut</u> \n\. White card 11.

Many students confuse this letter visually with <u>m</u>. It sometimes helps to remember that <u>m</u> stands for a great big <u>m</u>ountain and so has more humps than <u>n</u>, which stands for the little word <u>n</u>ut.

New Words: nag, nab, nap, not, nip, tan, ran, pan, man, ban, fan, bin, pin

<u>th</u> <u>this</u> \th\. White card 27a.

Several of the consonant digraphs are introduced before some of the single letters because they are easy and increase the available drill words. A digraph is explained "as two letters that stick together and have a single sound," but the correct term, *digraph*, is taught.

New Words: than, that

<u>u</u> <u>upper</u> \ə\. Salmon card 5a.

The symbol [ə], called schwa (\shwä\), is defined in Merriam-Webster's Elementary Dictionary (1994) as "an unstressed vowel that is the usual sound of the first and last vowels of the English word *America*."

New Words: run, gum, bun, pup, pun, nut, hut, but, rut, bug, hug, jug, mug, rug, pug, hub, rub, tub, hum

<u>ch</u> <u>chin</u> \ch\. White card 22a.

This digraph is taught before the letter <u>c</u>, because <u>c</u> has two sounds, neither of which is distinctively its own. The name <u>c</u> is taught and the form studied, but no sound is given for this letter by itself yet.

New Words: chug, chip, chop, chat, chap, chum, rich, much

<u>e</u> <u>eddy</u> \e\. Salmon card 2a.

New Words: fen, pen, hen, then, them, let, Ben, ten, ken, men, hem, net, pet, peg, beg

<u>s</u> <u>snake</u> \s\. White card 15a.

New Words: set, sit, Sam, sun, sob, sag, this, sin, sip

<u>sh</u> <u>ship</u> \sh\. White card 25.

Be sure that the student is able to call this a digraph when asked for this name.

New Words: shin, shut, sham, shop, hash, shun, rash, lash, gash, mash, sash, mesh, hush, rush, lush, gush, mush, fish

<u>d</u> <u>dog</u> \d\. White card 3.

New Words: bid, hid, kid, lid, did, mud, dot, den, had, shed, dish, Ned, bed, Ted, fed, don, dash, dug, fad, pad, lad, bad, mad, rod, dim, dam, dab, pod, dad, Dan

<u>w</u> <u>wind</u> \w\. White card 18.

The consonant <u>w</u> can occur only before a vowel sound, and cannot be pronounced without the following vowel. The attempt to pronounce it results in \wə\. The student is to place his lips in the <u>w</u> position and then say the words given on the drill card, e.g., <u>ag</u>-<u>wag</u>; <u>ent</u>-<u>went</u>. See back of <u>w</u> card.

<u>wh</u> <u>whistle</u> \ hw\. White card 28.

New Words: <u>w</u>, wed, wet, web, wag, wig, wit, win, wish
<u>wh</u>, whim, whit, whip, when, whet, which

It is best to teach these two phonograms together. There is no inherent reason for their giving trouble, for <u>w</u> begins <u>wind</u>, and <u>wh</u> has the distinct sound which begins <u>when</u> and <u>whistle</u>, like blowing out a candle. Insecure visual recall does not cause confusion since the two are entirely different in appearance. Some spellers with weak visual memory and/or recall reverse the <u>w</u> and <u>h</u> in spelling, e.g., <u>when</u>—<u>hwen</u>, but this is not a confusion with the <u>w</u> phonogram.

However, many people have difficulty pronouncing the <u>h</u> in \hw\ and so pronounce both symbols alike. This is especially common in America today. We say, "The wind wistles," "The snow is wite." The ears of children accustomed to such pronounciation do not perceive any difference. To them \w\ and \hw\ sound alike. If they are good visual spellers, they may spell <u>whistle</u> and <u>white</u> correctly, while saying both with initial \w\. The training required here is not to overcome visual confusion, but to develop keenness of auditory discrimination. We repeat, one cannot distinguish between one sound! It is therefore essential that the two symbols be placed side by side and their differences brought out.

<u>y</u> <u>yoyo</u> \y\. White card 20.

Consonant <u>y</u> occurs only as an initial sound in a word or syllable.

New Words: yam, yet

<u>v</u> <u>van</u> \v\. White card 17.

New Words: vat, vim

<u>z</u> <u>zebra</u> \z\. White card 21.

New Words: zip, zigzag, buzz, jazz

ONE-SYLLABLE WORDS ENDING IN CERTAIN DOUBLE CONSONANTS

Introducing the concept of a syllable is essential for learning the first spelling pattern.

Give students an explanation like the following:

> Little words such as we have been reading and spelling, which can be spoken by one impulse of the voice, are called *one-syllable words* or monosyllables.

So far most of these words have followed one pattern. A very few have contained only two letters, such as if and in. A few have had four letters if they contained digraphs (two adjacent letters representing a single speech sound, e.g., ee, oo, sh, or th). Most of them, however, have three letters: a consonant, a vowel, and a consonant.

There are three consonants that are usually doubled when they stand at the end of a one-syllable word. These consonants are f, l, and s. When you see a word like muff or fill or less, it is pronounced just as if there were only one f or l or s. Students do not have difficulty reading such words, but when they spell them, these words require special thought.

SPELLING PATTERN 1 (The "Floss" Pattern)

Words Ending in ff, ll, or ss

- Words of one syllable ending in f, l, or s (sounding \f\, \l\, or \s\) after one vowel, usually end in ff, ll, or ss.

This is the first spelling pattern. The student must learn and use this pattern whenever \f\, \l\, or \s\ follows a short vowel at the end of a word.

In the Jewel Case the following words are printed on yellow cards. The reading should provide no trouble, and before long many students will be alert to the fact that when spelling a phonetic word like *bell*, if it ends in l, they must double the l.

doll, doff, buff, huff, muff, puff, whiff

bell, fell, hell, sell, tell, well

ill, bill, dill, fill, hill, kill, mill, pill, rill, sill, till, will

gull, hull, mull

bass, mass, chess, less, mess, muss, hiss, kiss

For a more extended discussion of this pattern and its application, refer to page 130. The teacher must carefully select the words used at this point, avoiding those that contain vowel sounds not yet introduced and exceptions to the pattern. As soon as students have become fairly familiar with these words, the words should be shuffled in with the other cards for reading, graphing, and simultaneous oral spelling (S.O.S.).

Stories

Now that the student can read and write two- and three-letter, perfectly phonetic words (four-letter when digraphs and blends are included), these words can be included in the sentences and stories both for reading and dictation.

These stories are stapled into small books, illustrated by teachers or students, and referred to as *Little Stories*. It is very difficult to construct stories with only phonetic words. It is necessary to include a few words that the student cannot be expected to read at this stage. Note that the words that have not been taught are considered sight words (underlined in our text) and are to be explained at once without any attempt on the part of the student to read them. These *Little Stories* are offered for practice and should not be read with the "grunt and groan" intonation. The words are to be merged into sentences as fluently and naturally as possible. When the student is asked to read orally, he should read the paragraph silently to prepare. At this time, if he has any questions about some of the words or sentences, he should ask the teacher. The teacher should not hesitate to assist the student in his efforts to read the word (telling the student the word is also acceptable). When he decides that he knows everything, and that he can read it, he is then *responsible for the correctness* of every word.

STORIES—GROUP I

Containing: Unequivocal Consonants, Short Vowels, Pattern 1

Tom and Jip

This is Tom. This is Jip. Tom and Jip.
Jip is Tom's dog.* Jip is not a big dog.
Tom can run. Tom can hop. Tom can jump.
Jip can jump. Jip can not hop.
Tom and Jip can run and jump.
Tom will pat Jip. Tom will not hit Jip.
Tom can spin his top.
Tom will hit the ball. Jip will help Tom to get it.

Charlotte C. Pardee

---

* The word *dog* gives no real trouble, but it is not the short sound of o which is all that the students have encountered so far.

Tom <u>and</u> Nan

Tom <u>and</u> Nan sat on <u>the</u> rug. Tom had <u>a</u> pup. Nan had <u>a</u> hen. <u>The</u> hen <u>and</u> <u>the</u> pup sat on <u>the</u> mat. <u>The</u> big bug got on <u>the</u> mat. <u>The</u> pup got up. <u>The</u> hen ran at <u>the</u> bug. <u>The</u> bug got on <u>Nan's</u> lap. <u>The</u> bug got on <u>the</u> rug. Nan got up. Tom ran <u>and</u> got <u>a</u> rod. <u>The</u> bug ran up <u>the</u> big <u>box</u>. Nan and Tom fed <u>and</u> fed the pup. <u>The</u> pup got big <u>and</u> fat.

Mary Davidson

CONSONANT BLENDS

(Before proceeding with the consonant blends, the teacher should familiarize himself with the section on dictation, beginning on page 123, so that he may use some of it while continuing with the review and new work indicated here.)

Learning the consonant blends will increase the number of words that the student can read.

Up to this point, the focus has been on typical consonant-vowel-consonant syllables, and those containing digraphs formed with <u>h</u> (<u>ch</u>, <u>sh</u>, <u>th</u>, <u>wh</u>). These function as single letters with distinctive sounds. The teacher may now introduce words that contain four to six letters. Plurals may be mentioned as a special type of blend.

Most students have little difficulty grasping the idea that in the case of blends, unlike digraphs, both letter sounds are heard. For example, in the word <u>risk</u>, both the \s\ and the \k\ are heard. In the word <u>spend</u>, the sounds \s\ and \p\, \n\ and \d\ are all heard. Sometimes an amusing exercise helpful in training auditory discrimination is to ask students to locate one or the other of these letter combinations in sample words; e.g., <u>frisk</u> starts with a blend and ends with a blend; <u>chest</u> starts with a digraph and ends with a blend. (Final blends are more difficult for some students; they may need extra practice.)

WORDS

Words like the following, printed on yellow cards in the Jewel Case, can now be introduced and shuffled into the pack of phonetic words for daily reading, frequent graphing, spelling in the Four-Point Program, and dictating.

risk	blend	slit	skin	staff	brand
grunt	stamp	plant	trim	stiff	dress
strap	grip	slab	mend	snuff	press
trash	drift	plot	trot	sniff	still
brisk	from	lent	flash	smell	fond
print	drop	lend	sled	spell	grass
trust	spot	grand	hand	swell	brass

SENTENCES

Words containing blends can now be used in stories, both for reading and dictation.

STORIES—GROUP II

Containing: Previously learned phonograms and Pattern 1; consonant blends added.

Ted and Kip

That is Ted.
Ted is in bed.
Ted is ill.
Send Ted a pet.
Which pet can I send him?
The dog is the best pet to send.
Get a tag for him.
At ten, send Kip to Ted.
Send him with a man.
If Kip is hot, he will pant.
Ted will thank the man.
This dog will help Ted to be happy.
Then Ted will get well.
This is Kip.
Kip is not a big dog, but he can
  run and jump.
Tell Kip to sit up.
Kip sits up just when Ted
  tells him to.

Kip can beg.
How much can Kip beg?
Kip can beg for his rag doll.
Ted will send the man to get the
  rag doll.
Kip will rip the rag doll.
The doll will not last.
Kip will miss it.
Ted will send Kip to his pen.
In his pen is a box.
Kip's bed is in the box.
Kip will rip the bed.
Such a dog!
Such a dog!
Is he a bad dog?
He is not!
Kip is just a rascal puppy.

C. I. Berger

(*dog*—not short o)

The Fish

Ted can fish well. A big fish swam in a pond. Ted got a fat grub. He bent a pin. He had a rod.

The fish swam up and bit the grub. Up went the rod. Up went the grub. Up went the fish with the grub.

Ted let Bob sit on the bench. The fish in the pan felt hot. Bob bit it. "Yum!" Then Ted bit the fish. "Yum, yum!"

"I am glad Ted can fish well," said Bob.

Miriam Phelps Baggett

Effect of Silent Final E

Thus far only one sound has been taught for each of the five vowels. These sounds are \a\, apple; \e\, eddy; \i\, itchy; called respectively "short a", "short e", "short i" in the dictionary. o \ä\, octopus; this sound of o is called "two-dot a." \ə\, umbrella; this sound of u is called *schwa* in the dictionary, when it is pronounced as in *cut*.

Now we shall take up a new sound and a new pronunciation symbol for each vowel.

These new sounds are indicated by placing a bar (⁻) over each of the following letters: ā, ē, ī, ō, illustrated below.

\ā\, ape, salmon card 7; \ē\, eve, salmon card 12; \ī\, pine, salmon card 20; \ō\, home; salmon card 23.

The letter u, in situations similar to the above, may have either of two sounds: \yü\, mule, salmon card 31a; \ü\, ruler, salmon card 31b.

The sounds of all the vowels as changed by silent final e are given in one lesson. Students should call this a vowel-consonant-e syllable.

The teacher should now say, "You know the names of all the vowels. What are they? What sound do they stand for?"

After students name the vowels and their sounds, the teacher will continue,

Now I am going to show you a magic trick: Suppose you take the little word pin. The letter i says \i\, right? Now suppose we just put an e on the end. We get pine, a great pine tree. That e doesn't say anything at all. It is silent, but it performs a trick. It makes the letter i say its own name, and the little pin is changed to a great big pine tree. That silent e on the end of a syllable does the same thing to all other vowels. It usually makes them say their own names. There are exceptions, so we say *usually*. By knowing this, you are now able to read almost twice as many words as you could at the beginning of this lesson! Take this list and see how you can read these new words right away.

WORDS

The following list is longer than needed for the yellow phonetic word cards. It is sometimes worthwhile to have the student read rapidly from a long typed list of similar words. The hope is that the student can perceive the vowel-consonant-e syllable quickly.

hide	ate	more	pane	rode	bite	ripe
dime	tone	mate	wake	name	safe	hire
wine	wide	gaze	wove	mane	robe	kite
pipe	time	bone	late	sake	tame	pale
wire	vine	tide	pave	note	vane	home
fade	wipe	pile	lone	gate	rake	lame
sale	dive	pine	ride	gave	vote	Jane
yoke	made	bake	life	mule	fate	make
same	save	size	nine	side	hope	duke
Kate	pole	wade	tape	line	pure	date
lake	lane	wave	hive	tine	wife	rope
rate	take	hole	bale	tire	mine	tune

These words are to be shuffled in with the growing pack of phonetic words for reading and spelling.

STORIES—GROUP III

Containing: Previously learned phonograms and patterns; silent final <u>e</u> added.

Jake and Kate

This <u>is</u> Jake.
<u>He</u> <u>came</u> in at the wide gate.
Jake <u>has</u> a big rake.
This <u>is</u> <u>his</u> wife.
<u>Her</u> name <u>is</u> Kate.
Kate <u>can</u> bake fine <u>cake</u>.
<u>She</u> gave Jake a bone.
<u>He</u> <u>can</u> smile at the joke.
Then Kate made Jake take a big bite <u>of</u> <u>cake</u>.
Jake ate up the <u>cake</u>.

Minna R. Colton

Jane and Sam

This <u>is</u> Jane.
Jane met Sam.
Sam gave Jane a ride.
<u>She</u> wore a red <u>cape</u>.
<u>They</u> <u>came</u> <u>to</u> a wide lake.
Sam <u>can</u> dive.
Jane likes <u>to</u> wade.
Sam and Jane ran home <u>to</u> tell <u>Mother</u>.
"<u>I</u> like <u>to</u> dive."
"<u>I</u> like <u>to</u> wade."

Minna R. Colton

Summer Trip

Last <u>summer</u> <u>I</u> went on a trip.
<u>I</u> went <u>to</u> a lake <u>to</u> fish.
<u>I</u> swam in the lake and had a fine time.

Evelyn Kratz

The Whale

This <u>is</u> a ship. It went <u>to</u> get fish. A big wave broke on the ship.
The ship had a bad time. The nets tore and let the fish swim <u>off</u>. A man fell from the mast. Then the mast broke.
"The men must help," <u>said</u> the mate. "Get ropes! Mend the mast and the nets!"
A big hulk swam up. "A whale!" <u>said</u> the mate.
The whale ate up the fish from the nets. The mate shot a gun. The shot had a line on it. It hit the whale. The whale did not bump the ship. It swam <u>off</u> with the rope and the fish.

At last the ship is at home. The mate is glad the ship is safe. But he is sad that the whale ate the fish.

Miriam Phelps Baggett

The Trip

This is Mike.
He is my chum.
I like Mike a lot.
He has a red bike and mine is white.
We will go on a bike hike up on the hill.
I will not want to miss the hike.
We will go if the sun shines.
We like to have fun in the grove by the bog.
Mike likes to wade in the wet fen.
We will make a stove of stones.
We will make a fire inside the stones.
Then we will eat our lunch.
I have a flat tire on my bike.
Mike will help me fix it.
We will ride down hill for home.
It is late and we must go fast.
We do not want to miss supper.
We had a fine day.
We want to do it again some time.

Mary Davidson

In the Game

Jim likes football.
He will take the pigskin and hug it to him.
He will dive at a gap in the line. Then he will run like a flash.
This will bluff the other lads.
Jim will help his side win.
In the big rush he will cut a gash in his shin. He will hit his lip and hand.
That is the risk you take in a game. But the game will be fun!
Jim's dad will pat and hug him when the game ends.

Margaret T. Willier

SYLLABLE CONCEPT

Some students may not completely understand the concept of a syllable. We have known several students who, when asked how many syllables were in their names, responded thoughtfully with the number of letters.

With instruction and practice, they gradually acquire the idea that a syllable is a word or part of a word. It is composed of one or more letters with one vowel sound and is produced by one impulse of the voice (e.g., I, me, can). To increase the student's understanding of a syllable, the teacher may ask, "How many syllables are there in the word *chair*?" "In *window*?" "In *baseball*?" "In *automobile*?" and so on.

When the student understands the concept of a syllable and can identify and apply the syllable pattern, he then has a strategy for reading words that he has never seen. There are six syllable patterns. It is not necessary to introduce all six at one time.

Note to the Teacher: As soon as the student was able to read the word "at," she mastered the first syllable pattern informally. Now is the time to teach syllable patterns as a concept.

Syllable Patterns

SYLLABLE PATTERN 1—CLOSED SYLLABLE (cvc)
The purpose of this pattern is to help students decide on the appropriate vowel sound, which for this pattern is most always short. At this point the student is not able to divide words into syllables independently. The rules for syllabication will be given later.

A. A closed syllable ends with a consonant.
B. The vowel before the final consonant has a short sound (for example, it, at, cat, that, went).

To Teach This Pattern:
* The teacher should have lists of words that are all closed syllables.
* Through guided instruction and drill, the student perceives the pattern (visually) and then conceptualizes it and applies it to new words.
* The student soon realizes that he can read and spell words he has never seen.

Three or four times a week, as part of a daily lesson, the student should practice syllable exercises. Working with syllables should continue in successive steps, according to the maturity and skill level of the student.

SYLLABLE PATTERN 2—VOWEL-CONSONANT-E (vce)
Note to the Teacher: Once again the student has already encountered words that contain the silent e pattern.

A. The final e is silent in a vowel-consonant-e syllable.
B. The silent e at the end of the word makes the vowel before it have a long sound (e.g., mule, same, stripe).

To Teach This Pattern:
* The teacher should have lists of words that are all closed syllables (e.g., **pin**).
* The teacher then places an e at the end of the closed syllable, showing that the e is silent and makes the vowel before the consonant long (e.g., **pine**).
* Through guided instruction and drill, the student perceives the pattern (visually) and then conceptualizes it and applies it to new words.

Activities

• *Detached Syllables*

Practice with detached syllables is often a most constructive step on the road to reading. Before a student attempts to read words of more than one syllable, he must be able to read separate syllables that are parts of larger words. These are phonetic syllables and are not real words but appear as units within larger words.

The student who has attempted to learn words as ideograms, guessing a word from the context without looking at its form, often refuses to attempt a detached syllable such as *sep* or *dit*. "It doesn't make sense," he protests. It is essential to help him attempt any pronounceable combination of letters. Hundreds of big words are composed largely or entirely of phonetic syllables. When such meaningless syllables can be pronounced in sequence, they often produce a supposedly difficult long word.

The following is a list of the six syllable patterns (adapted from *How to Teach Spelling*, Laura Toby Rudginsky and Elizabeth C. Haskell, Cambridge, MA: Educators Publishing Service, Inc., 1985). The patterns should be introduced as needed.

The Six Kinds of Syllables:

1. **Closed Syllable (c)**
   a. A closed syllable ends with a consonant.
   b. The vowel before the final consonant usually has a short sound (*thăt, shŏt, strŭt*).
2. **Vowel-Consonant-e̲ Syllable (vce̲)**
   a. The final e̲ is silent in a vowel-consonant-e̲ syllable.
   b. The silent e̲ at the end of the word makes the vowel before it have a long sound (*mūlé, sāmé, strīpé*).
3. **Open Syllable (o)**
   a. An open syllable ends with a vowel.
   b. The vowel has a long sound (says its own name).
   c. An open syllable can be just one letter if that letter is a vowel (*ī, ā, ō/pen*).
4. **Diphthong Syllable (d)**
   a. A diphthong syllable usually has two adjacent vowels that are pronounced together.
   b. The diphthong syllable has a special sound (*sail, stay, snow/ing, light, eight, greet/ing*).
   c. Be sure to notice whether a vowel combination is reversed (for example, *io* instead of *oi* as in *vi/o/lin*). If the two vowels are reversed, divide between them.
5. **r̲-Combination Syllable (r̲-com)**
   a. An r̲-combination syllable always has at least one vowel followed by r̲ (*ar, er, ir, or, ur*, and *ear*). The r̲ gives the vowel a unique sound.
   b. You have already learned the sounds these r̲-combinations make (*start, bird, burn/ing, learn, port, doc/tor, beg/gar, work*).

6. Consonant-*le* Syllable (c-*le*)
a. A consonant-*le* syllable comes at the end of a word (*cra/dle*, *bub/ble*, *ti/tle*).
b. A consonant-*le* syllable has no vowel sound. The silent *e* at the end of the syllable is the only vowel. Only the consonant and the *l* are pronounced.

• *Words with Separated Syllables*

In the next exercise the teacher asks the student to read real words of more than one syllable printed with the syllables apart.

Words like the following should be typed on a card:

sus	pend	pave	ment	im	pel	an	vil
trip	lets	hum	drum	trum	pet	mis	take
stam	pede	in	dex	hob	gob	lin	ton	sil

• *Jumbled Syllables*

Building words out of their component syllables is a favorite exercise for students of all ages. Picking up syllables and moving them into position most effectively conveys the idea of syllables as units in a word.

The words below are most suitable at this time. The teacher should write each word part (syllable) on a separate card. He or she may enlarge the list as work and progress proceed.

vel	vet		en	gulf	sun	set	sub	lime
trum	pet		him	self	ad	mire	in	fant
prob	lem		mis	take	um	pire	em	pire
chil	dren		pump	kin	en	trust	mem	brane
splen	did		tan	dem	em	press	tin	sel
in	fan	tile	in	dig	nant	stam	pede	ham	let
es	tab	lish	as	ton	ish	gob	let	
hob	gob	lin	in	vest	ment			

Accent

Even though the jumbled syllables are correctly arranged to form a word, the student may not recognize the word unless one syllable is stressed more forcibly than another. The student should be required to place the accent on each syllable in succession and decide which trial produces a word he recognizes. Students differ greatly in their ability to place and recognize accent. Some younger students recognize the stressed syllable almost at once. Other students, older and perhaps more capable, may pronounce a word correctly, e.g., *napkin*, placing the stress on the first syllable, and then insist that the accent is on the second one. With practice, students can detect and place accent correctly, an essential skill for pronouncing unfamiliar words looked up in the dictionary.

The discussion of accent is introduced at this point because logically the student is ready for it. It may prove an interesting supplementary exercise while drill on previous phonograms continues. However, it must never hold up the introduction of new topics. The next chapter must be begun promptly whether or not the work on accent has been successful. In any case it should be an incidental recreational exercise, never consuming a large portion of any lesson period. By the end of the work contained in this chapter, all students except those with marked auditory confusion should have developed a relatively reliable discrimination of accent.

Such exercises with syllables never constitute the main part of the day's work, but two or three times a week, a part of the period may be given to them.

BUILDING WORDS WITH SYLLABLES—SPELLING PATTERNS

The most advantageous time to introduce a particular spelling pattern depends upon the student. For example, many lower grade students understand and apply Pattern 2 (compound words), while other students fail to grasp its full import until they are much older. Chapter 7 explains the development of each pattern.

Depending on the material covered, the logical place for the introduction of Pattern 2 is after the spelling of blends (see page 47).

Familiarity with Pattern 2 and consideration of accent determine the logical time to introduce Pattern 3. It is usually best to postpone the consideration of this pattern for a time because the words covered by it will not occur in the young student's vocabulary.

Familiarity with the spelling of words ending in silent final <u>e</u> (see page 48) leads logically to the introduction of Pattern 4.

REGARD FOR SYLLABLES IN SPELLING LONG WORDS

A great deal of misspelling in the upper grades might be prevented if the habit of always repeating the word had been established early, at least subvocally, with syllables distinctly separate. Not only must the whole word be repeated with clearly marked syllable division, but the spelling must follow this division. For example, when *pavement* has been dictated, the student must begin by saying, "\pāv\ [slight pause] \mənt\," so that each syllable is clear. He then begins to spell the word, syllable by syllable: "<u>p-a-v-e</u> [slight pause] <u>m-e-n-t</u>." If he spells the first syllable as <u>p-a-v</u> (without the <u>e</u>), then pauses in preparation for spelling the second syllable, he must be stopped before he makes the error of beginning the second syllable without correctly completing the first. The teacher must ask, "How do you pronounce <u>p-a-v</u>?" She should make it clear that without the silent <u>e</u> at the end of the syllable, <u>p-a-v</u> spells \pav\, not \pāv\. Similarly, if the student begins spelling the word *program* as <u>p-r-o-g</u>, he must be stopped and asked to pronounce what he has just spelled: \präg\. Since the teacher did not dictate \präg'-ram\, beginning the spelling with <u>p-r-o-g</u> is incorrect. The student must spell each syllable separately; for *program*, <u>p-r-o</u> <u>g-r-a-m</u>.

To insist upon the repetition of the word is not merely a teaching device, but a bit of daily diagnosis as well. Misspelling is often due to inability to retain the auditory sequence. If the practice words are lengthened too rapidly, they may exceed the span of immediate recall, and a student cannot be expected to spell a word that he cannot repeat correctly. For example, when he can spell monosyllables correctly but spells problem as poblem, or astonish as astonsh, as often happens when the student has practiced insufficient repetition, it means that he has not held the sound of the word from beginning to end. Perhaps it is not enough to insist upon the repetition of the word before spelling. He may need echo exercises to isolate his particular difficulty. He can be given several words each day to repeat after the teacher, e.g., transport trans/port, Atlantic At/lan/tic, election e/lec/tion, responsible re/spon/si/ble. Here, of course, spelling plays no part. The goal is to see how long an auditory sequence he can retain and repeat.

It may help some students to give them manipulatives (small blocks of wood, pennies, or other items) to use while echoing each syllable. Place several of them on the desk. Ask the student to move a block toward herself as she echoes each syllable. This will give the student a visual cue to assist her in keeping the syllables in the correct sequence and retaining the appropriate number of syllables in the given word.

The Dictionary

Although there are many different dictionaries in print, we have based this manual on *Merriam-Webster's Collegiate Dictionary*, tenth edition. The use of the dictionary in schools is confined largely to definitions, and the meaning of words is naturally very important. However, we do not emphasize this aspect of dictionary use in the technique of this manual. We are endeavoring to give the student skill in locating words efficiently and in pronouncing them by means of the symbolic representation of sounds.

Syllable Division

Now that he has worked with detached and jumbled syllables, the student is ready to begin to learn about the various syllable types. With this knowledge the student will be able to separate words into syllables and determine the appropriate vowel sound based on the syllable pattern he has identified.

PATTERN 1   A one-syllable word is never divided. It is composed of one or more letters with one vowel sound and is produced by one impulse of the voice (*I, me, can, plan, hug, it*).

PATTERN 2   A compound word is divided between the words that make it a compound word (*cowboy cow/boy, sunset sun/set, baseball base/ball*). Present the student with many examples of compound words to be certain that she understands the concept.

PATTERN 3   When two or more consonants come between two vowels in a word, the word is usually divided between the first two consonants (ve**l**vet ve**l**/**v**et, tru**mp**et tru**m**/**p**et, hu**ng**ry hu**n**/**g**ry). Before the student is ready to apply this syllabication pattern, he should have much practice in reading closed syllable words to become skilled in identifying the pattern and then ascertaining the vowel sound.

The following list contains the remaining patterns for dividing words into syllables. Introduce them as needed, using the above procedure.

DIVIDING WORDS INTO SYLLABLES

1. A one-syllable word is never divided.

    boat   good   small   knelt

2. A compound word is divided between the words that make the compound word.

    raincoat   sunset   airplane   baseball

3. When two or more consonants come between two vowels in a word, the word is usually divided between the first two consonants.

    hungry   better   suffer   picture

4. When a word has a suffix, it is divided between the root and the suffix.

    melted   softness   sewing   homeless

5. When a word has a prefix, it is divided between the prefix and the root.

    except   disturb   mislead   unsold

6. When a single consonant comes between two vowels in a word, the word is usually divided after the consonant if the first vowel is short.

    clever   lemon   robin   travel

7. When a single consonant comes between two vowels in a word, the word is usually divided before the consonant if the vowel is long.

    music   polite   paper   locate

8. When a vowel is sounded alone in a word, it forms a syllable by itself.

    disobey   alive   monument   uniform

9. When two vowels come together in a word and are sounded separately, divide the word between the two vowels.

    radio   diet   cruel   idea

10. When a word ends in <u>le</u> preceded by a consonant, the word is divided before that consonant.

turtle   cable   thistle   bicycle

11. When a word or syllable ends in <u>al</u> or <u>el</u>, usually these letters form the last syllable.

camel   jewel

12. When <u>ed</u> comes at the end of a word, it adds a syllable only when preceded by <u>d</u> or <u>t</u>.

landed   taunted   sported

Syllable Division

1. Determine and mark the vowels.
2. Determine and mark the consonants between the vowels.
3. Determine the syllable pattern and divide accordingly.
4. Pronounce the word by syllables.
5. Do you know the word?
6. Have you divided it correctly, or are there other possibilities?
7. If yes, start over again.

Words Phonetic for Reading but Not for Spelling

CHAPTER OVERVIEW

Chapter 3 begins with an explanation of how some words are phonetic for reading but not for spelling. Using the example *since*, students quickly learn that reading such words can be easy, while spelling them is a whole different ball game!

Although the history of written language has been reviewed and discussed in Chapter 1, the history of the English language is now reviewed more specifically. As before, the purpose of this dialogue helps to lay a foundation from which the student can better understand the complexities of our language and from where many of our words were derived. Adaptation and modification of this information is at the teacher's discretion.

The remainder of this chapter moves into the development of decoding skills, and covers new phonograms—their placement, sounds, and use.

The chapter also includes word lists and a variety of dictionary exercises.

Materials Needed

- Phonics Drill Cards*
- Phonetic Word Cards (Jewel Case—introducing blue cards)*
- Introduction of Diphthongs* (optional)
- *Merriam-Webster's Elementary Dictionary*
- Little Stories (Group IV)*
- World map/globe (optional)

---

* Gillingham Supplementary Materials

SEQUENCE OF LETTERS AND CONCEPTS PRESENTED IN CHAPTER 3

	Jewel Case Card Numbers:
y (as a vowel)	284–293
ph	294–298
x	299–309
qu	310–313
hard and soft c and g	314–333
s	334–347
*Syllable Concept**	page 71
*Dictionary Technique**	page 71
Final Syllables Ending in y	page 71
Vowel at the End of a Syllable	348–374
a, e, i, o, u, y /*i*/	New response: long vowel sound (see page 72)
ild, old, ind, ost Words	375–403
Diphthongs/Sight Words	Introduce as needed

Thus far we have dealt with a perfectly phonetic language, in which each phonogram has had only one sound and each sound has been represented by only one symbol. The long vowels and two-dot ü have been introduced, but only in the situation in which they are tagged by the silent final e̲. Separate cards are used for drill on this. Students have learned only one possible pronunciation or spelling for the words, and the reading and spelling have merely been the reverse of each other.

As soon as the first ambiguity is introduced, both the character and the relative difficulty of the processes change. If a phonogram has two sounds and the wrong one is tried first, the student can instantly self-correct, thinking about what makes sense, sounds correct, or fits context clues; for example, *stream* when read \strem\ will readily be changed to \strēm\. At this point, reading is still largely phonetic. Spelling a sound that can be represented by two or more phonograms is much more difficult. Drill, repetition, review, and knowledge of generalizations will help visual recall. Some students have brought out this distinction by describing certain words as "phonetic for reading but not for spelling." For example, *since* can be read in only one way, whereas the sound \sins\ could be spelled c-i-n-s-e, s-i-n-s-e, c-y-n-c-e, s-y-n-c-e, c-y-n-s-e, s-y-n-s-e, s-i-n-c-e, or c-i-n-c-e.

The introduction of a second sound for a symbol, or two spellings to represent one sound, is a momentous event for the student who has just begun to understand the notion of written language as a phonetic instrument. During the previous period of failure he may have wearily decided that English is senselessly complicated. He now naturally inquires why any letter should have more than one sound or any sound be spelled in more than one way.

---

* A few minutes each day should be given to these topics while presenting new phonograms.

The answer to this repeated and often indignant question cannot be really understood until the student has some understanding of the history of the English language. The idea that words change as they pass from country to country can transform what seemed a foolish muddle into a tale of adventure. The exact details of language change are often lost in antiquity and some are the subject of conjecture—even bitter controversy—among authorities, but one can follow the general course of English's development with sufficient accuracy.

No teacher can foresee all the questions that may arise in any lesson. Books on language history and illustrations of alphabet changes should be at hand. Encyclopedias usually give plates showing the origins of our alphabet. An unabridged dictionary is also helpful. Long before the student is ready for definite dictionary technique, he should have learned to regard the dictionary as a source of fascinating information. Some students are ready at this stage to understand only that words reach us from many languages, but something like the following gives the trend of attitude we would like the student to acquire, although it may not all come at once. For additional resources on the history of the English language, see the Appendix.

MORE HISTORY OF THE ENGLISH LANGUAGE

Anyone who gave himself the task could construct a perfectly phonetic language by assigning just one letter to each sound. Esperanto is one example; so is the Hawaiian language as written down by the early missionaries. No living language remains as simple as that, although some are relatively phonetic, such as the German, Italian, and Spanish languages. People move about and mingle with those who speak other languages, and they learn words from each other. Finally, over time, people change the way they pronounce words.

English, with over 350 million speakers (half the population of the world) and with its vocabulary of close to a million words, is rapidly becoming the first global language. It owes its huge vocabulary to its ability to absorb words from other languages. When we learn English, we are learning not one, but three languages—each with its own phonology and structure. Although English is classified as a Germanic language, less than one percent of English words are Germanic. Over half are based on Latin, and about eleven percent are Greek.

The Angles, Saxons, and Jutes came from northern Germany, bringing their language with them. Later the Vikings—known as the Danes, although they came from all over Scandinavia—invaded the land. The Danes spoke a northern branch of Germanic. Although relatively few in number, Germanic words are the common, everyday words in the language. All the words on the Dolch list, all the words on any list of the "100 most common words" are Germanic.

Germanic words are short because over time, the endings dropped off. Most of our one-syllable words are Germanic, such as *the, but, cold, sit.* Because they are the oldest words in the language, they are the least phonetic and the hardest to spell. Words such as *was, they, could, knee, write, old, most,* and *thought* are Germanic. Silent letters, vowel pairs, and the unfamiliar behavior of vowels are characteristics of the Germanic strain of the language.

While a handful of Latin words entered the language during the Roman era, most of them came by way of French. French is a *Romance* language: the word means *Roman* and French is closely related to Latin. Some of the Vikings had settled in northern France in Normandy (which means "north men") and adopted the French feudal ways and language. In 1066 they invaded England, bringing their language with them. For the next three hundred years, no king of England spoke English, every English king was also king of France, and French was the language of the court and of the educated people. Thousands of French words found their way into the English language. Later still, scholars in England borrowed words directly from Latin itself. The Christian Church, with its center in Rome, adopted Latin for its services. As Christianity spread over western Europe, the people attending services learned many Latin words. Latin also entered the language through the schools and universities where Latin was required.

Latin words are usually long and consist of a prefix, a root, and a suffix, as in the words *pre dic tion, dis tract able, con ver sion, in somni a, trans port ation*. Latin words seldom use vowel pairs, but use vowel-consonant-e or the vowel alone for the long sound, as in *denote, invade, complete*. Latin never uses <u>sh</u> for /sh/; instead, the sound is spelled <u>ti</u>, <u>ci</u>, <u>si</u>, or <u>xi</u>, as in *invention, social, permission, complexion*.

Greek words came into the language from two sources: by way of Latin, for every educated Roman knew Greek; or borrowed by scientists. Greek has become the language of science.

Greek words can be recognized by their spelling and structure. They use <u>ph</u> for /f/, <u>ch</u> for /k/ and <u>y</u> for /i/: *phone, nymph, chaos, school, gym, type, tyrant, physics, myth*. Often a Greek word consists of two elements joined by a connecting <u>o</u>: *photograph, monogamy, cryptogram, hydrogen, geography, psychology*. Scientists use Greek when they want a word for a new discovery or invention, as with *electron, neutron, proton, petroleum, cardiogram, cyclotron*.

As English spread throughout the world with the British Empire, it continued to acquire new words. The crusaders and the trade with medieval China had already brought back words such as *tea, sofa*, and *sherbet*, but as the British Empire spread throughout the world, English words from many countries entered the language. From India: *rajah, calico, curry, bungalow, jungle, pyjama*. From Australia and New Zealand: *kangaroo, kiwi, outback, dingo*. From Africa: *indaba, safari, impi*, and, adopting the words the Dutch settlers had used, *veldt, kiopje, springbok*.

With the move to the New World, foreign words flooded into the language. Because the Dutch were among the first settlers we have many Dutch words that we no longer think of as foreign: *coleslaw, cookie, waffle, caboose, landscape*. The French voyageurs and explorers contributed *chowder, pumpkin, levee, crevasse, portage*, and *prairie*, and those who settled Louisiana added to the list. African Americans contributed *banana, cola, goober, yam, gorilla, tote*, and *okra*.

The Native Americans who were here first contributed place names—of mountains, rivers, and landmarks from coast to coast—as well as the names of over half the states. Other native loan words include *caribou, toboggan, mackinaw, pone, terrapin, papoose, hammock, raccoon, tobacco*, and, by way of Spanish, *barbecue* and *canoe*.

The potato famine that began in 1845 brought the Irish immigrants. The 1848 revolution brought us the Germans who settled Pennsylvania and the Midwest. After the American Civil War came the Spanish, Italians, and Scandinavians. Czechs, Slovaks, and Poles followed. Chinese were hired to build the railways and stayed on. Japanese settled the West Coast. Refugees from all over Europe fled World War II. There followed a huge influx from Puerto Rico, China, Hong Kong, Korea, and Thailand. Each group brought new words into the language.

So, it is no wonder that English is a complicated language and that the spelling is particularly complex to master. Remember, when you teach or study English, you are dealing with more than one language, each with its own phonology, structure, and rules.

Our alphabet, like those of most western European languages, is practically the same as the Latin one, but some of the languages that words were borrowed from used very different alphabets. Often, borrowed letters were used in a new language to represent sounds they never had in their old home. For example, the Greeks had a letter pronounced unlike any Latin letter. The Romans used it in words borrowed from the Greeks. They probably tried very hard to give it the Greek sound, but it was not always pronounced the same. In some words it became more like u̱ and in others like i̱, but its form was still something like the Greek letter. We know it today as y̱; most of our words in which y̱ has a vowel sound in the body of the word came to us from the Greek, such as *type, style, tyrant, myth, physics*.

We also find y̱ as \ī\ or \ē\ at the end of words. These come to us from Latin directly or from Anglo-Saxon, Middle English, French, German, or other languages. The changes that take place in words during long periods of use by many sorts of people are hard to believe. We know that even in different parts of our own country—New England, the South, the West—people pronounce words differently. American English is different from British English. But the changes we are now describing took place during centuries among people of different races and training. Thus, strange as it may seem, Latin *gloria* became English *glory*, and Latin *victoria*, English *victory*. The Anglo-Saxon ending *-tig* has reached us today as *-ty*, e.g., *twenty*, and the German *lustig* has become English *lusty*. We have the Anglo-Saxon ending *-lic* or *-lice* transformed into *-ly*, in *fatherly, daily, badly, safely*.

The Latin suffix *-ficare*, "to make," was combined with other words, e.g., *magnificare*, "to make big." French people speaking such words for many years changed the ending to *-fier*. When English people took these words, the suffix became *-fy*, as in *satisfy, magnify*.

In the early Roman days there was no letter i̱. This new letter seems to have been a scribe's alteration of the letter i̱. Especially at the beginning of a word he sometimes let his pen run down below the line. For a long time i̱ and i̱ had the same sound, really only two forms of the same letter. But, as we can prove to ourselves, it is hard to say initial \i\ followed by a vowel without making it sound like a consonant. *Iustitia* came to be pronounced *yustitia*, from which comes our word *justice*. In other places this initial i̱ or i̱ took on a soft g sound. People from Norway and Sweden learning to speak English often find it very difficult to pronounce our \j\. They say *yust* for *just*, and *yelly* for *jelly*.

Our consonant sound for y̱ is always at the beginning of a word or syllable. If we look up such words we will find that a large proportion of them are from Anglo-Saxon words beginning with g, such as the following: y̱es from *gese*, y̱oke from *geoc*, y̱ield from *gieldan*. We find the Anglo-Saxon word *gung* spelled *jung* in German and coming to us as y̱oung.

Whenever we find one of our English letters with two sounds, or two symbols for one English sound, or silent in a word, we know that this is a record of the changes wrought by people of different languages who altered the original sounds as they pronounced them.

Such a background will give a student an understanding attitude. He should make no effort to remember exact changes, but he will have acquired interest in the derivations following words in the dictionary and will have some basis for recognizing language groups, such as seeing the differences between European languages and Asian ones. Our essential purpose is to bring order out of the chaos in words—an understanding of the surprising uses of letters.

Before starting the main work of this chapter on page 68 the teacher should read the intervening pages, in order to plan for the work to be done parallel with the progress in reading.

SYMBOLS WITH MULTIPLE SOUNDS

From the first day when a second sound is introduced for a phonogram or a second spelling for a sound, there must be a radical change in procedure.

Review of white and salmon cards (Association I—symbol with letter name and sound) must be continuous. Not only will the pack be enlarged by the addition of new cards, but some of the familiar ones will now acquire additional responses.

Association II (teacher gives sound, student gives letter name) and Association III (teacher says sound, student writes letter) are not applied to any of the *new* phonograms or responses in this chapter while practice in Association I is being pursued. The student should not spell any of the words following each phonogram. As this chapter's title implies, these words are for *reading only*.

All the phonograms here have more than one sound, and the student will become conscious of the sounds that have more than one spelling. It is possible to *read* such words by trying first one sound and then another. However, after the soft sound of g has been learned so that *suggest* or *germ* can be read, there is no way of knowing whether the correct spelling of the former is *suggest* or *sugjest*, or whether the latter is *germ* or *jerm*, as with the spellings of *since* on page 62.

The practice words following the phonograms in this chapter, prior to diphthongs, are typed on blue cards in the Jewel Case. *These are not to be spelled at this stage.* Since they require more thought and trial than the words on the yellow cards (also in the Jewel Case), they should not be recorded on the same graph. They can be assigned a separate graph of their own, however, and receive drill on different days.

The Four-Point Program for phonetic words (Chapter 2) should be continued every few days. Spelling from now on must receive greater and different emphasis than before.

In Chapter 2, spelling is the reverse of reading. The procedure now changes and increasingly we try to present *spelling as a thinking subject*. This new presentation of spelling is accomplished by means of the introduction of patterns and generalizations. The students following the technique are *not* to be asked to learn arbitrary lists of spelling words as they appear in the spelling textbook. The description of the notebook that follows will give the clearest idea of the development of spelling as a subject requiring careful thought. (See also Chapters 7 and 8.)

STUDENT'S NOTEBOOK

By this time, the student is producing various kinds of papers. These should all be dated and preserved as a record of the student's work. We have found that she takes great pride in a formal notebook with conspicuous headings under which she can file her papers.

Work can be easily organized using a standard three-ring binder, equipped with dividing pages and blank tabs to be labeled Tests; Patterns; Generalizations; Learned Words; Dictation.

TESTS

1. **Ordinary spelling tests**
   The regulation spelling test—words pronounced by the teacher that the student writes in columns, using S.O.S.

2. **Labeling tests**
   The teacher dictates the words he has carefully selected from Patterns, Generalizations, and Learned Words already covered, with a liberal sprinkling of phonetic words. In the second column the student indicates his reason for spelling the word as he has just written it.

   For example: hoping   Pattern 4
                          thrash   ph (phonetic)

   This test demands deeper thought than does merely writing words and hoping that they are correct.

LABELING TEST

TEACHER DICTATES AND STUDENT WRITES	REASON
hoping	Pattern 4
thrash	ph.
changeable	Pattern 4 (exceptions)
were	l. w.
jumping	Pattern 2
cliff	Pattern 1
beginning	Pattern 3

WRONG - RIGHT TEST

WORDS WRITTEN BY TEACHER	CORRECT	CORRECTED BY STUDENT	REASON
less	✓		Pattern 1 - 2 s's
steping	✗	stepping	Pattern 2 - baseword 1 c
chil	✗	chill	Pattern 1 - 2 l's
lifted	✓		Pattern 2 - baseword 2 c
shadded	✗	shaded	Pattern 4 - baseword silent e
lonesome	✓		Pattern 4 - suf. beg. with c.
admitted	✓		Pattern 3 - baseword 1 c.

3. The Wrong-Right Test

The teacher writes words that come under patterns and generalizations already taught. Some of these are spelled correctly, others incorrectly in violation of the patterns. The student checks the word as correct or rewrites it because it is incorrect. He is then required to give the *reason* for the correction. There is no danger of confusing the student about the correct spelling. *Words given in these tests must only be those that fall under patterns already studied.* The teacher or student can give reasons for each spelling. It is the best device we have discovered for training students to proofread their own work. Teachers should never allow a *learned word* to be written incorrectly under any circumstances.

SPELLING PATTERNS

As dictation exercises become longer, the number of words available for them should increase. New patterns are gradually added to those previously taught. Each pattern is developed, *applied,* and in time memorized. It is better not to teach a pattern at all than to leave it as a memorized statement without an established habit of use. (See Chapter 7.)

GENERALIZATIONS

There are some words that can be spelled by the simple process of translating sounds into symbols (such as the words presented in Chapters 1 and 2). However, some words are not easily encoded for spelling, and one needs to develop a "spelling sense" or strategy in order to spell words the student has never seen before. A generalization is the ability to apply previously learned patterns and knowledge to the process of spelling new words. When all the phonograms in this chapter that have the same sounds have been mastered, they should be assembled and repeated by the student whenever the teacher calls for them as they appear on the back of the yellow phonics drill cards (for spelling). (See Chapter 7.)

LEARNED WORDS

There should be very few learned words at this time. Every word learned for itself as an ideogram (picture or symbol representation) violates our fundamental concept of word building. No one can foresee the exact words that will be needed, but a few such as the following will be found essential for dictation: were, has, have, does, goes, come.

Such words are studied S.O.S., and are reviewed in the labeling test. They are recorded in the notebook, as they are essential in construction of dictation exercises.

DICTATION

Papers filed under this heading should be dictation exercises produced in accordance with the instructions in Chapter 6.

INTRODUCTION OF NEW PHONOGRAMS

We emphasize again that none of the practice words following the letters and phonograms introduced in this chapter are to be used in spelling. They are meant for reading only, and are printed on blue cards in the Jewel Case.

The consonant y \y\ as in *yes* has been familiar for some time. This letter is now shown on a salmon card, that is, with vowel sounds. These are the same sounds as those of the letter i and also e:

y	Salmon card 6a, b, c	y-e	type \ī\. Salmon card 33.
y	gym \i\	ey	valley \ē\. Salmon card 19.
y	cyclone \ī\	ey	they \ā\
y	candy \ē\		

New Words: system, symbol, nylon, python, whey, type, style, salty.

If suitable, the teacher can point out that a large number of the words in which y has a vowel sound come to us from the Greek and are likely to be scholarly and technical words.

The Greeks had another letter, Φ (pronounced "phi"), unlike any in the Latin alphabet and with a different sound. When the Romans borrowed Greek words containing this letter, they did not know how to represent it, so they made a new combination, ph. This phonogram was pronounced in several ways, \p\ and \b\ and \f\, but early scholars who were careful to speak correctly regarded the \f\ sound with contempt. In time, however, as more and more people spoke these words they made the sound more and more like \f\. After many centuries—by A.D. 500—the two symbols f and ph came to be pronounced exactly alike. Words in which \f\ is spelled ph have reached us directly from Greek or through Latin.

Students are often interested to learn that the same kind of changes are still going on. *Sea* and *tea* used to be pronounced \sā\ and \tā\. Another type of change is the acceptance of words formerly regarded as incorrect or slang. *Mob* is such a word and so is *bike*.

ph phone \f\. White card 24.

This digraph occurs for the most part in scholarly and scientific words. A few that would be familiar to students are unsuitable at this stage. These are the only ones appropriate at present:

New Words: Philip, Joseph, lymph, graph

x box \ks\. White card 19.

This is not a distinctive sound, merely a blending of \k\ and \s\. It is frequently mispronounced, even by teachers. We have heard it reversed \sk\ and, again, given an initial vowel \iks\, and both errors show up disastrously in spelling.

New Words: fix, six, mix, box, fox, wax, lax, tax, index, suffix, annex

In English, there are several sounds for x. However \ks\ is the most common. It seems better not to risk confusion by introducing the others; they can be considered later.

qu queen \kw\. White card 13.

If manuscript writing must be used, this letter should be taught as q so that it is kinesthetically not the reverse of p. The student should start as if writing an a and continue downward as for a g.

The body of the letter turns toward the picture of a duck on the wall.
The duck quacks. (See page 42.)

In English q never occurs alone. It is always followed by u and the sound is a blending of \k\ and \w\.

New Words: quit, quite, quiz, squint

We now come to one of the most interesting situations in our phonics teaching, hard and soft c and g.

In the early Latin days the Etruscans in Italy used k and c for the same sound, sometimes like \s\, sometimes like \k\, and sometimes like \g\. The sound seemed to depend partly upon the following vowel. We have already noted that g was often changed into consonant y in pronunciation and spelling.

After a long time the sounds of c and g have become fairly well settled in English usage, but it is not hard to understand that with so many languages influencing ours, there might easily be exceptions to any pattern. We must be careful about saying that any form of spelling or pronunciation is "always" one way. "Usually" is a much safer word.

In English c has two sounds, neither of which is wholly its own. One is that of s and the other is that of k. The letter g has a sound entirely its own, \g\, but in addition, it often has a soft sound exactly like that of j.

Some students who like to be dramatic explain emphatically that y and g each have a sound of their own and then also take on another sound. The letter c, poor thing, has no sound of its own and must always borrow from either k or s.

How are we to know when to read c as \k\ and when as \s\? When does g say \g\ and when \j\? We can learn these all at once in five minutes. However, practice and drill will be needed for a long time to form the appropriate habits.

Generalization

Before e, i, or y, c is soft. It sounds like \s\ as in city.
c cat \k\. White card 2.
g goat \g\. White card 5.
Before e, i, or y, g is *usually* soft, that is, it *usually* sounds like j. It sounds like \j\ as in gym.

Students can now read the following list. They may need help, but teachers can supply it, not by pronouncing the word, but by repeatedly restating the above facts. It is especially important not to use any of these words in a spelling lesson.

NEW WORDS

ice	gun	pencil	space	cramp	strange	crush
got	cub	age	race	clip	grin	globe
drug	cup	can	trace	cab	face	glade
mice	crunch	nice	cube	cat	congest	distance
rage	cut	beg	brace	sage	grip	crust
gem	grand	grade	grace	cob	grape	quince
cage	crib	drag	grate	slice	cent	huge
clove	since	cactus	crab	census	crisp	stage
page	prince	gas	crate	price	gibe	crept
face	crane	grave	grunt	twice	convex	fence
change	glide	gulf	crop	range	club	crystal
gum	cute	place	got	lace	glad	entrance

The reason for saying *usually* so forcibly in the Generalization is that there are a few words in which g before e, i, or y is hard. These are very common words with which the student may already be familiar, e.g., girl, get, begin.

A more extended list of g words, which are exceptions to this Generalization, is in the Appendix.

White cards 29 through 44 may now be introduced for drill but should always be kept separate from the main pack. In the case of all the other cards, the sound of the whole phonogram is to be given. In the case of these cards, the teacher gives only the sound of the c or g.

The teacher should ask, "What sound does this c have?" thus forcing attention upon the c or g.

The student will encounter a few words like the following: guess, guide, plague, guild, guest. In these, g would be soft if the u were not inserted before the e or i to make the g hard. Such words may be difficult for spelling but should present no problem for reading.

Generalization

s not only says \s\ as in snake but also \z\ as in nose. White cards 15a and 15b.

When the s stands between two vowels it frequently says \z\. At the end of many words, especially plurals and possessives, s can also say \z\.

New Words: as, has, is, his, pins, lids, rugs, hose, wise, rise, fuse, the boy's hat, phrase

The Little Story *The Ten White Mice* can be read at this time. See page 74.

SYLLABLE CONCEPT

The following parts of words for Separated and Jumbled Syllables can be placed on cards and used as an activity in which students will correctly join syllables into words and then correctly pronounce and accent them.

SEPARATED SYLLABLES.   Here we have ambiguous sounds like hard and soft c and g in separated syllables.

can	cel	pen	cil	in	quire
cam	pus	ath	lete	con	fis cate
ban	quet	con	fuse	dol	phin

JUMBLED SYLLABLES

tal	cum	sug	gest	pam	phlet
cos	tume	prin	cess	ex	cite
ran	cid	ad	vice	ex	cel

DICTIONARY TECHNIQUE

By this time most students will be ready to study dictionary technique as described in Chapter 10. The dictionary is an essential tool for the poor speller, and it is inadequately handled by large numbers of high school and college students. We believe that the little booklets of the Skeleton Dictionary, with the training they afford in encouraging use of the Guide Words, are of great value. They are simple to make according to the description in Chapter 10.

However, the pressing need is to introduce more phonograms and thereby progress to further reading. It should be possible to cover much of the material suggested for syllable concept and dictionary technique with brief lessons while the introduction of new phonograms proceeds.

INTRODUCTION OF VOWEL SOUNDS IN NEW SITUATIONS

We now find several instances of vowel sounds in new situations. (See also Chapter 4, page 108 for information.)

The vowels e, o, and y are pronounced as $\bar{e}$, $\bar{o}$, and $\bar{\imath}$ respectively at the end of several common monosyllables familiar to most students; for example:

> e   he, me, she, we, be
> o   no, so, go
> y   by, my, cry, dry, fly, fry

Some vowels are long at the end of a few longer words:

> o   as in banjo

There is one group of very common final syllables ending in y which must be learned: the <u>by</u>, <u>cy</u>, <u>ly</u> group.

Students must be repeatedly reminded that the vowel sounds of <u>y</u> (see page 68) are \i\, \ī\, or \ē\. The following words illustrate <u>y</u> sounding \ē\: \'bā-bē\, \'kan-dē\, \'sȯl-tē\.

Words ending in <u>ble</u>, <u>ple</u>, etc., such as <u>table</u> \'tāb-l\, <u>cradle</u> \'krād-l\, are often pronounced as if the <u>ble</u>, <u>ple</u>, were a terminal syllable: \'tā-bəl\, \'krā-dəl\. More accurately, it is the absence of a vowel sound, indicated by a hyphen, \d-l\, \p-l\, or the schwa in superscript: \d-ᵊ\, which the dictionary shows.

The mispronunciation of these words may not always be detected, but it leads to misspelling later. A common variation in pronunciation is the omission of the final consonant of a base word to which the suffix -<u>ly</u> has been added, as in <u>directly</u>, \də-'rek-tlē\, becomes \də-'rek-lē\. These alternate possibilities in pronunciation are indicated in the dictionary by placing the <u>t</u> in parentheses, \də-'rek(t)-lē\.

A new response is now taught for each of the six vowel cards:

<u>a</u> <u>apple</u> \a\. Salmon card 1.
<u>a</u> <u>baby</u> \ā\.
    A vowel at the end of an accented syllable is usually long.

<u>e</u> <u>eddy</u> \e\. Salmon card 2.
<u>e</u> <u>eject</u> \ē\.
    A vowel at the end of an accented syllable is long.

<u>i</u> <u>itchy</u> \i\. Salmon card 3.
<u>i</u> <u>spider</u> \ī\.
    A vowel at the end of an accented syllable is long.

<u>o</u> <u>octopus</u> \ä\. Salmon card 4.
<u>o</u> <u>pony</u> \ō\.
    A vowel at the end of an accented syllable is long.

<u>u</u> <u>upper</u> \ə\ pronounced as in *cut*. Salmon card 5.
<u>u</u> <u>music</u> \yü\.
    This vowel at the end of an accented syllable is \yü\ or \ü\.

<u>y</u> <u>gym</u> \i\. Salmon card 6.
<u>y</u> <u>cyclone</u> \ī\.
    This vowel at the end of an accented syllable is long <u>e</u> or <u>i</u>.

ILD-OLD WORDS

This is a special group of words in which the vowel sounds appear in new situations.

With a few minor exceptions, the vowels in all the words thus far have had the short sound except those at the end of an accented syllable within the word or those given the long sound by the final silent <u>e</u>.

There is a curious group of words in which a vowel in the middle of a word is long, but followed by two consonants instead of one plus final silent e. They are usually called the \īld\-\ōld\ words.

The principal ones follow:

child	bind	pint	old	host	roll	both
mild	blind		bold	most	toll	
wild	grind		cold	post	poll	
	hind		gold		stroll	
	kind		hold		scroll	
	mind		mold			
	rind		sold			
	wind		scold			
			told			

Logically, *scold* and *cold* should not be given for spelling until after the \k\ generalizations of Chapter 8 have been taught.

From the reading of these words it becomes evident that this situation applies only to i and o.

Contrary to statements about spelling in this chapter, -ild and -old words can be used for spelling after they have become familiar for reading. This is the reason that these words are printed on yellow cards in the Jewel Case.

Note: At this point the teacher should familiarize herself with pages 82 to 85 so that she can carry on as much of this material as is consistent with the ability of the student, while introducing the remaining phonograms.

STORIES—GROUP IV

The following stories originated through the efforts of various teachers in an attempt to develop controlled reading activities. They are to be read as the phonograms, including the first diphthongs, are taught.

The stories contain:

- previously learned phonograms and patterns
- hard and soft c and g (*The Ten White Mice* can follow the introduction of these concepts)
- a few diphthongs (ee, ou, ow, ai, oo, ea)
- ar, or, ir, ed, tch, ck, sion, tion, ch \k\, y and \ē\

The complete text of the stories that end in an ellipsis can be found in the Little Stories supplemental materials published by Educators Publishing Service, Inc. (Call or write for availability information.)

The Ten White Mice

Jane has ten white mice.
She got them at the pet shop.
The white mice came in a big cage.
It is made of wire.
Jane gave the mice a big cake.
The mice ate up the cake.
Then the mice ran to the top of the cage.
Jane made them sit up.
Tom gave Jane a cat.
His name is Sam.
Sam did not like the white mice.
He felt sad.
Jane sent the white mice to Jill.

Mary Davidson

The <u>Little</u> Red Hen

<u>Little</u> Red Hen had a <u>seed</u>.
<u>She</u> <u>said</u>, "<u>Who</u> will plant this <u>seed</u>? It will make more <u>seeds</u>."
"I will not," <u>said</u> the Rat.
"I will not," <u>said</u> the Cat.
"I will not," <u>said</u> the Pig.
"Then I will plant it," <u>said</u> the <u>Little</u> Red Hen.
And she planted it.
When the <u>seed</u> <u>was</u> ripe, she <u>said</u>, "<u>Who</u> will cut the <u>seeds</u> from the stems?"
"I will not," <u>said</u> the Rat.
"I will not," <u>said</u> the Cat.
"I will not," <u>said</u> the Pig.
"Then I will cut them," <u>said</u> the <u>Little</u> Red Hen.
And she cut them.
"<u>Who</u> will take them to the mill?" <u>said</u> the <u>Little</u> Red Hen.
"I will not," <u>said</u> the Rat.
"I will not," <u>said</u> the Cat.
"I will not," <u>said</u> the Pig.
"Then I will, "<u>said</u> the <u>Little</u> Red Hen.
And she did.
The mill crushed the <u>seeds</u>.
When the <u>seeds</u> got crushed, the <u>Little</u> Red Hen made a cake.
When it <u>was</u> baked, she cut it.
The Rat ate the cake.
The Cat ate the cake.
The Pig ate the cake.
The <u>Little</u> Red Hen ate the cake.
"That is a fine cake," <u>said</u> the Rat.
"It is a big cake," <u>said</u> the Cat.
"I like cake," <u>said</u> the Pig.
"I like to bake cake," <u>said</u> the <u>Little</u> Red Hen.
Then the Rat, the Cat, and the Pig felt <u>happy</u>.
And the <u>Little</u> Red Hen <u>was</u> <u>happy</u> and glad.

Adapted by Emma C. Barnhard

Tim <u>Tadpole</u>

Here is a <u>little</u> pond.
It is at the end of the <u>forest</u>.
In <u>wintertime</u> this pond is still.
In the <u>springtime</u> these <u>sounds</u> came from the pond.
Sing, sing, and sing.
Jump, jump, and jump.
Tim <u>Tadpole</u> felt sad.
<u>He</u> did not sing.
<u>He</u> did not jump.
Tim <u>Tadpole</u> went for a swim.
He met a big <u>brown</u> <u>turtle</u>.
"<u>Are</u> <u>you</u> <u>going</u> to sit in the sun?" asked Tim.
Tim <u>Tadpole</u> went to the <u>bottom</u> of the pond.
He did not like the <u>snails</u>.
He did not like the <u>little</u> fish.
He did not sing.
He did not jump.
He did not sit in the sun.
Big Fat Frog came down to the <u>bottom</u> of the pond.
"Jump, jump, jump," said Big Fat Frog.
"I can not jump. I can not sing. I can not sit in the sun," said Tim.
Then Tim <u>Tadpole</u> wept and wept.
"Can you swim?" asked Big Fat Frog.
"Yes, I can swim and swim," said Tim.
And Tim is not Tim <u>Tadpole</u>.
He is Tim Frog.
He can jump.
He can sing.
He can sit in the sun.
He is <u>happy</u>.

Adapted by Minna R. Colton

Much Fun—Ti<u>ck</u>-Tock

Ti<u>ck</u>-to<u>ck</u>, ti<u>ck</u>-to<u>ck</u>!
That's the big clo<u>ck</u>!
Ti<u>ck</u>-tock, ti<u>ck</u>-to<u>ck</u>!
It's <u>granddad's</u> clo<u>ck</u>!
Ti<u>ck</u>-Tock sat <u>itself</u> on the shelf.
It went ti<u>ck</u>, ti<u>ck</u>, ti<u>ck</u>, ti<u>ck</u>.
Ti<u>ck</u>-To<u>ck</u> has hands and legs. It can run.
Ti<u>ck</u>-To<u>ck</u> ticks ti<u>ck</u>-tock when it runs.
When Ti<u>ck</u>-To<u>ck</u> ticks six, I am still in bed as snug as a bug in a rug. That's
when I shun him. At seven, Dad and I get up and dress.

Much Fun—The Big Bug

A big plump bug crept on its six legs.
It went zig-zag, zig-zag.
It crept on the <u>velvet</u> rug.
Sh! Sh! Sh!
Jim and Rex crept on the rug.
Run, Jim, step on the bug.
The bug is still on the rug, Jim
Pick it up, Rex. Quick! . . .

Much Fun—Quack-Quack, the Duck

Quack-Quack is a big fat duck.
It has ten ducks that can quack, run, and swim.
The duck with black fuzz on its back is Bob's pet.
It taps Bob with its big bill.
It quacks just as well as Quack-Quack quacks.
Bob's pet duck swims in the pond.
It ran up the hill and fell on its back.
It got up and ran to the pond.
Then it swam on and on and on. . . .

Much Fun—Splish-Splash, the Fish

Splish-Splash is a fish. It has red fins. Flash! It can swim. It can twist and swish just as well. Splish-Splash gets wet when it swims. It can splash and splash and splash.

Bad-Cat can sit on the rim of the dish. Splish-Splash must not swim to the top of the dish. Bad-Cat can bend its back and get the fish. . . .

Much Fun—Peg's <u>Doll</u>

Is Peg's <u>doll</u> still in bed?
Yes, it is.
Pick it up <u>gently</u>.
Such a <u>doll</u>!
It has a silk dress with a red sash.
Its <u>bonnet</u> is red. . . .

Much Fun—Jack and Jill

This is Jack and this is his pal, Jill.
Jack and Jill went up the hill to get a bag of nuts.
Jack will get ten nuts that fell in the mud.
Jill will pick up six nuts that fell on the bench.
Then Jack and Jill will fill the bag with the nuts.
The man in the truck will help Jack and Jill and crack the shells. . . .

Much Fun—The Thrush

The thrush can hop.
It can hop on the bench.
It can hop from twig to twig.
It can hop to the man's hut.
The thrush can stand on its legs.
It can stand on the rim of the nest.
The thrush has a fresh nest.
It is on that twig.
It is not a big nest but it has six eggs in it.
The wind rocks the nest.
The thrush sits on the eggs when the wind rocks the nest.
The sun helps the thrush.
The wind has fun with the thrush.
The egg shells will crack.
The thrush gets bugs and insects.
Such a lunch!
Then it hops back to the nest and rests on its rim. . . .

Much Fun—Rat-a-Tat

Rat-a-tat-tat
That's the big rat.
It can tap-a-tap-tap
With a big pat-pat.
With a black hat
And a red <u>velvet</u> vest
Rat-a-Tat will dress
In his best.
Big Rat-a-Tat
Went to <u>visit</u> the mill,
The mill on the crest
Of yon hill.
It went with a run;
It went with a jump;
It went with a skip and a hop.
With a run and a jump
With a hop and a skip
It got to the top of the hill. . . .

Much Fun—Trit-Trot

Trot-a-trot-trot
And chump, chump, chump.
Trit-Trot has a big hump.
A hump to pack
A back with a hump
A hump, hump, hump
A hump on its back.

Jog-a-jog-jog.
Trit-Trot can jog.
It's fun, fun, fun
When it runs, runs, runs.
Trit-Trot can kick and run.
It can run on the sand.
It has a thick split lip.
It can crop twigs and shrubs.
It has a hump on its back.
The hump has much fat in it.
It is its <u>pantry</u> shelf. . . .

Much Fun—Jig, the Pig

Rub-a-dub-dub
And rig-a-jig-jig.
That big fat pig
Can scrub the tub.
Rat-a-tat-tat
Is the pig fat?
The pig is fat.
And can stand pat.
Jig-a-jog-jig
And grunt, grunt, grunt.
The pig in the pen
Went to <u>visit</u> the hen.
With a cut-cut-cut.
The hen did strut
With the cluck, cluck, cluck
The cock sat up. . . .

Clothilde D. Faria

Camp in the Hills

I am Stan. I like to hike. Dad and I went to camp on a flat rock <u>ledge</u> in the hills.

I cut <u>spruce</u> and <u>hemlock</u> <u>branches</u> and made a bed. Then I made a stone fire-place.

Dad had a skiff on the lake. With his rod and line he got five rock bass. We made a <u>campfire</u>. I ate twice as much as I can at home.

We slept well by the fire. At six we woke up. The sun had <u>risen</u>. A mist rose from the lake.

We <u>quickly</u> made up the fire and ate the rest of the fish. Since we did not have ice, we had to <u>finish</u> the fish up.

I made a trap on the next hill but did not catch a <u>rabbit</u>.

As I went back to camp and ran up the <u>rocky</u> <u>hillside</u>, I slipped on a stone. I grabbed a rock with my hand. From the rock came a buzz. I jumped back. Next to the rock a snake rested. He had a thick neck. His back end went buzz, buzz.

I slipped <u>gently</u> off and then ran fast to camp. Dad <u>said</u> I am lucky that the snake did not strike at me.

Miriam Phelps Baggett

Life at School

I <u>have</u> fun at <u>school</u>.
I go to art and shop.
I am <u>making</u> a game.
I go to lunch with the boys and girls.
I ride in the bus.

Evelyn Kratz

The Ranch

Bill and Dave Gold <u>live</u> on a ranch.
It is a big ranch in the west.
Bill and Dave help with the farm work.
In the spring <u>they</u> like to play <u>baseball</u>.
Bill can pitch a fast ball.
Dave can catch a wild fly.
The ball game is played on a hill in back of the barn.
When it <u>rains</u> Dave and Bill go <u>fishing</u> in the lake.
They fish with a pole and line.
Dave saw a big bass, but he did not catch it.
When it is hot, Dave and Bill swim in the pond.
Bill likes to dive from the dock.

Lucille L. Warren

The Camp

It is summer.
Fred and Jack go to camp.
The camp is by a lake.
The camp has tents.
The name of Jack's tent is White <u>Owl</u>.
Jack and Fred swim in the lake.
The lake is <u>some</u>times cold.
Fred likes to fish.
<u>Sunfish</u>, <u>catfish</u> and bass <u>are</u> in the lake.
Fred hopes to catch fish.

Lucille L. Warren

The Twins

Bob and Bab will go to the pet shop.
Bob and Bab will ride on the bus.
At the shop Bob will see a big, white cat.
But he will not take it with him.
Then Bab will see a fish swim and a rat run.
Bob is so sad and he will go home.
He can not see his pet.
But Bab can see the pet and here it is.
Just a cute tan pup.
See him jump.
<u>Oh</u>—he got the bone.

Mary Davidson

The Lordly Stork

A stork sat here and ate his pork.
He did this <u>nicely</u> with a fork,
Then <u>grandly</u> called the <u>unicorn</u>
To take his plate and fetch him corn.
With his corn he sipped his port,
(Or a red wine of that same sort)
And off he <u>trundled</u> in his Ford
As <u>happy</u> as a <u>little</u> lord.
He came at last to the <u>largest</u> fort
Up on the hill <u>beside</u> the port.
But he stumbled in the short, thick corn
And pricked himself on a <u>spiky</u> thorn.
He chopped and hacked at that <u>wicked</u> thorn
<u>Until</u> he felt quite tired and worn,
And hot, and <u>thirsty</u>, and <u>very</u> <u>forlorn</u>.

Miriam Phelps Baggett
(adapted from verses by Emily Walton Taft)

The Cow

(Phonograms up to diphthongs and <u>ow</u> \ou\)

The clown will ride a cow to town,
Up and down, up and down.
The cow is robed in a <u>purple</u> gown
When the clown rides her to town.
On her pate of <u>reddish</u> brown
<u>Sparkles</u> <u>rakishly</u> a crown.
Her pal, the <u>pony</u>, drags a plow;
How <u>elegant</u> the cow is now!

Miriam Phelps Baggett

At the Shore

(Ways of spelling \ā\ using <u>a-e</u>, <u>ay</u>, <u>ea.</u> Phonograms up to diphthongs. <u>against</u>)

At the shore I <u>wear</u> my <u>bathing</u> trunks all day. I like to romp on the sand and swim in the <u>breakers</u>. When the <u>great</u> waves <u>come</u> <u>dashing</u> in, I stand still, <u>bracing</u> my legs <u>against</u> the <u>backsurge</u> of <u>water</u> until the wave is almost <u>toppling</u> <u>upon</u> me. Then with a <u>sudden</u> plunge I dive <u>under</u> the white, <u>swirling</u> mass and <u>come</u> up in the <u>quiet</u> <u>water</u> <u>beyond</u>.

Miriam Phelps Baggett

Skip and <u>Sandy</u>

(All consonants, short vowels including vowel <u>y</u>, silent-<u>e</u>. Non-phonetic words: <u>to</u>, <u>of</u>, <u>says</u>)

The Grants will go to <u>Texas</u> in <u>June</u>. <u>Milky</u>, the cat, will ride with them, but Skip, the dog, will not.
"Skip will like the Hunt Dog <u>Kennels</u>," <u>says</u> <u>Mother</u>.
Skip is <u>very</u> sad. "Take Skip," he begs.
She says, "Skip is big and wide. Skip <u>cannot</u> ride to <u>Texas</u> with us."
"Let us get in and go to <u>Sandy's</u> home," <u>says</u> Dad. "Tell <u>Sandy</u> that the Grants will go to Texas."
When <u>Sandy</u> lets them in, he is glad that the Grants came.
"Take <u>Sandy</u> to Texas," he begs.
Dad says, "<u>Sandy</u> cannot ride to Texas with us. He has his home here. When <u>Sandy's</u> family goes to <u>Texas</u>, <u>Sandy</u> will ride with them."
<u>Sandy</u> is very sad. Skip licks his hands. He licks Sandy's face and chin. "It is <u>lonely</u>," says Sandy.
"Skip is <u>lonely</u>. He will not like the Hunt Dog <u>Kennels</u>. Let <u>Sandy</u> take care of Skip while the Grants go to Texas."
<u>Sandy</u> likes Skip <u>very</u> much. "<u>Sandy</u> will take care of Skip. Then Skip will be <u>happy</u> and <u>Sandy</u> will be <u>happy</u>."

Miriam Phelps Baggett

Mr. Mate

<u>Tony</u> has a black and white dog.
His name is <u>Mr</u>. Mate.
<u>Mr</u>. Mate likes to run and jump.
He likes to romp with Tony.
<u>Tony</u> takes <u>Mr</u>. Mate to the store with him.
The man in the store likes <u>Mr</u>. Mate.
When he sits up and begs, the man <u>gives</u> him a bone.
Then <u>Mr</u>. Mate licks his hand.

Evelyn Kratz

NEW PHONOGRAMS

The order for teaching the remaining phonograms is not important, though the following order is convenient. For the younger student some of the harder ones may be postponed.

Probably no two remedial teachers will agree completely about the make-up of the pack of drill cards; for instance, should there be a phonogram gh \f\, as in *enough*?

This covers very few words, and we have chosen to have these words learned. In general, we have tried to keep a balance between a too-heavy memory load and phonograms which would cover few words.

There is one other sound for <u>a</u>, and if it is taught now, salmon card 1 will be finished. The sound is \ȯ\ as in <u>all</u>, <u>ball</u>, <u>fall</u>, and seldom occurs when not followed by <u>l</u> or <u>ll</u>.

The letter <u>i</u> also has another sound but is considered too unusual to be given a place on the drill cards. In or as a medial syllable, <u>i</u> is sometimes sounded as \ē\.

er   <u>her</u> \ər\ pronounced as in *curl*. Salmon card 35.

ir   <u>bird</u> \ər\ pronounced as in *curl*. Salmon card 36.

ur   <u>burn</u> \ər\ pronounced as in *curl*. Salmon card 38.

These phonograms all stand for \ər\, with the \ə\ pronounced as in *curl*, in monosyllables and in the accented syllables of longer words. They say \ər\, with the \ə\ pronounced as in the first and third syllables in *banana*, in unaccented syllables. The teacher should note that the symbol schwa \ə\ is used to represent two different vowel sounds when it precedes the consonant <u>r</u>. The teacher would do well to use the term *schwa* until it becomes familiar. Otherwise the student will be thinking and saying "upside down <u>e</u>."

Words to give practice with \ər\, with two of its three pronunciations, include: shirt, churn, thirsty, lantern, thirty, stir, curl, sister, murmur, colder, faster, church, burst, firm.

ar   <u>car</u> \är\. Salmon card 34.
ar   <u>beggar</u> \ər\
ar   <u>arrow</u> \ar\

The phonogram <u>ar</u> has three sounds. When it is in a monosyllable or in an accented syllable, it says \är\. When <u>ar</u> is in an unaccented syllable, it says simply \ər\ as in *beggar* \'beg-ər\. In a very few words <u>ar</u> in an accented syllable sounds like \a\, e.g., *arrow, arid.*

New Words: lizard, blizzard, buzzard, custard, dollar
car, far, march, card, star, starch, hard, yard, bark, dark, arm, farm, charm, barn, cart, party, chart, start, large, charge, sharp, harvest

or   horn \ȯr\. Salmon card 37a.
or   doctor \ər\. Salmon card 37b.

The phonogram <u>or</u> has the sounds indicated. They appear in monosyllables, unaccented syllables, or accented syllables.

New Words: actor, border, visitor, elevator, torpedo, former, transform, horse, storm, horn

th   <u>this</u> \th\. White card 27a.
th   <u>thumb</u> \th\. White card 27b.

The student is already familiar with the sound of this digraph as in \<u>this</u>\. It makes no difference for spelling whether the sound is \<u>th</u>\ or \th\. Either sound will be spelled <u>th</u>.

New Words: thump, width, tenth, throb, thrive, than, those, thresh, thrush, thrift, myth, that

For reading there is sometimes more doubt. Here is an interesting group of words.
When the phonogram <u>th</u> is followed by a silent <u>e</u>, it sounds \<u>th</u>\.

lithe, writhe, bathe (contrast bath), scythe, clothe (contrast cloth)

-<u>ed</u>   <u>scolded</u> \əd\. White card 45a.
-<u>ed</u>   <u>sailed</u> \d\. White card 45b.
-<u>ed</u>   <u>jumped</u> \t\. White card 45c.

New Words: landed, asked, pinned, dashed, twisted, tanned

The sounds \sh\ and \k\ for <u>ch</u> are so unusual for young students that it sometimes seems better to omit them until needed, unless a particular student wants to finish the entire set. On the other hand, <u>tch</u> is very common.

tch   <u>catch</u> \ch\. White card 26.

New Words: patch, latch, hatch, match, itch, witch, pitch, hitch, ditch, notch, Dutch

ck   <u>clock</u> \k\. White card 23.

New Words: chick, quick, lick, smack, track, sack, back, sick, licked, ticked

White card 49—the <u>ing</u>, <u>ink</u>, etc., phonograms—is included tentatively. Most students will learn these phonograms easily and require little repetition. In certain localities, however, they are pronounced with a separation of the final consonant, as in \sing\, \sink\. In such cases the occasional exposure of this card may be useful. -<u>ing</u> has already been used in Chapter 2 as a suffix in applying Spelling Pattern 2.

Practice words: bang, string, thing, boxing, packing, strong, wishing, hung, spending, thank, ink, strung, drink, trunk, think, resting

The endings below can well be postponed, with the teacher always pronouncing the words in which they occur in the reading. On the other hand, they are not difficult, and some students feel satisfaction in completing the consonant combinations.

<u>sion</u>   <u>expansion</u> \chən\. White card 46a.
      <u>mission</u> \shən\. White card 46b.
      <u>television</u> \zhən\. White card 46c.
<u>tion</u>   <u>attention</u> \chən\. White card 47a.
      <u>station</u> \shən\. White card 47b.

Possible practice words: suspension, expulsion, explosion, invasion, conclusion, action, collection, connection, objection, nation, relation, invitation, vacation, notion, promotion, mention, intention

The student may be told that the ending <u>cian</u> \shən\ nearly always denotes a person, as in *physician*.

Similarly, an occasional student may be given the last of the <u>ch</u> card.

<u>ch</u>   <u>chin</u> \ch\. White card 22a.
    <u>Christmas</u> \k\. White card 22b.
    <u>chute</u> \sh\. White card 22c.

Words in which <u>ch</u> has the sound of \k\ come to us from the Greek, as in <u>echo</u>, <u>chorus</u>, <u>chasm</u>. The Greeks had a letter χ unlike any Latin letter. The

Romans did not know what sound to give it, but they finally settled upon \k\.

Words in which <u>ch</u> has the sound \sh\ come to us from the French. Some of these have a very interesting history. When the French were exploring North America, they came to an Indian settlement on the shores of Lake Michigan that had a name that sounded like \shi-kȯ-gō\. We would have spelled this name <u>Shicago</u>. But for the French explorers the sound \sh\ had to be spelled <u>ch</u> and that is the way the great city of the midwest got the spelling of its name Chicago.

Practice words: inch, pinch, porch, rich, ranch, lunch, starch, anchor, orchid, chaos, chorus, chrome, chronological, chute, parachute, Chicago

Now that the student knows that the phonograms <u>k</u>, <u>c</u>, <u>ck</u>, and <u>ch</u> may all have the sound \k\, it will be desirable to start the generalizations (Chapter 8). The very natural question is likely to be asked: "How am I to know which spelling to use for a certain sound?" The answer to this question will be found in the development of the generalizations.

INTRODUCTION OF DIPHTHONGS

The most superficial glance into the primer of any series of readers will show the investigator that diphthongs are introduced in the very beginning of the student's learning to read. That is done because the focus of these books is on learning words that fit into the story.

The entire plan of this manual rests upon an exactly opposite concept: the logical development of the construction of words.

In this study of phonetic units, we have now reached the point where diphthongs will fit into the sequence of topics. The student is told that a diphthong is a special sort of digraph which, as he has already learned, is two letters standing together to represent a single sound. These diphthong-digraphs, however, are made up of vowels.

They are to be introduced to the student as they occur in his or her reading material. We consider it very important to have two copies of the selected material for two reasons:

1. To spare the eyes of both teacher and student from straining to look at the same book or page.
2. To enable the teacher to mark his or her own copy in preparation for each lesson.

For the correct reading procedure see page 95 in this chapter.

Each diphthong, as it occurs in a given story, is taught on a salmon-colored drill card, which is then added to the pack for daily drill. The diphthong may be typed or printed at the top of a strip of tagboard (2¾″ × 11″) followed by practice words (triple spaced) that the student will gradually learn to read. "Miscellaneous" lists made up of words from lists already read are included for additional practice. When the student has mastered a number of diphthongs and words, he should be ready to read stories in which they appear.

The tagboard strips may be run through an envelope with a slot in it, wide enough to expose one word at a time, a homemade tachistoscope. Or the student may simply read down the strip held in his hand.

Green (or another color) should be used for strips with lists of sight words. For more information on the use of sight words, see page 96.

A copy of the strips follows.

1. <u>ay play</u> \ā\
   hay
   day
   bay
   tray
   clay
   may
   stray
   way

2. <u>ow plow</u> \au̇\
   howl
   growl
   brow
   plow
   town
   frown
   drown
   crowd
   drowsy
   how
   now
   dow

3. <u>Miscellaneous</u>
   howl
   stray
   may
   drowsy
   clay
   town
   crowd
   way
   tray
   plow

4. <u>ou ouch</u> \au̇\
   couch
   pouch
   loud
   proud
   hound
   found
   ground
   wound
   sour
   flour
   mouse
   shout
   sprout
   mouth
   south

5. <u>Miscellaneous</u>
   crowd
   loud
   tray
   way
   shout
   wound
   brow
   drowsy
   hound
   town
   clay
   proud

6. <u>oo food</u> \ü\
   proof
   cool
   spool
   gloom
   droop
   goose
   broom
   smooth
   troop
   tooth
   choose
   boost
   groove

7. <u>Miscellaneous</u>
   may
   troop
   wound
   how
   gloom
   tray
   found
   clay
   proof
   ground
   drowsy
   goose
   pouch
   smooth

8. <u>ew pew</u> \yü\
   few
   mew
   hew

9. <u>Miscellaneous</u>
hay
drown
sour
tooth
hew
mouse
frown
bay
mew
hoof
stew
south

10. <u>ee feed \ē\</u>
bee
three
tree
screech
speech
deed
need
seed
weed
bleed
see
feed

11. <u>Miscellaneous</u>
growl
bleed
pew
cool
flour
speech
couch
day
now
weed
dew
room
stray
broom

12. <u>ou soup \ü\</u>
group
croup
youth
you

13. <u>Miscellaneous</u>
spool
sprout
droop
beech
coupon
bay
frown
group
three
hew
tooth
plow
youth
seed
stew
loud

14. <u>oa boat \ō\</u>
coat
road
coal
float
loaf
toad
boast
coast
toast
soak
soap

15. <u>Miscellaneous</u>
down
soak
you
tray
mouth
coast
see
choose
dew
deed
boost
soap
croup
howl
way

16. <u>oo book \u̇\</u>
stood
foot
wood
cook
hook
took
wool
brook
good
hoof

17. <u>Miscellaneous</u>	18. <u>ow snow</u> \ō\	19. <u>Miscellaneous</u>	20. <u>ue true</u> \ü\
feed	flow	hook	flue
groove	slow	flow	construe
coupon	throw	hay	blue
wool	glow	brow	due
toast	grow	hound	glue
bee	blow	yellow	sue
mew	low	took	clue
smooth	yellow	proof	
shout	shadow	glow	
howl	follow	pew	
foot	elbow	elbow	
coat		loaf	
may		stood	
need		speech	
cook		road	
float		group	
good		shadow	
tree		coal	

21. <u>Miscellaneous</u>	22. <u>oy toy</u> \ȯi\	23. <u>Miscellaneous</u>	24. <u>ea eat</u> \ē\
wood	annoy	blow	tea
boast	joy	oyster	each
blue	enjoy	blue	teach
clay	oyster	day	reach
low	royal	drown	read
town	boy	joy	
proud		flue	
flue		found	
troop		goose	
throw		hew	
stew		boy	
weed		bleed	
toad		croup	
construe		enjoy	
youth		soap	
slow		royal	
brook		cook	
grow		annoy	
		follow	
		good	

25. <u>Miscellaneous</u>
construe
yellow
foot
sea
annoy
soak
you
tea
three
dew
each
gloom
pouch
beach
how
oyster
tray
reach
flue
read

26. <u>ai sail \ā\</u>
aid
laid
ail
rail
trail
claim
drain
chain
paint
raise
praise

27. <u>Miscellaneous</u>
enjoy
raise
blue
flow
rail
wool
coat
drain
beach
boy
group
paint
beech
mew
ail
each
cool
ground
claim
growl

28. <u>aw saw \ȯ\</u>
thaw
crawl
law
draw
dawn
straw

29. <u>Miscellaneous</u>
sea
joy
dawn
construe
now
law
stray
broom
draw
chain
tea
pew
crawl
aid
seed
thaw
reach
coupon
lawyer
trail

30. <u>ey valley \ē\</u>
turkey
hockey
jersey
trolley
barley

31. <u>Miscellaneous</u>
glow
took
turkey
coast
crawl
laid
royal
hockey
down
sour
praise
law
jersey
paint
elbow
stood
youth
trolley
see
draw

32. <u>ea steak \ā\</u>
break
steak

33. <u>Miscellaneous</u>
ail
slow
wood
break
jersey
dawn
rail
toast
steak
trolley
sea
flue
croup
bay
hoof
tree
lawyer
beach
oyster
stew

34. <u>au August \ȯ\</u>
cause
fault
vault
saucer
saunter

35. <u>Miscellaneous</u>
reach
annoy
vault
turkey
thaw
claim
throw
cause
hook
float
you
saucer
break
deed
plow
mew
fault
mouse
steak
saunter

36. <u>igh light \ī\</u>

(a vowel sound
though not made
up solely of vowels)

sigh
bright
flight
fight
might
night
right
sight
tight

37. <u>Miscellaneous</u>
hay
south
spool
dew
flight
fault
coupon
night
loaf
brook
steak
hockey
draw
bright
raise
grow
youth
sight
saunter
trolley

38. <u>ea bread \e\</u>
bread
spread
thread
breast
health
ready
meant
feather
leather

39. <u>Miscellaneous</u>
tray
crowd
leather
couch
fight
droop
bread
need
blow
breast
tight
cause
break
blue
health
right
vault
joy
each
crawl

40. <u>ew grew \ü\</u>
blew
crew
drew
flew
screw
shrewd
dew
stew

41. Miscellaneous
hew
group
flew
road
good
crew
thread
drain
jersey
blew
saucer
might
shrewd
feather
tray
frown
flour
sigh
screw
spread

42. eigh eight \ā
weigh
weight
freight
sleigh
neighbor

43. Miscellaneous
choose
sprout
neighbor
drew
feed
follow
freight
blew
meant
construe
enjoy
tea
weight
ready
trail
law
sleigh
bright
saunter
steak

44. eu feud \yü
feudal
feud
eulogy
euphony

45. Miscellaneous
turkey
cook
feud
weigh
crew
boast
croup
pew
shrewd
drowsy
way
mouth
feudal
freight
flew
tooth
feather
flight
fault
dawn

46. ei ceiling \ē
seize
seizure
leisure
either
neither
deceive
receive
perceive

47. Miscellaneous
bee
shadow
neither
feud
blue
boy
leisure
neighbor
beach
chain
receive
lawyer
break
cause
screw
perceive
weight
either
bread
sight

48. ei vein \ā
skein
rein
veil

49. <u>Miscellaneous</u>
clay
howl
loud
rein
proof
deceive
stew
sleigh
you
toad
skein
foot
seize
hockey
each
drew
seizure
freight
leather

50. <u>ie piece \ē\</u>
piece
field
yield
shield
niece
priest
shriek
thief
grief
chief

51. <u>Miscellaneous</u>
speech
yellow
grief
flue
royal
skein
praise
priest
thaw
steak
vault
field
night
leisure
yield
feudal
weigh
niece
either
thief

52. <u>ie laddie \ē\</u>
Freddie
prairie

53. <u>Miscellaneous</u>
may
seizure
brow
shield
wound
room
laddie
mew
piece
coupon
coal
wool
prairie
shriek
rein
sea
trolley
blew

54. <u>oe toe \ō\</u>
doe
foe
woe
hoe

55. <u>Miscellaneous</u>
weed
low
construe
prairie
oyster
do
claim
draw
foe
laddie
field
break
saucer
woe
skein
weight
right
thread
neither
hoe

56. <u>oi boil \ȯi\</u>
toil
spoil
join
joint
moisture
embroider
rejoice
hoist
oil
soil
boil
coil

57. Miscellaneous

day
town
toil
shout
boost
moisture
dew
youth
spoil
woe
soap
jersey
rejoice
flew
niece
joint
rein
doe
seize

58. ue rescue \yü\

hue
value
cue
argue
statue
virtue
avenue

59. Miscellaneous

bleed
took
issue
flow
avenue
join
foe
blue
joy
argue
reach
aid
crawl
yield
saunter
sleigh
fight
feud

GREEN

Sight Words

river
they
carry
there
everyone
water
cried
one
door
sometime
once
every
of
money
wagon
who
some
many

GREEN

Sight Words

give
were
another
thing
autumn
other
lovely
mother
thought
alone
where
enough
laugh

GREEN

Sight Words

friendly
beautiful
through
people
front
climb
know
eye
garage
treasure
worm
shoe
course
picture
o'clock
four
evening
minute
believe

GREEN

Sight Words

gone
fruit
machine
mountain
answer
iron
guess
aunt
their
any
tried
pasture
hungry
trouble
several
brought
ocean
question
straight

GREEN	GREEN	GREEN
Sight Words	Sight Words	Sight Words
color	wrote	replied
certain	ski	coffee
else	juice	frolic
fasten	toward	built
together	wrong	beauty
among	busy	palm
potato	month	weather
listen	bicycle	whether
discovery	reason	young
real	apron	journey
America	notice	
bought	woman	
knee	often	
done	cupboard	
buy	though	
twelve	caught	
key	imagine	
prove	meant	
shoulder		

MOTIVATION—GAIN IN SKILL

Most remedial programs stress finding books that will appeal to the personal interest of the student. Many teachers make a wide search for such books even for the beginning lessons when the student is unable to read at all.

Frequently this attempt to follow the student's lead in such expressed interests only results in the intensification of his baffling sense of frustration and overwhelming despair. Having asserted his desire to read about electricity, he finds the book an impossible jargon of words he cannot decode and discovers that he cannot derive from the text the satisfaction that he anticipated from the title. Instead of luring him to want to read, such an attempt often repels him from the whole reading business upon which his parents and teachers have laid such emphasis.

In choosing the Little Stories and other books for the development of our technique, we have given no heed as to whether the context will appeal to the student. Our thought has been solely whether by careful preparation on our part the book can serve as one stage in the growth of *skill* in the logical sequence of principles.

Occasionally a teacher, to whom this aspect of the process is new, protests that the child will reject such books as too babyish. After rather wide experience we are convinced that this protest is not valid. The teacher may be attributing her own attitude to the student.

Enthusiasm in realizing the growth in skill is a far more mature experience for the student than is the momentary enjoyment of a story or the temporary excitement of an adventure. It is easy to convince oneself of the student's willingness to endure drudgery for the sake of a future goal by watching the zeal, even the laborious perseverance, with which someone will voluntarily practice basketball or strive to acquire the correct stroke in tennis.

"I did it! I read it!" exults the student.

"Never till now did I fully realize what the whole reading process means in contrast to the endless memorizing (and forgetting) of particular words," says one college student who had thus far been carried along in the content material by having his mother, his roommate, or his wife read to him.

In its final analysis, pleasure is not the ultimate purpose of school activities. Rather, the goal is the acquisition of abilities and skills. This mastery of these abilities and skills should result in the exultant joy of success.

All that we are attempting at this stage is to establish the simple application of the Alphabetic Approach to words. This phase is comparable to practicing scales on a musical instrument. A person who is learning to play an instrument must spend hours in laborious practice, but he feels increasing satisfaction in his improvement. His love of music, meanwhile, is fostered by hearing and becoming familiar with great masterpieces.

Similarly our student is introduced to the world of books and shown that it is a delightful world, not by stumbling through his own reading, but by having great works of literature read to him. This procedure has been found far more successful in developing taste and fostering wide interests than has the method of seeking congenial books when mechanical difficulties are so great as to make all effort futile.

READING PROCEDURE

Ideally, the matter presented for the student to read from now on should contain only words he has never seen before but that fall under headings already mastered—typical monosyllables, blends, silent final e words, c and g words, remaining phonograms in the pack of drill cards, and words containing the diphthongs already learned. This goal may be impossible, but by careful manipulation a teacher may approximate it. For example, *stay* does not appear on the tachistoscope list of ay words, but the student should be able to decode it.

The student studies the first sentence, very soon a paragraph or page, and is told in advance any word for which he is not responsible. He asks for help on any word that he does not know. The help given demands quick thought by the teacher. If the word is *duck*, she merely reminds him of the phonogram ck, already learned, which he must apply to this situation. If the word is nonphonetic, like *said*, she tells him at once without comment and tells him again as often as needed. In her own careful preparation of the lesson she can predict with considerable accuracy which words he will not know, and can underline these in her book to save him from miscalling any word he is not expected to know.

On the other hand, a particular word thus marked may be remembered by the student from some previous encounter. In such an instance the teacher does not praise him for his success, which is pure chance. She is stressing the concept of the Alphabetic Approach, which the student can use to decode many words. The object of this preliminary study is for the student to attain that goal of wisdom that will enable him to determine what he knows and what he does not know. No guessing!

Being permitted, even encouraged, to guess a word that "will fit into the story," is one of the most devastating experiences encountered by the language-disabled student.

When the designated unit—sentence, paragraph, or page—has been prepared, and the student says that he is ready, he should read it perfectly, with no blundering or repetition, and with a smoothness and correctness of inflection that *sounds like talking*. If he makes errors in his reading, he should go back and restudy the entire unit.

SIGHT WORDS

Toward the end of this period of building up reading skills by the acquisition of phonograms, we begin to drill the sight words that the teacher thus far merely told the student. A green tagboard strip presents a list of these, to which other words are slowly added as needed, and the list read very frequently. It is interesting for both teacher and student to note how many such words are remembered from various tellings and how many must be learned afresh. This is a good place to repeat that in spite of its irregularity English is essentially a phonetic language, and that less than twelve to fifteen percent of our words are truly non-phonetic.

PHRASING

Increasingly, attention should be given to phrasing. Show the student that words in a sentence are not all spoken with equal stress. We do not say: "\thē\ dog runs along \thē\ street," but "\thə\ dog runs along \thə\ street." The symbol schwa \ə\ is pronounced as in the first and third syllables of *banana*. Certain words belong together. These should be read "trippingly on the tongue" for practice. It is essential, however, that the student become adept in discovering such groups of words in the text that she is reading.

WHAT NEXT?

When all the phonograms have been introduced, a critical point is reached. To what extent and of what nature should the continuation of remedial training be? It is clear that we believe students with reading and spelling disability should study the Alphabetic rather than the Sight Word Approach. However, since this idea may be difficult, there comes a time when we must decide, "What next?"

Even after the entire pack of drill cards has been introduced and all the books prescribed have been read, many students will still require further reading under expert supervision as a part of the emphasis upon skill—the idea of practicing scales.

SPELLING

It is not safe to stop definite remedial training in spelling until the material of Chapters 7, 8, and 10 has been thoroughly mastered. Many students who have had a successful course in remedial reading fail high school examinations because they cannot spell.[1] They should also learn carefully selected nonphonetic words by the S.O.S. procedure.

READING

The student is now encouraged to read all that he can of the material his fellow classmates read or study. There is one limit to be placed upon this participation: This student must not be held responsible for all the classroom assignments. It may be that he is not yet able to carry the full load. In such a situation he may hurry to cover the ground and thus break down his laboriously acquired accuracy, or he may not succeed and give up in despair. He should read as much as he can efficiently, and definite arrangements should be made for a family member, a peer tutor, or some other qualified person to read the remainder of his assignments to him.

NOTE

1. Anna Gillingham, "Is Writing Essential for Proof of Knowledge?" *The Independent School Bulletin*, November 1958.

Remedial Training for High School Students and Adults

CHAPTER OVERVIEW

Chapter 4 analyzes the reading and spelling problems of the older student with specific language difficulty. A scope and sequence of concepts that can be used as a guide for lesson planning and review is given. (Throughout this chapter, references will be made to other chapters in which teachers will find information necessary to complete a daily lesson.) Also included are lessons on vocabulary and dictionary skills, detached syllables and instruction on various pronunciations, including digraphs, blends, and vowels in different positions in words.

Materials Needed

- Dictionary
- Phonics Drill Cards
- Phonetic Word Cards (Jewel Case)
- Little Stories
- Affix and Root Cards
- *The Tea Cup Whale*

ANALYSIS OF THE PROBLEM

Significant Factors to Consider:

- Some students have no knowledge of the phonetic units on which words are built. If they have been taught phonics, they may not have had sufficient opportunity for review, and the information may not have been introduced systematically enough to ensure that important concepts were presented.

Failure to do so often results in a weak foundation of basic reading and decoding skills which may affect fluency of reading, and will ultimately affect reading comprehension.

- Although they may have been taught to read words as whole units, the students may often confuse the "little" words on which meaning so often depends (such as: if, is, it, on, of, off).
- Limited word attack skills make reading multisyllabic words a significant challenge. If students do not "slide over" these words, they often pronounce them with a meaningless sound, or substitute some word remotely resembling the given word.
- The dictionary may not be useful for them. Students may not understand what information the dictionary entry can provide.
- Their vocabulary may be limited.
- The only remnant of their study of literature may be a feeling of loathing for books that have been recommended to them as enjoyable to read.

In the previous chapters, the OGS technique has been presented in detail for teaching students in the elementary grades. Students who have received this instruction are able to move on gradually to more demanding and sophisticated books, and to learn the spelling patterns and generalizations presented in Chapters 7 and 8.

However, a student who has a reading problem that is not identified in elementary school may be called a "poor student" in high school. In giving a case history of the student, a parent may refer to her child's initial difficulty in learning how to read, unaware that the difficulty with reading still exists. The student may excel in mathematics and lab science classes, but graduation and college look doubtful. The primary reason for his difficulties may go unnoticed because students in the upper grades are seldom required to read aloud. Therefore, his teachers may be unaware that he is failing in his work because he cannot read the text with understanding. The student himself may reject the idea that he has a reading problem, although he may admit that he does not like history or lengthy novels, and has difficulty writing essays and compositions or doing research projects.

His reading difficulties may be a mystery to him because he is not aware that others have less difficulty. Never having read accurately, he has no conception of what real reading is. To miscall little words, often not even noticing them, slide over long ones, and catch only a point here and there seems perfectly natural to him.

A considerable number of high school students referred for remedial help can read with fair efficiency. Their obstacle is spelling. Therefore, lessons must be planned to give the student as much mastery as possible of the material in Chapters 7 and 8 with practice in the study of nonphonetic words by the S.O.S. procedure.

It is impossible to conduct the remedial work needed with the older student in exactly the same way as with a younger student. Fortunately, their greater maturity and the realization of what they are facing may make it possible to proceed more rapidly.

For such a student, reading may mean continual repetition of blundering and inaccuracy. If possible, the daily assigned textbook lessons should be read aloud to the student until skills are commensurate with grade-level reading demands. If there is time, supplementary books should also be read to him, to contribute to his understanding and enjoyment of literature and to extend his vocabulary.

Teachers of poor readers are familiar with the startling amount of misinformation that these students may derive from their textbooks by attributing wrong meanings to words. Only someone who has tested many of these students critically realizes how seldom they have any reliable knowledge of the letters to associate with sounds or how to make each letter contribute to the pronunciation of a word. If they normally pronounce a word incorrectly, and they happen to know that word in print, they will tend to pronounce it incorrectly with total disregard for the letters before their eyes. For example, *recognize* may be read \'rek-u-nīz\ just as they say it, while the unknown word *incredible* may be read \in-'kre-b'l\.

Knowledge of Phonics

Few of the remedial books written to help poor readers in the upper grades recognize phonics as a prerequisite to word attack. Currently, more materials have become available as it became clearer to those working with these students that more were needed. Many teachers have written material to address this need. As mentioned earlier, a list of some of these materials is available.

Much difficulty would be prevented if poor spellers had the opportunity to practice phonetically regular words before they were presented with words that require memorization. The following words, culled from one set of papers from a group of seventh and eighth grade students referred for help in spelling, show their attempts to represent the sounds:

Word	Spelling	Word	Spelling	Word	Spelling
spoonful	sponeful	hoping	hopping	Chinese	Chines
estimate	estamate	loaded	louded	angry	ongry
capitalize	capilize	burning	barning	"	angory
champion	champon	pressure	presser	concern	conceran
support	surport	luckily	luckley	perfume	perfulm

A superficial analysis shows that the errors are by no means confined to peculiar and erratic words. These students had had no early training in phonics and possessed little skill in handling words that should translate themselves into letters almost automatically.

The procedures in all the formal skills developed in the following pages depend upon a thorough preliminary knowledge of phonograms and presuppose almost daily practice with the drill cards, handled just as with the younger student—although older students' mastery can be expected more speedily and is more comprehensive. The teacher will need to refer to the previous chapters to learn the multisensory techniques with which to present the phonograms (see Associations, Chapter 2).

Although only white and salmon cards are mentioned here, the teacher will see that she should use the yellow cards from the start. However, these drills, if allowed to consume too large a portion of the remedial period, result in diminishing returns. Other phases of the work, such as the various topics listed in the scope and sequence table that follows, need to be carried on simultaneously.

In this table, under Roman numerals, we indicate the order in which the phonograms should be presented. In the second column, opposite each group of phonograms and under corresponding Arabic numerals, are the topics that may be safely introduced at that point before another group of phonograms is taught. Once introduced, each topic should be reviewed and expanded in subsequent lessons as necessary. However, mastery of the phonograms is of first importance at this stage and should not be unduly delayed in order to introduce all the topics suggested in the second column. Students with good memory and keen perception of sound may learn the phonograms so quickly that some topics in the second column will remain after all the cards have been finished. This can be dealt with satisfactorily by following the order in the second column.

On the other hand, new topics should not be introduced too rapidly, or before the card groups they are intended to supplement.

In the exposition after the scope and sequence table, the topics are discussed in detail. The order throughout is only suggested, not by any means the *one* order in which the material must be developed. However, we believe it to have the merit of logical presentation, and it is a definite plan. If it is considered unsuitable for a particular student, it can be adapted to her needs, but the altered procedure should be laid out just as definitely. It is a great comfort to the student for whom all language study has been vague and uncertain, to feel that she is following a precise course, in which all parts are logically integrated.

We repeat: the outstanding value of this plan is that while dealing with facts and skills fundamental to reading, for a time it excludes from the *remedial* periods all reading from books, and consequently the fumbling and disregard for detail which blocked intelligent interpretation for so long. Before he is allowed to return to a book, the student has become familiar with many new and interesting aids to a successful attack on the words that until now have always stood like barriers between his mind and the thought of the passage. Furthermore, no other approach could so clearly demonstrate to the student his habitual inaccuracy, and how this can be replaced by correct pronunciation, so that by this means alone many words carry to his mind the ideas they were intended to convey.

We are aware that excluding students from all reading except during instructional periods may be unrealistic, given that schools do not have enough staff to read everything to an individual student. It is important for the teacher and the students to understand from these statements that the strategies the student used to cope in the past need to be replaced by new skills and strategies. Much time should be devoted to the application and practice of these new skills.

SCOPE AND SEQUENCE TABLE

Phonograms	Parallel and Subordinate Topics
I. Consonants: b, d, f, h, j, k, l, m, n, p, r, t, v, w, y, z. White cards: 1, 3, 4, 6, 7, 8, 9, 10, 11, 12, 14, 16, 17, 18, 20, 21.	**1.** **a.** Language Function Explained **b.** Drill Cards Presented **c.** Key Words Explained
II. First Sounds of Vowels: a, e, i, o, u, y (short vowel sounds) Salmon cards: 1, 2, 3, 4, 5, 6	**2.** **a.** Detached Syllables and Made-Up Words (consonant-vowel-consonant syllables). **b.** Pronunciation Symbols of Letters Thus Far Introduced **c.** Consonant Blends **d.** Detached Syllables and Made-Up Words (blends) **e.** Spelling Patterns as Needed for Dictation
III. qu and x	**3.** Vocabulary Study Begun
IV. Consonants with Two Sounds: c, g, s White cards: 2, 5, 15 Hard and Soft c and g White cards: 29 through 44	**4.** **a.** Pronunciation of c̲, g, s̲ explained **b.** Dictionary
V. Digraphs: ch, ck, ph, sh, tch, th, wh White cards: 22, 23, 24, 25, 26, 27, 28	**5.** **a.** Digraphs Contrasted with Blends **b.** History of Our Language
VI. Syllable Types:	**6.** See Chapter 2, p. 53
VII. Silent Final e̲ a-e, e-e, i-e, o-e, u-e, y-e Salmon cards: 7, 12, 20, 23, 31, 33	**7.** **a.** Effect on Preceding Vowel **b.** Detached and Made-Up Syllables
VIII. Vowels Finished: (Refer to salmon cards: 1, 2, 3, 4, 5, 6)	**8.** **a.** Introduction of Vowel Sounds in new situations **b.** Detached Syllables and Made-Up Words and Sentences **c.** Accent (Stress) **d.** Practice with Pronunciation Symbols
IX. Syllable Division Patterns:	**9.** See Chapter 2, p. 56
X. ar and or Salmon cards: 34, 37	**10.** **a.** Pronunciation Explained **b.** Detached Syllables and Made-Up Words and Sentences **c.** Dictionary Continued
XI. Diphthongs: oa, ai, ay, ee, oe, eu Salmon cards: 24, 8, 11, 14, 25, 17	**11.** Pronunciation Explained

SCOPE AND SEQUENCE TABLE (continued)

Phonograms	Parallel and Subordinate Topics
XII. er, ir, ur Salmon cards: 35, 36, 38	**12. a.** Pronunciation Explained **b.** Practice with Pronunciation Symbols
XIII. Diphthongs: oi, oy, au, aw, ea Salmon cards: 26, 30, 9, 10, 13	**13.** Pronunciation Explained
XIV. 3 sounds of <u>ed</u>; ble, dle, fle, gle, kle, tle White cards: 45, 48	**14.** Pronunciation Explained
XV. Diphthongs: ey, ie, oo, ou, ow Salmon cards: 9, 21, 27, 28, 29	**15.** Pronunciation Explained
XVI. <u>tion</u> and <u>sion</u> White cards: 46, 47	**16.** Pronunciation Explained
XVII. Diphthongs: ei, ue, ew Salmon cards: 15, 32, 18 Phonograms eigh, igh Salmon cards: 16, 22	**17.** Pronunciation Explained
XVIII. ang, ing, ong, ung ink, onk, unk White card 49	**18. a.** Pronunciation Explained **b.** Spelling Generalizations **c.** Dictation **d.** Formal English **e.** Paraphrasing and Précis Work

DEVELOPMENT OF PARALLEL AND SUBORDINATE TOPICS

Some of these topics may have been discussed in a previous chapter, or will be more fully explained later in the Manual. In such cases a reference to that place will be listed. In other cases a brief discussion of the topic will follow immediately.

First Group of Topics

a. Language Function Explained.

The explanation of the language function should be given in simple form. This furnishes a background in the student's mind for his own difficulties. Knowing that people understand his difficulty, and do not attribute his poor work to stupidity, carelessness, or laziness, encourages the student to feel hopeful about the special lessons. See "For the Student," page 13.

b. Drill Cards Presented.

The order of introduction of the phonograms in the various groups given in the scope and sequence differs from that in Chapters 2 and 3. In some cases all the cards in a group may be presented in one day; in other cases two or three cards of a group may be introduced in one day, and others of the same group on a succeeding day. The order in which the cards within the group are taught may be changed from the order in the table.

c. Key Words Explained. See Phonograms and Key Words in the Appendix.

Second Group of Topics

Vocabulary Study Begun.

Noun	Adjective	Verb	Adverb
equality equalization equalizer	equal	equalize	equally
regularity regulation regulator	regular	regulate	regularly

Synonyms	Antonyms
regular, normal, typical join, combine, unite	irregular, abnormal, atypical separate, sever, disconnect

There should also be sentences that bring out the exact meaning of certain words that the student confuses, such as *extract* and *extricate*; *hurdle* and *hurtle*.

There should be sentences using synonyms correctly—*huge* suggests bulk; *vast* suggests extent. Such sentences should be worked out with the student and recorded in his notebook.

Most high schools have good English books to help with vocabulary, sentence structure, and the like. Teachers should take advantage of these as often as needed.

Third Group of Topics

a. Pronunciation of c, g, s explained. (See page 69.)
b. Dictionary

Some teachers assume that students will absorb information and acquire skill without explicit teaching. A dictionary is an example of a fundamental educational tool that is often neglected. The student never discovers its usefulness and wealth of information.

The material a student can find in the dictionary includes: the use of guide words, the alphabetical arrangement beyond the initial letters, the matter enclosed in slanted lines, how to locate a word when the spelling is unknown, even the peculiar phraseology of the definitions. Each of these should be specifically explained.

Each older student should have access to a current dictionary as an essential part of his or her remedial equipment. An elementary dictionary is not adequate at this point.

Fourth Group of Topics

a. Older students are familiar with many words. The object of the remedial techniques in this Manual is to acquaint the student with a new way of approaching reading and spelling—syllable by syllable, letter by letter if necessary. There is no value in his reviewing the many words which he already knows at a glance.

At this point three-letter detached or made-up syllables are introduced. Detached syllables are parts of real words; made-up syllables or nonsense words are not. They should be read so clearly that there can be no doubt regarding any of the sounds. This statement applies to all similar lists of detached and made-up syllables that follow in this chapter. The goal here is *application of concepts*.

When words have been carelessly enunciated for a long time without regard to structure, it is very difficult to correct mispronunciations. The student knows the word and is satisfied with it even though the final consonant is lost or the vowel blurred. Detached or nonsense syllables in which every letter must be sounded serve a unique purpose in developing precision.

das	zin	hom	hab	bix	jal	dem	vol
des	nup	lis	muz	med	kem	jit	mon
dis	wob	kel	pud	sug	hep	fol	quin
dos	yid	ron	fif	zon	daf	ros	saf
dus	deg	tet	sym	beb	peb	dib	heb
rom	min	vix	dal	vit	biv	reg	yat
bez	siz	hos	quiv	fas	sud	gav	pif
rus	lav	lig	sep	rol	vap	ket	nal
quib	rel	fis	pid	pam	wiz	nym	jus
ped	gom	bak	nov	gat	len	zep	gog

b. Pronunciation Symbols of Letters Thus Far Introduced. (See Chapter 5.)
c. Consonant Blends. (See Chapter 2, page 47).
d. Detached and Made-Up Syllables (Blends). Although the student who has been attempting to read for some years has become familiar with the fact that certain consonants blend their sounds at times, he is frequently unable to accurately handle detached syllables in which such blends occur. When he attempts to read words containing blends, a curious situation very often appears. The word is made longer by the additional consonants involved in blends, and he is

very apt to mispronounce the vowel sound, which he would not do in the case of the shorter and simpler three-letter word or syllable. For example, he might read correctly the detached syllable *len*; but in the longer sequence of letters in *slend* the vowel might be distorted, his pronunciation *slind*. It is as though his concentration on blending the consonants distracted his attention from the vowel sound. The following list of detached syllables and made-up words contains and illustrates blends:

hild	spond	fraz	scond	broc	griz	sorp	blad
flab	grif	reft	lusk	stant	sliv	flam	swiv
cren	plym	trast	stig	sniv	quent	glit	snaf
smol	nist	skag	zond	lect	brun	flod	nect
dult	drant	prob	glox	pleb	rupt	fract	strem
grap	clin	cremp	prof	brev	drog	trib	slom

   e. Spelling Patterns as Needed for Dictation. See Chapter 2, Pattern 1, page 45; Chapter 3, Patterns and Dictation, page 37; Chapter 7.

Fifth Group of Topics

   a. Digraphs Contrasted with Blends.
   A digraph is a phonogram composed of two letters having a single sound. A phonogram with three letters having a single sound is a trigraph. For the most part digraphs occur because a letter was taken into a language from a foreign language. When this foreign letter did not exist in the receiving language, it was given a sound already existing in that language. For example, the digraph p̲h̲ representing the Greek letter Φ came to have the sound of \ f \ , as in *phone*. (See page 68.)
   Blends, on the other hand, consist of two or three letters; the sound of each letter is heard in the combination. In the word *plot* the sounds of the letters p̲ and l̲ are both heard.
   b. History of English Language. See Chapters 1 and 3.

Sixth Group of Topics

   a. Effect of Silent Final e̲ on Preceding Vowels. See Chapter 2, page 48.
   b. Detached and Made-Up Syllables.

pute	lete	nide	labe	tate	sade	vate	bibe
vene	tave	buke	hume	zome	vule	gade	nive
ute	nize	nade	dyte	mide	ane	bule	yune
fide	ube	vive	pede	fute	mune	zene	ume
nate	sote	jole	ole	une	dite	tude	tave
voke	rene	ite	bine	mize	pote	vade	vule

Seventh Group of Topics

a. Introduction of Vowel Sounds in New Situations. See Chapter 3, page 71.

The vowels a̲, e̲, i̲, and o̲ sometimes have sounds that are simply their own names, in which case they are marked with a macron: \ā\, \ē\, \ī\, \ō\. This is most likely to occur at the end of an accented syllable in words of more than one syllable. In a similar location the vowel u sometimes has the sound of \yü\ as in *music*, at other times, \ü\ as in *ruby*.

The vowel y̲ never has the sound of its own name. When it occurs at the end of a final syllable, it usually has the sound of \ē\ as in the words *baby, candy, pretty*. Sometimes, however, at the end of a syllable other than the last it has the sound \ī\ as in *cyclone, dynamo*.

For students who may not be able to divide words into syllables on their own, the teacher must complete the division prior to the student's reading the following activity.

b. Detached Syllables and Made-Up Words and Sentences.

1. Flimsate pondeg lant.
2. Talcig mundit cymbap.
3. Rindem brid segmel.
4. Dactus flum elfic.
5. Judsul gast gatlol.
6. Crobe twidlum rindem.
7. Drivlabe glom widrad prave.
8. Enmide modraf quen kriskel.
9. Drastoc elbon hep gitlem.
10. Foltum igsote jum kalmeg.
11. Melzim strep lobsig lanreb.
12. Trumpim engant cribe funbot.
13. Hectis quet vindit banbine.
14. Uglol struct blenzam val.
15. Lectem rom sutlib vive.
16. Brant linvict hab juncile.

c. Accent (Stress). See Chapter 2.

d. Practice with Pronunciation Symbols. See Chapter 5, Types.

e. Spelling Generalizations Introduced. See Chapter 8.

f. Dictation. See Chapter 6.

g. Grammar.

In the latter part of Chapter 6 there are suggestions for helping the student with original compositions in addition to the exercises in dictation. Even more than dictation, original writing demands instruction in formal English: punctuation, sentence structure (aided greatly by diagramming), and grammar. Books on these topics will be found in the student's own high school, and can be looked up elsewhere. Such books should be on the desk of the remedial teacher, available for ready reference.

h. Paraphrasing and Précis Work.

READING RESUMED

Again, it is unreasonable to suggest that the student not be required to read any class materials. However, deriving information from print can be made easier. Peer readers and books on tape are two of the strategies that can be employed while reading skills are being developed. Much of what is available in print is also available on cassettes. Videos may also be a great aid in acquiring information. Reading machines or voice-synthesized text readers, such as the Kurzweil Reading Machine, are small computers with an optical scanner that converts printed words into synthesized speech. Teachers should check to see if a reading machine is in place at their local library. Recordings for the Blind and Dyslexic, Inc. (800-221-4792) will provide taped books and professional materials on loan to people who are dyslexic or learning-disabled. Providing suggestions and teaching the student how to become a good listener can also assist him with his studies.

Selection of the first book for reading enjoyment is of vital importance, and should be a joint decision between teacher and student. It is important that the student is not set up for failure and discouragement. If little consideration is given to which book the student chooses, he may become discouraged quickly when he discovers he cannot read the chosen selection. If a book is selected using the following criteria, a student can begin the process of reading literature for enjoyment and skill:

- student's skill level for reading independently
- student's major topics of interest
- teacher's knowledge of a given book for identification of potential difficulties (such as vocabulary or word attack level)

The teacher must make reading a book a successful experience. She may even do some of the reading herself, paraphrasing some sentences as she goes. Vivid description, plot development, and character portrayal should all be discussed, understood, and enjoyed.

The goal of speed reading is not addressed as part of this program. It is our experience that as skill and accuracy in reading improve, so does speed. In other words, speed will keep pace with increased skill. To set speed as a goal is to place emphasis at the wrong end of the process. Fluency and comprehension increase speed, but striving to read more words per minute does not bring fluency or comprehension.

Teachers should make every effort to prevent the resumption of old habits, such as omitting unknown words or substituting and adding words. The student must make an effort to apply newly learned skills and concepts. He must also recognize that reading, for him, means genuine study. When he says that he is ready to read a selection, he must be held responsible for correct pronunciation of words and explanation of meaning, and demonstrate use of all tools available to him (such as the dictionary). When possible, most of this early reading should be done orally, so the teacher can assess application of skills.

While the need for continued training and review in the translation of symbols into sounds must be continually emphasized, neither the teacher nor the student should forget that the purpose of reading is to gain meaning and enjoyment from the printed page. Someone who has been hindered in this process for years by his inability to recognize words at sight and has only hazy ideas of what he has read, has probably acquired only a limited vocabulary.

VOCABULARY STUDY CONTINUED

Many books have been written to improve word knowledge. Knowing the meaning of words brings the capacity to understand and express complex thoughts. We do not suggest teaching vocabulary as an isolated skill; rather, we present it in such a way that a student can use it to discover what the author means. The first step in presenting words is to use those found in stories the student is reading. The discussion of these words should take place within the context of the selection. The student is encouraged to share these words with the teacher or tutor, and he should place them in his notebook. We recommend that he use a looseleaf notebook with appropriate letter tabs, so pages can be added as the number of words grows. A page or several pages can be devoted to words with initial a, other pages for initial b, and so on. The words on the page will not be arranged strictly in alphabetical order since they will be added as they occur in the reading. The words can be put in alphabetical order later if desired.

In the beginning the teacher should express the definitions in simple statements and in her own words, so the meaning is clear. Each definition should give a clear idea of the word's function—noun, verb, adjective, and so on. It may be helpful for some students to create pictures along with sentences to represent the meanings of words. As we know, some students learn best when they can see and illustrate the material to learn. By using students' strengths, their comprehension improves, and recall is easier.

summary, *n.*	A brief account, containing the main points of a fuller account. "There is a summary at the end of the chapter."
summary, *adj.*	Quick, without delay. "The judge's decision brought summary justice to the prisoner."
summarize, *v.*	To make a summary; to express briefly the main points in a longer account. "Summarize this chapter."
summarily, *adv.*	Done quickly or without delay. "The lazy worker was summarily dismissed."

At first the teacher should write the definitions in the notebook, preferably after the lesson in which the word had been discussed. Introducing new words too rapidly is a common mistake. The student is not to memorize these definitions. During reviews, it will be necessary for him to explain the word clearly, with illustrations, rereading the definition from the notebook whenever his own statement is unsatisfactory.

Another section of the notebook may contain notes that in some way describe the relationship of words. Diagramming sentences seems to bring out this relationship more effectively than any other device.

ORAL EXAMINATIONS

Although a student may have considerable knowledge in various subject areas, she may have difficulty expressing this knowledge in writing. A student's inability to complete a written exam may result in a failing grade, and is a poor example of her true ability and knowledge.

Oral exams may take additional time from a teacher's point of view, but who is more worthy of that time than the student? Teachers sometimes reject the suggestion of the oral examination, feeling that it would give one student an advantage over his classmates. However, no one would deny crutches or a wheelchair to someone who can only succeed with their aid, simply because they are not supplied to those who can succeed without them. In many instances, the arrangements for oral examinations are an essential element of a successful remedial program.

Acquiring Familiarity with Sound Symbols

CHAPTER OVERVIEW

Chapter 5 provides the necessary information for teaching and presenting lessons on the pronunciation of multisyllabic words.

- Decoding—including patterns and steps to follow
- Accenting
- Blends and digraphs in syllable division
- Stable and unstable diphthongs
- Adjacent vowels that are not diphthongs
- Unexpected behavior of familiar letters and combinations (e.g., age, ine, ate, ege)

The techniques in this chapter will aid students in accurate pronunciation by familiarizing them with the sound pictures (symbols) used in the dictionary for analyzing and correctly pronouncing words. Practice in using this symbolism to indicate pronunciation not only fixes the associations between symbols and the sounds they represent, but also sharpens the student's discrimination of sounds; it therefore provides excellent phonetic training.

It should be noted that this is a "substance" chapter requiring much time and study.

Materials Needed

- Dictionary

ACQUIRING FAMILIARITY WITH SOUND SYMBOLS

Familiarity with the dictionary's *symbolic representation of sounds* is of great help in understanding and learning to correctly pronounce unknown words met in reading. In order to provide efficient training in acquiring this skill, the teacher must be familiar with the symbols used and the situations in which they most frequently occur.

- Slanting lines serve as frames for the sound picture.
  e.g., c in the word *city* stands for the sound of \s\
- A short vertical stroke (a "high mark") at the top of the letter, preceding a syllable, indicates that this syllable is given full stress.
  e.g., banish \'ban ish\
- A similar vertical stroke (a "low mark") at the bottom of the letter, preceding a syllable indicates that this syllable is given medium stress.
  e.g., incorrect \ˌin kə 'rekt\
- Pronunciation symbols (sound pictures) consist of single letters or digraphs sometimes modified by "one dot" (ȧ), "two dots" (ä), "bar" or "macron" (ā), and the schwa (ə).

When a student has learned to use these symbols to pronounce the words listed on the following pages, he often becomes quite skillful in pronouncing new words of the same general pattern.

For each exercise the teacher should type or print a list of several words from this Manual.

Sequence of Presentation

The **First Group** of words contains short vowels. The letters a, e, and i have the short sound, and in this case have no distinguishing mark in the sound picture, e.g., *dispel* \dis-'pel\. When a, e, and i have these short sounds, they are nearly always in stressed syllables where the vowel is followed by a consonant or consonant combination. The key words for these sounds as given on the drill cards are a \a\ as in *apple*; e \e\ as in *eddy*; i \i\ as in *itchy*.

- The letter o has no sound comparable to the short sounds of a, e, and i. Its very common sound is indicated by \ä\, as in *father*. The key word for the sound on the drill cards is *octopus*. Likewise, the letter u has no comparable short sound. One of its frequent sounds is represented by the schwa \ə\, when it is pronounced as in *cut. Upper* is the key word given on the drill card. In unstressed syllables the vowel before a final consonant is sometimes elided (to omit or slide over a syllable), as in *rascal* \ras-kəl\ or schwa, \ə\, is substituted, as in *signal* \sig-nəl\.
- When words of Type 1 can be read with some facility with the aid of their symbolic representation, a lesson with Type 2 words may be introduced.

The **Second Group** of words contains vowel-consonant-e and long vowels.

- When some proficiency with Type 2 words has been acquired, a miscellaneous list of ten or twelve words composed of Type 1 and Type 2 words can be presented for pronouncing. After this, as Types 3 to 11 are introduced, lists of miscellaneous words can be used for practice. For other symbols see the introduction of letters in Chapter 3 and Chapter 4.

The **Third Group** of words contains r-controlled vowels: <u>ar</u>, <u>er</u>, <u>ir</u>, <u>or</u>, <u>ur</u>.

The **Fourth Group** of words contains words with double consonants, with the consonant in the unstressed syllable elided.

The **Fifth Group** of words contains three-syllable words.

The **Sixth Group** of words contains one consonant between two vowels. The consonant can be in either the first or second syllable, depending on the sound of the vowel in the first syllable.

The **Seventh Group** of words contains digraphs.

The **Eighth Group** of words contains blends.

The **Ninth Group** of words contains diphthongs.

The **Tenth Group** of words contains unstable diphthongs.

Unexpected Behavior of Familiar Letters and Combinations, such as exceptions to words containing vowel-consonant-<u>e</u>, and final syllable <u>age</u>, <u>ate</u>, <u>ege</u>, and the **Foreign Pronunciation of Vowel Sounds.**

TYPE 1
WORDS CONTAINING SHORT VOWELS

velvet	\\'vel-vət\\	dispel	\\dis-'pel\\
tandem	\\'tan-dəm\\	quintet	\\kwin-'tet\\
bandit	\\'ban-dət\\	distill	\\dis-'til\\
signal	\\'sig-nl\\	dismiss	\\dis-'mis\\
magnet	\\'mag-nət\\	impel	\\im-'pel\\
rancid	\\'ran(t)-səd\\	pastel	\\pas-'tel\\
dismal	\\'diz-məl\\	misfit	\\mis-'fit\\
sandal	\\'san-dl\\	admit	\\əd-'mit\\
cymbal	\\'sim-bəl\\	embed	\\im-'bed\\
cancel	\\'kan(t)-səl\\		
sylvan	\\'sil-vən\\		
hamlet	\\'ham-lət\\		
system	\\'sis-təm\\		
vandal	\\'van-dl\\		
lintel	\\'lin-tl\\		
dental	\\'den-tl\\		
cygnet	\\'sig-nət\\		
candid	\\'kan-dəd\\		
vanish	\\'van-ish\\		
fiscal	\\'fis-kəl\\		
index	\\'in-dəks\\		
atlas	\\'at-ləs\\		
aspic	\\'as-pik\\		
syntax	\\'sin-taks\\		
antic	\\'an-tik\\		
lactic	\\'lak-tik\\		
pencil	\\'pen(t)-səl\\		

TYPE 1
continued

^ˈ —

limpid	\ˈlim-pəd\
jetsam	\ˈjet-səm\
raglan	\ˈrag-lən\
viscid	\vis-əd\
mantis	\ˈman-təs\
hectic	\ˈhek-tik\
catnip	\ˈkat-nip\

TYPE 2
WORDS CONTAINING VOWEL-CONSONANT-E
see long vowels

costume	\ˈkäs-t(y)üm\		confuse	\kən-ˈfyüz\
dictate	\ˈdic-ˌtāt\		sublime	\səb-ˈlīm\
vampire	\ˈvam-ˌpī(ə)r\		cascade	\(ˈ)kas-ˈkād\
capsule	\ˈkap-səl\		compete	\kəm-ˈpēt\
magnate	\ˈmag-nāt\		escape	\is-ˈkāp\
compote	\ˈkäm-pōt\		dispose	\dis-ˈpōz\
calcite	\ˈkal-sīt\		advise	\əd-ˈvīz\
umpire	\ˈəm-ˌpī(ə)r\		admire	\əd-ˈmī(ə)r\
alcove	\ˈal-ˌkōv\		excuse	\ik-ˈskyüz\
oblate	\ˈäb-ˈlāt\		inquire	\in-ˈkwi(ə)r\
inmate	\ˈin-ˌmāt\		endure	\in-ˈdu̇r\
empire	\ˈem-ˌpī(ə)r\		engage	\in-ˈgāj\
mundane	\ˌmən-ˈdān\		dispute	\dis-ˈpyüt\
			ignite	\ig-ˈnīt\
			invite	\in-ˈvīt\
			invoke	\in-ˈvōk\
			induce	\in-ˈd(y)üs\

TYPE 3
WORDS CONTAINING <u>AR</u>, <u>ER</u>, <u>IR</u>, <u>OR</u>, <u>UR</u>

hermit	\\'hər-mət\\	confirm	\\kən-'fərm\\
turban	\\'tər-bən\\	concern	\\kən-'sərn\\
verbal	\\'vər-bəl\\	incur	\\in-'kər\\
burlap	\\'bər-,lap\\	concur	\\kən-'kər\\
doctor	\\'däk-ter\\	confer	\\kən-'fər\\
luster	\\'ləs-tər\\	infer	\\in-'fər\\
vernal	\\'vərn-l\\	survive	\\sər-'vīv\\
turnip	\\'tər-nəp\\	pervade	\\pər-'vād\\
circus	\\'sər-kəs\\	disturb	\\dis-'tərb\\
murmur	\\'mər-mər\\	perturb	\\pər-'tərb\\
vesper	\\'vəs-pər\\	absurd	\\əb-'zərd\\
nectar	\\'nək-tər\\	surpass	\\sər-'pas\\

TYPE 4
WORDS CONTAINING DOUBLE CONSONANTS,
THE ONE IN THE UNSTRESSED SYLLABLE ELIDED

tennis	\\'tən-əs\\	commit	\\kə-'mit\\
rabbit	\\'rab-ət\\	rattan	\\ra-'tan\\
ballad	\\'bal-əd\\	commend	\\kə-'mend\\
fossil	\\'fäs-əl\\	suppose	\\sə-'pōz\\
gossip	\\'gäs-əp\\	success	\\sək-'ses\\
happen	\\'hap-ən\\	annex	\\ə-'neks\\
funnel	\\'fən-ᵊl\\	allot	\\ə-'lät\\
vellum	\\'vel-əm\\	offend	\\ə-'fend\\
ditto	\\'dit-(,)ō\\	assume	\\ə-'süm\\
dollar	\\'däl-ər\\	oppose	\\ə-'pōz\\
pepper	\\'pep-ər\\	efface	\\i-'fās\\
millet	\\'mil-ət\\	commute	\\kə-'myüt\\
		accede	\\ak-'sēd\\
		annul	\\ə-'nel\\
		effete	\\ə-'fēt\\
		pollute	\\pə-'lüt\\
		connote	\\kə-'nōt\\

TYPE 5
THREE-SYLLABLE WORDS

___ˈ___ ___

carpenter	\ˈkär-pən-tər\
peppermint	\ˈpep-ər-mint\
infancy	\ˈin-fen-sē\
turpentine	\ˈtər-pən-ˌtīn\
eglantine	\ˈeg-lən-ˌtīn\
extirpate	\ˈek-stər-ˌpāt\

ˈ___ ___ˌ___

thunderbolt	\ˈthən-dər-bolt\
underpass	\ˈən-dər-pas\
mizzenmast	\ˈmiz-ᵊn-mast\
malcontent	\ˌmal-ken-ˈtənt\

___ ___ˈ___ ___

abnormal	\(ˈ)ab-ˈnor-məl\
bandana	\ban-ˈdan-ə\
fantastic	\fan-ˈtas-tik\
important	\im-ˈport-ᵊnt\
assassin	\ə-ˈsas-ᵊn\
astonish	\ə-ˈstän-ish\

ˈ___ ___ ___ˈ___

incorrect	\ˈin-kə-ˈrekt\
circumvent	\sər-kəm-ˈvent\
opportune	\ˈäp-ər-ˈt(y)ün\
personnel	\ˈpərs-ᵊn-ˈel\

TYPE 6
ONE CONSONANT BETWEEN TWO VOWELS
Consonant in First Syllable

ˈ___ ___

solid	\ˈsäl-əd\
planet	\ˈplan-ət\
relic	\ˈrel-ik\
modest	\ˈmäd-əst\
profit	\ˈpräf-ət\
tribute	\ˈtrib-yüt\
camel	\ˈkam-əl\

ˈ___ ___

legend	\ˈleg-ənd\
banish	\ˈban-ish\
closet	\ˈkloz-ət\
punish	\ˈpən-ish\
tragic	\ˈtraj-ik\
comet	\ˈkäm-ət\
static	\ˈstat-ik\

Consonant in Second Syllable

ˈ___ ___

profile	\ˈprō-fīl\
tripod	\ˈtrī-päd\
crisis	\ˈkrī-səs\
climax	\ˈklī-maks\
zenith	\ˈzē-nəth\

ˈ___ ___

tyrant	\ˈtī-rənt\
iris	\ˈī-rəs\
unit	\ˈyü-nət\
vacate	\vā-ˈkāt\

TYPE 7
DIGRAPHS

franchise	\'fran-chīz\	nickel	\'nik-əl\
exchange	\'eks-chānj\	prophet	\'präf-ət\
urchin	\'ərch-n\	zephyr	\'zef-ər\
anchovy	\'an-chō-vē\	gopher	\'gō-fər\
strychnine	\'strik-nīn\	hyphen	\'hif-ən\
orchid	\'ȯrk-əd\	metaphor	\'met-ə-ˌfȯ(ə)r\
architect	\'är-kə-ˌtekt\	usher	\'əsh-ər\
nonchalant	\nän-sha-'lant\	bishop	\'bish-əp\
pitchfork	\'pich-ˌfȯ(ə)rk\	ashamed	\ə-'shāmd\
hackney	\'hak-nē\	cathode	\'kath-ōd\
pickle	\'pik-əl\	anathema	\ə-'nath-ə-mə\
duchess	\'dəch-əs\	antithesis	\an-'tith-ə-səs\
trachoma	\trə-'kō-mə\	epithet	\'ep-ə-thət\
mechanic	\mi-'kan-ik\	mythical	\'mith-i-kəl\
brochure	\bro-'shu(ə)r\	apathy	\'ap-ə-thē\
satchel	\'sach-l\	pathos	\'pä-thōs\
kitchen	\'kich-ən\	fathom	\'fa<u>th</u>-əm\
cricket	\'krik-ət\	rather	\'ra<u>th</u>-ər\
mackerel	\'mak-r(-)əl\		

TYPE 8
WORDS CONTAINING BLENDS

pantry	\'pan-trē\	algebra	\'al-jə-brə\
osprey	\'äs-prē\	perspire	\pər-'spī(ə)r\
belfry	\'bel-frē\	prospect	\'präs-pekt\
umbrella	\em-'brel-ə\	despair	\de-'spar\
partner	\'pärt-nər\	extra	\'ek-strə\
pamphlet	\'pam(p)-flət\	detriment	\'de-trə-ment\
synchronize	\'siŋ-krə-ˌnīz\	detract	\di-'trakt\
reflex	\'rē-fleks\	compact	\kəm-'pakt\
cathedral	\ke-'thē-drəl\	victim	\'vik-təm\
thermostat	\'ther-mə-stat\	correct	\kə-'rekt\
artist	\'ärt-əst\	dumpling	\'dəm-pliŋ\
disturb	\dis-'tərb\	campus	\'kam-pəs\
scalpel	\'skal-pəl\	pompous	\'päm-pəs\
umpire	\'əm-pīr\	handsome	\'han(t)səm\
fantastic	\fan-'tas-tik\	window	\'win-(ˌ)dō\
membrane	\'mem-brān\	standard	\'stan-dərd\
fabric	\'fab-rik\		

TYPE 9
WORDS CONTAINING DIPHTHONGS

maiden	\\'mād-ᵊn\\	money	\\'mən-ē\\
sausage	\\'sȯ-sij\\	besiege	\\bē-'sēj\\
hawthorn	\\'hȯ-ˌthȯ(ə)rn\\	mischief	\\'mis(h)-chəf\\
crayon	\\'krā-ˌän\\	approach	\\ə-'prōch\\
steak	\\'stāk\\	poison	\\'pȯiz-ᵊn\\
bearing	\\'ba(ə)r-ing\\	typhoon	\\tī-'fün\\
conceal	\\ken-'sē(ə)l\\	woodbine	\\'wu̇d-bīn\\
weapon	\\'wep-ən\\	thousand	\\'thȧuz-ᵊn(d)\\
steeple	\\'stē-pəl\\	acoustic	\\ə-'kü-stik\\
surveillance	\\sər-'vā-lən(t)s\\	double	\\'dəb-əl\\
leisure	\\'lēzh-ər\\	sparrow	\\'spar-(ˌ)ō\\
feudal	\\'fyüd-ᵊl\\	powder	\\'pȧud-ər\\
eschew	\\is(h)-'chü\\	voyage	\\'vȯi-ij\\
nephew	\\'nef-(ˌ)yü\\	recruit	\\ri-krüt\\
conveyance	\\kən-'vā-ən(t)s\\	pursuit	\\pər-'süt\\

TYPE 10
WORDS CONTAINING UNSTABLE DIPHTHONGS

mosaic	\\mō-'zā-ik\\	coerce	\\kō-'ərs\\
archaic	\\är-'kā-ik\\	coeval	\\kō-'ē-vəl\\
create	\\'krē-āt\\	egoist	\\'e-gə-wəst\\
ideal	\\ī-'dē-əl\\	coordinate	\\kō-'ȯrd-n(-)ət\\
linear	\\'lin-ē-ər\\	zoology	\\zō-'äl-ə-jē\\
deity	\\'dē-ət-ē\\	cooperate	\\ko-'äp(-ə)-ˌrāt\\
reinforce	\\re-ən-'fo(o)rs\\	duel	\\'d(y)ü-əl\\
spontaneity	\\spänt-en-'ā-ət-ē\\	duet	\\'d(y)ü-'et\\
nucleus	\\'n(y)ü-klē-əs\\	cruet	\\'krü-ət\\
museum	\\myü-'zē-əm\\	minuet	\\min-yə-'wet\\
lyceum	\\'lī-sē-əm\\	influence	\\'in-flü-ən(t)s\\
science	\\'sī-ən(t)s\\	fuel	\\'fyü-əl\\
client	\\'klī-ənt\\	suet	\\'sü-ət\\
orient	\\'ōr-ē-ent\\	fluid	\\'flü-əd\\
expedient	\\ik-'spēd-ē-ənt\\	druid	\\'drü-əd\\
oasis	\\ō-'ā-səs\\	altruism	\\'al-trü-iz-əm\\
coagulate	\\kō-ag-yə-ˌlāt\\	annuity	\\ə-'n(y)ü-ət-ē\\
boa	\\'bō-ə\\	ambiguity	\\am-bə-'gyü-ət-ē\\
poem	\\'pō-əm\\		

TYPE 11
VOWELS ADJACENT BUT NOT DIPHTHONGS

chaos	\\'kā-äs\\	hiatus	\\hī-'āt-əs\\
aorta	\\ā-'ȯrt-ə\\	raffia	\\'raf-ē-ə\\
neon	\\'nē-än\\	zodiac	\\'zōd-ē-ak\\
peony	\\'pē-ə-nē\\	viaduct	\\'vī-ə-dəkt\\
vireo	\\'vir-ē-ō\\	diary	\\dī-ə-rē\\
creosote	\\'krē-ə-sōt\\	lion	\\'lī-ən\\
meteor	\\'mēt-ē-ər\\	riot	\\'rī-ət\\
hideous	\\'hid-ē-əs\\	iodine	\\'ī-ə-dīn\\
bounteous	\\'baunt-ē-əs\\	oriole	\\'or-ē-əl\\
theory	\\'thē-ə-rē\\	serious	\\'sir-ē-əs\\
neophyte	\\'nē-e-fīt\\	tapioca	\\tap-ē'-ō-kə\\
geometry	\\jē-'äm-ə-trē\\	triumph	\\'trī-əm(p)f\\
theocracy	\\thē-'äk-rə-sē\\	premium	\\'prē-mē-əm\\
trial	\\'trī-əl\\	truant	\\'trü-ənt\\
pliant	\\'plī-ənt\\	casual	\\'kazh-(ə)-wel\\
vial	\\'vī-əl\\	virtuous	\\verch-(ə)-wəs\\
diamond	\\'di-(ə)mənd\\	tenuous	\\'ten-yə-wəs\\
dialect	\\'dī-ə-lekt\\	vacuum	\\'vak-yəm\\

UNEXPECTED BEHAVIOR OF FAMILIAR LETTERS AND COMBINATIONS

The remaining aids to pronunciation have no logical dependence upon one another. Their order here is purely arbitrary, and any shift in sequence may be made. They should be taken up as needed to answer a student's question or to prepare for a foreseeable difficulty.

Earlier, phonograms were described as having the sounds most commonly attributed to them. Exceptions that were avoided will now appear, although what seems an exception may simply be another correct but less common usage.

EXCEPTIONS TO LONG VOWELS IN VOWEL-CONSONANT-E The most common and striking of these occurs in words ending in i-consonant-e. Not only is i often "short," as in *expensive*, it may even have an \\ē\\ sound as in *machine*.

The final syllable age is often pronounced \\ij\\, not \\āj\\ as in the word age.

shortage	stoppage	cleavage	manage	cottage
breakage	tonnage	wastage	village	damage
coinage	savage	dosage	forage	orphanage

The pronunciation of the final syllable ate ranges from \\āt\\ through \\et\\.

ate \\it\\

'sen ate	'frig ate	'del i cate	'des o late
'cli mate	'choc o late	'tem per ate	de 'lib er ate

A large number of these words are adjectives with corresponding verbs ending in \āt\, e.g., *des o late*, *v.* \lāt\.

The word *privilege* illustrates the fact that <u>ege</u>, terminal in a word, may be pronounced \ij\ instead of \ēj\ as would be expected: \'priv(-ə)-lij\.

FOREIGN PRONUNCIATION OF VOWEL SOUNDS   Out of the complicated interplay of influences upon Old English from Norse, Roman, and Norman conquerors, Modern English emerged with very different vowel sounds from those of Romance languages, which for the most part retain very nearly the Latin sounds.

While there is no fixed rule about foreign names, many of which have been completely Anglicized (like Aristotle or Plato), it will still be very useful to become familiar with the Latin vowels, which have strongly influenced modern pronunciations. This must not be undertaken until the English sounds have been mastered.

Expressing Ideas in Writing

CHAPTER OVERVIEW

This chapter emphasizes the importance of tracing, copying, and dictation as separate but integrated elements in developing the ability to express ideas in writing.

Tracing letters and words helps to reinforce the kinesthetic picture of the letter shape or word pattern, and forms a fundamental link in the multisensory approach to integration of the language function. In copying exercises, students learn to copy sentences and information in sensible units to increase their visual memory span. Oral dictation helps to eliminate the complications students sometimes encounter when composing their own works, to reinforce visual memory of the written symbol or pattern, and to increase auditory memory.

Chapter 6 also reinforces the concept of proofreading as an important step in helping the poor speller detect his or her mistakes. It gives helpful techniques to teach students to proofread their work. Grammar and punctuation should be introduced as needed.

Materials Needed

- Dictation exercises
- Copying exercises
- Various writing surfaces (roughboard, sand, or other material)
- Tracing paper
- Student notebook/paper (for dictation and copying exercises)
- Dictionary

EXPRESSING IDEAS IN WRITING

Throughout the early chapters, there are frequent references to writing phono-grams, phonetic words, and combining these into sentences as rapidly as possible so that the student will be able to express himself in writing. It is the kinesthetic reinforcement that helps the student to process and keep the information.

The location of this chapter does not indicate the point at which written expression should be taught. Naturally, no one finishes reading practice before he learns to spell and write, and to demand written exercises without some training in spelling would be an absurdity. This chapter is placed here for convenience, and should be integrated with all that precedes and follows.

In Chapters 7 and 8 we state that spelling *patterns* and *generalizations* should not necessarily be taught in the order presented, but when needed by the partic-ular student. Recognizing such needs makes it obvious that written exercises should be worked on either in the regular classroom, aided by the remedial teacher, or as an integral part of the remedial sessions.

Although we are about to discuss tracing, copying, and dictation as separate elements in developing the ability to express ideas in writing, they are not to be regarded as graded steps, each to be finished before undertaking the next. They must all work together.

In order for the process of written composition to function normally in all its aspects, special exercises in which one function is isolated for training are often valuable.

TRACING

When teaching letter forms to students and training them away from mirror writ-ing tendencies, tracing is almost indispensable. For older students, it may help with correct letter sequences in spelling. Combined with the simultaneous oral naming of the letters, it forms a fundamental link in the multisensory approach to integration of the language function. Fernald attributed extraordinary potency to the simple process of tracing. (Fernald, Grace M. *Remedial Techniques in Basic School Subjects*. New York: McGraw-Hill, 1943.)

Procedures vary among teachers. We usually have the letters of words traced with a pencil on translucent paper. We have also applied the term tracing to the act of forming letters with pencil or finger in the air, in sand, or on roughboard, as a means of very basic kinesthetic training. Many adults do this spontaneously in order to assure themselves of correctly spelling the word about to be written. Fernald, on the other hand, regarded pencil tracing as of little value compared with having the student's finger move in direct contact with the model, without a pencil intervening.

Pronouncing the word and naming the letters as they are traced one by one should be followed by writing them S.O.S. after the model is removed. It is essen-tial that models be large enough to make a definite kinesthetic picture of the form traced. Students should trace the letters with enough force to involve the muscles in the upper arm.

COPYING

Exercises in copying serve as an informal diagnostic test. They provide the most convincing proof that the trouble is not due to any defect in vision. If the student looks at his copy letter by letter, he may produce a perfect result; but if he looks away from the words being copied, he is apt to make errors.

With practice, the student can lengthen the span of immediate visual recall. Some will find thoughtful copying using simultaneous naming of the letters (S.O.S.)—an association of visual, auditory, and kinesthetic elements—helpful in the permanent acquisition of spelling. The student so confused as to copy *go* as *og*, *of* as *fo*, *it* as *ti*, and see nothing wrong in her written product, may find it especially helpful to name each letter as she writes it.

Very few students copy in sensible units. Most of them refer to the book or the chalkboard for every word, or even parts of words, frequently losing their place and omitting important phrases. These faulty practices are time-consuming. For example, a homework assignment may not have been copied with sufficient accuracy to make its purpose clear when the writer attempts to carry it out. Many a lesson has been wrong for this reason.

Suggested procedure for copying (to build, strengthen, and lengthen the student's visual memory span):

- Teacher introduces a meaningful unit (letter, word, phrase, sentence).
- Student carefully studies the unit.
- Student reads the unit. (Any word unfamiliar to the student is practiced using the tracing technique until the word can be reproduced correctly.)
- When preparation is completed, *the model is removed* and the unit is written S.O.S. without assistance from the teacher or model.
- After each successive unit has been handled in the same way, the model is laid beside the student's paper, and he looks for discrepancies.

If he compares his paper with the model and finds several errors, he will become more cautious in estimating his ability the next time, and thus will take an intelligent interest in lengthening his visual memory span, which is the real purpose of the exercise. The teacher must carefully monitor the student's visual memory and slowly increase his visual memory span by selecting the units to copy. However, at some point in the remedial session, the student may be asked to read a selection and decide for himself which units he can safely attempt to reproduce.

DICTATION

Writing to dictation is the process of reproducing a model that has not been seen. For the student with reliable visual and auditory memory, the steps and the process are to

- first hear the sounds of the words,
- then think automatically how these words would look if written,
- finally transcribe the visual picture onto paper.

We have recognized from the beginning that we must not rely on the visual memory of our students but must reinforce it by every possible means, guiding them to think out the written symbols that represent the sounds heard. By taking dictation of meaningful sentences without the complication of composing them as in original writing, the student can focus on one skill—increasing auditory memory.

Periods, question marks, and capital letters should be introduced now. Intensive drill and review will probably be necessary. Introduction of more sophisticated punctuation (such as quotation marks, exclamation points, commas) should follow as needed.

The student should be responsible for correctly spelling words in dictation exercises. The teacher should only select words the student knows (phonetic words, learned words, spelling patterns already studied, etc.). If it is necessary to use words that the student does not know, they should be written in the form of penmanship the student uses and kept beside the student to copy. Doing this before beginning the dictation exercise will help the student maintain focus on the dictated material. The realization that no help will be given during the exercise usually stimulates careful listening to the passage as it is dictated. To provide opportunity for thoughtful listening, the teacher should read the entire selection slowly and distinctly, often more than once.

Dictation Exercises (Lengthening the Auditory Span)

Sentences too long for the student to remember are now divided, but always into meaningful units. The length of the units will depend on the student's ability.

- The student names and dates his paper so that progress may be noted. (A title may be added to add interest to the task).
- The teacher reads the first unit.
- The student repeats it and then writes it S.O.S. *from memory without prompting*; otherwise, the value of the lesson is lost. If the student asks for words to be repeated, the exercise becomes horizontal spelling.
- The teacher should make it clear when any sentence ends (through tone, not by dictating "period," or "question mark").
- When starting a new paragraph, the teacher should say: "The next sentence begins a new paragraph." One should never remind the student to use a period, or a question mark, or to indent a new paragraph. The mere statement that a sentence is ended or a new paragraph begins should be an adequate cue.
- When the last unit has been written, the student does all that he can to discover and correct his own errors.

Some students fail in dictation exercises because they cannot hold the sequence of words in memory. This indicates the need for still more preliminary training. An exercise called "oral dictation" is valuable. The teacher gives a large number of phrases or sentences to be repeated orally without any attempt to write them, and the span is gradually lengthened.

Selecting Material for Dictation

For young students progressing regularly through the work as planned in Chapter 2, dictation should be confined to material containing largely phonetic words (words that can be spelled only one way). Some of the Little Stories written by teachers may be used for such practice.

As new phonograms such as <u>ea</u> in *peach* and <u>ee</u> in *see* are taught, an occasional word containing one of them can be introduced (see Appendix 16). Later, when \k\ spellings are studied, a story may be written (such as one about a bla<u>ck</u> <u>c</u>at that li<u>ck</u>s her <u>k</u>ittens, that goes on to tell that they li<u>k</u>ed it). It is helpful if the teacher, who is the only one who knows what has been taught, composes the stories. Gradually the more difficult passages, proverbs, and short poems in Appendices 17 and 18 can be given. Students who have acquired more skill can be presented with longer, more difficult passages.

Since the chief value of dictation exercises is to give a feeling of continuous, meaningful writing, it is important that each selection interests the student. Passages taken out of a book often do not do this. It may be necessary for the teacher to write a suitable exercise himself or to adapt an interesting selection (see Appendix 19). It is not always possible to find or write a passage short enough to dictate at one sitting. Exercises can continue for several days. While it is appropriate to use selections just because they are interesting, it is possible and desirable for them to appeal to the student in content, and at the same time to reinforce formal drill.

They may

- Motivate the introduction of a new spelling pattern or test its mastery:
  A Sad Mishap gives a good review of Spelling Pattern 1
  A Pleasant Walk (Appendix 21) deals with Spelling Patterns 2 and 4 and with homonyms <u>heard</u> and <u>herd</u>, <u>there</u> and <u>their</u>
  An Unwelcome Gift (Appendix 22) is a thorough review of Spelling Pattern 12.
- Stress a new word:
  Palisades (Appendix 24) helps to establish this word in a student's vocabulary.
- Reinforce classroom studies:
  Marco Polo (Appendix 25) follows a study of this explorer.
- Enable the student, with intermediate double dictation (student to teacher, teacher to student), to translate his own thoughts into written material, as in *A Visit to a Vermont Quarry* (Appendix 26).

Original Stories and Themes

Some students will be interested in writing their own thoughts and stories. Some will express themselves regardless of incorrect spelling and usage. Teachers encourage this to a limited extent, but not to the point of fixing incorrect spellings in the memory of the student. There are different points of view regarding what some call "invented" spelling. Some feel it is important for students to learn to develop and express their ideas freely and not to be held back by lack of skill.

Perhaps some compromise can be made, such as holding the students responsible for the spelling patterns that have been introduced, yet allowing them some creative license.

The following activities provide some helpful techniques to increase fluency in expression. As with any suggestions, teachers must decide whether they are appropriate for the student.

- Student first dictates his experience or story to the teacher, who will then assist by paraphrasing the story or asking questions for clarification, content, details, sequencing, and vocabulary.
- Student dictates the story to the teacher. As the teacher listens, he or she writes down key phrases. The student can then use this as an outline for expanding a written composition.
- A tape recorder can allow the student to develop his story on his own.
- Devices such as outlines and graphic organizers may help to alleviate frustrations associated with the creative writing process, and can be more appealing to the visually-oriented student who may not think sequentially.
- Making it personal and fun helps the student to bring life into the story and become more involved. It also helps him to understand and find a connection with a topic.
- Use of word processing and a computer is efficient. With this technology, students can write with little worry about revisions and tiresome recopying.

The development of literary expression is not the primary function of this book. It is our purpose to address the student's ability to express his ideas in writing. In the classroom setting, pressure to complete written assignments can be alleviated by providing modifications. The sense of pressure engendered by the awareness that his classmates are finishing ahead of him can be paralyzing. If he must write his assignment during a class period, without modification, he may be doomed in advance. If forced to hurry, he may repeat old habits with careless mistakes.

Some Suggested Modifications for Classroom Assignments:

- extended time limits for written assignments
- modified assignments
- allowance for spelling or other errors

Self-Corrections

It is often helpful to have support when proofreading. A poor speller is poor because he does not retain clear visual images. It is important to train students to detect their own mistakes by providing more advanced and sophisticated knowledge about spelling patterns and generalizations. Teachers must include a careful course in self-correction, based on the needs of the individual student.

Helpful Techniques for Working toward Independence:

- For editing purposes it will be helpful to use double spacing.
- When the student has completed an exercise, he should read his own paper, aloud or subvocally, to see if he can discover any errors.
  - –The student should write the correct word above the mistake. We suggest that he be given a blue pencil for his corrections. Only after he has corrected in blue all the mistakes that he can detect does the teacher mark remaining errors with red pencil.
- Encourage the student to spell doubtful words aloud as an auditory check.
- Use the dictionary when in doubt. If using a computer, the student may use the "spellcheck" feature.
- Encourage the student to express his uncertainty about a word by underlining it.
- After he has examined his paper for spelling errors, he should inspect it again to see if every punctuation mark he has been taught is in place.

The teacher should use her red pencil with special consideration. In the earliest stages she may write the correction. Corrected misspelled words are to be studied and the necessary punctuation drill given in succeeding lessons.

For more advanced students she may indicate an error by a symbol placed above it. The teacher should use the same symbols that are used in the school. Where no symbolic code has been used before, we suggest the following, most of which are used in common manuscript correction:

- ∧ = insert or omission
- sp = spelling
- ¶ = paragraph
- lc = lowercase
- caps or ≡ (under the appropriate letter) = capitals
- p = punctuation
- w = wrong word

When an error is indicated, the student must apply his knowledge of patterns and generalizations or use the dictionary. This is preliminary to genuine self-discovery of an error. If *go* written as *og*, or *perceive* spelled *percieve*, is labeled *sp*, the student merely writes the other form with a minimum of thought. He must be helped to establish the habit of challenging each word and deciding whether it is right. As a means to this end, the teacher indicates that an error of a special type is in that line by the appropriate symbol in the margin.

The student assumes still more responsibility if the teacher does not indicate the character and place of mistakes, but merely puts "X" marks in the margin, each of which represents an error for the student to find and correct.

Spelling errors for which the student is not responsible, involving patterns and generalizations not yet introduced, are not marked at all, but are noted by the teacher for future instruction. The student should never feel chagrin for such errors.

The number of errors the student makes will depend upon many factors, such as the severity of the student's disability, how well the exercise was adapted to his ability, and so on.

This attitude of self-evaluation, fostered under controlled conditions, should carry over to original writing. Students will submit much better work if they form this habit. Many students hand in written assignments either without rereading at all or after a cursory glance that fails to reveal even glaring errors. This is a form of irresponsibility and demonstrates neglect in *applying* knowledge to practical situations. Students should be encouraged to take pride in their work by always putting forth their best effort.

Spelling Situations and Patterns

CHAPTER OVERVIEW

Chapter 7 presents the seventeen spelling patterns needed for a logical and organized approach to teaching and learning spelling.

Teachers should frequently review and refer to this chapter. They will need to learn its contents thoroughly before systematically presenting the patterns to the students.

Within the chapter are techniques and strategies to help students learn to spell confusing words. A quick-reference guide to the patterns is at the end of the chapter.

Materials Needed

- Student notebook (for spelling and dictation exercises)
- Word lists and dictation exercises
- Dictionary
- Phonetic Word Cards (Jewel Case—Spelling Pattern 1 word cards)

WHY LEARN SPELLING PATTERNS?

- They enable students (especially those with weak visual memory) to become better spellers.
- They help students make the connection between the sound and its appropriate symbol (phoneme/grapheme) and translate it into written form.
- They provide students with the structure that governs the English language. It is important for students to recognize that, for the most part, spelling is regular and predictable.

The key to the usefulness of spelling patterns is the time spent in application. A student may memorize a pattern in a lesson, but fixing a habit to ensure its application requires practice, review, and reinforcement.

After a pattern is taught and it is evident to the teacher that the student understands it, the pattern should be memorized and reviewed regularly. The student must now feel responsible for applying it in his written work. The student and teacher should regard a misspelled word as proof that further practice is needed. Spelling scores on tests may go down for the first few weeks as students begin applying the newly-learned spelling patterns to their written work.

The measure of success is not how few mistakes the teacher marks, but rather, how many errors the student discovers (see Self-Corrections, Chapter 6.)

SPELLING PATTERNS

It is impossible to predict the order in which to teach the patterns. They are presented here in a logical sequence, but their introduction will depend upon the age, previous training, and special learning needs of the student.

Patterns 1, 2, 4 and those relating to plurals are usually the ones first needed by younger students. For a statement concerning Pattern 3, see page 137.

PATTERN 1

Words Ending in <u>ff</u>, <u>ll</u>, or <u>ss</u>
(The "Floss" Pattern)

Words of one syllable, ending in <u>f</u>, <u>l</u>, or <u>s</u>
(sounding \f\, \l\, or \s\) after one vowel,
usually end in <u>ff</u>, <u>ll</u>, or <u>ss</u>.

Example: The cli<u>ff</u> is ta<u>ll</u> and covered with mo<u>ss</u>.

Sentences containing words from the following lists should be dictated to reinforce the spelling pattern. The student should spell only the words illustrating the pattern. Once the student has spelled the words in isolation, the teacher should provide meaningful sentences containing the spelling patterns for dictation.

The following procedure should be observed (S.O.S.):

- Teacher reads the sentence with the given word(s).
- Teacher repeats the word to be spelled.
- Student repeats the word.
- Student spells the word orally. (Only when he has spelled the word correctly can he take the next step.)
- Student writes the word, naming each letter as he writes.
- Student reads what he has written.

When a word is misspelled orally, the teacher should write what the student has misspelled, show it to the student and ask him what it says. Work to help the student identify errors and make corrections—*self-editing* is an important process.

Sample Sentences:

> Steve was <u>ill</u> and very <u>cross</u>.
> Beth made a silk <u>dress</u> and a fur <u>muff</u> for her <u>doll</u>.
> The <u>brass</u> knob <u>fell</u> from the <u>hall</u> door just now.
> The men toil to build the <u>wall</u>.
> The leaf blew <u>off</u> the roof.
> We found out Sis was a thief.
> The calf held his legs <u>stiff</u>.

Once the dictation exercise has been completed, the student is asked to state why he doubles or does not double (as in the *thief* sentence above) a final consonant. Remember, spelling needs to be viewed as a *cognitive task* (a thought process). Not until the pattern has been applied correctly in several sentences like those above should it be memorized. Until then, the student should be told about the pattern.

Exceptions to Pattern 1:

  a. Common words: if, pal, gas, this, us, thus, yes, bus, pus, plus
  b. Words in which <u>s</u> sounds like <u>z</u> (*is*) and <u>f</u> sounds like <u>v</u> (*of*)

Other double-consonant words are: miscellaneous double consonants (odd, ebb, egg, err, shirr, fizz, buzz, fuzz, add); monosyllable proper nouns (Penn, Grimm, Squibb, Todd, Rapp, Ann).

Most of the exceptions under **a** and **b** above are words which may have been previously learned. They should be discussed as exceptions so that the student will not attempt to apply the rule to *yes*, etc., and will remember exceptional doubling as in *add*, *egg*, and so on.

Pattern 1 Words
("Tester" Words in Last Column)

staff	all	bell	ill	doll	bass	bliss	soil
cliff	ball	cell	bill	cull	brass	miss	meal
stiff	fall	dell	dill	dull	class	hiss	wheel
whiff	gall	fell	fill	full	lass	boss	nail
sniff	hall	hell	gill	gull	mass	loss	coal
doff	mall	knell	hill	hull	pass	toss	loaf
buff	pall	sell	kill	lull	grass	cross	beef
cuff	squall	tell	mill	mull	chess	moss	thief
muff	tall	smell	pill	null	cress	fuss	roof
puff	stall	swell	quill		dress	muss	self
huff	wall	well	rill		less		half
ruff	small		sill		mess		wolf
			still		press		golf
			till				dwarf

AFFIXES
(Meaningful syllables placed before or after the base word.)

Before students can obtain satisfactory mastery of Patterns 2, 3, and 4, they should be familiar with the concept of *affixes* (the verb *affix* means "to fasten on").

A *prefix* is placed *before* the base word. *Pre* means "before," and occurs in such words as the following:

- <u>pre</u>*cede*, to go before
- <u>pre</u>*dict*, to say before, such as to predict what the weather is likely to be
- <u>pre</u>*pare*, to make ready before, as for a journey

A *suffix* is placed *after* the base word, in a word such as:

- <u>pre</u>dict*able*, able to be determined beforehand

Time should be devoted to *word building*. For example, words derived from the Latin *portare*, "to carry," serve well to illustrate the growth of words that are related in meaning, but have functions of their own. Taking *port* as a base word, we proceed to modify this idea by the use of an affix.

After explaining this to the student, the following words may be discussed: *porter, portable, export, import, transport, reporter*. The definition of the affix should be given briefly as each word is discussed; for example, the suffix <u>er</u> means "one who" or "that which performs some action." A *porter* is a person who carries objects, such as bags at a railroad station. In *portable* we have the suffix *able*, meaning "capable of being, fit to be." Anything that can be carried is *portable*. The word *reporter* (one who reports, especially one who gathers information and writes reports for a newspaper) is especially interesting with both the prefix <u>re</u> and the suffix <u>er</u> added.

<u>(Sample) Base Word Activity Sheet</u>
Base Word: port
Meaning: to carry

<u>Prefix</u>			<u>Suffix</u>
*ex*port _____		_____ por*ter*	
im _____		_____ *able*	
trans _____		_____ *al*	

re port *er*

The teacher may use the format above as a worksheet for students to complete exercises using other base words.

The student may not remember the meanings of all the prefixes and suffixes, but she should have a fairly clear idea of the function of affixes. Their meanings will grow clearer as she finds them added to different base words:

walk + er	sing + er	depend + able	laugh + able
trans + plant	re + deem	re + fund	de + port

As stated above, some familiarity with these is essential before the student can grasp the significance of Patterns 2, 3, and 4.

The student's knowledge of English usage will be extended by identifying affixes in different parts of speech.

For example,

- Mr. Verdi <u>imports</u> Chinese goods.
    v.
- Mr. Verdi buys Chinese <u>exports</u>.
    n.
- Ms. Rivera has a <u>portable</u> computer.
    adj.

After the idea of making new words by adding affixes to smaller words has been understood, the student is ready to observe that in certain cases the final consonant of a base word is doubled before a suffix and in other cases it is not.

PATTERN 2

Doubling the Final Consonant: Monosyllables
(1-1-1 Pattern)

One syllable, one consonant at the end, and one vowel before it—double the final consonant before adding a suffix that begins with a vowel, but do not double it when the suffix begins with a consonant.

Examples: flat, flatter, flatness

The student has already met the suffixes <u>er</u>, <u>ish</u>, and <u>ing</u>. Let him see what happens when one of these is added to a base word.

Examples: Final consonant *is* doubled.

rob	rob + er = robber
wet	wet + ish = wettish
drop	drop + ing = dropping

Examples: Final consonant *not* doubled.

loaf	loaf + er = loafer
small	small + ish = smallish
toil	toil + ing = toiling

By this time the student will be curious to know when he should double the final consonant before the suffix and when he should not. Analyzing the words will supply a partial answer: *One* syllable, *one* consonant at the end, and *one* vowel before it—double the final consonant.

Remember:

- Use the S.O.S. procedure.
- Work with words in isolation.
- Use sentence dictation.
- After successful application, the pattern should be reinforced until learned.

Lists similar to the following should be given. The requirements are to analyze the given word, decide whether the consonant before the suffix should be doubled, explain the reason behind the decision, and write the new word.

step + ing	hear + ing	flat + er	weed + ing
grin + ed	girl + ish	cold + est	rush + ing
tan + er	sun + y	big + est	pin + ed

Other lists may consist of words ending in suffixes; in these cases the student's part is to spell the original base word (before the suffix was added).

When he is accurate in performing such tasks and stating his reasons, the student is ready for further practice. The important thing to remember is that the doubling of the final consonant depends upon whether the suffix begins with a vowel or with a consonant.

Examples:

fretting, fretful	winning, winsome	dimmer, dimly

When he is familiar with all these elements he may begin to memorize the pattern. One good way to do this is to have the teacher say the pattern and the student join him in saying as much of it as possible. Meanwhile, the student should be doing exercises such as the following: Using a sheet of paper (preferably the double-ruled paper), he makes four columns, each with a proper heading as shown in the diagram on page 135.

PATTERN 2

WORD	REASON	FINAL CONSONANT DOUBLED	FINAL CONSONANT NOT DOUBLED
run + ing	1s, 1c, 1v + s-v	running	
feed + ing	1s, 1c but 2v		feeding
lift + ed	1s, but 2c		lifted
glad + ness	1s, 1c, 1v but s-c		gladness

In the first column of the diagram the teacher writes a word, the plus symbol (+), then the suffix (for example, <u>run</u> + <u>ing</u>). The student observes and thinks: **"one syllable, one consonant, one vowel, plus suffix beginning with a vowel,"** and then he records his response in the "reason" column as:

1s 1c 1v + s–v

Thinking over the coded pattern he has just made, the student decides whether or not the final consonant is to be doubled, and places the completed word in the third or fourth column.

The list of words that follows is a storehouse from which the teacher may select practice words.

FINAL CONSONANT DOUBLED

-ing, -ed		-er, -est	-er	-y	-ish	-en
drop	rob	wet	rob	mud	snap	red
step	plot	hot	run	stub	snob	fat
fan	bud	fat	blot	fun	prig	flat
fret	stop	big	plot	gas	fop	sad
plan	scrub	sad	rub	fog	red	glad
hop	scar	grim	snap	bag		mad
skip	fit	dim	win	wit		bit
nod	bar	slim	clip	fur		sod
rub	beg	trim	ship	star		bid
mop	clip	glad	hop	grit		hid
grin	quit	mad	chop	slop		trod
drag	grip	fit	tan	snap		
pad	stab	red	quit	sun		
ship	rip	flat	fit			

FINAL CONSONANT NOT DOUBLED

-ing, -ed		-er, -est	-er	-ish	-ness, -ly	-ly
heat	rush	deep	sleep	child	dim	man
roar	mend	warm	read	girl	grim	glad
wheel	sound	cool	steam	book	slim	sad
train	sport	light	cook	imp	trim	mad
fear	pack	bright	heat	fiend	flat	bad
need	reach	cold	loaf	dull	mad	thin
seem	pound	bold	feast		glad	dim
spoil	jump		point	**-y**	**-ness**	**-ful**
nail	wash		room			
pour	crack	**-en**	sing	rain	big	fit
loaf	act		hunt	leaf	wet	fret
fail	burn	ash	fish	soap	fit	sin
heap	rent	oak	farm	room	fat	
floor	match	wood	dust	weed	red	
roof	learn	gold	walk	fish		
feast	climb	lead	wash	mist		**-some**
weed	suit	light	mark	dirt		
	coast	fright	paint	dust		win
			learn	frost		glad
			rent			

PATTERN 3

Doubling the Final Consonant: Polysyllables

Words of more than one syllable, with one consonant at the end and one vowel before it, *double* the final consonant before a suffix beginning with a vowel, *if* the accent is on the last syllable.

Accent on last syllable: be 'g*in* + <u>ing</u>, beginning
Accent not on last syllable: 'o p*en* + <u>ing</u>,   opening

This pattern is actually an extension of Pattern 2, and it seems natural for it to follow at this point. However, it may be desirable to wait until some of the other patterns have been taught because young students use few multisyllabic words and can spend their time better by studying patterns which they can put to use quickly. Also, the application of this pattern can be difficult for some students and adults because they are unable to place the accent accurately. Many students have poor auditory discrimination skills, which are necessary for placing the accent. Therefore, if a student is unable to detect the stressed syllable, this pattern may not prove to be very useful, and the student will have to refer to the dictionary. Some students have been trained in various ways to detect the accent (see pages 54–55.)

Those students who can learn to apply the pattern will profit by exercises in adding suffixes to multisyllabic words (if the students always state the reason for doubling or not doubling the final consonant). During oral dictation exercises, the teacher should stress the accented syllable as he dictates.

For the older student, attention should be given to words derived from Latin verbs, e.g., *ferre,* "to bear," which can show irregularities when a suffix is added:

Examples: con<u>fer</u>   de<u>fer</u>   in<u>fer</u>   pre<u>fer</u>   re<u>fer</u>   trans<u>fer</u>

The student should be helped to discover for himself which derivatives of the English verbs are formed according to patterns, and which are not (see Exceptions, below). He will find that where the accent in the derivative changes to the first syllable, the final consonant of the verb is not doubled in the derivative.

Examples: pre 'fer   'pref er <u>able</u>   'pref er 'en <u>tial</u>

The student may not easily recognize all of the exceptions; therefore, he must be on the alert for them.

Exceptions:

1. **-<u>fer</u>** words double final consonant only with <u>ing</u>, <u>ed</u>, and <u>al</u>.

   Examples: re<u>fer</u>   refer<u>ring</u>   refer<u>red</u>   refer<u>ral</u>

2. **-<u>ff</u>** words never double the final consonant.

   Examples: suffer<u>ing</u>   offer<u>ing</u>   differ<u>ing</u>

3. **-<u>fit</u>** words:
   - Words with Anglo-Saxon origins (often having to do with size or clothing) double the final consonant.

   Examples: mis<u>fit</u>   misfitt<u>ed</u>   un<u>fit</u>   unfitt<u>ed</u>
                  re<u>fit</u>   refitt<u>ed</u>   out<u>fit</u>   outfitt<u>ed</u>

   - Words with Latin roots do not double the final consonant.

   Examples: profit<u>able</u>   benefit<u>ed</u>   discomfit<u>ing</u>

A few words, not accented on the final syllable, may be spelled with the final consonant doubled or not doubled:

   Examples: trav el   trave**ll**ed or traveled
                 ra vel   rave**ll**ed or raveled
                 shov el   shove**ll**ed or shoveled

FINAL CONSONANT DOUBLED

-ing • -ed	-ance	-al	-ence
omit	admit		occur
control	remit	transmit	concur
propel	transmit	acquit	recur
submit	acquit		excel
permit		**-en**	abhor
transmit	**-er**		intermit
regret		forgot	
befit	begin	forbid	**-able**
compel	propel		
commit	transmit		control
impel			regret
incur			forget

FINAL CONSONANT *NOT* DOUBLED

Ending in 2 Consonants	Final Consonant Preceded by 2 Vowels	Accent Not on Final Syllable	Suffix Begins with a Consonant
ing • ed	**ing • ed**	**ing • ed**	**ment**
prevent	contain	garden	allot
remark	refrain	number	annul
direct	remount	limit	inter
request	conceal	suffer	commit
depart	disdain	differ	equip
support	restrain	discover	confer
supplant	reveal	pilot	defer
contest		summon	prefer
respect	**ance**	gather	
resent		market	
divert	appear	blossom	
consult	forbear	blunder	
contend		benefit	
repent	**able**	remember	
transform		recover	
consent	conceal	deliver	
convert	reveal	solicit	
subsist		develop	
subtract		master	
transcend		profit	
depend		enter	
demand		quarrel	

Ending in 2 Consonants			
able	**ance**	**ant**	**ent, ence**
prevent	accept	expect	consist
remark	acquaint	descend	correspond
present	disturb	repent	depend
comfort	perform	resist	exist
perish	resist	defend	insist
transport		triumph	
report			

FINAL CONSONANT *NOT* DOUBLED (*CONTINUED*)

Accent Not on Final Syllable							
er	**ant**	**or**	**al**	**ance**	**ent, ence**	**able**	**y**
discover	vigil	conquer	critic	deliver	differ	credit	silver
slander	inhabit	solicit	cubic	inherit		alter	water
murder		visit				market	sugar
blunder						profit	powder
plaster						conquer	
loiter						inhabit	
deliver							
labor							
plunder							

NONSENSE SYLLABLES

Doubled		Not Doubled	
bap	thun	muth	riev
hin	wel	tush	dilt
con	shog	leck	fapp
pol	brav	enth	bleaf
jat	spal	sputh	vant
pof	drub	glash	lisk
fim	twen	froog	pliah
tas	plax	kirp	sliev
tog	prag	rond	tund
qued	stec	buft	spond
quop	crad	polt	slerd
whav	thet	cont	hend
chub	krel	lorg	bramp
chid	preg		

PATTERN 4

Silent <u>e</u>

For words ending in silent <u>e</u>, drop the <u>e</u> before a suffix beginning with a vowel. Do *not* drop the <u>e</u> before a suffix beginning with a consonant.

Examples: hope, hoping, hopeful

There are a few exceptions to this pattern, but they are not especially troublesome, and should be introduced only after students understand and master the application of the "non-exceptions" pattern.

An introductory opportunity should be provided to observe the behavior of several words ending in silent e when various suffixes are added. The word <u>tame</u> may be taken as a base. The student should note the effect of adding the suffixes <u>ing</u>, <u>ed</u>, <u>er</u> (one who), <u>er</u> (comparative degree), <u>est</u>, <u>able</u>, <u>ly</u>, <u>ness</u>. He will see that sometimes the e of <u>tame</u> is retained and sometimes it is dropped. He is likely to wonder: "How will I know when to drop the e and when to keep it?"

The answer will be apparent if the words are arranged as indicated below:

Word	+	Suffix	=	New Word	Reason
tame		ing		taming	e dropped, suffix beg. with a vowel
tame		ed		tamed	e dropped, suffix beg. with a vowel
tame		ly		tamely	e kept, suffix beg. with a consonant
tame		ness		tameness	e kept, suffix beg. with a consonant

Next, one should ask, *"Does this pattern work with other words?"* The word *measure* may be used, and the suffixes <u>ing</u>, <u>ed</u>, <u>able</u>, <u>less</u>, <u>ment</u> added. To provide additional practice, suffixes beginning with a vowel and suffixes beginning with a consonant should be added to a number of words; sometimes the e will be dropped and sometimes not.

The following list of words, to which specified suffixes should be added, will serve to test the student's understanding of the pattern:

hope	waste	slide	dance	use	home	name
noise	slope	expense	care	like	move	blame
endure	measure	tame	taste	bike	rope	tape

The completed words are to be arranged under these headings:

Final e Dropped	**Final e Retained**	**Reason**

When it is evident that the student understands the pattern and can apply it, it should be memorized.

Note: In words ending in two e's (see), neither e is silent; the diphthong <u>ee</u> produces the \ē\ sound. If one e were dropped when a suffix beginning with a vowel was added, the resulting word would contain another diphthong not necessarily sounding \ē\ (seing, agreable). The pattern also applies to the words ending in an e that is not silent (epitome).

FINAL E DROPPED

-ing, -ed	-able	-er
dance	blame	tune
carve	use	poke
smile	cure	trade
whine	sale	dive
raise	tame	provide
twine	like	office
chime	quote	engrave
wade	love	erase
cable	move	debate
release	observe	deceive
capsize	believe	examine
discharge	excite	
believe	endure	**-or**
receive	desire	
tremble	pleasure	educate
tumble	debate	operate
achieve	measure	radiate
revolve	admire	elevate
balance	imagine	navigate
twinkle		decorate
telephone	**-ance**	translate
		percolate
-ive	grieve	
	guide	**-ity**
expense	endure	
abuse	contrive	pure
create	insure	rare
repulse	persevere	docile
intense	resemble	active
decorate		hostile
illustrate	**-ation**	immense
appreciate		mobile
	quote	fragile
-ous	admire	agile
	inhale	ductile
nerve	exhale	immobile
fame	derive	
desire	combine	**-y**
virtue	incline	
rapture	declare	haze
membrane	imagine	laze
trouble	examine	pine
continue	continue	shine
ridicule	determine	brine
adventure		slime
		spice
		mouse

FINAL E NOT DROPPED

-some	-ment	-ly
lone	move	brave
blithe	excite	sure
awe	amuse	late
tire	announce	scarce
mettle	achieve	fine
trouble	amaze	like
	atone	time
-ness	enslave	wise
	replace	safe
base	abase	wide
like	manage	tame
wide	enlarge	sparse
late	engage	rare
fine	enhance	large
cute	debase	square
tame	entangle	base
lame		loose
sore	**-less**	lame
ripe		sincere
genuine	name	extreme
complete	blame	remote
	taste	entire
-ful	use	intense
	grace	complete
tune	guile	genuine
taste	home	absolute
use	care	accurate
peace	cease	intimate
grace	love	immediate
care	tire	affectionate
hate	noise	
hope	spine	
waste	life	
fate	time	
spite	wire	
pride	shame	
revenge	price	
distaste	sense	
disgrace		

Exceptions should be introduced only after various exercises like those suggested earlier, in which every word followed the pattern.

Exceptions:

- Words ending in <u>ce</u> or <u>ge</u> retain the <u>e</u> before a suffix beginning with <u>a</u> or <u>o</u>. See List 1 below.
- A few words retain the final <u>e</u> before a suffix beginning with a vowel (List 2).
- Some words drop the final <u>e</u> before a suffix beginning with a consonant. The important ones should be memorized (List 3).

Discussion of Exceptions:

- Since <u>c</u> and g are usually soft before <u>e</u>, <u>i</u>, or <u>y</u> and hard before <u>a</u>, <u>o</u>, or <u>u</u>, it will seem reasonable that the <u>e</u> of a word ending in <u>ce</u> or <u>ge</u> is needed before a suffix beginning with <u>a</u> or <u>o</u> to preserve the soft sound of <u>c</u> or <u>g</u>.
- The <u>e</u> is retained in the words *singeing* and *dyeing* to avoid confusion with *singing* and *dying*. <u>Toe</u> + <u>ing</u>, <u>hoe</u> + <u>-ing</u> and <u>shoe</u> + <u>-ing</u> spelled without the <u>e</u> might appear to be one syllable words with the <u>oi</u> pronounced \ȯi\, not \tō'ing\.
- There seems to be no reasonable explanation for this third exception. It must be accepted as a fact.

Students who memorize List 3 so thoroughly that they can reproduce it in writing find it very helpful.

EXCEPTIONS TO PATTERN 4

List 1		List 2		List 3*
-able		**-age**	**-ing**	
peace	change	mile	dye	due - - - - - - - - duly
trace	charge	acre	singe	true - - - - - - - - truly
notice	manage		hoe	whole - - - - - - wholly
service	exchange		shoe	
replace				awe - - - - - - - - awful
pronounce	**-ous**			judge - - - - - - - judgment
	outrage			argue - - - - - - - argument
	advantage			acknowledge - acknowledgment

* For some words the <u>e</u> is permitted, but seldom used, e.g., *judgement, acknowledgement*.

REVIEW OF PATTERNS 2 AND 4

After the student has studied Patterns 2 and 4, his ability to select the correct pattern when adding a suffix should be evaluated. Often he will need to apply both patterns when spelling words—*dropping the <u>e</u> and doubling the consonant.*

When the result is simply a misspelled word, e.g., *tammable* for *tamable*, it may not seem strange to the unsure speller. Sometimes, however, he may produce a word which is entirely different from that which he intended to spell. For example, with <u>hope</u> + <u>ing</u>, he may drop the <u>e</u>, leaving <u>hop</u>, then double the <u>p</u>, producing <u>hopping</u>. A sentence may be given that shows this to be incorrect.

Example: "He was <u>hopping</u> to get a watch for his birthday."

Lists like the following will foster the habit of thoughtful consideration. The student should practice with them frequently as work with other patterns progresses.

plan + ed	dance + ed	wet + ness	plane + ing
weep + ing	blame + able	scrape + ing	big + est
shine + ing	sun + y	blue + ish	time + ly
drip + ed	rob + er	red + ish	fish + ing

The secret of success is to think first of the base word without the suffix, and then of the pattern that tells what to do when adding that suffix to the given word.

PATTERN 5

Regular Plurals

The most common way of forming the plural of *nouns* is to add <u>s</u> to the *singular* form of the word.

Examples: dog, <u>dogs</u>   elephant, <u>elephants</u>   table, <u>tables</u>

This pattern should pose no problem since plurals ending in <u>s</u> are very common.

PATTERN 6

Plurals of Nouns Ending in <u>s</u>, <u>x</u>, <u>z</u>, <u>ch</u>, or <u>sh</u>

Nouns ending in <u>s</u>, <u>x</u>, <u>z</u>, <u>ch</u>, or <u>sh</u> form the plural by adding <u>es</u> to the singular form of the word.

Examples: gas, <u>gases</u>   tax, <u>taxes</u>   topaz, <u>topazes</u>
torch, <u>torches</u>   thrush, <u>thrushes</u>

The logic behind this pattern can be demonstrated easily by giving the student the following sentences. Ask him to read them orally, pronouncing the nouns so as to show which are singular and which are plural:

The <u>glass</u> fell on the floor and broke.
The <u>glasss</u> fell on the floor and broke.
See the <u>topaz</u> in her ring.
See the <u>topazs</u> in her ring.
The <u>box</u> came by mail.
The <u>boxs</u> came by mail.
Look at the <u>thrush</u> in the tree.
Look at the <u>thrushs</u> in the tree.

The student will soon realize that he cannot form plurals this way. The two hissing sounds merge into one. He will probably unconsciously add a separate \ez\ syllable as he reads the word.

With silent <u>e</u> words that end in the sounds of \s\ or \j\, the plural form will take on the syllable \ez\. However, in other silent <u>e</u> words only the <u>s</u> is added.

Examples: lace, laces   age, ages

It is unnecessary to give lists of words illustrating Pattern 5. Lists are provided for Pattern 6, so that teachers can devise exercises to give practice in deciding whether to form the plural by adding <u>s</u> or <u>es</u>.

Plurals—Pattern 6

s	x	z	ch	sh	ce
bus	ax	jazz	arch	ash	ace
gas	tax	waltz	coach	marsh	lace
mass	wax	quiz	touch	rush	case
pass	box	fez	crutch	blush	race
grass	fox	fizz	clutch	flush	mace
class	hoax	whiz	wretch	hash	place
dress	onyx	buzz	stretch	mesh	maze
cress	annex	fuzz	blotch	clash	haze
press	prefix	topaz	watch	bush	
miss	suffix		torch	brush	**ge**
kiss			porch	flash	
loss			match	slash	age
moss	**Two Plurals***		patch	sash	rage
lens			stitch	dash	page
guess	index		witch	squash	cage
truss	ibex		switch		edge
atlas	apex		birch		ledge
witness	vortex		perch		hedge
hostess	calyx		march		
illness	appendix		snatch		
actress	thorax		peach		
	sphinx				

Many of the words in these lists are also verbs.

---

* The dictionary indicates two acceptable spellings for the plural of these words, as in "index"—indexes, indices. Latin plurals are sometimes of interest to older students. See "Irregular Plurals" on page 149.

PATTERN 7

Plurals of Nouns Ending in y

- Nouns ending in y after a *vowel* form the plural by adding s.

  Example: boy, boys

- Nouns ending in y after a *consonant* form the plural by changing the y to i and adding es.

  Example: lady, ladies

It is especially important that students remember the illustrative words (boy, boys; lady, ladies) when the plural of a noun ending in y is to be formed. Even some poor spellers will recognize boies as the incorrect plural of boy. By associating these two words (boys and ladies) with this spelling pattern as a memory aid, students will be able to spell other nouns ending in y correctly.

Nouns Ending in y

day	key	quay	jitney	turkey	galley
ray	toy	relay	lackey	monkey	abbey
joy	tray	delay	display	journey	trolley
guy	dray	alloy	valley	medley	chimney
clay	buoy	money	decoy	alley	donkey
play	spray	tokay	lamprey	pulley	parley
fly	body	hobby	candy	country	boundary
spy	copy	berry	dairy	company	luxury
cry	duty	ferry	fairy	factory	industry
ivy	pony	gypsy	cherry	salary	variety
city	army	penny	puppy	victory	deformity
lily	party	daisy	enemy	mystery	secretary
baby	study	ally	county	peccary	territory
story	pansy	jelly	quarry	library	dictionary

Some of these words are also verbs.

PATTERN 8

Plural of Nouns Ending in o

- Nouns ending in o after a vowel form the plural by adding s.

  Example: studio, studios

- For the plural of nouns ending in o after a consonant, consult the dictionary.

There is much irregularity in forming the plurals of nouns ending in o preceded by a consonant; both s and es occur. A large number of those which add s are foreign words, but this fact is no help since there is no way for the student to know which are foreign words. The dictionary is the only sure guide.

Pattern 8 Examples

Vowels

taboo	nuncio	trio	portfolio	impresario
shampoo	radio	polio	punctilio	intaglio
bamboo	ratio	curio	scenario	embryo
cameo	folio	studio	oratorio	kangaroo
rodeo				

Consonants

s	s	s	es	<u>s</u> or <u>es</u>	es or s
	Italian	Spanish			
silo	cello	Spanish	echo	banjo	motto
ditto	solo	burro	hero	halo	fresco
chromo	alto	pinto	jingo	hobo	cargo
albino	basso	bronco	veto	zero	grotto
kimono	rondo	lasso	lingo	gecko	mango
dynamo	piano	poncho	torpedo	lasso	stucco
merino	soprano	rancho	embargo	proviso	tornado
pimento	libretto	pueblo	mosquito	indigo	buffalo
Filipino	falsetto	hidalgo	potato	flamingo	portico
	contralto	ranchero	tomato	memento	volcano
	piccolo	sombrero	innuendo	palmetto	fiasco
	violoncello		manifesto	stiletto	calico
					domino
					desperado

PATTERN 9

Plural of Nouns Ending in <u>f</u> or <u>fe</u>

- Most nouns ending in <u>f</u> or <u>fe</u> form their plurals regularly by adding <u>s</u>.

  Examples: roof, roofs   fife, fifes

- However, some of them form the plural by changing the <u>f</u> or <u>fe</u> to <u>ves</u>.

  Examples: leaf, leaves   knife, knives

  In the case of <u>hoof</u>, <u>scarf</u>, and <u>staff</u>, both ways of forming the plural are acceptable.

  Examples: <u>hoof</u>, hooves or hoofs   <u>scarf</u>, scarves or scarfs

Irregular Plurals

Familiar nouns that are alike in singular and plural (deer, sheep, moose), or form their plurals irregularly (foot/feet, mouse/mice, woman/women) should be taught separately.

It is difficult to predict the plurals of foreign nouns that have become a part of our English vocabulary. For example:

- Some retain the original plural, as radius, radii.
- Some have two plurals, as <u>fungus</u>—fungi or funguses.
- Some have two plural forms with different meaning, as <u>genius</u>—<u>geniuses</u>, <u>genii</u>.

Plurals of foreign nouns should not be taught as a pattern, but explained as needed.

REVIEW OF PATTERNS 5 THROUGH 9

Paper ruled in three columns with headings like the following should be available. In the first column, the student copies the singular nouns selected by the teacher from lists under various spelling patterns. He then writes their plurals in the second column. In the third column, the student states his reasons for forming the plurals as he does. These statements should be in abbreviated form as illustrated in the following example.

Singular	Plural	Reason
church	churches	Singular ends in <u>ch</u>.
pony	ponies	<u>y</u> preceded by a consonant.
vireo	vireos	<u>o</u> preceded by a vowel.
pencil	pencils	Regular—add <u>s</u>.
tax	taxes	Singular ends in <u>x</u>.
tray	trays	<u>y</u> preceded by a vowel.
hero	heroes	<u>o</u> preceded by a consonant—dictionary.

Exercises like this may reveal the fact that the student does not have a strong usable knowledge of some patterns. A student who gives the correct plural but expresses only superficial reasons shows no promise of future correct application, as in the example below.

Student's Example:

turkey	turkies	Change <u>y</u> to <u>i</u> and add <u>es</u>.
tray	trays	Because it ends in <u>y</u>.
church	churches	Ends in a consonant.

Remember: Memorizing the pattern is not enough. Correct application of the pattern is the goal.

PATTERN 10

Possessives

- The *singular possessive* of nouns is formed by adding **'s** to the singular form of the word. It is used to show ownership:

  Examples: Tom**'s** kite   the child**'s** toy

- The *plural possessive* is formed most often by adding an **apostrophe** to the plural. This is used to show ownership by more than one:

  Examples: the boy**s'** kites   the rabbit**s'** burrow

  The possessive of a plural not ending in s is formed by adding **'s**.

  Examples: men**'s** voices   women**'s** group
  children**'s** laughter

- The *possessive* of *personal pronouns* does not require an apostrophe. The form of the word indicates possession:

  Examples: his   her   their

- The *possessive* form of an *indefinite pronoun* does require an apostrophe:

  Examples: anybody's   one's
  nobody's   anyone's
  everybody's   everyone's
  somebody's   no one's

The following is a simple activity which may be used for younger students and those who have difficulty with the concepts just stated. The student who has not been exposed to, or who has not grasped the grammatical structure of the language, may find this a simpler way to learn possessives.

Use the following procedure:

1. Write the word in its basic form.

   Example: tree

2. Add an apostrophe.

   Example: tree'

3. (a) If the word is singular, add s.

   Example: The tree's branches.

   (b) If the word is plural and ends in s, add nothing, since the apostrophe has already been added.

Example: The beaches' lifeguards.

(c) If the word is plural and does not end in s, add s.

Example: The men's coats.

Singular Possessives

A paper is ruled and headed as in Fig. 1, and a list of words dictated for the student to write in the first column.

Fig. 1		Fig. 2	
Singular	*Plural*	*Singular*	*Plural*
horse		horse	horses
tiger		tiger	tigers
lion		lion	lions
man		man	men

The student then writes the plurals in the second column, as in Fig. 2, and is told to notice that there is not an apostrophe in sight—no apostrophe for the "plain singular" or for the "plain plural." (The plurals of figures and letters, explained on page 153, must not be introduced until the general pattern is firmly fixed.)

The next step is to consider how to show ownership.

The horse's harness - - - - - - - - - - - - - - add 's to the singular.
The tiger's tail - - - - - - - - - - - - - - - - - add 's to the singular.
The lion's roar - - - - - - - - - - - - - - - - - add 's to the singular.
The man's hat - - - - - - - - - - - - - - - - - add 's to the singular.

An apostrophe after a noun shows ownership. However, in the case of a singular noun, this is not enough. We must add an s to the apostrophe to represent the \z\ sound that we make when we say: the horse's harness, the tiger's tail, the lion's roar, the man's hat.

There is one exception: when the singular ends in a hissing sound and the added s would produce an unpleasant effect, it is sometimes omitted, as in Moses' law, conscience' sake, James' dog, Achilles' heel, Socrates' teachings.

Plural Possessives

We must next examine what happens when we need to show the plural possessive:

A number of horses together own something—the horses' stable.
Add an apostrophe to the plural.

A family of tigers owns its den—the tigers' den.
Add an apostrophe to the plural.

A number of lions own their home—the lions' cave.
Add an apostrophe to the plural.

In the case of these plural possessives, the <u>s</u> representing the \z\ sound is part of the plural, so all that is necessary is to add the apostrophe, showing ownership.

When the plural does not end in <u>s</u>, however, we must add an <u>s</u> to the apostrophe to produce the \z\ sound. Thus we have <u>men's hats</u>.

Fig. 3

Singular Possessive	*Plural Possessive*
horse's	horses'
tiger's	tigers'
lion's	lions'
man's	men's

We are now ready to dictate a list of nouns. We have both singular and plural possessive written in columns as shown in Fig. 3. The following lists have proved satisfactory for drill, both in the patterns for the formation of plurals and in those for possessives. They are arranged so that each group may constitute one exercise.

cow	goose	thief	child
bird	thrush	priest	boy
ox	crow	sailor	girl
deer	puppy	merchant	wife
dog	robin	farmer	elf
wolf	turkey	tailor	woman
monkey	junco	jockey	lady
pony	parrot	gypsy	baby
panther	chicken	attorney	husband
elephant	flamingo	minister	fairy
sheep	class	fly	ship
rat	flock	moth	friend
fox	army	vireo	voter
mouse	hero	wasp	captain
calf	jury	insect	speaker
swine	soldier	beetle	navy
snake	company	burro	citizen
rabbit	crusader	hornet	employer
donkey	committee	mosquito	employee
gorilla	family	grasshopper	enemy

There should be variety in the drills for thorough mastery. The following exercises have interested a number of students. They should use broad paper ruled in four columns and headed as shown below:

Singular	**Plural**	**Singular Possessive**	**Plural Possessive**

Give the student a list of various forms, such as monkey, lions, pony's, deer's, horses', ponies, rabbit, sheep, tigers'. His task is to write each word in the proper column.

Have another paper ruled in the same way. Give the student a list of nouns (all singular, all plural, or a combination) and have him write all four forms of each word in the proper columns.

It is necessary to emphasize the fact that the pronoun <u>its</u> follows the pattern for possessive pronouns, since almost all uncertain spellers confuse it with the contraction <u>it's</u>. Contractions are not included here because they are usually well-presented in any good spelling text.

The possessive forms of indefinite pronouns are troublesome. Their consideration should be postponed as long as possible.

PATTERN 11

Plurals of Letters, Figures, and Signs

The plurals of letters, figures, and signs are usually formed by adding an <u>s</u>.

Example: There are two 8s in 88.

However, a few illustrations show that in some cases confusion can be avoided only by the use of an apostrophe.

Examples:

- The plural of <u>a</u> = a's (How many A's did you get on your report card?)
- The plural of <u>i</u> = i's
- The plural of <u>u</u> = u's

Apart from clarifying meaning, an apostrophe is also sometimes used in forming the plurals of words. Changes in text formatting may also be used.

Example: There are too many *and's* in your sentences.

or

There are too many *and*s in your sentences.

However, this concept does not have to be taught until needed.

PATTERN 12

Pattern for <u>ie</u> and <u>ei</u>

Put **i** before **e** except after <u>**c**</u>, or when it sounds like \ā\ as in <u>neighbor</u> and <u>weigh</u>.

Note: Pattern 12 applies only to words in which <u>ie</u> or <u>ei</u> are diphthongs.

Examples: di et   the <u>**ie**</u> is not a diphthong.
         ch<u>ie</u>f   the <u>**ie**</u> is a diphthong

Examples of Exceptions:

1. **e** before **i** when the diphthong does not follow **c** and does not sound like \a\. Most of these exceptions are noted in this sentence:

Neither leisured foreigner seized the weird height.
(Associate <u>either</u> with <u>neither</u>.)

The following sentence contains some less common exceptional words:

The farmer will <u>forfeit</u> his <u>heifer</u> if she breaks the <u>weir</u> (dam).
(Associate <u>surfeit</u> and <u>counterfeit</u> with <u>forfeit</u>.)

2. **i** before **e** following **c**.

In the following exceptional words we are not considering **ie** as a diphthong. The significant part of each word is the **ci** phonogram. In the majority of these, this phonogram says \sh\: <u>glacier</u>, <u>species</u>, <u>deficient</u>, <u>efficient</u>, <u>proficient</u>, <u>sufficient</u>.

<u>Financier</u> is an exception to this exception.

Pattern 12 is relatively easy to learn and to apply, provided one knows that the vowel sound in a word is represented by either <u>ie</u> or <u>ei</u>, but there is no way for the uncertain speller to know whether \ē\ is spelled <u>e - e</u>, <u>ea</u>, or <u>ee</u> instead of either <u>ie</u> or <u>ei</u>. For example, why shouldn't the \ē\ in <u>green</u> be <u>ie</u>, or the \ā\ in <u>braid</u> be <u>ei</u>?

There are really very few words spelled with <u>ie</u> or <u>ei</u>, and the most important can be grouped as indicated (see Tables 1 and 2), so that they will be recognized easily when heard. Systematically arranged words stand a better chance of being recalled. A miscellaneous list may fade quickly from memory. The student may not be able to reproduce the entire table even after a few weeks, but will surely have a "feeling" for the words he has placed in it.

Introduce one group at a time. Discuss each one, so that if possible students may find a thread to tie the words together as a unit:

Group 1—All end in <u>f</u>
Group 2—All end in <u>ve</u>
Group 3—All terms applied to people
Group 4—Rhyming words
Group 5—Words associated with the storming of a walled town: "The *siege* was *fierce*. Finally the wall was *pierced* and the *shrieks* of those within were heard."
Group 6—Miscellaneous

While new groups are being added, there should be reviews of those already studied—"Write the group of words beginning with *chief*." Students will be more likely to remember the words if they are always in the same order, although the cue is not always the first word: e.g., "Write the group containing the word *friend*."

When groups 1 through 6 can be handled with some facility, a second paper, headed Table 2, is filled out like the first, with the words recorded and studied. After the student's familiarity with both papers is certain, the exceptions can be added, first from Table 1, later from Table 2.

Table 1 *"Put i before e"*	
1. chief thief brief grief belief relief	Exceptions neither—either leisure foreign seize
2. grieve believe relieve achieve reprieve retrieve	weird height forfeit—surfeit heifer weir
3. niece priest friend fiend	protein caffeine
4. field yield shield wield	
5. siege fierce pierce shriek	
6. pier tier piece sieve	

Table 2	
"except after c"	*"or when sounded like \ā\"*
1. ceiling conceit deceit receipt	**1.** eight freight eight
2. conceive deceive receive perceive	**2.** weigh sleigh neigh
Exceptions	**3.** neighbor heigh-ho
1. ancient species conscience glacier	**4.** vein skein rein reign deign veil
2. deficient efficient proficient sufficient financier	

When the lists of words can be recalled routinely, the teacher should give tests of the pattern and its exceptions. Words are drawn partly from the tables and partly from the supplementary list of less common words, which the teacher should explain also fall under the pattern.

Supplementary List:

veil	feint	eighteen	chandelier
Seine	sheik	heinous	chiffonier
fief	eighty	surveillance	cavalier
feign	diesel	frontier	chevalier
liege	reindeer	cashier	

To assess the student's knowledge, a paper is ruled in columns as shown below. Miscellaneous ie and ei words are dictated. The student is to place each word in the correct column with the reason stated.

Practice with ie–ei Pattern

ie	ei	Reason
relieve		i usually before e
	receive	e before i after c
	weigh	sounds like \ā\
	foreign	one of the exceptions

Have the student copy a list such as the following, inserting ie or ei in the blank and stating why:

br f	pr st	v l	fr nd
h ght	sl gh	r gn	l sure
gr f	sh ld	c ling	r n
n ghbor	surf t	y ld	n ther
th f	w rd	n ce	conc t

Still another type of drill in application of a pattern is a special dictation lesson. The exercise, "An Unwelcome Gift," (Appendix 22) is an excellent review of Pattern 12.

Mastery of the pattern can be assessed by dictating lists of words in which various spellings of the sounds \ē\, \ā\, \ī\, \e\, and \i\ occur. The following is a useful and interesting exercise.

To provide further daily practice in distinguishing <u>ie</u> from <u>ei</u>, the teacher may dictate the following words. Before the teacher dictates from the list of words, the student should be told that he is to write only the <u>ie</u> or <u>ei</u> words.

This study must continue for some time, with a few minutes of each lesson period assigned to it. It is not possible to predict how much time a specific student will need.

The list is:

tight	blight	inspire	gray
green	seen	**belief**	delay
chief	**height**	complain	**relief**
quaint	wait	**niece**	breeze
maze	faith	cyclone	**priest**
veil	**thief**	**freight**	**retrieve**
species	people	treaty	release
multiply	**seize**	**wield**	eagle
receipt	celebrate	sheet	**weir**
magnify	**shield**	**friend**	peacock
treaty	steal	leaf	**reprieve**
sufficient	**heifer**	**tier**	hear
seal	reveal	price	**field**
pierce	**conceit**	**relieve**	cleave
feet	treat	**neither**	heal
reed	**brief**	**glacier**	**pier**
surfeit	lend	search	**deceit**
cheese	decrease	lift	strip
neighbor	**foreign**	**fiend**	**piece**
refer	peach	disagree	stripe
ceiling	queen	**leisure**	disappear
sheaf	**grief**	appeal	**ancient**
inveigh	bleed	**deficient**	**conceive**
defeat	**reign**	fright	**siege**
grand	**deceive**	**receive**	**weight**
vein	lead	weevil	repeal
grieve	tremendous	**proficient**	squeak
speak	**conscience**	retreat	**believe**
weird	effective	**weigh**	please
sneeze	**either**	reveal	shelf
fierce	touch	**eight**	**forfeit**
delete	**yield**	increase	tease
mean	elevate	Greece	least
skein	**efficient**	**shriek**	**achieve**
speech	bleed	**perceive**	

PATTERN 13

The Suffix -ful

The suffix -ful differs from the word full. The suffix *never* has two l's.

The following words may be used for practice in applying this rule:

joy**ful**	harm**ful**	help**ful**	mind**ful**
peace**ful**	boast**ful**	law**ful**	taste**ful**
sin**ful**	waste**ful**	spite**ful**	fret**ful**

PATTERN 14

The Suffix -ly

When the suffix ly is added to a word, the spelling of this base word *does not* change:

Examples: soft + ly = softly
safe + ly = safely

> *Note:* Many of the words falling into this pattern are covered by Patterns 2, 3, and 4, but -ly is a troublesome suffix and requires extra attention.

To help clarify Pattern 14, it may be necessary to point out that when the original word ends in l, the new word will have two l's. If the original word does not end in l, the new word will have only one l in it.

Examples: hopeful + ly = hopefully   peaceful + ly = peacefully
war**m** + ly = warmly   grea**t** + ly = greatly

Exceptions:

- Words ending in **le**
  For words ending in **le**, the **e** is replaced by **y**

  Examples: humb**le** + ly = humb**ly**   gent**le** + ly = gent**ly**

- Words ending in **y**
  For words ending in **y**, the **y** is replaced by **i**.

  Examples: nois**y** + ly = nois**i**ly   happ**y** + ly = happ**i**ly

  > *Note:* By adding -ly to adjectives, they can become *adverbs* modifying a verb or another adverb. When the -ly word modifies a noun, it is an adjective, e.g., *This is a lonely road.*

The following words may be used in dictation exercises:

swift	glad	beautiful	light
safe	free	accidental	quick
sorrowful	late	merciful	neat
bad	love	lone	tyrannical
double	forcible	negligible	ample
subtle	despicable	indelible	capable
feeble	illegible	reliable	excitable
simple	invincible	incredible	acceptable
single	irascible	corruptible	probable
triple	indissoluble	responsible	suitable
treble	incorrigible	irrevocable	fashionable

PATTERN 15

Final y before a Suffix

When a final y follows a vowel, the y remains *unchanged* when adding any suffix.

Examples: pray + ed = prayed   pray + ing = praying

prey	+	ed	ing	pray	+	ed	ing	
bray	+	ed	ing	play	+	ed	ing	er
stray	+	ed	ing	buy	+		ing	er
fray	+	ed	ing	pay	+		ing	ment able
dismay	+	ed	ing	delay	+	ed	ing	
destroy	+	ed	ing	relay	+	ed	ing	
display	+	ed	ing	enjoy	+	ed	ing	ment able
				employ	+	ed	ing	ment able

Many of the words in this pattern are verbs.

Exceptions (learned words):

- In the following words the y changes to i.
  say, said   lay, laid   day, daily
  pay, paid   slay, slain
- The word \ 'gā lē \ may be spelled either gayly or gaily.
- When a final y follows a consonant, the y changes to i before any suffix,
  except one beginning with i (ing, ist).

Examples: pity + ful = pitiful   copy + ed = copied

Examples: copy + ist = copyist   copy + ing = copying

Note: accompanist is an exception.

The following is a sample word list for practice in adding suffixes.

-er, -est, -ly, -ness		-ous		-ance	-ed, -ing		-al	-ful
noisy	spooky	glory	melody	rely	spy	study	deny	mercy
lucky	crafty	fury	luxury	defy	cry	busy		fancy
plucky	ready	vary	harmony	comply	dry	pity	**-ant**	beauty
worthy	busy	study	industry	ally	shy	fancy		pity
heavy	merry	envy	perfidy	apply	try	occupy	ply	
murky	steady	mystery	ceremony		fry	justify	rely	**-ist**
dusty	healthy	injury	parsimony	**-able**	carry	fortify	comply	
moldy	dainty	victory			copy	multiply	defy	copy
moody	sleepy			ply	embody	supply		
jolly				pity				
				rely				
				justify				

Exceptions for Pattern 15:

1. The following words retain **y** before -**ly** and -**ness** but usually follow the pattern before other suffixes:

			but		
dry	dryly	dryness		drier	driest
shy	shyly	shyness		shier	shiest (y allowed)
sly	slyly	slyness		slier	sliest (y allowed)
spry	spryly			sprier	spriest (y allowed)
wry	wryly			wrier	wriest

2. In certain adjectives formed from nouns ending in **y**, the **y** is dropped and the suffix -**eous** is added: *pity, piteous,* not *pitious.* For a list of such words see page 215, List 4.

PATTERN 16

The Prefixes <u>dis</u>- and <u>mis</u>-

The prefixes <u>dis</u>- and <u>mis</u>- are placed before a word without altering its spelling:

Examples: <u>dis</u> + satisfy = dissatisfy
<u>mis</u> + spell = misspell

Before a student begins to write a word with the prefix <u>dis</u>- or <u>mis</u>-, he should be encouraged to think of the first letter of the base word—then he will know whether his new word will have two <u>s</u>'s.

The meaning of these prefixes should be studied before the pattern is taught. (See Affixes, page 132)

<u>Dis</u>- (not, away, apart)	**<u>Mis</u>- (not, bad)**
disadvantage	misspell
disbelief	misdeed
dissimilar	misbehave

Dis- (not, away, apart)	**Mis-** (not, bad)
discolor	mislead
discontinue	misshapen
discourteous	misfortune
dissatisfy	misstep

PATTERN 17

Prefixes Changed for Ease of Phonetic Blending and Pronunciation

The final consonant of a prefix may change to match or more easily blend with the following letter.

Example: con + lide (changes to) **col**lide

Double letters are frequently the result of this change, and therefore it is important that the student understand the chameleon-like behavior of certain prefixes.

Discussion of such words as <u>inactive</u>, <u>indirect</u>, <u>insecure</u> reveals that in these cases **in-** as a prefix means "not." Consideration of the following groups shows that **im-**, **il-**, and **ir-** can also mean "not."

<u>in</u>perfect	becomes	<u>im</u>perfect
<u>in</u>legal	"	<u>il</u>legal
<u>in</u>regular	"	<u>ir</u>regular
<u>in</u>mediate	"	<u>im</u>mediate
<u>in</u>legible	"	<u>il</u>legible

Similarly, when the prefix **in-** means "in" it becomes:

- **il-** before <u>l</u> as in <u>il</u>lumine (to let in light)
- **im-** before <u>b</u>, <u>m</u>, and <u>p</u> as in <u>im</u>bibe, <u>im</u>migrate, <u>im</u>prison
- **ir-** before <u>r</u> as in <u>ir</u>rigate

Such changes in prefixes account for many double letters. Consideration of other prefixes should follow. For example,

- **con-**
  with, together, jointly

  concur–to happen together
  connect–to join together
  convoke–to call together

In the following words, **con-** has changed its form because the combination of the prefix and combined base word is difficult to say and sounds unpleasant. Therefore, a change has been made for the sake of euphony, for ease of phonetic blending and pronunciation.

- <u>con</u>-

  collide
  correspond
  compress
  cooperate

The prefix **ex-** frequently changes when blended with a base word beginning with the letter f, as in **efface**, **effuse**, **effervesce**.

- **ad-** (to, toward, for) is another chameleon-like prefix.

When **ad** comes before		it becomes:	
c		ac	(accrue)
f		af	(affix)
g		ag	(aggression)
l		al	(allure)
n		an	(annex)
p		ap	(apply)
r		ar	(arrive)
s		as	(assault)
t		at	(attract)
sc, sp, st		a	(ascribe)

Certain words are decidedly puzzling. These include derivatives of a foreign word that have been adopted into English when the root word itself has not, such as *assembly* and *arrive*. In such cases the first syllable may not be recognized as a prefix. There is no such English word as *semble*. However, the word *assemble* carries the idea of separate units added together, and therefore the syllable **as-** is probably a form of the prefix **ad-**. The word derives from the Latin prefix **ad-** "to" and **simul** "together." *Arrive*, to get to a place, is clearly not related to the English word *rive*, "to tear asunder." The syllable **ar-** is probably a form of the prefix **ad-** which would become **ar-** only before the letter r; therefore, there should be two r's in *arrive*. The word comes from **ad-** and **ripa**, "the bank of a river," therefore, *arrive* meant "to come to shore," and has been extended to mean "to reach any destination." (Students should be encouraged to consult a dictionary about these words.)

Most elementary students cannot perform such feats of reasoning, but some older students find great satisfaction in doing so. This language study is of special value to fairly mature students with limited vocabularies, and to those who are not studying any foreign language and perhaps never will. There is excellent material of this kind in many spelling books. The more advanced student should explain the double letters in the following words:

collapse	effervesce	immemorial	illiterate
collision	effloresce	immodest	illogical
connote	effusion	immobile	immature
efface	immeasurable	immutable	

The student is now ready for the following exercise with double consonants.

The teacher dictates a word from the preceding lists illustrating Patterns 1, 2, 3, 14, 16, and 17 (pages 131, 136, 138, 159, 162). The student should write the word in one of the following columns, thus answering the question, "Why is there a double consonant in the dictated word?"

Word ends in f, l, or s	*1 syllable, 1 consonant, 1 vowel + suffix beg. with vowel*	*More than one syllable, accent on last syllable*

Prefix ends and word begins with the same letter	*Word ends and suffix begins with the same letter*	*Prefix changes to match the first letter of the word*

SUMMARY OF SPELLING PATTERNS

It is important to reinforce the idea that the student is responsible for applying the patterns she has been taught in all written work. She should organize a notebook for recording patterns learned for easy reference and review.

The following is an example of a high school student's summary, which she used as a permanent reminder:

Suffixes and Prefixes

1 s, 1 c, 1 v, + s beg. v   flat, flatter, flattest (Pattern 2)

More than 1 s: compel', compelled, o'pen, opened (Pattern 3)

Silent <u>e</u>:   hope, hoping, hopeful (Pattern 4)

Exceptions:

1. <u>ce</u> and <u>ge</u>: peaceable, courageous
2. mileage, acreage, dyeing, singeing
3. duly, truly

Final <u>y</u> preceded by a vowel, <u>y</u> unchanged: enjoy, enjoyed, enjoying, enjoyment

Exceptions: say, said, pay, paid (Pattern 7)

Final <u>y</u> preceded by a consonant, <u>y</u> changes to <u>i</u> except before a suffix beginning with <u>i</u>: copy, copied, copying

Exceptions: dry, dryly, dryness *but* drier, driest (Pattern 7)

Add -<u>ly</u> to a word as it is: kind, kindly; final, finally.

Exception: humble, humbl + y = humbly. (Pattern 14)

<u>dis</u>- and <u>mis</u>- are attached to a word as it is: disable, dissatisfy
Some prefixes change for the sake of euphony: <u>ad</u>- adhere *but* affix, annex, attract. (Pattern 16)

Plurals

<u>s</u>, <u>x</u>, <u>z</u>, <u>ch</u>, <u>sh</u>, add <u>es</u> (Pattern 5)

<u>y</u> preceded by a vowel, add <u>s</u>: boy, boys
<u>y</u> preceded by a consonant, change to <u>i</u> and add <u>es</u>: lady, ladies (Pattern 7)
<u>o</u> preceded by a vowel, add <u>s</u>: radio, radios
<u>o</u> preceded by a consonant—consult dictionary (Pattern 8)

Some nouns ending in <u>f</u> or <u>fe</u> change to <u>ves</u>: elf, elves (Pattern 9)

Miscellaneous

Singular possessive—add 's to singular: boy, boy's
Plural possessive—add ᴵ to plural: boys, boys'

Exception: Plural not ending in s—add 's to plural: men, men's (Pattern 10)

Past tense of regular verb—add -ed to present tense

Put i before e, etc.

Exception:

1. Neither leisured foreigner, etc.
2. ancient, species, etc. (Pattern 12)

ff, ll, ss: cliff, tall, moss, off (Pattern 1)

This paper was kept in the student's notebook and taken out for reference as she corrected a written exercise. She was also given a typed set of the patterns in complete form. Such a set can be found at the end of this chapter.

WORDS REQUIRING INDIVIDUAL ATTENTION

We have said that studying lists containing words of miscellaneous spelling patterns is not effective for confused spellers. Some cannot remember the correct spellings even for a day. Others learn and reproduce them in the next lesson, but forget them too quickly to benefit other written work. Furthermore, the attempt to remember a considerable number of arbitrary letter sequences breaks down habits of thoughtful consideration necessary for students with unreliable visual recall.

Nevertheless, some words do not fit any type of generalization but are so commonly used that no one can write freely without knowing them. Some are not phonetic and do not conform to spelling patterns.

Others are phonetic in a sense, but the student may choose the wrong phonogram from several that are possible, e.g., \brād\ braid or brade, \tōn\ tone or toan. How are such necessary words to be learned? Some suggestions follow.

Simultaneous Oral Spelling

We have already explained the fundamental procedure. Every poor speller should study spelling in this way. Frequently a student will spell a word aloud correctly that he has just misspelled in a composition. This is often mistakenly regarded as evidence of carelessness. One such boy said, "I see—I know it, but my hand does not."

"Exactly," replied his teacher without reproach. "It may be necessary for you to study it many times with S.O.S. before your hand can write it correctly when your mind is busy planning what you want to say."

A student will usually spell words correctly if he says the letters sub-vocally, whereas he would likely miss the spelling if he dashed words off simply by eye and hand. The threefold association of visual, auditory, and kinesthetic must never be neglected.

Spelling by Syllables

Another aid to study, mentioned in Chapter 3, is spelling by syllables instead of in a long breathless series of letters. It is much easier to spell a syllable than a string of six to ten letters composing more than one syllable.

Exaggerated Pronunciation

It is often desirable to overpronounce or even mispronounce an obscure letter or syllable, or a syllable in which a letter has an unusual sound. While this exaggerated emphasis will make the student conscious of the correct spelling, the mispronunciation is not likely to persist. Examples of words that may be treated in this manner include: sep-ā-rate, slep-t, ex-ak-t-ly, ar-k-tic, sar-dīne, automo-bīle, priv-ī-lege, rek-og-nize.

Nonsense Sentences and Jingles

Fun arbitrary associations often fix the spelling of a troublesome word in the student's mind.

You eat meat.
You go on your feet to meet a friend on the street and greet him with a sweet smile.
A piece of pie.
Mrs. Tate caught her naughty daughter and taught her to clean her face.
A fairy with fair hair flew gaily through the air.
Please bake a cake for me to take when we make the trip to the lake.
Ted was led to his bed. His head was as heavy as lead.
Do not waste the paste. A waist is an article of raiment.

Two, the t is followed by 2 different letters.
Too, the t is followed by too many o's for convenience!
To, the easiest and most common.
Too many people wanted to catch the two o'clock train to Albany.

I will be away for three weeks. Please give me weak tea.

does \dəz\
dose \dōs\ o is long because of the final silent e.
Does he need a dose of medicine?

Only the wise should advise others.

Advi<u>ce</u> to Mi<u>ce</u>

Don't nibble spice.
Sugared rice
Is twice as nice
For little mice.

	<u>ear</u>	
Sound	h<u>ear</u>	I h<u>ear</u> with my <u>ear</u>.
	h<u>ear</u>d	I h<u>ear</u>d with my <u>ear</u>.
	<u>here</u>	in this place
Place	t<u>here</u>	in that place
	w<u>here</u>	in what place
	her	We say "ladies before gentlemen," so
Possession	his	in *their* we take the <u>e</u> from h<u>e</u>r,
	<u>their</u>	and the <u>i</u> from h<u>is</u>—*their* home.

Different spellings for the same sound should relate to the context for correct word use and meaning.

Many a puzzled speller needs help in remembering which of the verbs ending in the syllable pronounced \sēd\ end in <u>cede</u>, which in <u>ceed</u>, and which in <u>sede</u>. There is only one ending in <u>sede</u>, <u>supersede</u>. Three end in <u>ceed</u>, and the rest in <u>cede</u>. If the student can remember the spelling of the three words that end in <u>ceed</u>, the problem will be solved. One teacher used the following anecdote with good results: When a speeding motorist was stopped by a police officer, he told of an emergency which seemed to justify his haste. The officer said, "Pro<u>ceed</u>. I hope you will suc<u>ceed</u>, but try not to ex<u>ceed</u> the s<u>peed</u> limit again." (The circumstances of the emergency can be elaborated to suit the locality and the interest of the student.)

There are times when, confronted by puzzling words, neither teacher nor student can think of a suitable mnemonic device like a sentence jingle. In such a case, the teacher must search for some artificial association which may fix the spelling of a troublesome word in the mind of a student. <u>Council</u> and <u>counsel</u> were two such words that one teacher kept in mind for several days. True, theoretically the final syllables should be pronounced differently, \sil\ and \sel\ respectively, but the average poor speller does not hear this distinction even if the speaker makes it, which he frequently does not; in fact, the two words are included in some lists of homonyms. It finally occurred to the teacher that a <u>circle</u> was a very probable arrangement for a coun<u>ci</u>l, especially in the councils of primitive people, with the participants seated around a central fire.

Sometimes the teacher's task is to eradicate a peculiar individual mistake. For example, such confusions as <u>take</u> with <u>tack</u> may have developed long before the presentation of these words. It is not unusual to find a small word, previously learned, inserted as part of a long, new word, e.g., in-<u>fear</u>-ior, <u>Pencil</u>-vania. A rhyme or other dramatic device is often more effective than any other explanation in breaking this habit.

Words that do not conform to a pattern and cannot be spelled according to a generalization require individual attention and must be learned individually. This is what we mean by "learned words."

On the following pages is a simplified list of the patterns explained earlier. Teachers and students may find it helpful to use this version for quick reference.

SPELLING PATTERNS SUMMARIZED

Pattern 1

(The "Floss" Pattern)

Words Ending in <u>ff</u>, <u>ll</u>, or <u>ss</u>

Words of one syllable, ending in <u>f</u>, <u>l</u>, or <u>s</u> (sounding \ f \, \ l \, or \ s \) after one vowel, usually end in <u>ff</u>, <u>ll</u>, or <u>ss</u>.

Example: The cli<u>ff</u> is ta<u>ll</u> and covered with mo<u>ss</u>.

Pattern 2

(1-1-1 Pattern)

Doubling the Final Consonant: Monosyllables

One syllable, one consonant at the end, and one vowel before it—double the final consonant before adding a suffix that begins with a vowel, but do not double it when the suffix begins with a consonant.

Examples: flat, flatter, flatness

Pattern 3

Doubling the Final Consonant: Polysyllables

Words of more than one syllable, with one consonant at the end and one vowel before it, *double* the final consonant before a suffix beginning with a vowel, *if* the accent is on the last syllable.

Examples: Accent on last syllable: be ′gi**n** + <u>ing</u> = beginning
Accent not on last syllable: ′o pe**n** + <u>ing</u> = opening

Pattern 4

Silent <u>e</u>

For words ending in silent <u>e</u>, drop the <u>e</u> before a suffix beginning with a vowel. Do *not* drop the <u>e</u> before a suffix beginning with a consonant.

Examples: hope, hoping, hopeful

There are a few exceptions to Pattern 4, but they are not especially troublesome, and should be introduced only after the student has mastered understanding and application of the regular pattern.

Pattern 5

Regular Plurals

The most common way of forming the plural of *nouns* is to add s to the *singular* form of the word.

Examples: dog, <u>dogs</u>   elephant, <u>elephants</u>   table, <u>tables</u>

This pattern should pose no problem since plurals ending in s are very common.

Pattern 6

Plurals of Nouns Ending in s, x, z, ch, or sh

Nouns ending in s, x, z, ch, or sh form the plural by adding es to the singular form of the word.

Examples: gas, <u>gases</u>   tax, <u>taxes</u>   topaz, <u>topazes</u>

torch, <u>torches</u>   thrush, <u>thrushes</u>

Pattern 7

Plurals of Nouns Ending in y

- Nouns ending in y after a vowel form the plural by adding s.

  Example: boy, boys

- Nouns ending in y after a consonant form the plural by changing the y to i and adding es.

  Example: lady, ladies

Pattern 8

Plural of Nouns Ending in o

- Nouns ending in o after a vowel form the plural by adding s.

  Example: studio, studios

- For the plural of nouns ending in o after a consonant, consult the dictionary.

Pattern 9

Plural of Nouns Ending in f or fe

- Most nouns ending in f or fe form their plurals regularly by adding s.

    Examples: roof, roofs   fife, fifes

- However, some of them form the plural by changing the f or fe to ves.

    Examples: leaf, leaves   knife, knives

In the case of hoof, scarf, and staff, both ways of forming the plural are acceptable.

    Examples: hoof—hooves or hoofs   scarf—scarves or scarfs

Pattern 10

Possessives

- The *singular possessive* of nouns is formed by adding 's to the singular form of the word. It is used to show ownership:

    Examples: Tom's kite   the child's toy

- The *plural possessive* is formed by adding an **apostrophe** to a plural word ending in s. This shows ownership by more than one:

    Examples: the boys' kites   the rabbits' burrow

and by adding 's to a plural not ending in s:

    Examples: men's voices   women's group   children's laughter

- The *possessive* of *personal pronouns* does not require an apostrophe. The form of the word indicates possession:

    Examples: his   her   their

- The *possessive* form of an *indefinite pronoun* does require an apostrophe:

    Examples: anybody's   one's
                   nobody's   anyone's
                   everybody's   everyone's
                   somebody's   no one's

Pattern 11

Plurals of Letters, Figures, and Signs

The plurals of letters, figures, and signs are formed by adding an s:

Example: There are two 8s in 88.

Pattern 12

Pattern for <u>ie</u> and <u>ei</u>

Put **i** before **e** except after **c**, or when it sounds like \ā\ as in <u>neighbor</u> and <u>weigh</u>.

Note: Pattern 12 applies only to words in which **ie** or **ei** are diphthongs.

Examples: **di et**, the <u>ie</u> is not a diphthong.
ch<u>ie</u>f, the <u>ie</u> is a diphthong.

Pattern 13

The Suffix -<u>ful</u>

The suffix -<u>ful</u> differs from the word <u>full</u>. The suffix *never* has two <u>l</u>'s.

Examples: joy<u>ful</u>, peace<u>ful</u>

Pattern 14

The Suffix -<u>ly</u>

When the suffix -<u>ly</u> is added to a word the spelling of this base word *does not* change:

Examples: soft + <u>ly</u> = softly   safe + <u>ly</u> = safely

Note: Many of the words falling under this pattern are covered by Patterns 2, 3, and 4, but -**<u>ly</u>** is a troublesome suffix and requires extra attention.

Pattern 15

Final y before a Suffix

- Final <u>y</u> after a vowel remains *unchanged* when adding any suffix.

  Examples: pray + <u>ed</u> = prayed   pray + <u>ing</u> = praying

- Final <u>y</u> after a consonant changes to <u>i</u> before any suffix.

  Examples: pity + <u>ful</u> = pitiful   copy + <u>ed</u> = copied
  except one beginning with <u>i</u> (ing, ist).

  Examples: copy + <u>ist</u> = copyist   copy + <u>ing</u> = copying

  Note: *accompanist* is an exception.

Exceptions:

- In certain adjectives formed from nouns ending in <u>y</u>, the <u>y</u> is dropped and the suffix -<u>eous</u> is added.

Pattern 16

The Prefixes <u>dis-</u> and <u>mis-</u>

The prefixes <u>dis</u>- and <u>mis</u>- are placed before a word without altering its spelling:

Examples: <u>dis</u> + satisfy = dissatisfy   <u>mis</u> + spell = misspell

Pattern 17

Prefixes Changed for Ease of
Phonetic Blending and Pronunciation

The final consonant of a prefix may change to match or more easily blend with the following letter.

Example: con + lide (changes to) **coll**ide

Chapter 8

Generalizations

CHAPTER OVERVIEW

Chapter 8 contains spelling generalizations for sounds (less definite than the spelling patterns) and procedures that will help students spell words when their visual memory fails them. Since this chapter contains vast amounts of information, it will require a lot of study and rereading. It is full of exercises to help students make educated spelling choices when confronted with more than one spelling possibility. There are twenty-five sounds, with corresponding generalizations and effective exercises. (A list of the generalizations is presented here for easy reference.) This chapter also contains comprehensive word lists for all the sounds presented.

Our mission is to make spelling a "thinking subject," with application as the goal, rather than glib repetition of rote information.

Materials Needed

- Student notebook (to collect lists of learned words)
- Yellow drill cards

SPELLING GENERALIZATIONS BASED ON PHONICS

Conflicting views concerning poor spelling have prevented its being recognized as a skill worthy of serious study. However, it is a skill that can be improved upon. If a student cannot read, we know we must do something, but some people's attitude toward spelling is likely to be, "Spelling, what difference does spelling make? I can't spell myself." On the other hand, correct spelling is essential for educated people. Misspelled words count against the college applicant and have caused the loss of many a job opportunity. "His application wasn't even spelled correctly."

Perhaps the underlying reason for this is that spelling is so easy for many people that it is taken for granted. Furthermore, someone who fails to acquire this skill is often assumed to be careless or limited in intellectual ability. This assumption of negligence, together with ridicule, casts a stigma upon a poor speller. Some people find their difficulty not only a handicap, but a humiliation. Fortunately, new technology such as the spellcheck feature in word processing programs can be an invaluable support for people with spelling difficulties. However, these tools may not always be available. A thank-you note, a letter congratulating a friend on a special occasion, or a get-well wish will all still have to be handwritten. More important, not all students or school systems can afford such equipment.

In many spelling textbooks there are statements to the effect that there could be no possibility of misspelling the simple monosyllables such as *and* or *to*. Yet we have seen papers written by intelligent, careful, and conscientious people, which contain numerous spelling errors, such as:

and	written as *nad* or *dan*
but	as *tub* or *ubt*
go	as *og*
man	as *amn*

Adults who tend to spell incorrectly have often learned labored coping strategies. Through concentrated thought, they may prevent errors, and by painstaking revisions eradicate others. At the cost of extreme effort and much time, they may match their knowledge of a spelling pattern against the sound of the word carefully pronounced, or if possible, consult the dictionary. In short, some people with spelling trouble work out for themselves, through laborious efforts, ways to keep their readers from discovering their weaknesses.

There are definite procedures to improve spelling. The purpose of this chapter is to organize and explain these procedures.

Many spelling programs adopted by schools and classroom teachers incorporate compiled lists of words occurring most frequently in textbooks and magazines. Students are to learn these words through the grades. The methods presented here differ radically from this type of ordinary instruction and are not offered as a substitute for usual classroom procedure.

Suggestions to aid in this learning process include:

- keen observation of the word to be studied/spelled
- pronunciation of the word syllable by syllable
- visualizing the word with closed eyes
- writing the word several times
- writing on a rough surface, for kinesthetic reinforcement

Teachers using these textbooks and methods find that the spelling of many of their students improves. As in the case of reading instruction, we disclaim any effort to replace established methods for those students for whom they succeed. Our concern is with those individuals, found in every class, whose spelling still remains weak—often to the point of the ludicrous and bizarre—despite traditional spelling instruction.

Many students cannot form a reliable visual picture of a word, so devices for visualizing are exactly the wrong ones for them. There would be fewer poor spellers if we all had photographic visual memory. The natural speller does not *think* about the spelling of the words she writes. She merely transcribes from the picture in her mind.

However, when trying to "remember how the word looks" brings confusion rather than help, assistance must be sought elsewhere. Spelling must be viewed as a subject that can be mastered with careful thought.

Not only is it difficult for the nonreader to recognize particular words, but the attempt to do so in the beginning fosters the wrong attitude for him. He must master skills that will enable him to attack words he has never seen before, because the words conform to general trends and principles he has learned. Similarly, the attempt to memorize the spelling of lists of words breaks down the attitude toward spelling as a subject controlled by patterns and generalizations.

For practical reasons it is necessary that some important common words (such as *does, goes, know, enough*), which are not phonetic and do not conform to any pattern, should be memorized by the S.O.S. process. *A list of such learned words should be kept in a special notebook section for ready reference.* However, the knowledge of such words does not increase general spelling ability. These memorized words must be tested again and again at frequent intervals; restudy is often necessary. The selection of a limited number of unclassifiable learned words for intensive study and repeated review must not be confused with the regular procedure of assigning lists of words from a spelling book to be learned for daily lessons. If spelling is taught as a subject apart from writing, as it usually is, a student may have high marks in spelling day after day and yet fail to retain the same skill level in his daily written work. His "spelling sense" is not being developed.

It is this spelling sense that we hope to develop in the procedures we suggest. The categories are presented separately as an aid to the logical development of each. However, we do not intend that all of the subject matter of one topic be finished before the next is taken up. Several different types of activities should appear in a daily lesson—introduction of a new spelling pattern, a generalization, phonics drills, dictionary technique, and review and application of previously taught skills, such as handwriting.

Multiple Spellings

Phonetic skill-building must continue, just as the most accomplished musician needs to practice to keep her fingers supple. However, in every list of words, there will be a considerable number that should never be studied in remedial procedure. These are the perfectly phonetic words that can be spelled by the simple process of translating sounds into symbols.

In Chapter 2, only one spelling was possible for each sound employed. As reading progressed through the introduction of phonograms with more than one sound (Chapter 3), the complicated array of spellings thus made possible was ignored in practical daily work. We are now ready for a thorough study of the possible spellings of ambiguous sounds. The ways of representing a sound, as listed on the back of the yellow phonics drill cards, must become so familiar to the student that he will recall the correct spelling of the sound almost automatically when he hears it.

In the case of certain sounds with multiple spellings, practice in spelling detached syllables and made-up words is very effective. Pages 178–180 contain syllables and words that are useful for this purpose.

All syllables having the sound of real words have been omitted from these lists because the student might remember the incorrect form, causing him to misspell real words. Most of the syllables chosen are parts of real words. Some have been used to emphasize the idea of *theoretically* possible spellings. We believe that such syllables conform to English usage and may safely be regarded as possible. While most of the syllables chosen can be spelled more than one way, syllables with only one spelling have been introduced to keep the student alert. The teacher should ask, "Is there only one way to spell this or are there several ways?"

If the teacher attempts to create lists of detachable syllables, he or she must be careful to avoid combinations that do not conform to English spelling patterns. For example, j almost never occurs at the end of a syllable. The student should not have to spell a made-up word in which the j occupies this position. The various spellings of the sound \k\ are so dependent on the position of the sound in the word—initial, final, medial—that it should not be used until the generalization is taught. The uses of s and z for the \z\ sound are not entirely interchangeable and the spelling of a detached syllable with both letters may result in confusion.

To summarize: In these lists we emphasize consonant sounds that can be spelled more than one way: \f\, \j\, \s\, and \sh\. Two spellings of \ī\—i and y—are used, but there is only one spelling for the other vowels. With the exceptions of syllables containing a vowel-consonant-e combination, no long vowel sounds are included. Other sound combinations will be introduced later in the chapter.

The First Lesson

If the work on unambiguous syllables has been thorough, the student, when asked to spell \thet\, should respond promptly and with assurance "t-h-e-t." The same should be true for \twen\.

The teacher might say: "You have spelled \thet\ and \twen\ each in only one way. That was right. How do you spell the syllable \fant\?"

If he does not think of the two spellings for the sound \f\, the teacher must remind him and then ask him to spell this syllable in two ways.

When he has done this, he is told to write the syllable first one way, then the other—of course, he repeats the syllable before beginning to write and names the letters as he forms each one. It must be clearly understood that he does not write these detached syllables again and again the way he frequently repeats the letter sequence of a difficult word that he is trying to learn. The object of S.O.S. is:

- to give visual, auditory and kinesthetic associations of the alternative spellings
- to give further training in forming the letter they are naming (some students say one letter and write another)
- to establish the habit of using S.O.S.

The teacher should insist on large, clear writing. Otherwise, the kinesthetic impressions will be indistinct and therefore unreliable. Some students enjoy knowing that both spellings of the syllable \fant\ occur in real words—in<u>fant</u> and ele<u>phant</u>.

The syllable \fal\ gives practice in the spelling of \f\ again, and the words <u>fallow</u> and <u>asphalt</u> may be mentioned.

The alternative spellings of \sh\ in the syllable \shan\ should be treated like those of \f\ in \fant\. <u>Sh</u>anty and <u>ch</u>andelier illustrate the use of these alternative spellings.

The Second Lesson

This lesson might take up \ques\, \sim\, \chig\, \stran\, \taf\, \gant\, and \shev\. New sounds should be introduced gradually while those already familiar should be reviewed in varied combinations.

Real words that contain the spellings of the syllable \sim\ are <u>sim</u>ple, <u>sym</u>pathy, and <u>cym</u>bal. Syllables that have many spellings always prove interesting. For \taf\ we find <u>taf</u>fy and epi<u>taph</u>; for \shev\, di<u>shev</u>el, <u>chev</u>ron.

Not all syllables with alternative spellings need to occur in real words. However, practice in reading and spelling these detached syllables will make reading real words easier. Students will often suggest words themselves. They should be encouraged to do this in the first few lessons and continue to do so as the lessons progress.

No one but the remedial teacher will be able to tell how much drill, review, and reinforcement a particular student will need. The teacher may need to supplement the lists in this book with materials of his or her own making.

Multiple Spellings
(Phonetically Regular)

Sound Dictated	Responses			Illustrative Words		
\ j \ spelled j and g *						
\ jit \	jit	git	gyt	jitney		
\ jip \	jip	gip	gyp	gipsy or gypsy		Egyptian
\ jith \	jith	gith	gyth			
\ jen \	jen	gen		jennet	general	
\ jelt \	jelt	gelt				
\ jep \	jep	gep				
\ jeb \	jeb	geb				
\ jinth \	jinth	ginth	gynth			
\ jelt dal \	jeltdal	geltdal				
\ jith nad \	jithnad	githnad	gythnad			
\ jep ral \	jepral	gepral				
\ jit lat \	jitlat	gitlat	gytlat			
\ f \ spelled f and ph						
\ fon \	fon	phon			fondle	phonic	siphon
\ dif \	dif	dyf	diph	dyph	different	diphtheria	
\ prof \	prof	proph			profit	prophet	
\ taf \	taf	taph			taffy	epitaph	
\ lef \	lef	leph				telephone	
\ ef \	ef	eph			effort	ephemeral	
\ fos \	fos	phos			fossil	phosphorus	
\ fēm \	feme	pheme				blaspheme	
\ af \	af	aph			affable	Aphrodite	
\ fid \	fid	fyd	phid	phyd	fiddle	aphid	
\ fal \	fal	phal			fallow	asphalt	
\ fren \	fren	phren			frenzy	phrenology	
\ rif \	rif	ryf	riph	ryph	riffle	periphery	
\ saf \	saf	saph			saffron		
\ sof \	sof	soph			soffit	sophomore	
\ fleg \	fleg	phleg				phlegmatic	
\ flet \	flet	phlet				pamphlet	
\ fant \	fant	phant			infant	elephant	
\ prof mel \	profmel	prophmel			infant	elephant	
\ sen fem \	senfem	senphem	cenfem	cenphem			
\ fid lat \	fidlat	phidlat	fydlat	phydlat			
\ lam fren \	lamfren	lamphren					

---

* The letter **j** is seldom or never followed by **y** in English words.

Sound Dictated	Responses				Illustrative Words		

\s\ spelled s and c

Sound Dictated	Responses				Illustrative Words		
\sep\	sep	cep			September	reception	
\sis\	sis	cis	sys	cys	sister	cistern	system
\sen\	sen	cen			sentinel	center	
\sinth\	sinth	cinth	synth	cynth	absinthe	hyacinth	
\sim\	sim	sym	cim	cym	simple	symbol	cymbal
\sig\	sig	syg	cig	cyg	signal	cigarette	cygnet
\sib\	sib	cib	syb	cyb	sibyl	Sybarite	Cybele
\sem\	sem	cem			Seminole	December	
\seb\	seb	ceb					
\seg\	seg	ceg			segment		
\sib tal\	sibtal	cibtal	sybtal	cybtal			
\sis nal\	sisnal	sysnal	cisnal	cysnal			
\sib lon\	siblon	syblon	ciblon	cyblon			
\tum sig\	tumsig	tumsyg	tumcig	tumcyg			
\sim dal\	simdal	symdal	cimdal	cymdal			
\sim bam\	simbam	symbam	cimbam	cymbam			
\sib ol sis\	sibolsis	sibolsys	sybolsis	sybolsys			
	cibolsis	cibolsys	cybolsis	cybolsys			

\sh\ spelled sh and ch

Sound Dictated	Responses				Illustrative Words	
\shif\	shif	shyf	shiph	shyph		
	chif	chyf	chiph	chyph		chiffonier
\shiv\	shiv	shyv	chiv	chyv	shiver	chivalry
\shan\	shan	chan			shanty	chandelier
\shev\	shev	chev			dishevel	chevron
\shat\	shat	chat			shatter	chatelaine
\shas\	shas	chas			Shasta	chassis
\shem\	shem	chem			Shemite	chemise
\shaf\	shaf	chaf	chaph	shaph		
\shat lab\	shatlab	chatlab				
\shas ōl\	shasole	chasole				
\neb tash\	nebtash	nebtach				

\i\ spelled i and y

Sound Dictated	Responses				Illustrative Words		
\stig\	stig	styg			stigma		
\div\	div	dyv			dividend		
\tim\	tim	tym			timber	tympanum	
\trib\	trib	tryb			tributary		
\stim\	stim	stym			stimulate		
\glim\	glim	glym			glimmer		
\stip\	stip	styp			stipple	styptic	
\vē\	vi	vy	ve		enviable	envy	Venus
\mir\	mir	myr			mirror	myriad	
\trin\	trin	tryn			trinity		
\trig\	trig	tryg			trigger		
\trich\	trich	trych					
\splin\	splin	splyn			splinter		
\rinth\	rinth	rynth			labyrinth		
\lig\	lig	lyg			lignite		
\glif\	glif	glyf	glyph	gliph	hieroglyph		
\glit\	glit	glyt			glitter		
\lith\	lith	lyth			lithograph		

Sound Dictated	Responses				Illustrative Words
\s\ spelled s and c (cont.)					
\lib\	lib	lyb			liberty
\rin mant\	rinmant	rynmant			
\gran rinth\	granrinth	granrynth			
\rath min\	rathmin	rathmyn			
\trig nant\	trignant	trygnant			
\grol dil\	groldil	groldyl			
\chig lan\	chiglan	chyglan			
\gat sim\	gatsim	gatsym	gatcim	gatcym	
\sim lat\	simlat	symlat	cimlat	cymlat	
\bram sinth\	bramsinth	bramsynth	bramcinth	bramcynth	

Sound Dictated	Responses	Illustrative Words
No ambiguity		
\sump\	sump	sumptuous
\ques\	ques	question
\em\	em	emblem
\blem\	blem	blemish
\wheth\	wheth	whether
\tral\	tral	central
\en\	en	enemy
\el\	el	elegant
\empt\	empt	exempt
\grat\	grat	gratitude
\nant\	nant	indignant
\ət\	ut	utter
\splen\	splen	splendor
\strel\	strel	minstrel
\ag\	ag	agate
\cham\	cham	champion
\səs\	sus	suspect
\ap\	ap	apple
\tav\	tav	tavern
\vōk\	voke	provoke
\vēn\	vene	intervene
\trēm\	treme	extreme
\tüd\	tude	attitude
\pret\	pret	interpret
\rəpt\	rupt	interrupt
\jan\	jan	January
\jas\	jas	jasper
\slen\	slen	slender
\bes\	bes	asbestos
\smat\	smat	smattering
\stam\	stam	stampede
\stat\	stat	static
\sten\	sten	stencil

SELECTING PROBABILITIES FROM MANY POSSIBILITIES

We have said that perfectly phonetic words should never be studied. But how is a student to know how to spell a word "as it sounds" after he has learned that he can no longer depend upon there being only one symbol to represent a sound?

In this chapter, exercises are provided in which multiple spellings of certain sounds are contrasted with sounds that can be spelled in only one way. These exercises provide the student with practice in using his intellectual skills to assist in spelling. For \stan\ and \ret\, for example, there is only one possible spelling, but \lin\ might be either *lin* or *lyn*, and for \frāz\ there are *frase* and *phrase*.

How is the student to know which of the possible spellings is probably correct in a particular word? For example, is the word *phrase* spelled with an f or a ph?

We will now attempt to provide the student with the answers to these types of questions.

GENERALIZATIONS

Spelling must be a thinking subject. Generalizations and intellectual deductions provide a foundation that the confused speller can depend on when his visual imagery fails him.

The lessons in generalizations are for the nonspeller who can use his power of abstract thought to circumvent his unreliable visual recall. Some students lack ability to handle abstractions and cannot apply these generalizations. Their needs will be better served by fewer words, which they must learn with the aid of phonics, the simpler spelling patterns, and S.O.S.

As we have seen in Chapter 7, spelling patterns are very important. However, generalizations based on phonics should be introduced from time to time according to the needs of the student and the discretion of the teacher. Each of the twenty-five "Ways of Spelling" sections contains several generalizations for spelling a particular sound. Generalizations, although less definite than patterns, give more fundamental training in thoughtful word attack and spelling.

Starting with the student's normal random guessing, the teacher will try to direct it into thoughtful spelling, controlled by increasing recognition of probabilities based on the patterns and generalizations.

The fact that sometimes there can be no decision between two or more possibilities does not minimize the importance of thorough acquaintance with them. Suppose the choice lies between a and ai; between a-e and ai; between k and ck; among e-e, ea, and ie; or among any other array of phonograms, all equally probable as far as the student knows at this point. The dictionary—or the teacher if dictionary technique has not yet been sufficiently mastered—must decide. It is clear that the student must develop dictionary skills as soon as possible, so that this tool may become a companion, always at hand to make decisions when the student cannot do so and when no teacher is present. It must never be forgotten, however, that unless the student is thoroughly acquainted with the possibilities of various spellings, the dictionary will be of little use. He may stumble upon a word, but he will not be able to search for it intelligently. When advised to refer students to the dictionary, well-educated adults, even experienced teachers, often exclaim, "How can anyone look up a word in the dictionary if he does not know how to spell it?"

The sounds are introduced without regard to their difficulty. The teacher must be prepared to take them up in any order that fits the needs of a particular student. Moreover, certain uses of a phonogram may be helpful in the early stages, whereas other uses would be of no practical value at this time and would even prove confusing. Therefore, such uses should not be mentioned until later. For example, \sh\ spelled <u>sh</u> (page 201), occurs in many words that young students need to use, whereas the spelling <u>ch</u> is seldom needed, and <u>ci</u>, <u>si</u>, <u>ti</u> as \sh\ spellings, found in such words as effi<u>ci</u>ent, compul<u>si</u>on, and par<u>ti</u>al, are likewise seldom used by young students.

Except in the case of the long vowels and \yü\ and \ü\, no attempt has been made to represent the relative frequency of the various spellings by the length of the lists. Some of the lists could be greatly extended. In other cases there are few or no examples beyond those given.

As will be evident, more material is presented than the student can assimilate quickly. Each "Ways of Spelling" section is followed by lists of words. This extensive amount of material is available for the teacher to use to assist in planning his or her lessons according to the interests and abilities of the students.

Under no conditions are these lists to be studied and reviewed as spelling lessons, nor are the general conclusions to be memorized one by one. There should be ample opportunity to scrutinize certain types of words and to draw conclusions about their spelling. From time to time, the teacher should select and dictate words the student has not studied. The student's attempts to choose intellectually and to give reasons for his choices of spellings will serve to familiarize him with the generalizations until their application becomes almost automatic.

The point of the exercises is to provide ample practice so that memorizing word lists is avoided. Students should strive for *automaticity*.

1. WAYS OF SPELLING \k\. Yellow card 24.

\k\ is spelled <u>c</u> as in <u>cat</u>, <u>k</u> as in <u>kite</u>, <u>ch</u> as in <u>Christmas</u>, <u>ck</u> as in <u>clock</u>.

How to Teach Spelling, by Laura Toby Rudginsky and Elizabeth C. Haskell, gives a useful introduction to the \k\ sound:

\k\ can be spelled <u>k</u> or <u>ck</u>.
- Use <u>ck</u> at the end of a word or syllable directly after a single short vowel.
- Use <u>k</u> or <u>ke</u> after a long vowel sound and after two vowels (page 39).

Complete information is as follows:

a. Initial \k\:

1. c̲ is by far the most common spelling for \k\. In *Merriam-Webster's Collegiate Dictionary*, tenth edition, 127 pages are devoted to initial c̲ and only 11 to initial k̲. The c̲ pages include soft as well as hard c̲'s, but decidedly more than half are hard.

2. k̲ as an initial letter occurs for the most part before e̲ and i̲, where c̲ would not function as \k\, as in k̲ite, k̲ettle, k̲ing, k̲itchen. Most of the words in which initial k̲ is followed by a̲, o̲, or u̲ are taken with little or no change from some foreign language:

kapok (Javanese)	kopek (Russian)
kayak (Eskimo)	kosher (Hebrew)
koala (native Australian)	kaput (German)

3. c̲h̲ is used as an initial spelling of \k\ though less frequently than c̲, (e.g., c̲h̲orus, c̲h̲aracter).

   The c̲h̲ spelling of \k\ in any situation, initial, final, or medial, occurs most frequently in words of Greek derivation. The c̲h̲ words are in one list. The student's attention should be called to their general form and the meaning of some of them should be discussed, to help the student be more selective about the c̲h̲ spelling for \k\ in familiar everyday words (see List 7, page 186).

4. c̲k̲ is never initial in a word.

b. Final \k\:

1. In monosyllables:

   \k\ preceded by a consonant sound is spelled k̲, e.g., san̲k̲, tus̲k̲ (List 1).

   \k\ preceded by a long vowel sound is sometimes spelled k̲, e.g., soa̲k̲, or vowel-k̲e, e.g., bro̲k̲e (List 2).

   \k\ preceded by a short vowel sound is usually spelled c̲k̲, e.g., spe̲c̲k̲ (List 3).

   Final \k\ is spelled c̲ in a very few one-syllable words, e.g., tal̲c̲ (List 4).

2. In dissyllables and polysyllables:

   In words of more than one syllable c̲ is almost the universal spelling of final \k\, e.g., publi̲c̲ (List 5).

   A few words of more than one syllable end in c̲k̲, e.g., hammo̲c̲k̲ (List 6) and a few in c̲h̲, e.g., stoma̲c̲h̲ (List 12).

c. In the body of the word:

1. At the beginning of a syllable, c̲ is the most common spelling, e.g., tal c̲um (List 7), but k̲ occurs in some words, e.g., jun k̲et (List 8), also c̲h̲, e.g., c̲h̲orus (List 12). c̲k̲ never begins a syllable.

2. At the end of a syllable:

   c̲ is the most common spelling, e.g., o̲c̲ to pus (List 7).

   c̲k̲ ends the first syllable:

In derivatives from monosyllables ending in <u>ck</u>, as in <u>sick ness</u> (List 9).

In words ending in <u>et</u> and <u>le</u>, e.g., <u>pick et</u>, <u>pick le</u> (List 9).

In a few words that do not fit into either of the above groups, as in <u>nick el</u> (List 9).

In a few derivatives formed by adding a suffix beginning with <u>e</u>, <u>i</u>, or <u>y</u> to a word ending in <u>c</u>, a <u>k</u> is used to preserve the hard sound of the <u>c</u>, as in <u>picnicker</u>, <u>picnicking</u>, <u>frolicked</u>, <u>panicky</u>, <u>trafficker</u>.

<u>ch</u> is fairly frequent at the end of syllables, e.g., <u>mech a nism</u> (List 12).

3. Medial in a syllable:

\k\   may be spelled <u>c</u>, <u>k</u>, or <u>ch</u>, but <u>c</u> is the most common.

<u>sc</u>   as a spelling of \sk\ occurs three times as often as <u>sk</u>.

<u>sk</u>   is found before <u>e</u>, <u>i</u>, or <u>y</u> where <u>c</u> would not function as \k\, as in <u>skein</u>, <u>ski</u>, <u>sky</u>, <u>skeleton</u>, <u>sketch</u>. Since these are all in initial syllables they can readily be found by the teacher, and no list is given here. Two Scandinavian words, <u>skull</u> and <u>skulk</u>, and the Algonquin Indian word <u>skunk</u> are exceptional in having <u>sk</u> before <u>u</u>.

<u>c</u> occurs in the common combinations <u>act</u>, <u>ect</u>, <u>ict</u>, <u>oct</u>, <u>uct</u>, and <u>inct</u> (List 10).

For <u>ch</u> within a syllable, as in <u>school</u>, see List 12.

Monosyllables ending in \k\ are very common and are puzzling because this final \k\ may be spelled <u>k</u>, vowel-<u>ke</u>, or <u>ck</u>. The use of a record sheet, ruled and headed as shown below, on which the student lists words after he has spelled them, serves greatly to reduce uncertainty.

k	k	ke	ck
bank	cloak	make	neck

If final \k\ is heard preceded by a consonant sound, the \k\ will be spelled <u>k</u> as in <u>bank</u>. When a short vowel sound precedes the \k\, the spelling will be <u>ck</u> as in <u>neck</u>.

These facts are easily mastered, but when the final \k\ is preceded by a long vowel sound, that sound may be represented by a diphthong as in <u>cloak</u>, or the spelling may be vowel-<u>ke</u> as in <u>make</u>.*

After discussing and writing on the record sheet a number of words, e.g., <u>fleck</u>, <u>rank</u>, <u>bake</u>, <u>click</u>, <u>soak</u>, <u>frisk</u>, <u>speck</u>, <u>speak</u>, <u>smoke</u>, <u>pluck</u>, <u>pork</u>, the student should be able to say confidently of \lärk\, "It is spelled <u>l-a-r-k</u> because I hear a consonant sound before \k\." Of \pek\ he should say, "That will be <u>p-e-c-k</u> because there is a short vowel before \k\."

---

* <u>Break</u> and <u>brake</u>, <u>steak</u> and <u>stake</u> are excellent illustrations, but discussion of them should be postponed until the student is familiar with homonyms.

But for the spelling of \chōk\ there are two possibilities, and he should say, "I don't know. It may be c-h-o-a-k or it may be c-h-o-k-e. I must look it up." Or, in case he is not yet able to locate words in the dictionary, "You will have to tell me."

There are very few monosyllables ending in c and they will be needed by high school or older students only. However, they should be discussed briefly even with beginners, who will readily see that it would not be sensible to end ordinary monosyllables with c. The homonyms bloc and block are illustrative. After the meanings have been discussed, bloc might be listed among several members of the "block family": lock, rock, clock, bloc, stock. Bloc looks out of place. It doesn't resemble the other members.

On the other hand, final \k\ in dissyllables and polysyllables is most frequently c. The teacher can demonstrate this by listing words under the headings:

c	ck	ch
music	hammock	stomach

Since the important fact is that c is the most frequent spelling of final \k\, this normal frequency should be indicated by the length of the columns of words on the student's record sheet.

Final \k\ spelled que will be used only by mature advanced students. Such words should be studied S.O.S. when needed (List 11).

The fact that \k\, both initial and final in syllables within a word, is most frequently spelled c, can be highlighted by writing lists of words, divided into syllables, in columns headed respectively:

Initial in a syllable	Final in a syllable

Words may be selected from List 7.

The conditions under which k, ck, and ch are used in the body of a word should be discussed. See *c* (1) and (2), pages 183–184.

The sound \k\ followed by \t\ within a syllable is troublesome. Many people omit the \t\ in pronunciation. Very often young students do not hear the sound and must be trained to do so by repeated exercises in pronouncing and spelling such words as fact, conduct, and distinct. The dissyllable arctic \'ärk-tik\, almost universally mispronounced, also needs special attention.

This plan of study must convince the student that it is safest to use c for \k\ unless he knows, or has good reason to suspect, that another spelling is necessary. In other words, "Use c whenever you can."

Other facts brought out in the generalizations should be considered as they come to have practical value to the student.

ILLUSTRATIVE \k\ WORDS

List 1	List 2	List 3	List 5	List 7
bank	make	back	cubic	recall
rank	lake	lack	relic	arcade
tank	bake	tack	music	alcohol
thank	cake	track	tropic	volcano
prank	wake	quack	static	encumber
ink	rake	neck	rustic	encampment
mink	flake	deck	heroic	incomplete
think	like	peck	poetic	agriculture
drink	spike	check	elastic	calico
honk	strike	fleck	angelic	article
sunk	joke	lick	gigantic	democrat
trunk	poke	nick	historic	lexicon
chunk	smoke	click	dramatic	ridicule
shrunk	stroke	trick	terrific	musical
milk	speak	lock	despotic	historical
silk	creak	clock	lilac	methodical
bulk	sneak	flock	shellac	theatrical
fork	streak	frock	zodiac	nectar
pork	squeak	stock	maniac	picture
brisk	tweak	luck	ipecac	lecture
frisk	meek	pluck	almanac	dictate
husk	soak	stuck	havoc	factory
rusk	cloak	struck	manioc	octagon
dusk	croak	truck		fracture

List 4	List 6	List 7 (cont.)
lac	derrick	rectify
sac	paddock	sacrifice
roc	haddock	nocturnal
bloc	hammock	reduction
disc	shamrock	particular
talc	rootstock	ridiculous
bric-a-brac	flintlock	gesticulate
	ransack	matriculate
	Cossack	satisfaction
	tamarack	cactus
	woodchuck	accuse
		acclaim
		occult
		occupy
		peccary
		piccolo
		moccasin
		tactical
		practical
		macrocosm

List 8	**List 9**	**List 10**	**List 11**	**List 12**
yokel	jacket	fact	pique	ache
market	pocket	compact	unique	chaos
basket	locket	detract	oblique	chorus
trinket	rocket	contract	antique	Charon
blanket	bucket	subtract	physique	chrysalis
tinkle	wicket	elect	technique	Charybdis
twinkle	cricket	insect	Basque	chalcedony
wrinkle	cackle	expect	clique	chronology
welkin	tackle	connect	bisque	epoch
firkin	grackle	neglect	mosque	stomach
lambkin	pickle	evict	grotesque	monarch
manikin	sickle	predict	humoresque	triptych
cannikin	trickle	restrict	picturesque	Petrarch
	locker	interdict		lichen
	rocker	decoct		troche
	wicker	concoct		orchid
	sticky	induct		archive
	plucky	conduct		Bacchus
	sickly	instruct		echidna
	reckon	obstruct		Achilles
	lackey	construct		architect
	nickel	instinct		anchorite
	cuckoo	distinct		trachoma
	package	adjunct		bronchitis
	buckram	defunct		synchronize
	stricken			sepulcher
	reckless			catechism
	stocking			melancholy
	hickory			Andromache
	mackerel			echo
	mackintosh			drachma
				technical
				lachrymal
				anachronism
				scheme
				school
				scholar
				schedule
				schooner
				scholastic

2. WAYS OF SPELLING \ch\. Yellow cards 28 and 29.

\ch\ is spelled <u>ch</u> as in <u>chin</u>, <u>tch</u> as in <u>catch</u>, <u>si</u> as in <u>expansion</u>, and <u>ti</u> as in <u>attention</u>.

      a. The sound \ch\ at the beginning of a word or syllable is spelled <u>ch</u>, never <u>tch</u>.

      b. If \ch\ is preceded by a short vowel sound or schwa in a one-syllable word it is usually spelled <u>tch</u> (List 1), otherwise <u>ch</u> (List 2).

      A few very common words are exceptions to *b*. It is good to teach these words S.O.S. before the generalizations are discussed. For young students, bring up <u>rich</u>, <u>which</u>, <u>much</u>, <u>such</u>. Later <u>niche</u>, <u>attach</u>, <u>detach</u>, <u>ostrich</u>, and <u>sandwich</u> will require attention.

ILLUSTRATIVE \ch\ WORDS

List 1		List 2		
batch	itch	branch	crunch	each
catch	ditch	ranch	hunch	beach
latch	flitch	stanch	punch	beech
match	hitch	staunch	munch	bleach
patch	kitchen	bench	lunch	leach
ratch	pitch	clench	luncheon	leech
ratchet	quitch	drench	puncheon	peach
hatch	stitch	French	truncheon	preach
hatchet	witch	quench	belch	reach
satchel	switch	stench	squelch	screech
snatch	botch	trench	mulch	beseech
scratch	blotch	entrench	larch	teach
thatch	notch	trencher	march	broach
etch	Scotch	wrench	parch	coach
fetch	splotch	inch	starch	loach
ketch	clutch	clinch	perch	poach
sketch	crutch	finch	search	brooch
stretch	Dutch	pinch	smirch	couch
vetch	hutch	winch	porch	grouch
wretch	smutch	bunch	scorch	pouch
			torch	slouch
			church	youch
			lurch	

3. WAYS OF SPELLING \f\. Yellow card 22.

\f\ is spelled f as in fish, and ph as in phone.

The ph spelling of \f\ is chiefly in words of Greek derivation, few of which are encountered except by high school students. However, such words as telephone, elephant, alphabet, Philip, and Joseph are needed by all students, and therefore all should be familiar with the phonogram ph.

Some of the unfamiliar Greek derivatives should be discussed so that the student may form an idea of their character: delphinium, amphibian, phosphorus, encephalitis—scientific terms; photostat, cellophane—words connected with invention; Aphrodite, Persephone, Philomela—characters in Greek mythology.

The overwhelming nature of these words may keep the student from suggesting ph for \f\ in words with which he is familiar but which he does not know how to spell. If students find all spelling difficult, it seems reasonable to some of them to choose the most extraordinary form.

Some older students will be interested to discover that when new words are needed for inventions or scientific discoveries, they are apt to be made by combining Greek or Latin word elements, as in pyroxylin, (*pyro* Gr. fire + *xylon*, wood), a flammable substance made from wood. Teachers should note that knowing a few of these elements will make it easier to spell many words that might otherwise be difficult. The following Greek prefixes and suffixes are especially useful:

phono-	sound	-phone	sound; voice
photo-	light	-graph	a writing; an instrument for recording
micro-	small	-graphy	a writing; a branch of knowledge
macro-	large	-scope	an instrument for viewing or observing
tele-	far; operating at a distance		

With these word elements before him, the student will be able to understand the meanings of such words as photograph, photography, telephone, telegraph, telegraphy, television, microphone.

The above words stand out in contrast to fall, father, feather, find, defend, effort—words in which ph would be quite out of place.

Our aim is to show the student that in attempting a new word, he should use f unless he has some reason to suppose that the word may be a Greek derivative. He should be so conditioned that he will assume that in a word like physics, a scientific term, the \f\ would probably be spelled ph, whereas in feather, a very common word, it would most likely be f; that the final syllable \fī\ in ordinary words, such as beautify, terrify, solidify, would be -fy, not -phy. Knowing that the suffix -fy means "to make, to form" will also be helpful in drawing this conclusion.

A few words in which gh is used to spell \f\ should be taught by S.O.S., such as cough, trough, laugh, rough, tough, slough, enough. The phonogram is not included in our drill cards because if gh is given with f and ph as possible spellings for the \f\ sound, there is likely to be trouble. In attempting to spell new words, the poorest spellers frequently suggest gh as the appropriate spelling for \f\.

The following lists will provide practice in educated choosing, developing the idea of the difference between f and ph words.*

ILLUSTRATIVE \f\ WORDS

<table>
<tr><th colspan="2">f</th><th colspan="2">ph</th></tr>
<tr><td>leaf</td><td>belfry</td><td>orphan</td><td>diaphragm</td></tr>
<tr><td>golf</td><td>defeat</td><td>dolphin</td><td>atmosphere</td></tr>
<tr><td>dwarf</td><td>confine</td><td>Orpheus</td><td>stratosphere</td></tr>
<tr><td>drift</td><td>refresh</td><td>morphine</td><td>monograph</td></tr>
<tr><td>shift</td><td>defect</td><td>symphony</td><td>multigraph</td></tr>
<tr><td>life</td><td>benefit</td><td>lymphatic</td><td>diphtheria</td></tr>
<tr><td>knife</td><td>interfere</td><td>cellophane</td><td>telegraph</td></tr>
<tr><td>perfume</td><td>justify</td><td>physics</td><td>Philip</td></tr>
<tr><td>confide</td><td>simplify</td><td>phonograph</td><td>emphasis</td></tr>
<tr><td>conflict</td><td>glorify</td><td>elephant</td><td>physical</td></tr>
<tr><td>wafer</td><td>magnify</td><td>geography</td><td>Joseph</td></tr>
<tr><td>muffin</td><td>intensify</td><td>telephone</td><td>phantom</td></tr>
<tr><td>office</td><td>electrify</td><td>alphabet</td><td>prophet</td></tr>
</table>

It is not necessary to conduct a series of elaborate lessons to teach this idea. It can be done more or less incidentally. If a student continually uses ph for common words, two lists headed respectively f and ph should be gradually built up. After the meaning of a word has been discussed, e.g., finger or lithograph, the student should say in which column to place it and give the reason for his decision. Of course, beginners are not expected to attempt the spelling of lithograph or other long words. For these, they should merely say "f" or "ph." Students thoroughly familiar with the phonetic elements will be able to spell most of them.

Whether written by the teacher or by the student, these lists should be added to from time to time, and shown to the student if, in a written exercise, he uses ph when it is out of place.

4. WAYS OF SPELLING \s\. Yellow card 25.

\s\ is spelled s as in snake, c before e, i, or y, sc as in science.

   a. The student finds that if he wishes to spell a word in which the \s\ is followed by l, or by one of the sounds of a, o, or u, he must use s and not c. For example, in sand, solid, sun only s can be used. The substitution of c for s sometimes produces a word different in meaning as well as sound, as in sap–cap, sold–cold, soil–coil.

---

* Words with initial f or ph are not included because they are easy to find in the dictionary.

b. One must not infer that \s\ followed by <u>e</u>, <u>i</u>, or <u>y</u> will always be spelled with a <u>c</u>, since <u>s</u> is frequently used, and one cannot predict which letter will be used in a particular instance. For instance, the words <u>c</u>enter, <u>c</u>ider, <u>c</u>ylinder, and <u>s</u>elf, <u>s</u>ilk, <u>s</u>ystem. There are also homonyms such as <u>cell–sell</u>, <u>cent–sent</u>, <u>cite–site</u>.

c. The more mature students may be helped by the knowledge of some prefixes and suffixes, like the prefixes <u>semi</u>-, <u>syn</u>- (<u>syl</u>- before <u>l</u>, <u>sym</u>- before <u>b</u>, <u>p</u>, and <u>m</u>), and the suffix -<u>cy</u>. Words ending in the suffix -<u>cy</u> (meaning "state, quality, rank, or office") are exceedingly numerous, e.g., <u>infancy</u>, <u>presidency</u> (List 1).

A few words end in <u>sy</u>, but in this case the terminal syllable \sē\ is obviously not a suffix (List 2). Some words end in <u>sy</u> pronounced \zē\, e.g., <u>pansy</u>, but these do not concern us here.

d. Final \s\ may be spelled <u>s</u>, <u>se</u>, or <u>ce</u>—<u>crisis</u>, <u>else</u>, <u>quince</u>—never <u>c</u> which, so placed, would be pronounced \k\ (Lists 3 and 4).

When final \s\, in a monosyllable, is preceded by any long vowel, or by \ü\ or \yü\, it is most often spelled -<u>ce</u>: <u>place</u>, <u>nice</u>, <u>truce</u>. The same generalization applies to the stressed syllables of longer words.

e. In some words \s\ is spelled <u>sc</u>, e.g., <u>scene</u>. This happens only if the following letter is <u>e</u>, <u>i</u>, or <u>y</u>. The fact that this possible spelling exists should be called to the student's attention, so that, if he fails to find his word in the dictionary with \s\ spelled <u>s</u> or <u>c</u>, he will think to look for <u>sc</u> (List 6 contains mostly unfamiliar words). For initial <u>sc</u> consult the dictionary.

f. List 7 is made up of words in which the sound \s\ spelled <u>s</u> or <u>c</u> occurs at the beginning or end of a syllable within the word.

In most instances, the dictionary will be the only safe guide as to which spelling to use. Just how puzzling the decision may be is illustrated by the possible uses of <u>c</u> and <u>s</u> in spelling the word \sin- 's(ə)ir\. It might be <u>sincere</u>, <u>cincere</u>, <u>cinsere</u>, sinsere. Consult the dictionary!

However it is important to impress upon the student that he must be alert to realize whether, in a given instance, he can decide for himself which phonogram to use or whether he must consult the dictionary. Two gradually growing lists, headed respectively, "Must be <u>s</u>," "Might be <u>s</u> or <u>c</u>," will tend to increase this alertness.

For young students short words beginning with \s\ are desirable. These they can easily check by referring to the dictionary. List 7 provides words to add as students are able to handle them. It consists of words with \s\ at the beginning or end of a syllable.

ILLUSTRATIVE \s\ WORDS

List 1

decent - - - - - - - decency
potent - - - - - - - potency
fervent- - - - - - - fervency
regent- - - - - - - - regency
secret - - - - - - - - secrecy
urgent - - - - - - - urgency
supreme - - - supremacy
buoyant- - - - - buoyancy
pliant - - - - - - - - pliancy
competent - competency
accurate - - - - - accuracy
persistent - - persistency
obstinate - - - - obstinacy
occupant - - - occupancy
proficient - - proficiency

List 2

curtsy
courtesy
ecstasy
embassy
controversy

List 3

atlas
cactus
crocus
focus
Madras
fracas
pathos
asbestos
sassafras
Osiris
emphasis
ellipsis
osmosis
case
chase
cease
house
moose
gorse
else
lapse
copse
glimpse
elapse
base
lease
chrysalis
bronchitis
gastritis
tonsilitis
metropolis
diagnosis
twice
trice
mace
space
embrace

List 4

entrance
fragrance
clearance
distance
countenance
elegance
forbearance
ignorance
inheritance
deliverance
consequence
occurrence
difference
confidence
evidence
existence
insistence
correspondence
circumference
intelligence

List 5

dense
tense
sense
expense
dispense
defense ⎫ also <u>ce</u> in
offense ⎬ British
pretense ⎭ spelling
condense
intense
nonsense
immense
recompense

List 6

descent
transcend
abscess
rescind
plebiscite
coalesce
effervesce
evanesce
proscenium

List 7

except
pasture
osprey
cascade
decide
plastic
vestry
stencil
jasper
pepsin
proceed
postern
rustic
placid
insult
recent
absorb
princess
gypsum
precede
mascot
ostrich
escape
deficit
insipid
palisade
pacify
establish
desolate
infancy
obsolete
taciturn
assassin
isolate
homicide
fratricide
incinerate
reciprocate
necessary
potassium
obsidian
accessible
poinsettia
felicity
phagocyte

5. WAYS OF SPELLING \z\. Yellow card 27.

\z\ is spelled z as in <u>zebra</u>, s as in <u>nose</u>, and x as in <u>xylophone</u>.

a. Initial \z\ is spelled <u>z</u>. <u>x</u> is used in a very few words.

b. There are two classes of words ending in \z\, both of which are needed by younger students.

    1. Several familiar monosyllables end in <u>s</u>, e.g., <u>is</u>, <u>was</u>, <u>has</u>, <u>his</u>. A few less useful monosyllables end in <u>z</u>: <u>buzz</u>, <u>fuzz</u>, <u>fizz</u>, <u>fez</u>, <u>quiz</u>.

    2. The \z\ endings of certain plurals, possessives, and verb forms are spelled <u>s</u>: <u>dogs</u>, <u>boy's</u>, <u>runs</u>.

    The statement on page 70, that <u>s</u> between two vowels frequently sounds like \z\, should be reviewed. The student must be warned, however, not to assume that the \z\ sound heard between two vowels is always to be spelled <u>s</u>, for <u>z</u> is employed in a number of words, e.g., <u>gaze</u>, and there is no way of knowing which to use without consulting a dictionary.

c. Lists 1 and 2 are given to provide training in recognition of this uncertainty. The student should be so trained that when she hears a word like one in these lists she will not attempt to spell it unless she remembers it from past experience. Otherwise, she will say, "There is no way for me to know. I must be told or look it up in the dictionary."

d. When \z\ is heard within a word of more than one syllable, a student should consult the dictionary. No dependable generalization has been found for the spelling of \z\ at the beginning of a syllable (Lists 3 and 4). At the end of a syllable \z\ is usually spelled <u>s</u> (List 5). Both classes of words are likely to be needed by fairly young students.

e. For older students there are two useful generalizations:

    1. The final syllable pronounced \-īz\ is regularly spelled -<u>ize</u>. This is a verb-forming suffix, as in <u>magnetize</u> (List 6). In a few instances <u>t</u> or <u>at</u> is inserted before the suffix, e.g., <u>drama-tize</u>, <u>system-a-tize</u>, the <u>t</u> being taken from the original Greek root.

    A less common suffix is -<u>lyze</u>, used in verbs with corresponding nouns ending in <u>lysis</u>, e.g., <u>analysis</u>, <u>analyze</u>; <u>electrolysis</u>, <u>electrolyze</u>.

    In some word \-īz\ is spelled <u>ise</u>. Usually it is not a suffix. The most common of these words are

advise	franchise	enterprise	advertise
surprise	exercise	compromise	merchandise

    Many verbs ending in \īz\ spelled <u>ize</u> are the base for nouns ending in \i'zā shun\ -<u>ization</u>, as in <u>naturalize</u>, <u>naturalization</u> (List 7).

2. The suffix \iz'm\ is spelled -ism, as in barbarism (List 8). In the few words we have found which suggest an exception, e.g., paroxysm and aneurysm, the final syllable is not a suffix.

In a few final syllables other than \iz'm\, \z\ before \m\ is spelled s, as in protoplasm, endoplasm, microcosm, macrocosm.

ILLUSTRATIVE \z\ WORDS

List 1	List 2*	List 3	List 4	List 5**
rise	gaze	easel	lazy	busy
wise	glaze	miser	hazel	basil
pose	craze	music	plaza	dismal
those	froze	pansy	blazon	cosmos
close	gauze	tansy	Brazil	muslin
chose	sneeze	flimsy	stanza	wisdom
prose	breeze	clumsy	frozen	plasma
noise	wheeze	poison	benzol	present
cause	squeeze	resort	benzene	pleasant
cheese	trapeze	result	gazelle	bismuth
abuse		chosen	bonanza	misery
amuse		mosaic	citizen	deposit
propose		roseate	damozel	miasma
dispose		reprisal	mazurka	abysmal
infuse		partisan	azalea	hesitate
		resolute	influenza	president
			trapezium	prismatic

List 6	List 7	List 8
minimize	organization	heroism
economize	nationalization	idealism
criticize	capitalization	criticism
galvanize	rationalization	galvanism
ostracize	Americanization	ostracism
barbarize	mobilization	barbarism
organize	authorization	organism
nationalize	generalization	nationalism
capitalize	crystallization	capitalism
rationalize		rationalism
Americanize		Americanism
mobilize		Darwinism
authorize		militarism
generalize		alcoholism
crystallize		Socialism

---

* The following words could be included in this list, but because each might be confused with its homonym, they must be used with care if at all: size–sighs; please–pleas; prize–pries; maze–maize; graze–grays; daze–days; freeze–frieze, frees.

** A few exceptions are noted: hazard, wizard, cozen, tweezers.

6. WAYS OF SPELLING \j\. Yellow card 23.

\j\ is spelled j as in <u>jam</u>, or g before <u>e</u>, <u>i</u>, or <u>y</u>, usually.

a. The student has learned that g followed by <u>e</u>, <u>i</u>, or <u>y</u> is usually pronounced \j\, and followed by <u>a</u>, <u>o</u>, <u>u</u>, <u>l</u>, or <u>r</u> is \g\, page 71. Therefore, he should know that if the \j\ in a word he wishes to spell is followed by one of the sounds of <u>a</u>, <u>o</u>, or <u>u</u>, he must use the letter j. In <u>pajama</u>, <u>banjo</u>, and <u>justice</u> no letter but j can be used for the sound \j\ (List 1). The combinations <u>jl</u> and <u>jr</u> do not occur in English.

Students must not assume, however, that the sound \j\ followed by <u>e</u>, <u>i</u>, or <u>y</u> will always be spelled g, since j is also used. It is true that the letter j is less frequent than g. In fact j is a letter little used in English. In *Merriam-Webster's Collegiate Dictionary*, tenth edition, there are forty-three pages given to initial g and only twelve to initial j. Of course this includes only the initial position and a large number of initial g's are hard, but it gives some idea of the relative frequency of the two letters, and it is true that there are more words beginning with \j\ spelled g than j.

b. There is no way for the student to make an intelligent choice as to which letter will be employed when the sound is initial in a word and followed by a sound of <u>e</u> or <u>i</u>. We find <u>jest</u>, <u>jelly</u>, <u>jitney</u> and <u>gentle</u>, <u>giant</u>, <u>gymnast</u>. (There are no words beginning <u>jy</u>, but several beginning <u>gy</u>.)

c. Initial in a syllable, other than the first, when the \j\ is followed by one of the sounds of <u>e</u> or <u>i</u>, the usual spelling is g, e.g., <u>re gent</u> and <u>en gine</u> (List 2).

In a small group of words, all derived from the Latin *jacere* (past part. *jectus*), to throw—<u>abject</u>, <u>eject</u>, etc.—we find the letter j representing the sound \j\ at the beginning of a syllable (List 3). The syllables <u>ger</u> and <u>gy</u> are sometimes pronounced \gr\ and \gē\, e.g., <u>anger</u> and <u>porgy</u>. However, j never represents the \g\ sound.

d. The common spellings for \j\ at the end of a word are <u>ge</u> and <u>dge</u> (Lists 4 and 5).

Comparison of Lists 4 and 5 reveals two dependable generalizations.

If there is a long vowel or a consonant sound before the \j\, the spelling is <u>ge</u>. In monosyllables, if a short vowel sound precedes the \j\, the spelling is <u>dge</u>. In words of more than one syllable, however, the spelling is uncertain and the dictionary must be consulted.

e. At the end of a syllable—followed in the next syllable by <u>e</u>, <u>i</u>, or <u>y</u>—the \j\ may be spelled g as in <u>frig id</u>, or dg as in <u>fidg et</u>. There seems no serviceable generalization to offer except that g alone is more common (Lists 6 and 7).

<u>Prej u dice</u>, <u>proj ect</u>, and <u>maj es ty</u> are in the *Collegiate Dictionary* as exceptional examples of j at the end of a syllable. There are also a few foreign words like this, mostly Asian, such as <u>Raj put</u>.

When the student has become familiar with the facts stated above under *a*, *b*, and *c*, the teacher should pronounce words beginning with \j\ followed by <u>a</u>, <u>o</u>, or u, chosen from Lists 1, 2, and 3. The student should be able to tell with assurance which spelling of the \j\ sound to use in each of these words and to state the reason for his choice without hesitation. In many instances he should be able to spell the entire word. When this is true, the exercise is doubly valuable, testing his knowledge of other phonograms as well.

A typical lesson might deal with the following words: jasper, majority, strategem, dejected, origin, prodigy, jumbo, margin.

Model Dialogue

Teacher: I am going to pronounce several words. You will hear the sound \j\ in each of them. When you have heard the word, you are to tell me what letter to use to spell the \j\ sound. Be sure to give the reason for your choice. If you can spell the whole word, do so. The first word is jasper.

Student: I'd use j because if I used g, the word would sound \'gas-pər\.

T: Right. Now take majority.

S: j again, because g followed by a, o, or u is always \g\. Oh, I can spell it: m-a j-o-r i-t y.

T: Digest.

S: g. Except in a very few words, the \j\ sound at the beginning of a syllable is followed by e, i, or y is spelled with a g: d-i g-e-s-t.

T: Dejected.

S: That is one of the few words where \j\ at the beginning of a syllable is spelled j. They all have jec or ject in them. D-e j-e-c-t e-d.

It would be very unusual for a student to give such complete answers as the imaginary ones quoted above, but it would be satisfactory if his replies gave some indication that he could apply what he had learned. It would not be necessary to finish the list of words selected for the lesson, but brief reviews at frequent intervals should be given.

A second type of lesson would include not only words for which the student should be sure of the spelling, but also some for which it cannot be predicted with certainty and for which he is able to state only the alternatives. For such a lesson the teacher selects from the dictionary words with initial \j\ followed by e, i, or y and others from Lists 4 to 7 inclusive. A typical list might be tinge, cogitate, projector, jolly, badger, gymnasium, privilege, jovial, cartridge.

It must not be forgotten that these are lessons solely on the spelling of \j\. Other parts of the words contain sounds not yet studied and the teacher must not demand such spellings. Failure to give the correct, or alternative, spelling of \j\ indicates need for further practice.

ILLUSTRATIVE \j\ WORDS

List 1	List 2	List 3	List 4	List 5	List 6	List 7
cajole	agent	object	stage	trudge	tragic	budget
Trojan	cogent	reject	page	fledge	frigid	badger
enjoy	congest	eject	urge	grudge	magic	cudgel
major	angel	inject	large	dodge	vigil	midget
adjutant	manger	subject	verge	badge	legend	fidget
perjury	margin	objection	fringe	pledge	regiment	gadget
adjacent	elegy	objective	range	judge	magistrate	lodger
marjoram	longitude	interject	strange	dredge	legislate	lodging
conjunctive	digestion	conjecture	tinge	lodge	regicide	edging
Elijah	diligence	dejected	flange	hedge	tragedy	pledging
Benjamin	divergent	dejection	gorge	sedge	vigilant	
injustice	prodigy	adjective	plunge	smudge	legible	
majolica	stratagem	projectile	singe	sledge	vegetable	
coadjutor	origin	projector	deluge	partridge	menagerie	
maharaja	fugitive		expunge	porridge	original	
majority	energetic		vestige	hodgepodge		
rejuvenate	eligible		indulge			
	emergency		infringe			
			salvage			
			advantage			

7. WAYS OF SPELLING \ks\. Yellow card 32.

\ks\ is spelled <u>x</u> as in <u>box</u>, and <u>ks</u> as in <u>banks</u>, <u>cks</u> as in <u>racks</u>, <u>cs</u> as <u>relics</u>, <u>chs</u> as in <u>monarchs</u>, vowel-<u>kes</u> as in <u>rakes</u>.

  a. The sound \ks\ is never initial.

  b. Nouns ending in the \k\ sound form their plurals by adding <u>s</u>, producing a final \ks\: ban<u>ks</u>, ra<u>cks</u>, reli<u>cs</u>, monar<u>chs</u>.

  Verbs ending in \k\ add an <u>s</u> in the third person singular: <u>think</u>, <u>thinks</u>.

  To young students who know little or nothing of grammar, one may say, "Some action words end in the \ks\ sound."

  In other cases, final \ks\ is spelled <u>x</u>, that is, in singular nouns, and in some verbs and adjectives: <u>fox</u>, <u>perplex</u>, <u>duplex</u> (List 1).

  c. Within a word \ks\ is most frequently spelled <u>x</u> (List 2).

  In some words \ks\ is produced by two <u>c</u>'s, the second followed by <u>e</u>, <u>i</u>, or <u>y</u>: <u>accent</u>, <u>accident</u>, <u>coccyx</u>; or by <u>c</u> followed by <u>s</u>: <u>tocsin</u> (List 3) (there is also a word spelled as one would expect, <u>toxin</u>, but with a different meaning).

The sound \gz\ is not sufficiently important or troublesome to warrant a yellow card and drill. It should be pointed out at a suitable time, however, that this sound heard in many common words is not spelled gz, but x as in exist. Care must be taken to avoid this or any of the other sounds of x while considering the \ks\ sound.

The nouns and verbs referred to in the first two paragraphs under *b* above are seldom misspelled. Since the \k\ is already present, the natural thing to do is to add the s. Once sure of this generalization, a student should not have trouble with the final \ks\ in other words. Words ending in ks and others ending in x should be dictated, with the student—as in all such exercises—telling the reason for the spelling he chooses.

The \ks\ within a word may give trouble. Perhaps the best help to offer the student is to have a copy of List 3 always ready for him to consult until he becomes familiar with such words. The list is fairly complete, except that it does not contain derivatives made by adding prefixes and suffixes.

ILLUSTRATIVE \ks\ WORDS

List 1	List 2	List 3
mix	next	tocsin
flax	text	coccyx
flex	pretext	vaccine
apex	sexton	accent
annex	mixture	accept
index	dexterous	access
prefix	expand	succeed
suffix	expend	success
relax	expect	succinct
convex	expense	accident
triplex	explode	occident
thorax	exploit	eccentric
prolix	external	occipital
pharynx	pixie	accelerate
	toxic	
	Texas	
	Saxon	
	maxim	
	waxen	
	vixen	
	flaxen	
	maximum	
	fixative	
	flexible	
	galaxy	
	peroxide	
	paroxysm	

8. WAYS OF SPELLING \d\ AND \t\.

\d\ is spelled <u>d</u> as in <u>dog</u> or <u>ed</u> as in <u>sailed</u>. Yellow card 21.
\t\ is spelled <u>t</u> as in <u>tot</u> or <u>ed</u> as in <u>jumped</u>. Yellow card 26.

Words selected miscellaneously from the following lists can be dictated. When the student hears \d\ or \t\ at the end of a word, he must decide whether the word is the past tense of a verb (or action word) that shows the action has already taken place. If, for example, when he hears \plād\ he can think \plā\ or when he hears \līkt\ he can think \līk\; then he will know that the \d\ or \t\ will be spelled <u>ed</u>: play<u>ed</u>, lik<u>ed</u>.

Otherwise, the \d\ or \t\ will be spelled simply <u>d</u> or <u>t</u>, as in <u>world</u>, <u>head</u>, <u>child</u>, <u>sand</u>, or <u>not</u>, <u>coat</u>, <u>print</u>, <u>cheat</u>.

ILLUSTRATIVE \d\ AND \t\ WORDS

<u>d</u>		<u>t</u>	
seemed	hand	slipped	first
raised	cloud	jumped	crust
bloomed	yard	placed	swift
lived	found	chased	plant
seized	crowd	fished	glint
grabbed	scold	lashed	grunt
pulled	goad	marched	twist
enjoyed	thread	reached	grant
returned	defend	remarked	tumult
opened	surround	talked	marmot
supposed	stipend	poked	combat
snowed	friend	waked	violet
closed	Cupid	looked	comment
happened	limpid	picked	resent
smelled	salad	soaked	forget

The student who has accepted the idea that \d\ and \t\ heard at the end of a past tense word are to be spelled -<u>ed</u> often needs definite introduction to the irregular past tense in which the vowel sound is changed from its form in the present tense. Following the pattern he may spell \slept\ <u>sleeped</u>. He must be shown that the past tense formed by -<u>ed</u> must contain the present with \d\ or \t\ added: \brusht\ <u>brushed</u>, \klēnd\ <u>cleaned</u>. <u>Sleeped</u> should be right, but it is not what we say. It sounds like "baby talk." There is no present <u>slep</u> and the irregular form is spelled phonetically <u>s-l-e-p-t</u>. Other examples are <u>keep</u>, <u>kept</u>; <u>creep</u>, <u>crept</u>; <u>sell</u>, <u>sold</u>; <u>behold</u>, <u>beheld</u>; <u>bind</u>, <u>bound</u>; <u>leave</u>, <u>left</u>.

The -<u>ed</u> added for the past tense to verbs ending in <u>d</u> or <u>t</u> is pronounced \əd\ which causes no trouble and does not concern us here, as in <u>landed</u>, <u>crowded</u>, <u>waited</u>, <u>wanted</u>, and so on.

9. WAYS OF SPELLING \sh\. Yellow cards 30 and 31.

\sh\ is spelled <u>sh</u> as in <u>ship</u>, <u>ch</u> as in <u>chute</u>, <u>ci</u> as in <u>physician</u>, <u>si</u> as in <u>mission</u>, <u>ti</u> as in <u>station</u>.

a. Students in the lower grades seldom encounter the <u>ch</u> spelling of \sh\, whereas the <u>sh</u> spelling occurs in many familiar words (lists below).

b. The phonograms <u>ci</u>, <u>si</u>, <u>ti</u> for the spelling of \sh\ occur in many words used by older students. These spellings are usually in the final syllable: fero <u>ci</u>ous, controver <u>si</u>al, ingra <u>ti</u> ate.

In a very few scientific terms the spelling <u>ce</u> is found. Only students of zoology and botany are likely to need words like crusta <u>ce</u>an.

c. In a few words \sh\ is spelled <u>s</u> or <u>ss</u>: <u>s</u>ure, <u>s</u>ugar, i<u>ss</u>ue, ti<u>ss</u>ue, fi<u>ss</u>ure, pre<u>ss</u>ure, in<u>s</u>ure, a<u>ss</u>ure.

<u>sh</u> *or* **<u>ch</u> Spellings.** It will probably be enough to emphasize the character of the words in which <u>sh</u> spells \sh\ and the words in which <u>ch</u> is to be expected. (The latter are words from the French and are less common.) Two lists, headed respectively <u>sh</u> and <u>ch</u>, help to make the distinction. They should be added to at intervals and referred to when the wrong phonogram is used in written exercises. Teachers may start such lists when students are too young to be expected to spell the unfamiliar French derivatives, but the lists should only tell which spelling to use for \sh\; the teacher should write the word and keep the list on file with others for reference.

ILLUSTRATIVE \sh\ WORDS

<u>sh</u>			<u>ch</u>	
thrush	tarnish	demolish	cache	machine
thresh	skirmish	establish	chute	mustache
thrash	polish	diminish	chamois	ruching
trash	cherish	extinguish	chenille	fichu
swish	banish	distinguish	chateau	sachet
mesh	finish	bashful	chambray	brochure
squash	vanquish	bishop	champagne	cachalot
selfish	mackintosh	cashmere	chiffon	seneschal
foolish	succotash	beshrew	chiffonier	parachute
childish	calabash	cashew	chandelier	pistachio
wolfish	abolish	dishevel	chivalry	nonchalant

<u>ci</u>, <u>si</u>, *or* <u>ti</u> Spellings. When a student attempts to spell a new word in which she hears \sh\, she will naturally use <u>sh</u> to spell this sound as she has in the words with which she is familiar—she will spell <u>glacial</u>, gla<u>sh</u>al; <u>Venetian</u>, Vene<u>sh</u>an.

To spell such words correctly, it is necessary to know that \sh\ is frequently represented by <u>ci</u>, <u>si</u>, or <u>ti</u>. This is true of the suffixes -<u>sion</u>, -<u>tion</u>, and -<u>cian</u>, which have been recognized and read in such words as <u>station</u> \shən\, <u>mission</u> \shən\, and <u>technician</u> \shən\. Other syllables in which the <u>ci</u>, <u>si</u>, <u>ti</u> spellings occur should be discussed and words containing them spelled, e.g., <u>gracious</u>, <u>martial</u>.

Having accepted these new spellings for \sh\, the unsure speller will have difficulty in deciding which one of the new phonograms to use in spelling the syllables \shəl\, \shən\, or \shəs\.

Except in the suffix -<u>sion</u>, <u>si</u> occurs very seldom. The only words that most students will need are <u>controversial</u> and <u>transient</u>, and these should be added to the list of "learned words."

<u>ti</u> occurs somewhat more frequently than <u>ci</u>. In deciding which spelling to use, it is helpful to associate the word to be spelled with a word related in meaning.

A few adjectives ending in <u>cial</u> are related to nouns ending in <u>ce</u>, such as ra cial.

A knowledge of Latin often helps. Students who have not studied Latin may find useful associations by looking up the derivations of words. For example, the student knows that <u>Venetian</u> has some connection with the city of Venice. It might reasonably end in <u>cian</u>, but if he knows that <u>Venice</u> is the Anglicized form of <u>Venezia</u> (the <u>z</u> having a <u>ts</u> sound), the Italian name, then the <u>t</u> in <u>tian</u> is more easily remembered.

Similarly, a number of words ending in <u>tial</u> would be expected to end in <u>cial</u> because words ending in <u>ce</u> often do. However, <u>space</u> becomes <u>spatial</u>, and <u>palace</u> becomes <u>palatial</u>. Finding the derivations shows that <u>space</u> and <u>palace</u> reach us from the French forms of the words, and <u>spatial</u> and <u>palatial</u> directly from the Latin roots.

The syllable \shənt\, with \ə\ sounded as in the first and third syllables of <u>banana</u>, occurs in comparatively few words. Most of those ending in <u>cient</u> are medical terms. The average person needs three: <u>ancient</u>, <u>efficient</u>, <u>deficient</u>.

Two words ending in <u>tient</u> will be commonly needed: <u>patient</u> and <u>quotient</u>.

The syllable \shəs\ may prove troublesome because the sound \ə\ is represented by <u>ou</u>, as in <u>tious</u> and <u>cious</u>. This spelling in the suffix -<u>ous</u> is discussed on page 214.

Teacher and student should be on the lookout for a helpful cue when any of these words proves difficult. If they cannot discover one, the student must consult the dictionary when he needs to use a word and cannot recall the correct spelling.

ILLUSTRATIVE \shəl\, \shən\, \shənt\, \shəs\ WORDS

martial	tertian	spacious	satiate
tertial	Venetian	gracious	negotiate
nuptial	Lilliputian	specious	ingratiate
spatial		ferocious	tertiary
palatial	ancient	astrocious	minutia
equinoctial	patient	tenacious	
	quotient	pugnacious	nuncio
racial			glaciate
social	fractious		associate
glacial	cautious		appreciate
commercial	facetious		
	vexatious		

<u>tion</u> and <u>sion</u> Spellings, pronounced \shən\. Yellow cards 30 and 31.

<u>sion</u> and <u>tion</u> are considered here as suffixes and as units, even though in the dictionary they are divided into their component sounds \sh\ and \ən\, as in <u>station</u> and <u>compulsion</u>.

Probably with no other group of words does a knowledge of Latin give more assistance in spelling than with those ending in \shən\. The suffix <u>-ion</u> is added to the past participial stem of a Latin verb to form an English noun. A Latin student familiar with the conjugations of verbs recognizes at once the participial stem and then knows whether the English stem will end in <u>-tion</u> or <u>-sion</u>. He also understands why related English verbs and nouns are sometimes similar (<u>educate</u> and <u>education</u>) and sometimes very different (<u>admit</u> and <u>admission</u>). But many students no longer study Latin as a foreign language, and remedial students may be even less likely to. We must give them as much generalized help as we can, based on Latin, but expressed very simply and without many grammatical terms. To students who know some English grammar, the information might be given more or less as follows:

- Most nouns ending in the suffix \-shən\ spelled <u>-tion</u> or <u>-sion</u> are closely related to verbs, since the noun and verb derive from the same Latin verb. This is obvious in pairs such as <u>collect</u>, <u>collection</u>; <u>situate</u>, <u>situation</u>; <u>ascend</u>, <u>ascension</u>.
- In other cases the verb and noun are so dissimilar in form, though related in meaning, that someone who knows no Latin might not detect the relationship, as with <u>compel</u>, <u>compulsion</u>. Such peculiar situations are more understandable when we find that the verb and noun are derived from different parts of the Latin verb, which are sometimes surprisingly unlike, just as in English <u>am</u>, <u>is</u>, <u>was</u>, <u>been</u> are unlike. The English verb <u>compel</u> comes from the present infinitive, *compellere*, and the noun <u>compulsion</u> from *compulsum*, the past participle of the same Latin verb.

A student should be told that there are many words which we can think of in pairs because they have somewhat the same meaning, such as <u>collect</u>, <u>collection</u>. <u>Collect</u> means "to gather together." <u>Collection</u> means "the things that are gathered." Peter is going to <u>collect</u> shells. All the shells that he gets will be his <u>collection</u>. <u>Locate</u> means "to establish or find something in a certain place." <u>Location</u> is "the place where something is."

It is worthwhile to teach the terms <u>noun</u> and <u>verb</u>, if these are not already known, in order to avoid the clumsy, time-consuming circumlocutions "naming words" and "action words." Then the student can be told that words ending in \-shən\ are nouns, and that it will help him to spell such words if he can think of a verb related to each. The ending of the verb will often enable him to decide whether to use <u>-tion</u> or <u>-sion</u> in spelling the noun.

Teacher: There is a noun, <u>invention</u>; do you know a companion verb?

Student: Yes, <u>invent</u>.

The teacher can continue this exercise with other easily recognizable pairs: <u>objection</u>, <u>object</u>; <u>education</u>, <u>educate</u>.

Later the student must search his mind for the verb when the relationship is less obvious: <u>pretension</u>, <u>pretend</u>; <u>expansion</u>, <u>expand</u>.

He should then be shown the parts of the Latin verbs from which the English verbs derive, not that he should be expected to remember them, but so he may understand why the form of the word changes before the suffix.

He can also have his attention called to nouns with companion verbs ending in -<u>fy</u>. The Latin suffix -*ficare*, "to make," was used in Latin compounds and when taken over from the French became -<u>fy</u>, e.g., <u>simplify</u>, (*simplex* + -*ficare* = to make simple). When these verbs are altered into English nouns, the <u>c</u> returns and we have <u>simplification</u> and <u>glorification</u> (see page 205).

The older student with no Latin can be told that when he can think of a verb ending in -<u>fy</u>, the noun will usually end in -<u>cation</u>: <u>gratify</u>, <u>gratification</u>. Similarly, verbs ending in -<u>ize</u> often have companion nouns and these regularly end in -<u>ation</u>: <u>naturalize</u>, <u>naturalization</u> (see page 195, List 7).

Sometimes there is no corresponding English verb. These nouns most often end in <u>tion</u>. They are usually derived from the stem of the Latin noun, as in <u>nation</u> (L. *natio, nationis*), and <u>ration</u> (L. *ratio, rationis*). In these words -<u>tion</u> is not a suffix.

After close observation and comparison of many -<u>tion</u> and -<u>sion</u> words, the following generalizations will emerge:

a. For many nouns ending in \-shən\, the suffix is spelled -<u>tion</u>, frequently preceded by <u>a</u>, and occasionally by <u>e</u>, <u>o</u>, or <u>u</u>.

Most of these are related to English verbs ending in <u>te</u> or <u>t</u>, as in the list that follows.

Other nouns ending in -<u>tion</u> are so dissimilar to their companion verbs that their relationship is not easily detected. They should cause no trouble, however, because the verb endings are not those designated under *b* as forming nouns in -<u>sion</u> (List 2).

List 3 contains a few examples of the many -<u>fy</u> and -<u>ize</u> verbs with companion nouns in -<u>ication</u> and -<u>ization</u>, and also contains a few nouns with no corresponding English verbs.

b. In a smaller number of words the \shən\ ending is spelled -<u>sion</u>: Nouns related to verbs ending in <u>pel</u>, <u>ge</u>, <u>vert</u>, and <u>d</u> end in -<u>sion</u>, with one <u>s</u> because there is only one in the participial form of the Latin verb (List 4).

NOUNS ENDING IN -<u>tion</u>

List 1: Companion Verb Similar

Verb Ending in <u>te</u>		Verb Ending in <u>t</u>	
operation	completion	distraction	exemption
education	devotion	construction	exhaustion
execution	promotion	corruption	affection
relation	translation	direction	objection
regulation	gyration	suggestion	affliction
substitution	illustration	distortion	infection
contribution	hesitation	detraction	connection
institution	arbitration	invention	election
distribution	congratulation	desertion	
investigation	communication		
gesticulation	cooperation		
deliberation	administration		

Verb with Other Endings and -<u>ation</u> Added

taxation - - - - - - - - tax		conversation - - - - - converse	
accusation - - - - - - accuse		conservation - - - - - - conserve	
admiration- - - - - - admire		dispensation - - - - - - dispense	
foundation- - - - - - found		examination - - - - - - examine	
condemnation - - - condemn		recommendation- - - recommend	
temptation- - - - - - tempt			

List 2: Companion Verb Very Dissimilar

suction- - - - - - - - suck		junction - - - - - - - - - join	
absorption - - - - - - absorb		destruction - - - - - - - destroy	
detention - - - - - - - detain		consumption- - - - - - consume	
description - - - - - describe		reduction- - - - - - - - - - reduce	
reception - - - - - - - receive		abstention - - - - - - - - abstain	
redemption- - - - - - redeem		revolution - - - - - - - - revolve	
solution - - - - - - - - solve		explanation- - - - - - - explain	

List 3

Companion Verb Ending in -<u>fy</u>		Companion Verb Ending in -<u>ize</u>	
notification	simplification	equalization	mobilization
glorification	ratification	crystallization	dramatization
modification	beautification	fertilization	hospitalization
purification	deification	authorization	Americanization
justification	verification	standardization	industrialization

No Companion Verb

nation ration lotion motion notion
station traction caution fraction friction emotion

NOUNS ENDING IN -sion

List 4: Companion Verb Ending in:

pel	ge	vert*
[L. *pellere, pulsum*]	[L. *mergere, mersum*]	[L. *vertere, versum*]
compulsion	emersion	aversion
expulsion	immersion	conversion
impulsion	submersion*	diversion
propulsion		inversion
repulsion		reversion
		subversion

	d	
[L. -*scendere, -scensum*]	[L. *prehendere, prehensum*]	[L. *tendere, tensum*]
ascension	apprehension	tension
condescension	comprehension	extension
	reprehension	pretension

[L. *pendere, pensum*]	[L. *pandere, pansum*]
suspension	expansion

There should be no attempt to have any student master all these facts, but even young students may be given considerable assurance about the spelling of most of the \shən\ words that they will need to use by observing the following points:

- If they can think of a companion verb ending in <u>te</u> or <u>t</u>, they should have no trouble.
- If the verb is very different as in List 2, e.g., <u>destruction</u>–<u>destroy</u>, they must think whether it has any of the endings included in List 4 and 5, which form their companion nouns with -<u>sion</u>. If not the ending will be -<u>tion</u>.
- If there is no companion verb the spelling is probably -<u>tion</u>, as in <u>nation</u>.
- In a very few words the sound \-shən\ is spelled -<u>cion</u>, e.g., <u>coercion</u>, <u>suspicion</u>.

---

* Although the preferred pronunciation of these words is now \zhən\, they are included here because they are still sometimes pronounced \shən\.

It is not expected that any student should attempt to memorize all the verb endings given above, and the spelling of the nouns must be gradually learned by repeated reference to the dictionary. The memory load must not be made too heavy.

NOUNS ENDING IN -<u>sion</u> PRECEDED BY <u>es</u>, <u>is</u>, OR <u>us</u>

Companion Verb Ending in <u>ss</u>

[L. *premere, pressum*]

compression
depression
expression
impression
oppression
repression
suppression

[L. *gradi, gressum*]

digression
progression
transgression
retrogression

[L. *discutere, discussum*]

discussion
percussion

[L. *fateri, fessum*]

confession
profession

[L. *possidere, possessum*]

possession
dispossession
prepossession

Companion Verb Ending in <u>cede</u> and <u>ceed</u>

[L. *cedere, cessum*]

accession   secession
concession   intercession
precession   procession
recession   succession

Companion Verb Ending in <u>mit</u>

[L. *mittere, missum*]

admission   remission
commission   submission
omission   transmission
permission

The spelling of nouns ending in -<u>ssion</u> is easy if the student can remember the corresponding verb. No one would suggest changing the second <u>s</u> to a <u>t</u> in such words as <u>compress</u> and <u>confess</u>. The group of nouns with companion verbs ending in a syllable pronounced \sed\ and those ending in \mit\ are both short. Those in each group are so closely related in meaning that many students will be able to remember them.

Spelling of \zhən\. \zhən\ spelled -<u>sion</u> as in television. Yellow card 33.
This sound deserves consideration entirely distinct from \shən\. It cannot be given a numbered place in this chapter on parallel spellings and generalizations, however, because once recognized it presents no ambiguity. The sound \zhən\ is spelled only -<u>sion</u>. The following words can be used to direct attention to this fact:

ILLUSTRATIVE \zhən\ WORDS

conclusion	evasion	abrasion	elision
exclusion	invasion	dissuasion	derision
inclusion	pervasion	fusion	decision
occlusion	persuasion	confusion	division
preclusion	allusion	infusion	provision
seclusion	collusion	suffusion	revision
intrusion	corrosion	transfusion	precision
obtrusion	erosion	profusion	
protrusion	explosion	contusion	

For some words, the pronunciations \shən\ and \zhən\ are both allowed, but this need cause no trouble. If aversion or reversion is heard with the sound \shən\ it is spelled -sion rather than -tion (see page 206, List 4). If words are heard ending in the unambiguous sound \zhən\ the endings are spelled -sion.

10. WAYS OF SPELLING \e\. Yellow card 4.

\e\ is spelled e as in eddy and ea as in bread.

Most of the words in which \e\ is spelled ea are Anglo-Saxon derivatives—short, common words having to do with everyday life. However, there are more words just as short and just as common in which \e\ is represented by e, so this bit of word history does not help with spelling monosyllables and dissyllables. It simply explains the presence of the seemingly unnecessary phonogram in our language.

One fact stands out clearly—we do not expect to find \e\ spelled ea in polysyllables.

As for the short words, no generalizations come to our aid. Since most of these words will be needed by very young students, we must devise ways of mastering them either as separate words or in groups. A sentence containing several of these ea spellings often serves to impress them on the memory: *His head felt as heavy as lead.* Similarly feather, heather, leather, weather might be worked into a sentence, with the student himself originating it if possible.

The following list of words in which \e\ is spelled ea is fairly complete:

ILLUSTRATIVE \e\ WORDS

dead	dread	deaf	breadth	breast	meadow
head	spread	dealt	health	heavy	treadle
lead	stead	sweat	wealth	ready	heaven
read	tread	death	realm	steady	pleasant
bread	thread	breath	meant	weapon	measure

11. WAYS OF SPELLING \i\. Yellow card 6.

\i\ is spelled i as in <u>itchy</u>, y as in <u>gym</u>.

a. Initial \i\ is spelled <u>i</u> in all but three or four words, and most of these are of foreign origin, like <u>Yggdrasil</u>, a huge tree in Norse mythology.

b. Final \i\ is spelled <u>i</u> in a very few words, most of which are not in common use. The student should be shown the list of such words so he will realize how unusual they are (see Appendix 14).

c. The \i\ sound—initial, final, or medial—in a syllable is spelled <u>i</u> in some words and <u>y</u> in others (List 1), but in the case of initial and final syllables note *a* and *b* above.

Knowing that syllables in which <u>y</u> is medial are usually in words of Greek derivation may sometimes guide the student to the correct choice. He should be reminded of what he was told when considering the <u>ph</u> spelling for \f\, namely that many scientific words and terms used in connection with discoveries and inventions are Greek derivatives. However, he will find that <u>y</u> frequently is used in one syllable of such a word and <u>i</u> in another syllable. <u>Glycerol</u>, obviously a scientific term, should not present any difficulty, but <u>symbolic</u> would. Should it be simbolyc, symbolic, simbolic, or symbolyc? If the student has a confused visual memory of the word, he must consult the dictionary. List 1 furnishes considerable material for practice in attempting the spelling of \i\ in various locations.

d. A knowledge of certain prefixes and suffixes will help to solve some of the problems presented by the \i\ sound. A few such prefixes include <u>dis</u>- and sometimes <u>di</u>-. In these cases \i\ is pronounced \dī\ or \də\, with \ə\ sounded as in the first and third syllables of <u>banana</u>. <u>Dis</u>- and <u>di</u>- can mean "apart, away from," as in <u>dismiss</u> and <u>divest</u>; and "the reverse of, not," as in <u>disconnect</u>– <u>dishonest</u>.

The Greek prefix <u>dys</u>- is used in medical and other scientific terms, such as <u>dyspepsia</u>, <u>dysentery</u>, but need concern the student very little. <u>Mis</u>- can mean "amiss, wrong, wrongly," as in <u>mislead</u>; or "bad," as in <u>misconduct</u>. In the half dozen words beginning with <u>mys</u>, the syllable is clearly not a prefix: <u>mysterious</u>, <u>mystery</u>, <u>mystic</u>, <u>mystical</u>, <u>mysticism</u>, <u>mystify</u>. The suffix -<u>ish</u> is also very common (List 2). There is no suffix <u>ysh</u>.

On page 48 the fact that vowels are long in the vowel-consonant-<u>e</u> combination was introduced; on page 119 certain exceptions to this rule were mentioned, and it was stated that <u>i</u> is the vowel most apt to present exceptions. It is frequently used when the sound is \i\. This should again be called to the student's attention (see Appendix 15).

The final syllable \iv\, whether suffix or not, is spelled <u>ive</u>. Final \id\, \ib\, \im\ are spelled <u>id</u>, <u>ib</u>, <u>im</u>. But final \il\, \in\, \is\, \it\ may be spelled <u>il</u>, <u>in</u>, <u>is</u>, <u>it</u> or <u>ile</u>, <u>ine</u>, <u>ise</u>, <u>ice</u>, <u>ite</u>. The student conditioned to be alert for the <u>i-e</u> possibility will at once think to consult the dictionary for a word with these final sounds if she does not know the word at hand. Words of this kind should be included sometimes in miscellaneous spelling exercises (see Appendix 15).

The need for the \i\ spellings covers a range of ages. The general treatment is suggested here. Specific exercises suitable for a particular student can be organized by the teacher.

ILLUSTRATIVE \i\ WORDS

List 1	List 2
terrific	elfish
onyx	impish
pharynx	boyish
brigade	girlish
mythology	mannish
film	British
dish	Turkish
ridge	Swedish
picnic	selfish
pickle	foolish
hither	greenish
simple	feverish
pillow	
cinder	
napkin	
commit	
predict	
distinct	
daffodil	
manuscript	
myth	
crypt	
cygnet	
system	
hyssop	
pyramid	
symphony	
sycamore	
cyclamen	
amaryllis	
chlorophyll	
oxygen	

12. WAYS OF SPELLING SCHWA \ə\. YELLOW CARD 34.

Spellings

a. u as in <u>bun</u>; <u>o</u> as in <u>cover</u>. Never before <u>r</u>. (See List 1.)

b. <u>u</u> as in <u>curl</u>; <u>e</u> as in <u>fern</u>; <u>i</u> as in <u>stir</u>. Always before <u>r</u>. (See pages 222–223.)

c. <u>a</u> as in <u>banana</u> (first and third syllables); <u>e</u> as in <u>ticket</u>; <u>i</u> as in <u>peril</u>; <u>o</u> as in <u>carrot</u>; <u>u</u> as in <u>sulphur</u>. (See List 2.)

The name of this symbol is schwa, an unstressed mid-central vowel. Although not a letter seen in written or printed English, it appears frequently as a pronunciation symbol in the dictionary. Schwa has three different sounds, all of them vowel sounds. Two of these sounds occur only in stressed syllables; (*a* and *b* above); the third sound occurs only in unstressed syllables (*c* above). The illustrative words indicate the pronunciations. Note that \ə\ in unstressed syllables may be spelled by any one of the five vowels, but is always sounded in the same way. When sounded this way, \ə\ may appear in initial, medial, or final syllables, providing they are unstressed.

For guidance in spelling choices when \ə\ is sounded as in <u>cut</u> and <u>cover</u>, see the following discussion of "Scribal <u>o</u>." For guidance when \ə\ is sounded as in <u>curl</u>, <u>fern</u>, and <u>stir</u>, see Ways of Spelling \ər\, page 219.

When \ə\ is sounded in unstressed syllables, and any one of five letters may represent it, there are fewer reliable indications of the correct spelling choice. In general, it may be said that the spelling of \ə\ in this situation is influenced by adjoining consonants, if \ə\ and the adjoining letters form a familiar syllable, or part of a syllable. See Ways of Spelling \əs\, page 213; \ər\, page 219; \sh\, page 201; \d\ and \t\, page 200. Increasing acquaintance with common prefixes and suffixes, especially the latter, and with Latin roots is of further help. Knowledge of allied words, such as <u>prepare</u>, <u>preparation</u>, is also clearly of service.

Scribal <u>o</u>

Spelling in the Middle Ages was phonetic. All books were written by scribes who copied every page by hand. Letters hastily written were likely to be poorly formed and so misread, just as they are today. Certain combinations were especially liable to this danger, as they still are. For example, think of the word <u>summer</u>. Written hastily such a word becomes just a series of humps. So when <u>u</u> came next to <u>m</u>, <u>n</u>, <u>r</u>, <u>u</u> scribes in many places fell into the habit of writing the <u>u</u> as <u>o</u> to avoid trouble.

The original \ə\ when sounded as in <u>bus</u> is clearly retained in some words, as in <u>son</u> from Anglo-Saxon *sunnu*, Middle English* *sone* or *sune*. In Modern English it is always written <u>o</u>, but is still pronounced \ə\. We have already learned that <u>y</u> is another form of <u>u</u>. There was an Anglo-Saxon word *cymlich*,

---

*Middle English was spoken from about 1100–1500; Modern English from about 1500 on.

which in Middle English became sometimes *cumlich* and at other times *comlich*. Today we have this word spelled <u>comely</u> and pronounced \\'kəm-lē\. Sometimes we cannot trace the original <u>u</u> because when first written by scribes in France or Ireland it was spelled with <u>o</u>. This <u>o</u> substituted for <u>u</u> is sometimes called "scribal <u>o</u>." *The Oxford English Dictionary* states that it was a change due to writing, not to phonetic development. Not only was the change in spelling not consistent, but the pronunciation of the words in which <u>o</u> had been substituted for <u>u</u> was not always regular.

The "scribal <u>o</u>" does not explain situations where the adjacent letter is not <u>m</u>, <u>n</u>, <u>r</u>, or <u>u</u>.

There are a few generalizations which may be of real service:

a. Initial \ə\ is spelled <u>u</u> with very rare exceptions, a few being <u>onion</u>, <u>other</u>, <u>oven</u>.

b. When the sound \ə\ occurs at the end of a word, it is not spelled <u>u</u> because in that position <u>u</u> is always pronounced \ü\ or \yü\ (see Appendix 14). Final \ə\ is always unaccented and is spelled <u>a</u>, as in <u>drama</u> and <u>hyena</u>.

c. Medial in initial syllables \ə\ is almost always spelled <u>u</u>, e.g., <u>cumber</u> and <u>sullen</u>. Some exceptions are: <u>covenant</u>, <u>cover</u>, <u>covey</u>, <u>smother</u>, <u>sloven</u>, <u>monkey</u>, <u>frontier</u>, <u>shovel</u>, <u>somersault</u>. Others are: <u>brother</u>, <u>done</u>, <u>glove</u>, <u>Monday</u>, <u>month</u>, <u>mother</u>, <u>other</u>.

d. In a final syllable the \ə\ sound is more likely to be represented by <u>o</u> than by <u>u</u>, especially in \ən\ which is regularly spelled <u>on</u>.
There are two definite exceptions to this. Final \əm\ is much more frequently spelled <u>um</u> than <u>om</u> and final \əs\ in nouns is regularly spelled <u>us</u> (see page 213).

Most of the <u>um</u> words are Latin, taken into English without change (List 3), or are classed as New Latin. This term should be discussed, as it will serve to create further interest in the growth of the language: *New Latin*, Latin as used since the end of the medieval period especially in scientific description and classification.* (List 4.)

The much shorter list of words in which final \əm\ is spelled <u>om</u> contains perhaps more words that younger students may use. The suffix -<u>dom</u> accounts for a number of these words, e.g., <u>kingdom</u>, <u>officialdom</u> (List 5).

---

* Reprinted by permission of Merriam-Webster, Inc.

ILLUSTRATIVE \ə\ WORDS

List 1	List 2	List 3 *Latin*	List 4 *New Latin*	List 5
muss	allow	magnum	capsicum	atom
runner	Alaskan	cerebrum	lithium	bottom
thunder	diagram	cerebellum	holinium	custom
reluctantly	catacomb	solarium	thulium	seldom
injunction	opera	maximum	sodium	ransom
rebuttal	resistant	medium	radium	random
begun	eleven	minimum	ascidium	fathom
engulf	effusive	museum	planetarium	transom
percuss	parentage	premium	sanitarium	symptom
	delegation	vacuum		dukedom
	honest	asylum		earldom
	silence	Colosseum		wisdom
	capital	arboretum		freedom
	testify	desideratum		martyrdom
	commit			Christendom
	pollute			arson
	reciprocate			cotton
	introduce			crimson
	until			season
	succeed			pardon
	prejudice			mutton
	resume			mason
				glutton
				poison
				emblazon
				horizon
				wagon

13. WAYS OF SPELLING \əs\.

\əs\ is spelled -<u>us</u> as in <u>circus</u> and -<u>ous</u> as in <u>dangerous</u>.

Since the sound \ə\ spelled <u>ou</u> is very rare except in the suffix -<u>ous</u>, we did not include this phonogram among the drill cards. However, the student will eventually encounter \əs\ as a final syllable in the spelling of certain nouns and adjectives. The following facts should be available at that time:

a. Almost all words ending in -<u>us</u> are nouns (List 1).

b. Words ending in -<u>ous</u> are adjectives.

The suffix may be added directly to a noun (List 2).

If the noun ends in e (fame), the e will be dropped before the suffix (famous). (Spelling Pattern 4, pages 140–141.)

If the noun ends in y, the y will usually be changed to i before the suffix: victory, victorious. (Spelling Pattern 15, pages 159–160.)

The noun and adjective may be quite different: fable, fabulous. (List 3.)

    c.   Some adjectives end in -eous, -ious, -uous. (Lists 4, 5, 6.)

With few exceptions the words ending in -us are Latin nouns taken into English with little or no change. Some exceptions are the adjectives minus, bogus, emeritus, and citrus (also spelled citrous, however), and the preposition versus. Minus and versus are needed by all but very young students.

A few adjectives are made by adding the suffix -ous to a verb, such as blasphemous, ponderous, prosperous. In some cases there is no companion noun or verb, but it seems unnecessary to complicate the situation for students by introducing this exception to *b* above.

In the case of some nouns ending in y, Spelling Pattern 15 is not applicable. The y is eliminated and the suffix -eous is added. It is necessary to be careful when attempting to spell adjectives when the companion noun ends in y, as in pity, piteous (List 4, last six words).

In some instances where the noun and the adjective stem preceding -ous differ entirely in spelling, e.g., number, numerous, the adjective is formed directly from the original Latin. The English noun, derived from the same Latin root, comes from the French. This is not given as a spelling aid, but as an interesting fact in language development.

If a student's auditory discrimination is not well developed, he may have to seek aid from the teacher or the dictionary when attempting to spell a word ending in -eous, -ious, or -uous. In some cases the e or i is silent, its function being to preserve the soft sound of g, as in courageous, religious (see page 144). The suffix -ious is often used to form adjectives from nouns ending in -ion: caution, cautious (List 5, last eight words).

Such words as ambitious may prove difficult (see page 202).

Drills should consist of listing words under the headings -us and -ous. To do this the student must know whether the word is a noun or an adjective. It is a good idea to use the word in a sentence, or have the student do so if he or she can.

Teacher: The word is famous. Can you put it into a sentence?

Student: Yes, Lincoln was a famous man.

T: Is it a noun or an adjective?

S: It is an adjective. It describes Lincoln.

T: Then which column will you put it in?

S: In the -ous column.

ILLUSTRATIVE \əs\ WORDS

List 1

crocus
fungus
lotus
humus
sinus
typhus
census
focus
Janus
Remus
Romulus
Arcturus
Tantalus
Oceanus
Olympus
hibiscus
papyrus
octopus
nautilus
detritus
exodus
terminus
omnibus
radius
colossus
hippopotamus

List 2

joyous
dangerous
perilous
humorous
marvelous
thunderous
mountain-
ous
ruinous
hazardous
odorous
traitorous
vaporous
libelous
clamorous
villainous
circuitous

List 3

luster- - - - - - lustrous
tremor- - - - tremulous
monster- - - monstrous
wonder- - - wondrous
fiber - - - - - fibrous
fable- - - - - fabulous
miracle- - - miraculous
mischief - - mischievous
nebula- - - - nebulous
pest- - - - - - pestiferous
omen- - - - - ominous
chivalry- - - chivalrous

List 4

hideous
extraneous
igneous
aqueous
gaseous
erroneous
spontaneous
simultaneous
contemporaneous

duteous
piteous
plenteous
bounteous
miscellaneous
beauteous
courteous

List 5

previous
curious
odious
illustrious
laborious
imperious
fastidious
hilarious

cautious
infectious
contagious
contentious
ambitious
nutritious
suspicious
superstitious

List 6

conspicuous
continuous
impetuous
tempestuous
tumultuous
virtuous
deciduous
incongruous

14. WAYS OF SPELLING \aủ\. Yellow card 14.

\aủ\ is spelled <u>ou</u> as in <u>ouch</u> and <u>ow</u> as in <u>cow</u>.

There appears to be only one dependable usage concerning <u>ou</u> and <u>ow</u>, which is that the sound \aủ\ at the end of a word or syllable is spelled <u>ow</u>. When this sound is encountered in other locations the teacher or the dictionary must be consulted.

Some of these words will be needed so frequently even by young students that they should be memorized if possible.

ILLUSTRATIVE \aủ\ WORDS

<u>ou</u>			<u>ow</u>		
trout	our	loud	how	trowel	gowan
about	scour	proud	plow	powder	clownish
bound	mouse	blouse	brown	allow	rowdy
found	house	county	drown	powwow	prowess
abound	ounce	countess	growl	dower	cowslip
surround	flounce	thousand	crowd	flower	howitzer
pouch	mouth	scoundrel	drowse	drowsy	dowager
vouch	south	catamount	towel	blowsy	endowment

The phonogram <u>ough</u> is another spelling of \aủ\, but is so infrequent that it was not placed on a drill card. Examples are <u>slough</u>, <u>sough</u>, <u>plough</u> (also spelled <u>plow</u>).

15. WAYS OF SPELLING \ȯi\. Yellow card 13.

\ȯi\ is spelled <u>oi</u> as in <u>boil</u> and <u>oy</u> as in <u>toy</u>.

a. Initial \ȯi\ is found in only a very few words and compounds. The greater number follow in <u>oil</u>, <u>oily</u>, <u>ointment</u>, <u>oyster</u>, and some compounds— <u>oilcake</u>, <u>oysterplant</u>, <u>oilskin</u>, <u>oilcloth</u>.

b. Final \ȯi\ is spelled <u>oy</u>, e.g., <u>boy</u>.

c. Within a word <u>oi</u> is much more common than <u>oy</u>.

The <u>oy</u> spelling other than final is found in some dissyllables and polysyllables, as in <u>boycott</u> and <u>loyal</u>. In monosyllables <u>oi</u> is almost universal, as in <u>toil</u>. Exceptions are the Swedish derivative <u>sloyd</u>, and some proper nouns like <u>Boyle</u>, <u>Lloyd</u>. Students must use the dictionary!

ILLUSTRATIVE \ȯi\ WORDS

oi			**oy**		
coil	quoin	exploit	coy	annoy	voyage
toil	void	thyroid	joy	alloy	loyal
moil	joist	moisture	soy	employ	royal
spoil	hoist	adenoid	cloy	deploy	boycott
join	devoid	celluloid	Troy	destroy	arroyo
joint	anoint	maladroit	enjoy	viceroy	gargoyle
point	rejoice	embroider	decoy	corduroy	flamboyant
quoit	coinage	boisterous	Savoy		clairvoyant
	poison	poinsettia			

16. WAYS OF SPELLING \u̇\. Yellow card 12.

\u̇\ is spelled oo as in book in so many common words that we thought it the only spelling necessary for the drill card. However, other phonograms are used, sometimes also in very common words, e.g., ou in could, would, and should, which are usually learned as a group; u as in full, pull; u in the suffix -ful and o as in wolf.

A few lists follow which can be used for reference. No generalizations are apparent regarding choice among the phonograms, except that o and ou are extremely rare.

ILLUSTRATIVE \u̇\ WORDS

oo	**ou**	**u**	**o**
book	could	full	wolf
foot	would	pull	woman
cook	should	put	wolverine
hook	gourmand	puss	wolfsbane
took	gourmet	push	
look	tourist	bush	
nook	tambour	bulrush	
rook	tourmaline	cuckoo	
brook	tournament	butcher	
shook	tourniquet	bullion	
crook		bullock	
good		bulwark	
hood		bushel	
stood		bushman	
wood		Buddha	
wool		bullet	
understood		insurance	
childhood			
woodbine			
livelihood			

17. WAYS OF SPELLING \ȯ\. Yellow card 9.

\ȯ\ is spelled <u>a</u> as in <u>all</u>, <u>au</u> as in <u>August</u>, <u>aw</u> as in <u>saw</u>.

a. Initial \ȯ\ is usually spelled <u>o</u> or <u>au</u>, but in a few words it is spelled <u>a</u> or <u>aw</u>.

b. Final \ȯ\ is always spelled <u>aw</u>, as in <u>flaw</u>.

c. Whenever <u>o</u> is used for \ȯ\ it is followed by <u>r</u>: <u>cord</u>. However, the phonograms <u>a</u> and <u>au</u> are also sometimes followed by <u>r</u>: <u>dwarf</u> and <u>laurel</u>. Indeed the <u>a</u> spelling for \ȯ\ is seldom followed by any letter other than <u>l</u> or <u>r</u>, as in <u>salt</u> and <u>warp</u>. A common exception is <u>water</u> \'wȯt-ər\.

Most of the words in which initial \ȯ\ is spelled <u>a</u> or <u>aw</u>, as in <u>all</u> and <u>awning</u>, are in very common use and definite effort should be made to remember them. The word <u>all</u> will be needed by the youngest student; words beginning with the syllable \ȯl\ as in *almost* needed by those only slightly more advanced.

Knowing the spelling of the word pronounced \ȯl\, the student tends to use two <u>l</u>'s for all words beginning with the syllable of the same sound. The seven common words beginning with <u>al</u> should be memorized:

<u>almighty</u>, <u>almost</u>, <u>already</u>, <u>also</u>, <u>although</u>, <u>altogether</u>, <u>always</u>.

They should be reviewed frequently, called for suddenly at odd moments. (Special attention should be called to the spelling of <u>all right</u>. This is not a single word, but a two-word phrase, which may be remembered as coupled with the corresponding two-word phrase <u>all wrong</u>—not commonly misspelled.) The student should also learn to spell <u>awe</u>, <u>awestruck</u>, <u>awful</u>, <u>awkward</u>, and <u>awning</u> and should know that these are the only words with initial <u>aw</u> which he is likely to need.

Words selected from the following lists should be dictated and placed by the student under the proper headings, <u>o</u>, <u>a</u>, <u>au</u>, or <u>aw</u>. Such exercises will involve frequent reference to the dictionary as there are so few reliable guides. The chief doubt concerns the use of <u>au</u> or <u>aw</u> within a word. There is no way for the student to know which to choose in an unknown word.

Many words beginning with <u>o</u> and <u>au</u> should be included to demonstrate the frequency with which these phonograms are initial. Eventually, words in which the different spellings of \ȯ\ occur should be included in miscellaneous spelling tests.

ILLUSTRATIVE \ȯ\ WORDS

o	a	au	aw
cork	all, ball, etc.	daub	saw
cord	salt	cause	paw
scorn	malt	fault	craw
scorch	talk	vault	squaw
border	walk, etc.	haul	thaw
retort	bald	daunt	taw
formal	scald	saunter	seesaw
morsel	dwarf	centaur	coleslaw
sordid	wharf	laurel	pawpaw
absorb	thwart	pauper	macaw
reform	war	applause	outlaw
escort	warp	jaunty	awkward
torment	warm	caustic	dawdle
mortal	alter	faucet	tawdry
portrait	altar	fauna	hawser
hornet	walnut	saucer	crawfish
corbel	walrus	laureate	lawyer
portent	water	nautical	tawny
corpulent	quarter	fraudulent	drawer
fortitude	warble	tarpaulin	hawthorn
abnormal	caldron	cauliflower	pawn
porcupine		mausoleum	prawn
subordinate		laudatory	crawl
horticulture		tautology	squawk

18. WAYS OF SPELLING \ər\, \r\. Yellow cards 17 and 18.

There are two sounds of \ər\, depending on whether it is an accented or an unaccented syllable. When in an accented syllable it is always sounded as in person; in an unaccented syllable, it is sounded as in baker. See Ways of Spelling \ə\, page 211.

In an accented syllable \ər\ may be spelled as ur, er, or ir. In an unaccented syllable any one of the five vowels, followed by r, may be the spelling: ar, er, ir, or, ur.

For ways of spelling \ər\ in an accented syllable see Ways of Spelling \ə\. The ir spelling is the rarest, in all situations. In all three spellings of \ər\ in a stressed syllable (ur, er, or, ir) it is sounded as in curl.

In unaccented syllables, \ər\ sounded as in baker may be spelled ar, er, ir, or, or ur. Note that ar and or have their own peculiar sounds in stressed syllables, but these sounds are not \ər\ so they are not dealt with here. See pages 82–83. In a small group of words, where or is preceded by a w it is sounded as \wər\. This pronunciation is exceptional for or. Examples of such words are in the illustrative word list of this section.

The \r\ illustrated in the heading is a reminder that unstressed medial or final syllables may have a single \r\ to represent the syllable, in order to denote less vocalization than would \ər\. Consonants other than r are used alone in many cases where one might look for a \ə\ before the consonant.

The following generalizations may be helpful for spelling \ər\ in an unstressed syllable, as in baker:

Uses of ar
- As a suffix:
    In nouns (infrequently) to denote "one who, that which"
        Example: beggar

    In adjectives denoting "of or pertaining to"
        Example: circular

- -ar- in the suffix ward \wərd\:
    In adjectives and adverbs denoting "tendency toward"
        Example: backward

- Not as a suffix, occurring (infrequently) in nouns
    Example: dollar

- ar followed by d, not as a suffix, \ərd\, in nouns
    Example: orchard

Uses of er
- In monosyllables and stressed syllables
    Example: her

- As a suffix, with the meaning, "one who, that which"
    Example: farmer
    Many words ending in -er are Anglo-Saxon derivatives—short, simple words of everyday living.

- In comparatives of adjectives and adverbs
    Example: warmer, kindlier

- "An inhabitant of"
    Example: Londoner

- Miscellaneous unstressed syllables
    Example: certificate

Uses of ir
- In monosyllables and stressed syllables
    Example: bird

- In miscellaneous unstressed syllables
    Example: extirpate

Uses of <u>or</u>
- Preceded by <u>w</u>
  Example: w<u>or</u>k

- -<u>or</u>, as a suffix, "one who, that which"
  Example: act<u>or</u>

- In many nouns
  Examples: harb<u>or</u>, od<u>or</u>, terr<u>or</u>

Uses of <u>ur</u>
- In monosyllables and stressed syllables
  Examples: b<u>ur</u>n, f<u>ur</u>nish

- In unstressed syllables. See list of illustrative \ər\, \-r\ words.

<u>ear</u>, <u>our</u>, and <u>yr</u> are exceptional spellings of \ər\. See list of illustrative \ər\, \-r\ words, <u>ur</u> section, last column.

ILLUSTRATIVE \ər\, \-r\ WORDS

ar	er, -er			
liar	berg	baker	ponderous	
beggar	fern	walker	numerous	
scholar	berth 3	runner	generous	
hangar	germ	teacher	reverent	
pedlar	herd 1	builder	reservoir	
bursar	serf ..	ringer	interval	
	tern ..	folder	intervene	
circular	merge	rower	camera	
angular	serge ..	player	exercise	
muscular	verge	avenger	hinterland	
globular	nerve	consumer	pulverize	
granular	perch	propeller	superfine	
singular	serve	+	peppermint	
lunar	terse		countermand	
solar	verse	warmer	desperate	
stellar	+	colder	moderate	
popular		taller	temperate	
insular	certify	kinder	government	
	dervish	sooner	dexterous	
homeward	fertile	faster	treacherous	
backward	germinate	later	temperament	
outward	hermit		reservation	
westward	jerkin	foreigner	conversation	
+	mercy	islander	toleration	
	nervous	villager	heterodox	
dollar	serpent	northerner	superscription	
pillar	sterling	New Yorker	——	
grammar	termite	Londoner	recovery	
mortar	thermal		discovery	
nectarine	verdict	certificate	cantankerous	
calendar	+	fertility	itinerant	
collar		jerboa	inveterate	
cellar	internal	perhaps	incinerate	
+	commercial	thermometer	consideration	
	preferment	verbena	confederation	
hazard	diversion	+	+	
orchard	imperfect			
coward	reversal	gallery	cavern	
lizard	exterminate	livery	bittern	
wizard	hyperbole	misery	modern	
blizzard	assertion	energy	western	
standard	aspersion	property	filbert	
sluggard	+	innermost	culvert	
steward		mineral	——	
custard	concern	liberal	lobster	
mustard	intern	literal	bolster	
scabbard	divert	asterisk	monster	
tankard	revert	asteroid	amber	
+	reverse	average	ember	
	transverse	different	larder	
	converge	conference	pilfer	
	preserve	haversack	spatter	
	reserve	cumbersome	render	
	assert		tender	
	——		character	
	confer		remember	
	prefer		sinister	

Two dots (..) after a word indicate a homonym on the same line in another column.

A numeral after a word indicates a homonym with the corresponding numeral on another line in the same or another column.

ILLUSTRATIVE \ər\,\-r\ WORDS

ir	or	ur	
squirt	work	burn	pursue
sir	worm	curt	pursuit
dirk	word	church	surprise
dirge	world	fur 4	surpass
birth 3	worse	furl	survive
fir 4	worst	surf ..	curmudgeon
firm	worth	turn ..	liturgy
firth	worthy	purl 2	measurable
girth	worry	surge ..	femur
girl	worship	urge	lemur
kirk		lurk	augur
quirt	actor	nurse	auburn
squirm	editor	spur	sulphur
swirl	inspector	spurn	
twirl	conductor	purse	ear
birch	collector	+	early
chirp	inventor		earl
bird	visitor	furnish	earn
+	instructor	burnish	earnest
circle	aggressor	curfew	earth
firkin	confessor	furtive	heard 1
girdle	professor	gurgle	learn
hirsute	supervisor	hurdle	yearn
kirtle	councilor	murder	pearl 2
sirloin	doctor	nurture	pearly
skirmish	+	purpose	search
squirrel	illustrator	surplus	hearse
thirsty	navigator	turban	rehearsal
virtue	educator	Thursday	
+	elevator	incursion	our
	decorator	insurgent	journey
confirm	operator	recurrent	journal
affirm	translator	refurbish	adjourn
infirm	radiator	refurnish	sojourn
	legislator	precursor	flourish
extirpate	imitator	excursive	nourish
affirmation	regulator	resurgence	courage
confirmation	refrigerator	disturbance	yr
	investigator	concurrence	myrrh
tapir	+	regurgitate	myrtle
elixir		diurnal	
triumvir	error	nocturnal	martyr
	terror	nasturtium	satyr
	valor	metallurgy	zephyr
	candor	concur	
	splendor	incur	
	odor	recur	
	color	absurd	
	armor	disturb	
	vapor	perturb	
	mirror	suburb	
	parlor	usurp	
	harbor	return	
	camphor	disburse	
	major		
	minor		

A plus (+) indicates that the list could easily be extended.

The lines (___) separate groups arranged according to location of the phonogram: in monosyllables; initial or final in word; in initial, medial, or final syllables.

19. WAYS OF SPELLING LONG VOWELS, \ü\, AND \yü\

"Ways of Spelling," numbers 19–25 (yellow drill cards 1, 3, 5, 7, 10, 11), deal with spelling the long vowel sounds and \yü\ and \ü\.

They belong together in a group. There are many ways of representing each of these sounds and they occur in a great number of common words. These facts make them both more difficult and more important than the other multiple spellings. Therefore, we have found it necessary to handle them somewhat differently and to develop their presentation in more detail.

Before we discuss the steps to be taken in dealing with the generalizations that follow, we reiterate our earlier warning. The attempt to present spelling as a thinking subject cannot succeed with very young or low-I.Q. students who lack the ability to handle abstractions.

We emphasize this warning because we have discovered third and fourth grade teachers attempting to get their classes to generalize in this way and remedial teachers trying to incorporate this procedure into their work, with children whose I.Q. was too low to enable them to solve arithmetic problems or to reason about historical situations. We regard such attempts as distinct misapplication of a method devised for students of average-superior intelligence, but handicapped by specific spelling disability, who have been carefully trained in phonics and familiarized with the concept of multiple spellings.

If the young student must use any of these long-vowel words they should be given to him to copy without comment. There are many children with no spelling difficulty who can spell almost any word once they have seen it in print. None of this work is for them.

Words to be used in considering the possible spellings of each long vowel sound are assembled on charts, so that all necessary data will be at hand. These will be referred to as "word charts."

Although each of these word charts has its own special features, they have all been prepared with one general plan, except the one for \yü\ and \ü\, which will be discussed later.

In the first column of each chart are words in which the vowel sound ends a syllable.* The second column of each chart contains vowel-consonant-e words. Next are columns in which the long vowel sound is followed by a consonant and others in which it is final in the word. The phonograms heading these columns are arranged in alphabetical order, as they are most easily recalled when so placed. For example, on the \ā\ word chart we find a, a-e, ai, ay, ea, ei, eigh.

Reference to the note at the bottom of any one of the word charts will show that homonyms are clearly indicated, a plus sign indicates that a list might easily be extended, and short lines separate groups within a column so that the type of word needed at the moment may be readily located.

In the first column of the \ō\ word chart (page 236) the first and third groups consist of words accented on the first syllable. This is true of the second group, but here the initial syllable consists of one letter, as in opal. In the fourth group the stress falls on the second syllable, as in component.

---

* In words ending in o the last syllable is seldom stressed, but with rare exceptions the o is given the long sound, as in tomato.

To accompany each word chart there is a "ratio chart" showing frequency of occurrence. Under representative words, vertical lines represent the relative lengths of the columns of words on the word chart. While some columns on each word chart could be greatly extended, others contain all or nearly all the words in which a particular phonogram is used. If words were added to these long columns, their ratio to the short ones would be even greater. Therefore, neither word charts nor ratio charts are mathematically accurate, but both may serve as rough guides in selecting more common and less common ways of spelling a sound occurring in a particular location. For example, the column headed o-e is longer than that headed oa, so we know that o-e is more frequently used than oa.

The ratio charts enable the student to select the most probable spellings without looking at the word charts, where he might discover spellings he should work out for himself. It must not be forgotten that the exercises in this chapter are not spelling lessons to be memorized. Their purpose is to establish the habit of "intelligent guessing" of the probable spellings.

There is no inflexible sequence in which these vowel sounds should be taught. We have found the following order satisfactory: \ō\, \ī\, \ā\, \ē\, \yü\, \ü\.

Before beginning lessons on the spelling of a long vowel sound, the teacher must, of course, be thoroughly familiar with the generalizations to be taught, and must plan how best to present them.

Let us now consider the generalizations that are helpful in selecting the phonogram to use in spelling \ō\ in a particular word.

20. WAYS OF SPELLING \ō\. Yellow card 7.

\ō\ is spelled o as in pony, o-e as in home, oa as in boat, oe as in toe, ow as in snow.

a. In polysyllables, when \ō\ is heard at the end of a syllable or is a syllable by itself, the most common spelling is o alone. Even at the end of a final syllable \ō\ may be spelled o. In fact, this spelling is quite common, and the syllable is seldom if ever accented.

A few monosyllables end in o: go, no, so.

b. There are three ways of spelling \ō\ at the end of a word: o alone, as noted above; ow, which the student will have encountered frequently in his reading; and oe, known in toe and perhaps in hoe and doe. It is the least common, and ow is the most frequent.

c. When \ō\ is heard within a syllable which ends in a consonant sound, it may be represented by o-e or oa. In final syllables, with very rare exceptions, o-e is used. The o-e spelling is used in the first syllable of some compounds or derivatives, e.g., forestall, colewort, boredom.

oa is found most frequently in monosyllables.

Words in the "old" and "ost" families—bold, cold, most, host, and so on—will have become familiar before this work is undertaken, and are not included on the \ō\ chart.

The two familiar words <u>floor</u> and <u>door</u>, probably the only ones in which \ō\ is spelled <u>oo</u>, should be memorized.

The letter <u>o</u> followed by <u>r</u> in the same syllable is usually marked \ȯ\ by the dictionary, e.g., <u>born</u> \bȯrn\, <u>for</u> \fȯr\; but sometimes with the line above the vowel, e.g., <u>worn</u> \wōrn\, <u>fore</u> \fōr\. In some words people have difficulty distinguishing \ȯ\ from \ō\, but in other cases the distinction is easier to detect. This situation is so confusing that none of the \ȯ\ words have been included on the \ō\ word chart.

Words in which \ō\ is followed by <u>r</u> in the next syllable do appear on the chart. The teacher must take care to divide these words in such a way when pronouncing as to make clear the \ō\ sound; for example, <u>story</u> as \'stō-rē\ not \'stȯ-rē\ which the student might reasonably spell s-t-a-u-r-y or s-t-a-w-r-y.

There is a small group of words in which \ō\ is spelled <u>ou</u>. In most of these the diphthong is followed by <u>r</u>, as in <u>four</u>. We have seen that <u>r</u> somewhat alters a preceding vowel sound. We have omitted the <u>ou</u> spelling from the lists. The words can be dealt with when the need arises.

In readiness for the first \ō\ lesson the teacher should prepare for the student a record sheet ruled in columns headed with phonograms and key words as follows:

WAYS OF SPELLING \ō\

o	o-e	oa	oe	ow
pony	home	boat	toe	snow

It is difficult if not impossible to find paper wide enough for from five to seven columns, each of which will allow large, clear writing. If the paper is too narrow, two sheets should be used. If obliged to use paper with narrow spaces between the lines, the student should skip every other line.

Older students often resist writing in large letters. Small writing is a symbol of growing up for them and they resent being asked to form large letters, which may seem babyish. Furthermore, small and indistinct letters have proven to be a refuge for many poor spellers. A somewhat pointed hump may stand for an <u>i</u> without a dot or for an <u>e</u> without a loop; an oval with a line out from the middle may be either an <u>o</u> or an <u>a</u>. Students often confess that they write indistinctly on purpose in the hope of "getting by with it." One can scarcely blame them. It is important, however, to make them understand that inaccurate kinesthetic impressions mean blurred kinesthetic memory.

The teacher should make a wall-sized ratio chart for each vowel. It should be tacked on the wall for ready reference.

Lesson 1. Begin with a review of the five phonograms that spell \ō\, already learned for reading. Then the student may be given the record sheet.

Model Dialogue

Teacher: This is a record sheet on which you will write in columns words that belong under the various phonograms. To decide where the words belong will be an even better guessing game than any we have had. Before you can guess sensibly about new words you must observe the kind of words that belong in each column. Look at the word at the top of the last column. In what part of the word is the \ō\ sound?

Student: At the end.

T: Yes. Do you know any other word that might go in that column?

S: Crow, slow, blow—there are lots of them.

T: You're right, there are many such words. Should we decide that \ō\ at the end of a word is always spelled ow? Before we do so, let's look at the other key words.

S: The word toe ends in the \ō\ sound.

T: Are toe and snow the only key words ending in \ō\?

S: Yes.

T: What do we hear at the end of the other key words?

S: In pony it is \ē\ and home ends in \ē\.

T: Listen to the word as I say it: \hōm\. Do you hear \ē\ at the end?

S: No, I hear \m\.

T: You forgot that e at the end of a word is almost always silent. We hear the sound of the consonant before the e. What about the final sound of the other words?

S: I hear \t\ at the end of boat.

T: You see that under some of the phonograms there are two columns. You must think of these words as all one list. If the page were long enough they would make one long column. Here is a ratio chart, which shows this. It is smaller than the word chart, but the lines are in the same proportion to each other as are the columns of words. The first line on this ratio chart represents the two columns under pony added together. This line under home also stands for two columns of words. The other lines represent the columns as they are in the book. This chart will help you to make reasonable deductions in spelling new words. The line under home is much longer than the line under boat. That tells us that o-e is used more often than oa. Which is the shortest column?

S: The oe column.

T: Yes. It would be foolish to suggest oe over and over again to spell the sound \ō\ at the end of words. We will work with words from the word chart many times until you become a skillful deducer.

It is not to be expected that the student will always answer questions so fully. If a rephrasing of the question fails to bring a satisfactory response, the teacher should give the answer herself. Much valuable time is wasted in futile attempts to draw from students something they cannot give. A question which seems perfectly clear to the teacher may have no significance for the student; facts he has seemed to know may have escaped his memory. Whatever the reason for his failure to respond, the lesson should not be allowed to drag. One of the main objectives is to stimulate interest in the subject.

For the second lesson the student will need a trial paper on which to write his deductions. This, also, should provide space for large, clear writing. Trial papers should be dated and kept in his notebook.

Lesson 2. Review of the facts discovered during the first lesson:

T: In what kind of word will you find \ō\ spelled by <u>o</u> alone?

S: In a word of more than one syllable.

T: In what part of the word?

S: At the end of the first syllable.

T: Listen again to this word, \lə-'nō-lē-əm\. Is the \ō\ sound at the end of the first syllable?

S: No, I should have said at the end of one of the syllables.

T: There is another thing you should know. You have read and spelled words like <u>mon u ment</u> and <u>tel e gram</u>, in which one of the vowels by itself makes a syllable. It may even be an initial syllable, as in '<u>o pen</u>, so you must be ready to find <u>o</u> in such positions as well as after a consonant, as in '<u>po ny</u> and <u>li 'no le um</u>.

In what ways can \ō\ be spelled in words ending in a consonant sound? Think of the key words.

S: <u>Home</u>, <u>o-e</u> and <u>boat</u>, <u>oa</u>.

T: Good! How may \ō\ be spelled at the end of a word?

S: It may be <u>oe</u> and it may be <u>ow</u>.

[For the time being, final <u>o</u> in a word is disregarded.]

T: Think of the ratio chart we looked at yesterday. Do you remember which line was longer? The one under <u>oe</u> or the one under <u>ow</u>?

S: No.

T: Let us look at it again.

S: The <u>ow</u> column is much longer.

T: Yes. It will be worthwhile for you to remember that fact. Now I think you are ready to make some educated choices for \ō\. How might you spell \ glō\? Write it on your trial paper.

S: <u>gloe</u>.

T: Yes. Is there any other way? Look at the key words.

S: <u>glow</u>.

T: Write that beside the other. Which way do you think is more likely to be correct?

S: I don't know.

[A look at the ratio chart is in order.]

T: Now check the one you think is the more likely to be right. Yes, <u>glow</u> is correct. From now on you will write your choices on your trial paper and check the spelling you think is most probable. In that way we can see how rapidly you become a more successful detective. You must be sure which way is correct before you write the word in the proper column on your record sheet. I must tell you or you must consult the dictionary.

The next word attempted might be \\'mō ment\\. The student should be quite sure of the spelling of the \\ō\\ sound if he remembers the <u>o</u>-alone column. He may spell \\ment\\ <u>m-e-a-n-t</u>, in which case he should be reminded that the syllable \\-ment\\ is spelled <u>m-e-n-t</u>. He has written the word <u>meant</u>.

<u>Moment</u> should be recorded.

T: Now try to spell \\flōt\\.

S: F-l-o-a-t.

T: Yes. Why did you spell it that way?

S: Because I know how to spell it.

This is disconcerting, but teachers must be prepared for unexpected answers. Even a very poor speller will have mastered a few words. Though its spelling was not "guessed," <u>float</u> should be recorded.

It is most important that the majority of the words discussed should be those of which the student cannot be expected to know the spelling. The point is not to list words she already knows but, we repeat, to give practice in "intelligent choosing" of the probable spelling, "guessing" based on the knowledge of usage which will become more and more familiar during these lessons.

Some students do not want to try to spell a word unless they know its meaning. Others are pleased with the idea of being able to make reasonable choices about unknown words, an attitude to be encouraged in all, for the ability to find unfamiliar words heard in conversation or in a lecture is a very valuable step in dictionary technique (see Chapter 10). The search for such a word can be successful only for the person with a fairly good idea of how such a word might be spelled.

T: Did you ever hear of a roan horse? It is brown or gray with some white mixed in. How might you spell \\rōn\\? Look at the key words and you can come near to the right spelling if you choose sensibly.

S: It might be <u>r-o-n-e</u>.

T: Yes. Why?

S: Because I hear \\n\\ after the \\ō\\, just as I hear \\m\\ after the <u>o</u> in <u>home</u>.

T: Right. Is there any other way that it could be spelled?

S: <u>r-o-a-n</u>. That \\n\\ comes after the \\ō\\ sound, and \\t\\ comes after <u>oa</u> in <u>boat</u>.

Such incomplete answers must be expected at first, but the time should come when the choice of phonograms and the reason for the choice is given at once and not in response to repeated questioning.

T: Now look again at the key words. Is there any other way?

S: No, but I don't know which of these is right.

T: What are we going to do about it?

S: Unless you tell me, I have to look it up in the dictionary.

Other words suitable for consideration in this lesson or the next are <u>foe</u>, <u>Dover</u>, <u>crow</u>, <u>tome</u>, <u>woe</u>, <u>joke</u>.

The amount that can be accomplished in one lesson depends upon several factors. The lessons outlined here are planned for a student who has had thorough training in phonics as a prerequisite of this work, and they assume that for a few days the entire forty-five minute remedial period will be devoted to these long vowel spellings. The student should never be hurried in order to accomplish all that had been prepared for one lesson.

Material for lessons should be planned in advance in order to maintain a proper balance, and to accustom the student to the relatively common uses of the different phonograms. A teacher's hit-or-miss selection of words during a lesson period will not accomplish these ends.

Some teachers prefer to plan one lesson at a time. Others like the long look ahead and plan a list for a series of lessons, feeling that in this way the complete record sheet will be better balanced.

For some students shorter lists may suffice, while others may need more illustrations of each use of the phonograms. However, this record sheet shows how the generalizations can be developed. For some students with especially severe spelling difficulty, easier and more familiar words should be selected.

When the student's record sheet has two words in each of the five columns it is wise to devote a lesson or two to the study of homonyms. Some students may not have heard the word, indeed may not even have the concept, in which case it must be developed during the consideration of the first pair introduced. These might be <u>rode</u> and <u>road</u>.

Lesson 3

T: How would you spell \rōd\? Tell me all about it. Don't wait for me to ask "why."

S: <u>R-o-a-d</u> or <u>r-o-d-e</u>, because I hear \d\ after the \ō\ and <u>oa</u> and <u>o-e</u> are the ways to spell \ō\ when you hear a consonant sound after it.

T: Good! Which way do you choose?

[Both are written on the trial paper.]

S: R-o-a-d.

T: Yes, that is a correct spelling. What does the word <u>road</u> mean? Can you show me by writing it in a sentence?

S: Tom <u>road</u> on horseback.

T: You have chosen the wrong \rōd\. <u>R-o-a-d</u> means a street or highway. We spell the \rōd\ in your sentence, <u>r-o-d-e</u>. Tom did something. You might say, "Tom <u>rode</u> on the <u>road</u>." You see that they are both real words. This is a good time to learn a new name, *homonyms*. Homonyms are words that sound alike, but have different meanings and different spellings.

Write these homonyms on your record sheet and place two dots after each one. When you see the dots you will know that the word is a homonym and will look in another column for its companion.

S: How am I going to remember which is which?

T: R-o-d-e is an action word (a verb) and is related to the word r-i-d-e. You use ride if you mean the present time and rode if you mean the past.

From now on the lessons on \ō\ words should occupy a shorter part of the remedial period in order that other types of work are not crowded out—S.O.S. study of words, reading, dictation, and so on.

The teacher should usually select the words to be attempted from different columns in order to keep the student alert to the possibilities in varying situations. The words in the teacher's word list on page 234 were selected with this end in view as well as for the maintenance of proper ratio between the columns on the finished record sheet.

Since the number of words taken up each day will vary from student to student there is no further attempt to divide the teacher's word list into lesson units. Suggestions are given here in regard to certain words that offer opportunities to introduce important points or that present difficulties.

Gopher, no. 28. If the syllable -pher gives trouble, a quick review of the spellings of \f\ is needed, and the student is told to find in the dictionary which spelling of \er\ is used.

Opal, no. 32, has a one-letter syllable and this spelling should be emphasized. The word chart may be consulted for other examples.

Boast, no. 34, differs from the other words in which the oa spelling occurs—the \ō\ sound is followed by two consonants. If asked to suggest other words in which this situation occurs, the student will probably name coast, roast, toast, and may include most, post, ghost. This is a chance to stress the fact that rhyming words may differ in the phonograms used to spell an identical sound, and to dwell on the necessity for verifying the spelling chosen by consulting the dictionary.

Doe, no. 35, will suggest its homonym dough, but the ough spelling for \ō\ is so unusual that no column has been provided for it.

Chorus, no. 43, should be pronounced by the teacher clearly: \ˈkōr-əs\, not \ˈkȯr-əs\.

Polite, no. 45, \pə-ˈlīt\. In the dictionary o is marked ə because it is not accented, but is heard unmistakably as \ō\ and therefore gives no trouble.

Woeful, no. 51. Since the first syllable ends in \ō\, the student would probably think the proper spelling wo. The word should be discussed as a derivative of woe, and therefore spelled w-o-e-f-u-l. After it has been discussed and recorded, a look at the ratio chart will call to mind the fact that the oe column should be shorter than the others on the complete record sheet.

The teacher can then say, "The oe column is now long enough for the sheet you are making; I won't give you any more words for that column because then it would be out of proportion."

Burrow, no. 57, and burro, no. 58. The oe spelling for final \ō\ having been eliminated, \'bər-ō\ will naturally be spelled with ow and placed in the last column. If the \bər\ gives trouble the teacher spells it. The meaning of the word is discussed and then the teacher points out that there is a homonym (burro). A description of the animal may be given. Since, being a homonym, this word cannot end in ow, it presents a problem. Some students may have noticed words ending in o in the first column and suggest that it belongs there. Others will have to be told.

Since these two words do not appear on the same line of the record sheet, the fact that they are homonyms cannot be indicated by dots, and numbers are used, 1 and 1. Other such pairs are given on the word chart, the first being no and know. It will be interesting to look over the chart and locate such homonyms. Toe and tow are discovered, numbered 7 and 7. As a key word, toe is already on the student's record sheet. Tow may be added and numbered 2 and 2, which is suitable in this instance, since the individual record is to be shorter than the word chart.

The discovery that final \ō\ may be spelled with o alone may serve as an introduction to final vowels in general. Comparatively few words in English end in vowels, and in only a small proportion of those are the final vowels long (see Appendix 14)—a, never; i and u rarely; while final e is usually silent. Final o is therefore an outstanding exception.

On the other hand, many words in several foreign languages end in vowels. The final o's in English usually come to us from Spain or Italy—burro from Spain.

Soprano, no. 61. A schwa and a stressed o, but both belong in the first column.

Provoke, no. 62. Students must be taught to distinguish between justifiable mistakes and careless ones. The syllable \vōk\ could be spelled v-o-a-k as well as v-o-k-e. As the work progresses it will become clear that in final syllables the o-e spelling is almost always used. If, on the other hand, the student offers v-o-k as the spelling for \vōk\, he should be asked to pronounce what he has written. When he hears himself say \vok\ he will realize that he was not sufficiently thoughtful. Students find it interesting to discover that a word like provoke \prə vōk\ belongs in two columns. After it has been recorded in the o-e column, it may also be placed in the first column after Mongolia.

Groan, no. 65. Asked to spell \grōn\, a moaning sound, the student will probably think of g-r-o-a-n. He may not be able to think of a spelling for the homonym grown, "fully developed," no. 66, since ow has been learned as a spelling for final \ō\ in a word. It must be explained that grown is related to grow in which the ow is final. Add growth, no. 67, and slowly, no. 68, related to grow and slow respectively, and discuss such words as crowbar and towline.

Telescope, no. 70. On the word chart we have grouped together certain words related in meaning. The study of such words with older students can be made an initial step to a more detailed study of derivations of microscope, gyroscope.

A younger student may sometimes be permitted the same sort of observation, according to her ability and with greater direction from the teacher if necessary.

Never forget that the spelling of the particular words on the word charts is not to be studied, but there will be steady gain in the student's power to select the most probable spelling for each word considered. In time the student can feel complete assurance in many instances that her spelling of a new word is correct. In others her knowledge will enable her to use the dictionary very effectively, often merely to verify her intuitive feeling.

Baritone, barytone, no. 73, provides an opportunity to discuss the fact that for some words two spellings are allowed, the first one being preferred.

No one can predict how long such exercises should continue. If a student has gained the power to attack \ō\ spellings with reasonable success it may be unnecessary to give him all the words in the Teacher's \ō\ List (page 234).

Another student may make disappointingly slow progress in selecting the most probable spelling. Indeed, the point of diminishing returns may be reached. The \ō\ spellings should then be dropped. After a series of lessons devoted to another type of work, another vowel sound should be introduced. Return to \ō\ after the behavior of other long vowel sounds has been observed, for contrast and similarity will do more toward mastery than will exclusive attention to one vowel. The "Student's Record Sheet" can be completed from the Teacher's \ō\ List. This suggested list was prepared with an average student in mind. It may be that some, while obviously making gains, need more practice in applying the generalizations. Additional words can be selected for them from the word chart on pages 236–237. In selecting these new words teachers must be careful to maintain the relative length of the columns.

We have emphasized regarding the word charts largely as reservoirs for the teacher, not to be closely observed by the student. By way of introduction he is allowed a mere glance at the general arrangement. His thoughts should focus on working out for himself the spelling of new words to place on his record sheet.

After this procedure has been established, however, there are often situations in which close examination of some portion of a word chart may prove exceedingly valuable, especially for the older student. For example, he may be helped by thoughtful scrutiny which will fix in his mind the typical characteristics of a group of words. During such an examination to compare the o-e and oe columns, the suffix -scope may be discovered and its meaning emphasized.

Immediately before each of the long vowel double pages and ratio charts, there is a list distributed in two ways.

The first is the Teacher's List. After the generalizations for a particular vowel have been discussed carefully, the teacher dictates the words in his list, *in the exact* order as printed. Any deviation from this order will throw out the sequence. The student:

- considers all possible spellings for the word
- writes them down for comparison
- decides which is the best one
- has it verified by teacher or dictionary
- places the word in the proper column on his record sheet.

No word is to be placed on his chart until its correctness has been established.
When all the words in the Teacher's List have been thus placed, the Student's Record Sheet will look like the list following the Teacher's List. The length of the columns must conform to the length of the lines in the ratio chart.

In most cases homonyms appear on the same line and are labeled with two dots (..) after each.

The concept to establish is that of multiple spellings with a choice of the most probable one. Many times even the ratio chart does not give an infallible decision and the student must look up his tentative choice in the dictionary.

Repeatedly the teacher says, "But you can't look up two or three words simultaneously. Which will you look up first as the *most* probable?"

The teacher will often need several lists and the student several charts before this concept has been firmly established.

Because much thought, liberal allowance for errors, and expectation of several rearrangements are required of the teacher in constructing such lists, we here give one list for each of the vowel sounds.

A simpler but less graphic procedure has been followed for the \ü\ and \yü\ spellings.

Words selected from the large two-page lists are arranged to approximate carefully the relative length of the lines on the ratio chart, but with no regard for the location of the homonyms. These proportional lists are then completely jumbled and are dictated without regard to homonyms. Thus the student may, for example, find himself with one word halfway down a column and its homonym near the top of another column. No matter. He gives each the same numerical label and goes on.

The first method is more graphic, the second more practical in terms of teacher-hours.

TEACHER'S \ō\ LIST

1. glow	18. roe	35. doe	51. woeful	67. growth
2. moment	19. flow	36. potentate	52. borrow	68. slowly
3. float	20. floe	37. alone	53. episode	69. flamingo
4. roan	21. rodent	38. goad	54. toboggan	70. telescope
5. foe	22. clove	39. devotion	55. narrow	71. oakum
6. Dover	23. grocer	40. Mongolia	56. coax	72. obey
7. crow	24. dome	41. cajole	57. burrow	73. baritone
8. tome	25. Roman	42. tallow	58. burro	74. semaphore
9. woe	26. shoal	43. chorus	59. tow	75. crowbar
10. joke	27. crocus	44. croak	60. lasso	76. roadster
11. rode	28. gopher	45. polite	61. soprano	77. approach
12. road	29. grope	46. billow	62. provoke	78. bemoan
13. coal	30. rove	47. verbose	63. shadow	79. boredom
14. cole	31. trophy	48. pekoe	64. anecdote	80. canopy
15. moat	32. opal	49. mellow	65. groan	81. coleslaw
16. mote	33. Odin	50. Crusoe	66. grown	82. begonia
17. row	34. boast			

STUDENT'S COMPLETED RECORD SHEET

Ways of Spelling \ō\

o	o-e	oa	oe	ow
pony	**home**	**boat**	**toe 2**	**snow**
moment	tome	float	foe	glow
Dover	joke	roan	woe	crow
rodent	rode ..	road ..	roe ..	row ..
grocer	cole ..	coal ..	floe ..	flow ..
Roman	mote ..	moat ..	doe	tallow
crocus	clove	shoal	pekoe	billow
gopher	dome	boast	Crusoe	mellow
trophy	grope	goad	woeful	borrow
opal	rove	croak		narrow
Odin	alone	coax		burrow 1
potentate	cajole	groan 3		tow 2
devotion	verbose	oakum		shadow
Mongolia	episode	roadster		grown 3
chorus	provoke	approach		growth
polite	anecdote	bemoan		slowly
toboggan	telescope			crowbar
burro 1	baritone			
lasso	semaphore			
soprano	boredom			
provoke	coleslaw			
flamingo				
obey				
canopy				
begonia				

ILLUSTRATIVE \ō\ WORDS

o		o-e	
pony		**home**	

moment	devotion	cote	..		condole
rodent	commotion	rode	..		parole
motion	begonia	lone	..		cajole
frozen	custodian	bore	..		backstroke
rotate	linoleum	ore	..		explode
locate	Mongolia	sore	..		anode
clover	—	cole	..		electrode
Dover		mote	..		episode
crocus	testimonial	rote	3		Seminole
bonus	tuberculosis	wrote	3		casserole
focus	+	hole	4		pinafore
grocer		whole	4		commodore
gopher	chorus	throne	5		stevedore
potent	borax	drone			semaphore
mohair	thorax	dote			baritone
program	dory	quote			monotone
profile	quorum	joke			cellulose
protest	oriole	Coke			bellicose
pronoun	porous	choke			comatose
Mohawk	—	probe			diagnose
trophy	arboreal	globe			varicose
cobra	pictorial	dome			grandiose
coma	no 1	tome			hippodrome
soda	burro 2	pose			metronome
toga	halo	prose			anecdote
Roman	banjo	node			telephone
Trojan	motto	strode			microphone
broken	grotto	dole			gramophone
token	veto	mole			interlope
local	lasso	core			telescope
vocal	cargo	clove			microscope
floral	volcano	rove			baroscope
donate	potato	lope			horoscope
quota	tomato	grope			stethoscope
profile	kimono	core			ophthalmoscope
	soprano	wore			+
opal	flamingo	—			
omen	albino	abode			boredom
odor	portfolio	alone			forecast
ozone	+	cyclone			forestall
okra		trombone			wholesome
oleander	polite	postpone			coleslaw
	rotund	intone			chokecherry
motivate	donation	invoke			
foliage	flotilla	revoke			
protocol	toboggan	provoke			
zodiac	proboscis	inclose			
potentate		disclose			
chromium	obey	suppose			
stoical	omission	remote			
	opossum	denote			
component		connote			
mimosa	canopy	verbose			
factotum	decorate	lactose			
anchovy	eloquence	jocose			
erosive		morose			
October	economy	ignore			
	antagonist	implore			
	+				

Two dots (..) after a word indicate a homonym on the same line in another column.

A numeral after a word indicates a homonym with the corresponding numeral on another line in the same or another column.

ILLUSTRATIVE \ō\ WORDS

oa		oe		ow	
boat		**toe 7**		**snow**	
coat	..	roe	..	row	..
road	..	floe	..	flow	..
loan	..	sloe	..	slow	..
boar	..	throe	..	throw	..
oar	..	doe		tow	7
soar	..	foe		bow	
coal	..	hoe		low	
moat	..	woe		crow	
float		—		glow	
gloat		aloe		know	1
stoat		pekoe		grow	
groan	6	Crusoe		blow	
moan		Defoe		—	
roan		Tahoe		fallow	
loaf		mistletoe		mallow	
goad		shallow		tallow	
toad				arrow	
boast		roebuck		harrow	
coast		woeful		marrow	
toast		woebegone		sparrow	
foal				narrow	
shoal				shadow	
soak				meadow	
croak				elbow	
broach				below	
coach				yellow	
poach				mellow	
coax				fellow	
hoax				billow	
soap				window	
oath				windrow	
loath				winnow	
loathe				widow	
hoar				borrow	
roar				sorrow	
hoard				follow	
board				hollow	
coarse				burrow	2
—				tomorrow	
coarsen				bungalow	
oaken					
oakum				known	
coating				thrown	5
gloaming				grown	6
roadster				growth	
—				towed	
soapstone				slowly	
approach				crowbar	
encroach				crowfoot	
reproach				lowboy	
cockroach				towline	
clapboard				towhead	
bemoan				+	

A plus (+) indicates that the list could easily be extended.
The lines (___) separate groups arranged according to location of the phonogram: in monosyllables; initial

RATIO CHART OF \ō\ SPELLINGS

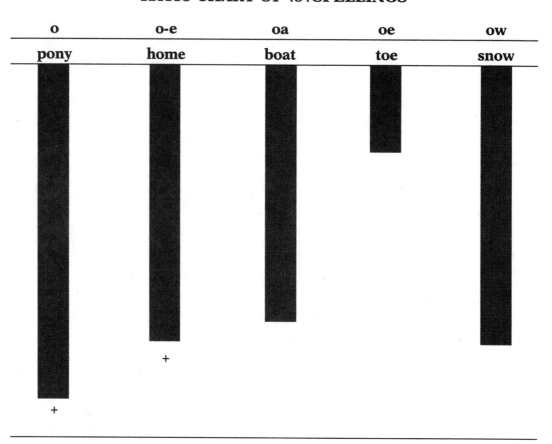

o	o-e	oa	oe	ow
pony	home	boat	toe	snow

21. WAYS OF SPELLING \ī\. Yellow card 5.

\ī\ is spelled i as in <u>spider</u>, i-e as in <u>pine</u>, igh as in <u>light</u>, y as in <u>my</u>, y-e as in <u>type</u> and ie as in <u>pie</u>.

a. \ī\ at the end of a syllable in a dissyllable or polysyllable may be represented by either <u>i</u> or <u>y</u>; <u>i</u> is more common.

The <u>y</u> spelling at the end of a syllable within a word is likely to occur in scientific terms and words connected with industrial processes, most of which are derived from Greek. However, it must be noted that not all such terms use the <u>y</u> spellings for \ī\. We have <u>microbe</u> [Gr.], <u>siphon</u> [F. fr. L. fr. Gr.], <u>biped</u> [L.], <u>micrometer</u> [F.]. In Greek names we expect the \ī\ to be spelled <u>y</u>. When \ī\ forms a syllable by itself, it is usually spelled <u>i</u>, e.g., '<u>i</u>vory.

b. Final \ī\ is almost always spelled <u>y</u>.

Some words end in the letter <u>i</u> but the sound is usually \ē\ as in <u>broccoli</u>, and \ē\ as in <u>ski</u>. Most of these words are foreign and retain their original spelling (see Appendix 14). Close observation of these words, derived from many different languages, will tend to prevent the use of a final <u>i</u> in common words, e.g., <u>beautifi</u>.

In a very few familiar monosyllables, final \ī\ is spelled ie: die, lie, pie. These should be studied when needed, as should the even more unusual ye words: bye, dye, rye. It seems unnecessary to complicate the \ī\ chart by including ie and ye columns, but some students are sure to suggest doing so.

The igh spelling for final \ī\ occurs in four words, high, nigh, sigh, thigh. These must be learned when needed.

c. When \ī\ is heard within a syllable that ends in a consonant sound, it may be represented by i-e, y-e or igh; i-e is the most common spelling. y-e occurs in a very few unfamiliar words: compare time, mile, line with lyre, gyve, enzyme, neophyte.

All the words in the igh column end in t. They are familiar rhyming words that should give no trouble. Comparatively few words ending in the sound \īt\ are spelled with ight. Many more end in ite or yte: bite, sprite, electrolyte. However, it is necessary to give special attention to this final syllable because uncertain spellers are often intrigued by peculiar spellings.

It should be made clear that igh words are not used as syllables in longer words, except when combined with prefixes or suffixes as in insight or frighten, or joined with another word as in limelight. The frequent display of a list of ight words typed on a card may serve as a warning against their use as syllables.

If a student is asked to spell epiphyte he should be told that it is the scientific name for an air plant. If he proposes e-p-i-f-i-g-h-t, he is reminded that f-i-g-h-t is a word. True, it is used as a syllable in fighting and fighter, but these words are made from fight and epiphyte is not. The possible spellings for the syllable \fīt\ are discussed: f-i-t-e, f-y-t-e, ph-i-t-e, ph-y-t-e. Epiphyte is a scientific term. The fact that it is from Greek is discussed. The student familiar with the history of the English language will know that ph and y are the safest guesses.

The rhyming words bind, find, kind, and so forth, will be familiar to any student undertaking this work and are not on the chart.

TEACHER'S \ī\ LIST

1. fight	15. cycle	29. ivy	42. confine	55. defiant
2. tiger	16. diagram	30. recite	43. violin	56. stile
3. dine	17. rite	31. tripod	44. sublime	57. style
4. dyne	18. write	32. gyroscope	45. magnify	58. tirade
5. tiny	19. right	33. white	46. defile	59. smile
6. hyphen	20. wright	34. diamond	47. deprive	60. bright
7. mite	21. pyre	35. twice	48. biography	61. item
8. might	22. cypress	36. library	49. horizon	62. provide
9. giant	23. cite	37. pile	50. variety	63. hibernate
10. lyre	24. site	38. cry	51. alibi	64. columbine
11. hydrant	25. sight	39. vice	52. Siamese	65. reply
12. Bible	26. biplane	40. vise	53. contrive	66. typhoon
13. title	27. gyve	41. dry	54. describe	67. paralyze
14. tyrant	28. tidy			

STUDENT'S COMPLETED RECORD SHEET

Ways of Spelling \ī\

i	i-e		igh		y	y-e	
spider	**pine**		**light**		**cyclone**	**type**	
tiger	dine	..	fight		hyphen	dyne	..
tiny	mite	..	might	..	hydrant	lyre	
giant	rite	1	right	1	tyrant	pyre	
Bible	write	1	wright	1	cycle	gyve	
title	cite	2	sight	2	cypress	style	4
diagram	site	2	bright		gyroscope	paralyze	
biplane	recite				cry		
tidy	white				dry		
ivy	twice				magnify		
tripod	pile				reply		
diamond	vice	3			typhoon		
library	vise	3					
violin	confine						
biography	sublime						
horizon	defile						
variety	deprive						
alibi	contrive						
Siamese	describe						
defiant	stile	4					
tirade	smile						
item	provide						
hibernate	columbine						

ILLUSTRATIVE \ī\ WORDS

i		i-e	
spider		**pine**	
tidy	diadem	dine ..	feline
tiny	diamond	fife	confine
liar	quiescent	knife	combine
giant	pliable	smile	imbibe
tirade	privation	mite ..	subscribe
tripod	libation	write 2	describe
lichen	citation	rite 2	inscribe
Bible	violin	site 3	prescribe
title	violet	cite 3	incite
rifle	triumphant	bite ..	recite
trifle	bicycle	while	despite
stifle	tricycle	hive	ignite
divan	hiatus	nice	graphite
Midas	hibiscus	twice	inquire
bivalve	dinosaur	thrice	inspire
biplane	biology	mine	expire
tiger	biography	slime	retire
miser	criterion	prime	admire
microbe	——	fire	provide
siphon	untidy	mire	confide
Zion	decisive	lime	decide
final	derisive	bride	deride
rival	defiance	strike	surprise
spinal	reliance	drive	devise
spiral	denial	stripe	revise
trial	proviso	snipe	despise
siren	compliant	pike	exercise
trident	detritus	strike	enterprise
migrate	horizon	wise	crocodile
stipend	acclimate	rise	infantile
mica	bronchitis	jibe	appetite
cipher	gastritis	tribe	extradite
quiet	entitle	prize	erudite
client	unrivaled	size	dynamite
strident	environment	vise	stalactite
silo	variety	——	stalagmite
crisis	sobriety	concise	memorize
science	society	precise	pulverize
——	proprietor	sublime	galvanize
iris	leviathan	exile	fertilize
ivy	excitation	revile	oxidize
item	annihilate	defile	victimize
ibis	advisory	derive	columbine
Isis	revisory	deprive	eglantine
ivory	maniacal	connive	valentine
iodine	——	contrive	turpentine
itinerant	modifier	survive	regicide
iridium	purifier	revive	paradise
——	multiplier	endive	+
Siamese	undeniable	incline	
library	justifiable	divine	hireling
priory	indecipherable	opine	likeness
diagram	+	supine	fireproof
dialect		quinine	livelihood
	alibi		likelihood
	alkali		

Two dots (..) after a word indicate a homonym on the same line in another column.

A numeral after a word indicates a homonym with corresponding numeral on another line in the same or another column.

ILLUSTRATIVE \ī\ WORDS

igh	y	y-e
light	**cyclone**	**type**
bright	hyphen	dyne ..
fight	hydrant	lyre
night 1	tyrant	byre
knight 1	typhoon	pyre
might ..	thyroid	gyve
right 2	cycle	style
wright 2	cypress	———
sight 3	Cyclops	enzyme
tight	dryad	neophyte
fright	python	proselyte
blight	pylon	epiphyte
plight	phylum	bryophyte
———	stylus	leukocyte
affright	gyrate	electrolyte
delight	gyration	electrolyze
foresight	gyroscope	analyze
insight	dynamo	paralyze
limelight	dynasty	
	cyanide	
	myopia	
	hydrogen	
	hydraulic	
	hydroplane	
	hyacinth	
	pyrites	
	hypothesis	
	hyperbole	
	hydrometer	
	Hyperion	
	cyclometer	
	dehydrate	
	encyclopedia	
	carbohydrate	
	cry	
	dry	
	fly	
	why	
	wry	
	pry	
	spry	
	July	
	deny	
	defy	
	rely	
	reply	
	imply	
	occupy	
	magnify	
	gratify	
	ratify	
	identify	
	+	

A plus (+) indicates that the list could easily be extended.

The lines (____) separate groups arranged according to location of the phonogram: in monosyllables; initial or final in word; in initial, medial, or final syllables.

RATIO CHART OF \ī\ SPELLINGS

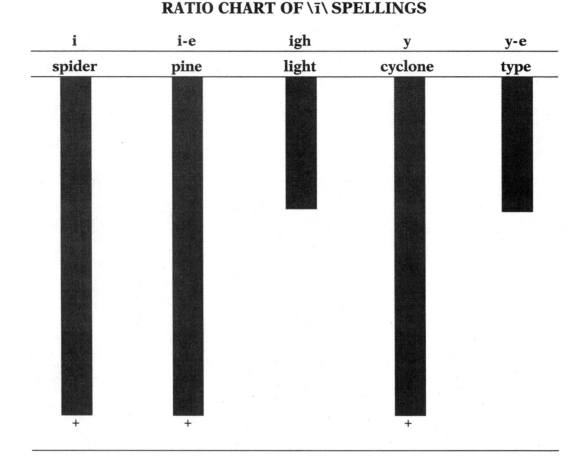

i	i-e	igh	y	y-e
spider	pine	light	cyclone	type

22. WAYS OF SPELLING \ā\. Yellow card 1.

\ā\ is spelled <u>a</u> as in <u>baby</u>, <u>a-e</u> as in <u>ape</u>, <u>ai</u> as in <u>sail</u>, <u>ay</u> as in <u>play</u>, <u>ea</u> as in <u>steak</u>, <u>ei</u> as in <u>vein</u>, <u>ey</u> as in <u>they</u>, <u>eigh</u> as in <u>eight</u>.

   a. In dissyllables and polysyllables, \ā\ at the end of a syllable other than the last, or when the sound constitutes an entire syllable, is most commonly spelled with the letter <u>a</u> alone. When <u>a</u> occurs at the end of a word it is not pronounced \ā\ but is \ə\ or rarely \ä\: <u>ze brə</u>; <u>Pan ə mä</u> (see Appendix 14).

   b. Final \ā\ is spelled <u>ay</u> (play), or very rarely <u>eigh</u> (sleigh).

     The spelling <u>ey</u> for final \ā\ is needed by younger students only for <u>they</u>, <u>obey</u>, and perhaps <u>whey</u>; by older students for such words as <u>convey</u>, <u>survey</u>, <u>purvey</u>, to be learned as needed.

   c. In syllables ending in a consonant sound, \ā\ may be spelled <u>a-e</u>, <u>ai</u>, <u>ea</u>, <u>ei</u>, or <u>eigh</u>. The first two spellings are decidedly the most common, but in many instances there is no way to predict which of the two is more probable.

d. a-e is seldom found except in monosyllables, and in final syllables of longer words: trade, forsake. In compounds and derivatives a-e may be followed by another syllable: brakeman, pavement.

e. ai occurs in monosyllables, in final syllables (at the end of words), and at the end of syllables that are part of multisyllabic words: praise, complain, raisin.

Closely approximating \ā\ is another sound, spelled a, ai, or ea followed by r. Many students hear it as long a. Since they fail to detect any difference between the a in fame \fām\ and that in stare \ster\, or between the sound of ai in mail \māl\ and that in fair \fer\, for purposes of spelling the difference is negligible and all may be regarded as long a. Words containing a, ai, or ea modified by r are common and groups are on the word chart. The symbol \e\ should be discussed with the student when the first word from such a group is given. Otherwise, if he spells \chār\ c-h-a-r-e and c-h-a-i-r and, checking in his dictionary, finds c-h-a-i-r pronounced \cher\ he may think it is not the word he is looking for.

The ea, ei, and eigh spellings should be treated as exceptional and the columns on the student's record sheet headed by these phonograms should be disposed of as promptly as was the oe column (see note under woeful, page 231). It would be a waste of time if all possibilities were considered for each word ending in a consonant sound, e.g., for \flāl\, f-l-a-l-e, f-l-a-i-l, f-l-e-a-l, f-l-e-i-l, f-l-e-i-g-h-l. When the ea, ei, and eigh columns have been disposed of, it will be apparent that f-l-a-l-e and f-l-a-i-l are the reasonable probabilities.

In the ea column, great and break and their derivatives, together with steak and yea, are the only words in which ea is used to spell \ā\ in standard English pronounciation. The study of the first three involves consideration of their homonyms: grate, brake and stake. Drill and memorization may be deferred for a time, but they should be added gradually to the student's list of learned words. Some catchy expressions may be helpful, such as "*Great waves break* on the shore." If the student associates great and break, he will be fairly sure that "the other ones" are grate and brake.

Before beginning to make his record sheet, a student who has worked with the \ō\ and \ī\ spellings may be interested in predicting the generalizations helpful in attempting the spelling of words containing long a.

TEACHER'S \ā\ LIST

1. maple
2. weigh
3. way
4. bait
5. lady
6. fable
7. sleigh
8. slay
9. ladle
10. yea
11. jail
12. gravy
13. veil
14. vale
15. shady
16. pagan
17. steak
18. stake
19. hatred
20. canine
21. neigh
22. nay
23. David
24. skein
25. great
26. saber
27. dismay
28. inveigh
29. vein
30. vain
31. vane
32. neighbor
33. bray
34. break
35. brake
36. wear
37. ware
38. rein
39. reign
40. rain
41. pray
42. macron
43. Dane
44. deign
45. stay
46. proclaim
47. data
48. heigh-ho
49. sustain
50. haven
51. say
52. stair
53. stare
54. craven
55. bay
56. tailor
57. save
58. raisin
59. gray
60. blame
61. station
62. sway
63. fairy
64. slate
65. basis
66. ray
67. mail
68. male
69. gracious
70. pain
71. pane
72. decay
73. bail
74. bale
75. lace
76. blatant
77. dame
78. relay
79. paint
80. crayon
81. came
82. dray
83. repair
84. gale
85. creation
86. betray
87. drape
88. scrape
89. display
90. vase
91. domain
92. breakage

STUDENT'S COMPLETED RECORD SHEET

Ways of Spelling \ā\

a	a-e		ai		ay		ea		ei		eigh	
baby	**ape**		**sail**		**play**		**steak**		**vein**		**eight**	
maple	vale	..	bait		way	..	yea		veil	..	weigh	..
lady	stake	..	jail		slay	..	steak	..	skein		sleigh	..
fable	vane	..	vain	..	nay	..	great		vein	..	neigh	..
ladle	brake	..	rain	1	dismay		break	..	rein	1	inveigh	
gravy	ware	..	proclaim		bray		wear	..	reign	1	neighbor	
shady	Dane	..	sustain		pray		breakage		deign	..	heigh-ho	
pagan	stare	..	stair	..	stay							
hatred	save		tailor		say							
canine	blame		raisin		bay							
David	slate		fairy		gray							
saber	male	..	mail	..	sway							
macron	pane	..	pain	..	ray							
data	bale	..	bail	..	decay							
haven	lace		paint		relay							
craven	dame		repair		crayon							
station	came		domain		dray							
basis	gale				betray							
gracious	drape				display							
blatant	scrape											
creation	vase											

ILLUSTRATIVE \ā\ WORDS

a		a-e		ai	
baby		**ape**		**sail 1.**	
maple		gate ..	behave	gait ..	constraint
ladle	stabilize	bale ..	concave	bail ..	restraint
fable	patronize	hale ..	inane	hail ..	bewail
lady	radio	pale ..	mundane	pail ..	derail
gravy	radiate	male ..	membrane	mail ..	retail
shady	gradient	tale ..	inhale	tail ..	afraid
pagan	maniac	pane ..	impale	pain ..	mislaid
latent	drapery	mane ..	abrade	main ..	portrait
sacred	rapier	made ..	invade	maid ..	complain
hatred	capable	cane ..	brigade	Cain ..	chilblain
canine	radium	ale ..	disgrace	ail ..	domain
saline	vagrancy	maze ..	replace	maize ..	sustain
David	vaporous	raze ..	amaze	raise ..	restrain
baker	——	plate ..	enrage	plait ..	arraign
saber	temptation	wave ..	rampage	waive ..	campaign
wager	striation	plane ..	erase	plain ..	entertain
Janus	creation	sale 1	stockade	faint 14	monorail
macron	vacation	grate 2	cascade	rain 15	+
pathos	decadence	brake 3	cavalcade	fain 16	
datum	equator	stake 4	palisade	wait 17	tailor
data	abrasion	vale 5	everglade	bait	daily
gala	evasion	sane 6	ambuscade	trait	gaily
haven	hiatus	lace	retrograde	slain	daisy
raven	impatience	mace	marmalade	raid	raisin
craven	sagacious	dame	cellophane	braid	naiad
graven	Titania	blame	counterpane	faith	complaisant
hazel	uranium	nave	perforate	wraith	complai-
label	geranium	lave	granulate	praise	sance
nation	Pygmalion	crave	palpitate	jail	traitorous
station	——	flake	fabricate	flail	lackadaisical
famous	ignoramus	safe	evacuate	trail	
basis	digitalis	drape	inoculate	claim	fair 7
gracious	percolator	scrape	+	maim	hair 8
matrix	generator	case		quaint	stair 9
calyx	rutabaga	vase	blameless	paint	pair 10
vacant	nomencla-	jade	graceful	——	air
blatant	ture	glade	bracelet	painting	chair
fragrant	veneration	sage	brakeman	painless	lair
halo	hibernation	stage	trademark	plaintiff	dairy
phalanx	graduation	glaze	baneberry	dainty	fairy
placate	quantitative	graze	——	wainscot	despair
nasal	legislative	dale	cordate	maiden	repair
papal	——	whale	duplicate	bailiff	impair
fatal	recuperative	swale	graduate	sailing	
fracas	refrigerator	phase		ailment	
Hades	repudiation	phrase	fare 7	strainer	
——	+	——	hare 8	maintenance	
able		mistake	stare 9	bailiwick	
agent	fatality	retake	pare 10	——	
apex	chaotic	forsake	bare 11	remainder	
April	vacation	elate	tare 12	retainer	
amen	gradation	innate	ware 13	attainment	
——	atonal	ornate	square	acquaintance	
	——	ingrate	glare	appraisal	
	canary	abate	declare	——	
	various	rebate	beware	acclaim	
	malaria	gyrate		proclaim	
	librarian	mandate		acquaint	
	vegetarian	sulphate		complaint	
		inflate			

Two dots (..) after a word indicate a homonym on the same line in another column.

A numeral after a word indicates a homonym with corresponding numeral on another line in the same or another column.

ILLUSTRATIVE \ā\ WORDS

ay	ea	ei	eigh
play	**great 2.**	**vein**	**eight**
gay	break 3	veil 5	weight 17
bay	steak 4	skein	freight
day	yea	seine 6	eighteen
tray		feint 14	eighty
gray	greatly	rein 15	eighty-one
way ..	greatness	reign 15	weigh ..
slay ..	breakage	feign 16	sleigh ..
nay ..	breaker	deign	neigh ..
may	breakable	beige	neighbor
hay	breakneck	geisha	inveigh
lay	breakwater	obeisance	heigh-ho
pay	beefsteak	surveillance	
say			
pray	pear 10		
stay	bear 11		
stray	tear 12		
clay	wear 13		
ray			
bray			
dray			
flay			
spray			
sway			
decay			
delay			
relay			
allay			
inlay			
Malay			
display			
essay			
betray			
array			
portray			
moray			
defray			
dismay			
crayon			
Dayton			
payment			
haymow			
layman			
waylay			
wayward			
bayberry			
bayonet			
mayonnaise			

A plus (+) indicates that the list could easily be extended.

The lines (____) separate groups arranged according to location of the phonogram: in monosyllables; initial or final in word: in initial, medial, or final syllables.

RATIO CHART OF \ā\ SPELLINGS

a	a-e	ai	ay	ea	ei	eigh
baby	safe	sail	play	great	vein	eight

+ (under a-e)

+ (under a)

+ (under ai)

23. WAYS OF SPELLING \ē\. Yellow card 3.

\ē\ is spelled e as in eject, e-e as in eve, ea as in eat, ee as in feed, ei as in ceiling, ie as in piece, y as in candy, ey as in valley.

The fact that in a word ending in a consonant sound \ē\ may be spelled e-e, ea, ee, ei, or ie makes the \ē\ list perplexing, especially as ea and ei are also spellings for \ā\.

The confusion can be lessened by studying the spelling pattern for the ie–ei words (see page 153) *before beginning work on the student's \ē\ record sheet if possible.* When the lists ie–ei have become familiar, the range of guesses for a word in which \ē\ is followed by a consonant sound will not include the ie–ei phonograms (except as a last resource), because the student will be reasonably sure whether the word he is attempting belongs or does not belong in the fifth or sixth columns of the \ē\ word chart.

Since not all the ie–ei words are included on page 255, he may have to try one of those spellings if none of the other possibilities proves satisfactory; for example, sheik and liege are included on the word chart but not in the lists given under Pattern 12.

A good way to demonstrate the value of this pattern is to review the \ē\ spellings, and then ask for the possible spellings of an unfamiliar word, e.g., \tēl\. The possibilities are t-e-l-e, t-e-a-l, t-e-e-l, t-e-i-l, t-i-e-l. Knowledge of the lists under Pattern 12 reduces the probabilities to t-e-l-e, t-e-a-l, and t-e-e-l.

a. In dissyllables and polysyllables, when the \ē\ sound is heard at the end of a syllable other than the last, or by itself constitutes a syllable, e.g., edict, the most frequent spelling is e alone. The spellings ea (eager) and ee (eel) occur, but are rare.

b. Final \ē\ is most often spelled ee, but y and ey do occur, e.g., family and chimney. Compare the ea and ee columns. In a very few monosyllables \ē\ is spelled e—me, we, he, she, be—but final e is usually silent.

Most words in which final e is sounded are relatively uncommon words, taken unaltered from a foreign language, and the original pronunciation is frequently retained, e.g., adobe (see Appendix 14).

c. Observing now the \ē\ in a syllable ending in a consonant sound (exclusive of ie and ei) we find three spellings, e-e, ea, ee.

e-e occurs in monosyllables and in final syllables. If the student examines the e-e column on the word chart, he will see that the few monosyllables are somewhat unusual words. This fact reduces the probabilities for the \ē\ in monosyllables to ea and ee.

\ē\ followed by a consonant sound in the final syllable of dissyllables and polysyllables is most frequently spelled e-e, though ea and ee do occur. The dictionary must decide.

We have found only one word, Cleveland, in which e-e is used in a syllable other than the last.

There is yet another possible spelling for \ē\, i-e, a most unexpected combination, as in machine. Nearly all such words are from French or reach us from some other language through French. Since it is exceptional, we did not include this spelling on the word chart or among the drill cards. However, the student may already have encountered it in reading and it should be presented again here. We have found no example of this spelling except in words in which the consonant following \ē\ was l, n, s, or soft c, as in automobile, sardine, valise, police (see Appendix 15).

The sound \ē\ is spelled with the letter i in another situation: in a few instances where i is either part of, or constitutes by itself, a medial syllable before a vowel, it is pronounced \ē\, as with me di al.

TEACHER'S \ē\ LIST

1. sea	19. egret	37. cathedral	55. recent	73. seem
2. see	20. teeth	38. weak	56. field	74. neon
3. deceit	21. premium	39. week	57. Siamese	75. cream
4. veto	22. neither	40. ether	58. brief	76. need
5. these	23. fever	41. speech	59. mean	77. beat
6. Venus	24. breve	42. leakage	60. mien	78. beet
7. leisure	25. peace	43. athlete	61. fleece	79. precept
8. regret	26. piece	44. shriek	62. recipe	80. delete
9. shield	27. mete	45. weird	63. feat	81. beach
10. frequent	28. meat	46. team	64. feet	82. beech
11. flea	29. meet	47. teem	65. equator	83. heave
12. flee	30. heliotrope	48. wield	66. plead	84. speed
13. pretext	31. grieve	49. completion	67. genteel	85. peony
14. conceit	32. Korean	50. peal	68. gleam	86. sheath
15. scheme	33. heal	51. peel	69. sincere	87. degree
16. zenith	34. heel	52. priest	70. exceed	88. appeal
17. niece	35. intercede	53. convene	71. seam	89. referee
18. history	36. monkey	54. gravity	72. journey	90. honey
				91. lady

STUDENT'S COMPLETED RECORD SHEET

Ways of Spelling \ē\

e	e-e	ea	ee	ei	ie	y	ey
eject	**eve**	**eat**	**feed**	**ceiling**	**chief**	**candy**	**valley**
veto	scheme	sea	see	deceit	shield	history	monkey
Venus	breve	flea	flee	leisure	niece	gravity	journey
regret	delete	peace	teeth	conceit	piece	lady	honey
frequent	mete	meat	meet	neither	grieve		
pretext	intercede	heal	heel	weird	shriek		
zenith	athlete	weak	week		wield		
egret	convene	leakage	speech		priest		
premium	Siamese	team	teem		field		
fever	sincere	peal	peel		brief		
heliotrope		mean	fleece		mien		
Korean		feat	feet				
cathedral		plead	genteel				
ether		gleam	exceed				
completion		seam	seem				
recent		cream	need				
recipe		beat	beet				
equator		beach	beech				
neon		heave	speed				
precept		sheath	degree				
peony		appeal	referee				

253

ILLUSTRATIVE \ē\ WORDS

e		e-e	ea	
eject		**eve**	**eat**	
being	prehistoric	theme	eat	leaflet
fever	secrecy	scheme	pea	leakage
meter	——	plebe	sea ..	teamster
neon	completion	breve	tea ..	ceaseless
peon	ideal	mete ..	flea ..	weakling
veto	magnesia	eke	lea ..	weakfish
sepal	primeval	eve	meat ..	peacemaker
legal	Korean	scene 2	beat ..	deanery
regal	hyena	cede 3	feat ..	freakish
Venus	pantheon	——	peal ..	——
female	cathedral	accede	steal ..	demeanor
feline	immediate	recede	weak ..	appeasement
femur	ingredient	secede	peak ..	——
helix	comedian	concede	leak ..	appeal
pretext	gardenia	precede	beach ..	repeal
precept	panacea	intercede	leach ..	conceal
prejudge	Colosseum	supersede	team ..	congeal
rebate	mausoleum	extreme	seam ..	reveal
regent	Galilean	supreme	read ..	repeat
frequent	neurasthenia	impede	grease ..	retreat
decent	inappreciable	stampede	heal ..	defeat
trefoil	+	complete	peace 5	increase
thesis		athlete	mean 6	decrease
Creole	be 1	delete	leaf 7	release
sego	recipe	deplete	cream	+
sequel	simile	obsolete	scream	
sequence	aborigine	replete	squeal	ea gle
zenith		secrete	squeak	ea glet
——	begin	serene	tweak	ea ger
edict	debate	convene	feast	ea sel
egret	prefer	achene	least	bea ver
egress	regard	benzene	cease	dea con
eland	eclipse	gangrene	lease	rea son
equal	elastic	trapeze	sheath	trea ty
ether	equator	intervene	heat	crea ture
eon	equality	supervene	wheat	fea ture
equinox	——	kerosene	bead	mea ger
egotism	+	Japanese	lead	mea sles
		Siamese	plead	pea cock
peony	abalone	blaspheme	leave	pea nut
helium	catastrophe	velocipede	heave	tea spoon
premium			heap	
medium	hero	Cleveland	reap	dear 8
realize	zero		glean	hear 4
theory	serum	here 4	clean	shear 9
deity	query	mere	meal	tear 10
sepia	Erie	sphere	teal	clear
reappear	cereal	——	league	gear
reappoint	period	adhere	each	near
reassemble	serious	sincere	ease	rear
devious	ethereal	revere	eaves	sear
deodorize	+	severe	——	spear
heliotrope		cashmere	easy	year
		interfere	Easter	——
		persevere	eastern	weary
		atmosphere	beaker	wearisome
		hemisphere	heater	——
				appear

Two dots (..) after a word indicate a homonym on the same line in another column.

A numeral after a word indicates a homonym with corresponding numeral on another line in the same or another column.

ILLUSTRATIVE \ē\ WORDS

ee	ei	ie	y	ey
feed	**ceiling**	**chief**	**candy**	**valley**

ee — feed

bee	1	tepee	
		Shawnee	
see	..	Pawnee	
tee	..	rupee	
flee	..	settee	
lee	..	disagree	
meet	..	pedigree	
beet	..	filigree	
feet	..	chimpanzee	
peel	..	chickadee	
steel	..	bumblebee	
week	..	manatee	
peek	..	jubilee	
leek	..	repartee	
beech	..	fricassee	
leech	..	referee	
teem	..	refugee	
seem	..	nominee	
reed	..	absentee	
Greece	..	employee	
heel	..	appointee	
		+	
seen	2		
seed	3	beetle	
freeze	11	feeble	
kneel		needle	
queen		steeple	
sheen		wheedle	
fleece		cheetah	
reel		leeward	
reef		leeway	
cheese		peevish	
breeze		weevil	
speech		teetotal	
bleed		squeegee	
teeth		deer	8
teethe		beer	12
seethe		sheer	9
creed		peer	13
speed		veer	
meek		cheer	
greedy		———	
needful		peerage	
tweezers		steerage	
———		career	
exceed		veneer	
proceed		———	
succeed		engineer	
canteen		volunteer	
careen		profiteer	
tureen		privateer	
between		pamphleteer	
indeed		domineer	
genteel		muleteer	
parakeet		charioteer	
———			
agree			
degree			
decree			

ei — ceiling

sheik	
seize	
seizure	
leisure	
either	
neither	
conceit	
conceive	
deceit	
deceive	
receipt	
receive	
perceive	
weir	
weird	

ie — chief

piece	5
mien	6
lief	7
frieze	1
field	
yield	
shield	
wield	
niece	
priest	
fiend	
fief	
liege	
shriek	
brief	
thief	
grief	
grieve	
diesel	
relief	
relieve	
belief	
believe	
achieve	
reprieve	
retrieve	
besiege	
Siegfried	
bier	12
pier	13
tier	10
fierce	
pierce	
frontier	
cashier	
financier	
cavalier	
chiffonier	
chandelier	
species	

y — candy

agency
academy
baby
biology
dairy
daisy
economy
eighty
———
factory
family
faculty
fancy
gallery
geography
gravity
happy
harmony
history
immunity
inquiry
integrity
jelly
jewelry
lady
laundry
liberty
machinery
majesty
majority
navy
notary
novelty
occupancy
quality
quarry
raspberry
sixty
sympathy
tardy
tendency
territory
university
vacancy
vanity
variety
yearly
zoology
pansy
pastry
pony
worry
weekly
yearly
+

ey — valley

abbey
attorney
barley
chimney
cagey
covey
dickey
donkey
galley
———
hockey
honey
jersey
jitney
jockney
journey
key
kidney
lackey
money
monkey
motley
parsley
parley
pulley
surrey
turkey
trolley
volley

A plus (+) indicates that the list could easily be extended.

The lines (____) separate groups arranged according to location of the phonogram: in monosyllables; initial or final in word; in initial, medial, or final syllables.

RATIO CHART OF \ē\ SPELLINGS

e	e-e	ea	ee	ei	ie	y	ey
eject	eve	eat	feed	ceiling	chief	candy	valley

| + | | + | + | | | | |

24. WAYS OF SPELLING \ü\. Yellow card 11.

\ü\ is spelled <u>oo</u> as in <u>food</u>, <u>ou</u> as in <u>soup</u>, <u>ew</u> as in <u>grew</u>, <u>u</u> as in <u>ruby</u>, <u>u-e</u> as in <u>ruler</u>, or <u>ue</u> as in <u>true</u>.

<u>oo</u> is the most common spelling for \ü\. However, this spelling is infrequent for \ü\ at the end of a syllable. In that position the phonogram <u>u</u> is the most common spelling, as in <u>ru by</u>. Also when \ü\ constitutes a syllable by itself it is usually spelled <u>u</u>. Since the sound is represented by \ü\, <u>oo</u> is given the first place on the word chart in spite of the fact that it seldom occurs at the end of a syllable, as do the other long vowels.

a. Final \ü\ in a syllable of a dissyllable or polysyllable may be spelled <u>u</u>, <u>ou</u>, or <u>oo</u>, e.g., <u>ruby</u>, <u>cougar</u>, <u>booty</u>, with <u>u</u> as the most frequent.

While <u>ou</u> is a relatively uncommon spelling for \ü\, it requires special attention. Many unsure spellers have a particular liking for the diphthong <u>ou</u> in a wide range of situations and must be impressed with the necessity of avoiding <u>ou</u> when spelling a new word until they have exhausted other possibilities. Close observation of the <u>ou</u> column should give some idea of the sort of word in which this spelling is to be expected. Most of the words come to us directly from French with little or no change; younger students seldom need them.

b. Final \ü\ may be spelled <u>ew</u>, <u>ue</u>, <u>oo</u>, very rarely <u>ou</u> or <u>u</u>. See Appendix 14 for a list of words ending in <u>u</u> pronounced \ü\.

c. In a syllable ending in a consonant sound the spelling may be <u>oo</u>, <u>ou</u>, or <u>u-e</u>.

Two possible spellings, not noted on the chart, remain: <u>o</u> and <u>ui</u>. Words in which they occur should be added to the student's list of "learned words" when needed. The <u>o</u> spelling occurs in <u>do</u>, <u>to</u>, <u>who</u>, <u>lose</u>, <u>prove</u>, <u>tomb</u>, and their derivatives.

In a very few common words <u>ui</u> is found as a spelling for \ü\. The following sentences contain most of them and are easily memorized: "The recruit drank the juice of bruised fruit on the cruise." "A light suit is suitable for a suitor, but may be a nuisance in case of pursuit."

In preparing for this lesson, the teacher makes a record like the following, with the columns approximately proportional to the lines on the ratio chart. In cases where there are very few words in one column, the column has been slightly lengthened to afford more practice with that particular spelling.

Ways of Spelling \ü\

oo	ou	ew	u	u-e	ue
food	**soup**	**grew**	**ruby**	**rule**	**true**
gloom	route	yew	truly	yule	rue
broom	troupe	blew	gruel	jute	blue
balloon	stoup	flew	druid	brute	flue
root	youth	slew	fluent	chute	construe
droop	group	strew	frugal	rude	
troop	caribou		prudent	dupe	
stoop	goulash		brutish	preclude	
shoot	roulette		rumor	include	
harpoon	uncouth		scruple		
baboon	recoup		truism		
maroon			juniper		
poodle			July		
whirlpool			plutocrat		
shampoo			rutabaga		
pontoon			inconclusive		
mongoose			rejuvenate		
kangaroo			incongruous		
mushroom			adjutant		
festoon					

The teacher jumbles the words on the above chart and dictates them to the student in the order below.

1. gloom	14. droop	27. group	40. goulash	53. kangaroo
2. route	15. frugal	28. scruple	41. whirlpool	54. uncouth
3. truly	16. stoup	29. harpoon	42. July	55. inconclusive
4. broom	17. prudent	30. brute	43. rude	56. mushroom
5. gruel	18. troop	31. flew	44. shampoo	57. prelude
6. yew	19. blew	32. baboon	45. slew	58. rejuvenate
7. balloon	20. youth	33. caribou	46. roulette	59. recoup
8. yule	21. brutish	34. truism	47. pontoon	60. incongruous
9. troupe	22. stoop	35. maroon	48. plutocrat	61. festoon
10. druid	23. jute	36. chute	49. dupe	62. strew
11. root	24. rumor	37. juniper	50. mongoose	63. include
12. rue	25. blue	38. poodle	51. rutabaga	64. adjutant
13. fluent	26. shoot	39. flue	52. construe	

The student places the words in the appropriate column, thus making a record sheet that corresponds to the one made by his teacher. The only difference is that as he recognizes a word as a homonym, he places a numerical label after it corresponding to its twin homonym.

STUDENT'S COMPLETED RECORD SHEET

Ways of Spelling \ü\

oo		**ou**		**ew**		**u**	**u-e**		**ue**	
food		**soup**		**grew**		**ruby**	**rule**		**true**	
gloom		route	1	yew		truly	yule		rue	
broom		troupe	2	blew	5	gruel	jute		blue	5
balloon		stoup	3	flew	6	druid	brute		flue	6
root	1	youth		slew		fluent	chute	4	construe	
droop		group		strew		frugal	rude			
troop	2	caribou				prudent	dupe			
stoop	3	goulash				brutish	preclude			
shoot	4	roulette				rumor	include			
harpoon		uncouth				scruple				
baboon		recoup				truism				
maroon						juniper				
poodle						July				
whirlpool						plutocrat				
shampoo						rutabaga				
pontoon						inconclusive				
mongoose						rejuvenate				
kangaroo						incongruous				
mushroom						adjutant				
festoon										

ILLUSTRATIVE \ ü \ WORDS

oo		ou	ew
food		**soup**	**grew**
root ..	buffoon	route ..	yew 1
troop ..	bassoon	troupe ..	slew
stoop ..	cartoon	stoup ..	crew
shoot ..	cocoon	croup	screw
rood ..	dragoon	group	strew
gloom	festoon	mousse	shrewd
droop	harpoon	rouge	eschew
mood	lagoon	dour	unscrew
brood	lampoon	ghoul	dew
moon	maroon	youth	new
soon	monsoon	youthful	stew
croon	platoon	cougar	newel
swoon	poltroon	foulard	steward
room	pontoon	louver	sewer
broom	tycoon	trousseau	sewerage
zoom	typhoon	toupee	anew
swoop	macaroon	routine	bedew
whoop	caboose	roulette	renew
loot	mongoose	goulash	curlew
scoot	mushroom	souvenir	mildew
boost	whirlpool	accouter	
roost	forsooth	acoustic	
booth	nincompoop	acoustical	
tooth	boo	accouterment	
soothe	coo	uncouth	
goose	moo	recoup	
moose	too	you 1	
noose	zoo	sou	
roof	booty	caribou	
proof	goober	marabou	
cool	poodle		
pool	igloo		
spool	taboo		
spook	tattoo		
groove	bugaboo		
smooth	kangaroo		
schooner	hoodoo		
rooster	voodoo		
doomsday			
loophole			
rootlet			
schooling			
schoolmaster			
gloomy			
moody			
soothsayer			
boomerang			
foolhardiness			
balloonist			
cartoonist			
harpooner			
buffoonery			
balloon			
baboon			

Two dots (..) after a word indicate a homonym on the same line in another column.

A numeral after a word indicates a homonym with the corresponding numeral on another line in the same or another column.

ILLUSTRATIVE \ ü \ WORDS

u		u-e		ue
ruby		**rule**		**true**
ruin	frugality	yule		rue
bruin	fluorescence	jute		blue
cruet	rutabaga	brute		flue
gruel	intrusion	chute ..		glue
druid	exclusion	rude ..		accrue
fluid	seclusion	plume		construe
frugal	inclusive	flume		misconstrue
gluten	exclusive	ruse		due
truant	perusal	June		sue
cruel	Peruvian	rune		ensue
fluent	rejuvenate	prune		issue
prudent	inscrutable	fluke		tissue
prudence	excruciating	spruce		pursue
tuna	inconclusive	truce		indue
brunette	incongruous	include		subdue
julep	hallelujah	exclude		virtue
brutish	+	conclude		residue
brutal	jujitsu	preclude		avenue
crucial	tumor	intrude		retinue
crusade	stupor	extrude		revenue
rhubarb	student	obtrude		
rumor	suet	recluse		
rupee	tunic	peruse		
rubric	tumult	jejune		
scruple	tumid	parachute		
truism	lucid	picayune		
July	stupid	assume		
jubilee	duel	dune		
juniper	dual	tune		
judicial	duplex	duke		
juvenile	duty	dupe		
crudity	ducal	lute		
crucible	tuba	tube		
crucify	tuber	dude		
crucifix	tulip	dilute		
fluency	lunar	salute		
fruition	duplicate	tribute		
plutocrat	tuberous	pollute		
glutinous	studious	minute		
ruinous	luminous	elude		
petunia	numerous	exude		
intuitive	dubious	allude		
enthusiasm	nutritive	exhume		
evolution	nutriment	resume		
revolution	stupefy	presume		
resolution	studio	obtuse	introduce	
continuity	superintend	reduce	reproduce	
opportunity	superhuman	induce	attitude	
ingenuity	stupefaction	produce	gratitude	
incredulity	elusive	opportune	quietude	
impromptu	solution	absolute	solitude	
superb	illuminate	institute	interlude	
ruminant	vituperate	resolute	ingratitude	
ruminate		substitute	irresolute	

A plus (+) indicates that the list could easily be extended.

The lines (____) separate groups arranged according to location of the phonogram: in monosyllables; initial or final in word; in initial, medial, or final syllables.

RATIO CHART OF \ü\ SPELLINGS

oo	ou	ew	u	u-e	ue
food	soup	grew	ruby	rule	true

25. WAYS OF SPELLING \yü\. Yellow card 10.

\yü\ is spelled <u>u</u> as in <u>music</u>, <u>u-e</u> as in <u>mule</u>, <u>ue</u> as in <u>rescue</u>, <u>eu</u> as in <u>feud</u>, <u>ew</u> as in <u>pew</u>.

We save the consideration of <u>u</u> for the last of the long vowels because it is particularly difficult for some students.

a. As we should expect after observing the other long vowels, in dissyllables or polysyllables at the end of a syllable other than the last or forming a syllable by itself, \yü\ is most often spelled <u>u</u>. An unexpected spelling is <u>eu</u> (<u>euphony</u>, <u>Europe</u>).

Very few of the words in which \ yü \ is spelled <u>eu</u> are used by young students and these can be taught separately as needed. The fact that initial \yü\ is sometimes spelled <u>eu</u> makes it imperative that older students be familiar with this diphthong, otherwise they would never think to look in the <u>e</u> section of the dictionary for a word beginning with the \yü\ sound. They will be interested in the fact that <u>eu</u> is found in words derived from Greek.

b. \yü\ in a syllable ending in a consonant sound is usually spelled <u>u-e</u> or <u>eu</u>, rarely <u>ue</u> or <u>ew</u>: <u>cube</u>, <u>feud</u>, <u>newt</u>.

c. Final \yü\ may be spelled <u>ue</u> (<u>rescue</u>) or <u>ew</u> (<u>pew</u>).

Very few words end in the letter <u>u</u> and in some of these the <u>u</u> sounds \yü\. As in the case of the final <u>e</u> and <u>i</u> words, most of them are from foreign languages. The list is very brief (see Appendix 14).

In America the practice of pronouncing \yü\ as \ü\ is widespread and seems to be increasing. In certain localities there are many people who actually do not detect a difference in the two sounds, while others consider the \yü\ an affectation in such words as <u>duty</u> and <u>student</u>. It may not be possible to alter their pronunciation, but they should be helped to avoid errors in spelling.

While working with the \yü\ words, be careful to pronounce the \yü\s very distinctly and to demand clear pronunciation from the student.

If a particular student has no difficulty in recognizing and representing the two sounds, he needs no special training, but those who have difficulty in detecting a difference may be helped by exercises featuring words in which, according to common usage, the letter <u>u</u> is pronounced \yü\ and others where it is always \ü\. All agree that <u>u</u> following <u>b</u>, <u>c</u>, <u>f</u>, <u>h</u>, <u>m</u>, and <u>p</u> is pronounced \yü\; after <u>j</u> it is \ü\; usually after <u>ch</u>, <u>r</u>, <u>s</u>, <u>z</u>, and <u>th</u> the sound is \ü\.

Begin by pronouncing <u>bugle</u> first as \'byü-gəl\, then as \'bü-gəl\. "Do they sound the same? Which is correct? Do we say, 'He is blowing a \'bü-gəl\' or 'He is blowing a \'byü-gəl\'?"

Discuss also <u>cube</u> and <u>June</u>. "Is it a \küb\ of sugar or a \kyüb\? Do we say \jün\ or \jyün\?" Other illuminating words are: <u>human</u>, <u>pupil</u>, <u>choose</u>, <u>fuse</u>, <u>root</u>, <u>ruby</u>.

A second step in training the ear to distinguish these sounds is to dictate words from the \ü\ and \yü\ lists, having the student decide in which list each word belongs.

If these exercises are consuming a disproportionate amount of time, they should be discontinued. Some students seem unable to make this auditory distinction. Someone who is conscious that there are two confusing sounds and that he cannot trust himself to distinguish them will know that he should consult the dictionary when in doubt.

Of course, the fact that the student has decided in which list the word belongs, \yü\ or \ü\, will not help him to know which of the spellings for \yü\ or \ü\ to use. However, if he has recognized the word as belonging in the \yü\ list, he will know that he must not choose <u>oo</u>, <u>ou</u>, or <u>o</u> to represent the vowel sound, since they are not used to spell \yü\; on the other hand, if it belongs in the \ü\ list he must not choose <u>eu</u> since this phonogram usually does not spell \ü\. The following arrangement of drill cards demonstrates these facts.

\ü\	<u>oo</u>	<u>ou</u>		<u>ew</u>	<u>u</u>	<u>u-e</u>	<u>ue</u>
\yü\			<u>eu</u>	<u>ew</u>	<u>u</u>	<u>u-e</u>	<u>ue</u>

In preparing for this lesson, the teacher makes a record like the following with the columns approximately proportional to the lines on the ratio chart.

Ways of Spelling \yü\

u	u-e	ue	eu	ew
music	**mule**	**rescue**	**euphony**	**skew**
bugle	fuse	cue	feudal	hew
fusion	spume	revue	eulogy	pew
human	muse	hue	eugenics	curfew
humor	cute	continue	eucalpytus	
cubit	cube	argue	euphonious	
humid	commute	value	neurology	
unit	tribute		euphemism	
uniform	huge			
usual	refuse			
mutiny	mute			
fuel	ridicule			
pupa	accuse			
pupil	vestibule			
fumigate	execute			
cupola	refuge			
cucumber				
community				
menu				
humane				
fugitive				

The teacher jumbles the words on the above chart and dictates them to the student in this order:

1. bugle	12. cute	23. tribute	34. mute	45. vestibule
2. fuse	13. cubit	24. usual	35. pupil	46. menu
3. cue	14. revue	25. eugenics	36. euphonious	47. curfew
4. fusion	15. cube	26. huge	37. fumigate	48. execute
5. feudal	16. student	27. mutiny	38. ridicule	49. humane
6. spume	17. eulogy	28. continue	39. cupola	50. value
7. human	18. hue	29. skew	40. argue	51. refuge
8. hew	19. unit	30. fuel	41. cucumber	52. fugitive
9. muse	20. commute	31. refuse	42. accuse	
10. humor	21. pew	32. eucalyptus	43. euphemism	
11. euphony	22. uniform	33. pupa	44. community	

The student places the word in the appropriate column, thus making a record sheet that corresponds to the one made by his teacher. The only difference is that as he recognizes a word as a homonym, he places a numerical label after it corresponding to its twin homonym.

STUDENT'S COMPLETED RECORD SHEET

Ways of Spelling \yü\

u	u-e	ue	eu	ew
music	**mule**	**rescue**	**euphony**	**skew**
bugle	fuse	cue	feudal	hew 1
fusion	spume	revue	eulogy	pew
human	muse	hue 1	eugenics	curfew
humor	cute	argue	eucalyptus	
cubit	cube	value	euphonious	
humid	commute		euphemism	
unit	tribute			
uniform	huge			
usual	refuse			
mutiny	mute			
fuel	ridicule			
pupa	accuse			
pupil	vestibule			
fumigate	execute			
cupola	refuge			
cucumber				
community				
menu				
humane				
fugitive				

ILLUSTRATIVE \ yü \ WORDS

u	u-e
music	**mule**
bugle	fuse
human	muse
humus	spume
humor	mute
fusion	cute
Cuban	cube
cubit	huge
cubed	dispute
cubic	commute
humid	compute
Cupid	tribute
fuel	acute
pupil	misuse
puny	refuse
pupa	infuse
puma	accuse
unit	abuse
usage	perfume
usual	commune
unity	tribune
universe	immune
unicorn	profuse
uniform	refuge
fumigate	ovule
mutiny	granule
mutilate	molecule
unite	ridicule
humidity	vestibule
museum	disrepute
utensil	execute
humane	persecute
mutable	electrocute
fugitive	hypotenuse
cupola	+
cucumber	
abusive	
profusion	
communicate	
community	
impecunious	
+	
emu	
menu	

Two dots (..) after a word indicate a homonym on the same line in another column.

A numeral after a word indicates a homonym with the corresponding numeral on another line in the same or another column.

ILLUSTRATIVE \ yü \ WORDS

ue	eu	ew
rescue	**euphony**	**pew**
hue ..	feudal	hew
cue	eugenics	mew
ague	eulogy	few
argue	euphemism	skew
value		ewe
revue		pewter
imbue		ewer
continue		curfew
curlicue		nephew
		sinew

A plus (+) indicates that the list could easily be extended.

The lines (____) separate groups arranged according to location of the phonogram: in mono-syllables; initial or final in word: in initial, medial, or final syllables

Handwriting

CHAPTER OVERVIEW

This is an especially helpful chapter for teachers whose students do not learn to write legibly despite traditional classroom handwriting programs. It covers handedness, slant position, and retraining. It also supports the use of keyboarding for students whose significant difficulty with handwriting interferes with production.

HANDWRITING

"Writing, like other fractions of the language faculty, is intimately related to the problem of unilateral dominance, since it is frequently lost in the adult as a result of destructive lesions of the dominant hemisphere and is not disturbed by lesions of comparable extent and locus in the subjugate hemisphere."

This paragraph is quoted from "Special Disability in Writing," by Samuel T. Orton and Anna Gillingham, and the following introduction to handwriting closely paraphrases or quotes from the same article.

"Special disability in writing" describes the challenge for students whose written output is faulty. Their difficulty with handwriting impedes their ability to express themselves in written form.

Cases of marked problems in learning to write may be grouped as follows:

1. Those in which there is clinical evidence of injury to the cortical motor system, as with birth injuries. Here the difficulty is chiefly an expression of the general motor disintegration.
2. The second group is made up of left-handed individuals who have met difficulties because of training unsuited to their needs. These are of two types:

   a. Those who have been permitted to use their left hand in writing but who have been allowed or compelled to place the paper in the right-hand position and to employ a slant abnormal for them.
   b. Those who have been taught to use the right hand in writing but have retained the use of the left hand in all other activities, showing little or

no evidence of mixed dominance. Not only are such students usually slow and awkward in writing, but not infrequently the left hand, although untrained for writing, does almost as well on examination as does the experienced right hand, and after a very brief period of training does much better than the right hand ever did.

3. The "third and by far the largest group is composed of those students whose difficulty in writing coexists with other problems which we relate to delays or failures in acquisition of clear-cut unilateral dominance. . . . These cases show good manual dexterity except in writing and their symptoms are held to be added evidence of interhemispheric rivalry." Several subgroups are found here:

   a. Those associated with reading and spelling disabilities.
   b. "An interesting group . . . who in spite of good intelligence and good muscular strength, encounter an unusual degree of difficulty in learning any motor patterns which require a high degree of complexity of muscular movements. Such individuals we interpret as cases of congenital *apraxia*."
   c. There can be an association of exceedingly poor handwriting with stuttering.

"The highly individual character of the organization of skills and abilities in a given student emphasizes the need of full analysis of each case and an approach to treatment without fixed methods but rather as an experiment."

PRELIMINARY INVESTIGATIONS

Determination of Hand to Be Trained

The first thing to decide when a student comes for handwriting reteaching is which hand the student should use. This decision is not always easy. Some students are so nearly equal in skill (or lack of skill) with both hands that the choice is difficult. Sometimes, although the student was originally inclined to be left-handed and was shifted to be right-handed, a change back seems inadvisable. Mastery was not well established in either hand and while very awkward, the trained right hand has become more capable than the left. Now and then we find that the untrained left hand has kept its natural dominance, and a very short period of training solves the problem; the student soon becomes an average writer with his left hand.

Position of Paper

The next step in the case of the left-handed student is to consider the position of paper and hand. A left-handed person who has good penmanship is somewhat rare. Even though he may have good motor control and form separate letters well, the general result is usually poor. A little questioning reveals the fact that most left-handers and their parents and teachers have accepted poor writing as inevitable, saying, "Oh, yes, he is left-handed, you know." This is very largely because they have been permitted, if not actually required, to turn the paper in the position used for the right-handed majority of students.

Punahou School afforded us an unusual opportunity to draw conclusions regarding widespread school procedure because it had students from public, private, and military schools from New England to Florida and across the continent. The preparation of the left-handed students from these widely scattered schools showed the same range as that of the right-handed, with only one exception. Some were strong students and some weak, some good readers and some poor, but their writing was usually poor and cramped, and they dragged their fingers across their written words, because they held paper and hand in the position pictured below.

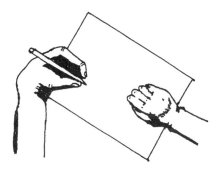

Fig. 1

Students often protest against the first suggestion of straightening the wrist, saying that teachers have told them to keep their wrists straight, but that they "just couldn't do it." The second picture shows how painful the effort would be with the paper still turned at the angle suitable for the right-handed.

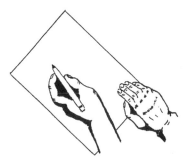

Fig. 2

The position of the paper should be different for the left-handed writer. Instruction can be slow and arduous; rarely does one encounter a miracle. One of the nearest approaches to the miraculous is sometimes found in the simple process of turning the paper to a position that is the exact reverse of that suitable for the right-handed person and insisting that the arm be parallel to the edge, thus preventing the sharply bent wrist, the writing down from above, and the fingers trailing over each word as it is written.

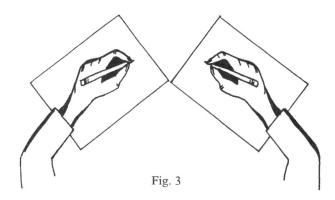

Fig. 3

Some teachers who appear convinced of the correct position for left-handed students still allow them to write with the paper at the wrong angle, declaring that they remind them frequently and are trying to form the habit gradually. This is not a matter for patient training. It is a technique to employ consistently. It cannot be effective if the paper is turned first in one direction, and then in the other. Every return to the previous, twisted position tears down the newly acquired skill. White lines painted on the desk or strips of tape to show how the paper is to be placed have helped in some cases. Teachers should do everything possible to make the new position interesting as an individual adjustment, just as shoes, gloves, glasses, and other items are fitted to the user. Not one lapse should be permitted. Of course, it is better if students never form the wrong habit. Even kindergartners with their free drawing on floor, easel, and desk should not be allowed to establish the habit of the bent wrist.

In the case of those who have learned to write in the wrong position there is at first a feeling of strangeness in the shift, but this soon passes. It has been the means of completely altering a student's school outlook by speeding up her work and reducing stress and strain. However, no simple formula will remove the trouble for students whose writing disability results from genuine kinesthetic confusion. These students, whether right- or left-handed, will need long practice. Even among them, however, the left-handed ones will be considerably helped by the correct position as a first step.

In some schools, especially those employing manuscript or vertical cursive script, one can sometimes observe another position that is equally disastrous for both right- and left-handers—holding the paper so that its front edge is parallel to the table. It is physiologically impossible to write at this angle with any power. One rarely sees an adult with the paper so placed unless it is a teacher demonstrating to students. Older students shift to a comfortable angle as they speed up. Although they shift later, this early position leaves its mark in habits of cramped wrist and fingers.

With the paper in the position shown in Fig. 3, the elbow is the center of a circle, the arm its radius, and the pencil describes a small portion of a large arc. The paper can be moved with the other hand, just as typewriter paper moves in order to keep each letter at the same spot on the carriage. The arm is straight and can exert control. If one must write on a horizontal line parallel with the table edge, neither hand can exert such power. The wrist can be straight only when the hand is directly in front of the shoulder and elbow, as in Fig. 4.

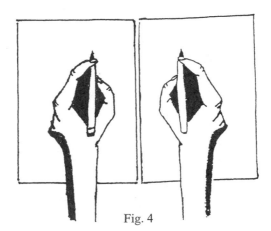

Fig. 4

The elbow must be on the desk! One of the worst obstacles to freedom of movement is the habit of writing with the wrist on the desk edge, elbow sticking out behind or hanging down, so that the weight of the whole arm drags upon the hand. A corollary of this is that no writing should ever be done with the paper fastened in the notebook. The broad cover pushes the hand toward the edge, leaving no room for the elbow on the desk.

This paper position precludes reaching the inner corners of the sheet or even the median line with either hand without bending the wrist, Fig. 5.

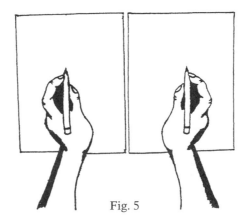

Fig. 5

This position is not very common and the student unconsciously corrects it. The right-handed paper position allowed or required of left-handed students gives evidence of a much more permanent misunderstanding, namely failure to recognize that the position in which the left hand can function efficiently is the exact reverse of that for the right hand. Also, the student himself is much less likely to change the position.

Determination of Slant

After handedness and the position of paper and arm have been settled, there is still a very important decision to make—the slant most comfortable for the student in question. This is of the utmost importance in the case of both right- and left-handed students. Indeed, the adoption of the best slant has occasionally been the only training factor necessary to produce almost magical improvement.

There are still some teachers who do not accept the backward slant, who are determined that slant should be uniform on all papers. It is comparatively easy to convince almost anyone, however, that just as in rowing and swimming the movements of the two arms are the same but in reversed pattern, so the natural movements of both hands in writing are outward from the median line, the left thus producing a mirrored copy of the right-hand form. So natural is this that frequently when right-handed persons attempt to write with the left hand for fun, they find themselves starting at the center and running outward in mirror writing. In a perfectly rational setup, left-handed people would write toward the left, as Leonardo da Vinci did in his notebooks.

Fig. 6

Because this mirror writing, natural for the left-handed, does not meet the practical demands of legibility, the best that we can do is to accept the backward slant, which maintains the outward thrust for each letter, even though the hand moves along the line toward the center.

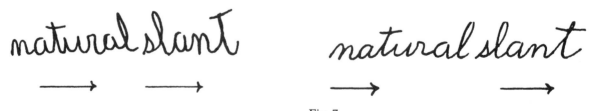

Fig. 7

Our files contain scores of samples showing the great improvement in form and neatness when backward slant and correct paper and arm position were required. The reproduction in Fig. 8 was written a few days after the writer was turning out almost illegible and very untidy papers. He was jubilant over the discovery that he could at last write really well.

The American Boy

Of course what we have a right to expect of the American boy is that he shall turn out to be a good American man. Now the chances are strong that he won't be much of a man unless he is a good deal of a boy. He must not be a coward or a weakling, a bully, a shirk, or a prig. He must work hard and play hard. He must be clean-minded and clean-lived, and able to hold his own under all circumstances and against all comers. It is only on these conditions that he will grow into the kind of American man of whom America can be really proud.

A more radical innovation in the classroom, often harder for the conventional teacher to accept, is the recognition that backward slant is more desirable for some right-handed students, unprejudiced observation and experimentation leave no doubt of this. Our goal is to assist all students to attain the slant most satisfactory for them, not to force upon them a preconceived notion of what is "correct."

However, it is not enough to remove objections and let the student take his course. The investigation should be made carefully, and slant should not be mentioned at all for several lessons. We use such devices as the following, which are good teaching procedure as well as tests for slant:

1. Freehand exercises like these below; the student is told to make the downward strokes as nearly vertical as possible.

Fig. 9

2. Freehand loops.

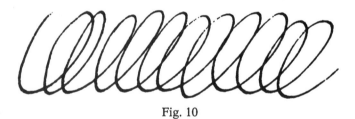

Fig. 10

3. Exercises 1 and 2 are often done with eyes looking away from the paper.
4. Each day some writing is done without looking.

Study these exercises, as well as the student's regular class papers, for evidence of slant. Even an occasional backward stroke is significant, since the full force of the student's training has given the push in the conventional direction. It is especially important to study the last lines of a long paper executed when the writer was becoming tired.

With few exceptions we can be reasonably sure almost at once that the natural slant of the left-handed student is toward the left. With the right-handed we must proceed more slowly. Especially in the case of weak spellers we may find that many lines in Exercises 1 and 2, and most likely of all in 3 and 4, will turn backwards.

Frequently we meet opposition from the student when we first suggest that the backward slant may be best. We must assure her that we are asking her to experiment with us to discover which slant is more comfortable, thus breaking down the idea that there is one fixed appearance which all must attain. We say: "You have used this other slant for several years. Will you use this new way for just one week, and then let's talk about it?" If our preliminary investigation has been careful, there is seldom a student who does not feel greater ease and freedom in the new slant long before the end of the trial week. Naturally, handwriting models for these cases are all written in backward slant.

The teacher will make his model letters, both for tracing and writing, according to the handwriting system used in his school.* Some people find it difficult to write in backward slant. For this reason we are inserting model letters for both right- and left-handed students (Figures 11 and 12).

While we can hope for success in a large number of cases in the predetermination of the more comfortable slant, teachers must be cautious in regarding it as fixed for all time. All early writing, whether of young students or reteaching cases, bears considerable resemblance to drawing in being slow and consciously directed; therefore it lacks rhythm. As skill increases and the hand moves more rhythmically, a slant that is even more "natural" than the one used earlier often develops. Many older right-handed students who had written well as children and had seemed entirely comfortable with the conventional slant discover that they can write more rapidly and rhythmically if they slant backwards. Many people admire this style of writing, and it is often employed to lend distinction to advertisements and formal notices.

RETEACHING

With correction of posture and slant the miracles cease. Training for specific writing disability is slow and can be discouraging. Almost every teacher of handwriting employs his or her own exercises and devices for relaxing the hand and arm before writing begins, and for securing some degree of rhythm. These are often ingenious and probably at times very beneficial. However, as we have observed them they are usually unsatisfactory in two respects. First, they are preliminary. The student relaxes and lets his hand lie limp or flops it loosely as directed. He then proceeds to write with fingers pressed white, knees drawn hard together, feet bearing down upon the floor, thus merely transferring tension from the hand to the rest of the body. Second, minute directions are often given for holding the pencil "loose and easy." The student follows them—the thumb, *here*; this finger, *there*; pencil *so*, across *this* finger; hand lying at ease, *so*, not turned over. All this centers the entire attention upon the hand.

It is best to get the student to forget his hand by fixing his attention elsewhere. We try to enlist his interest in making kinesthetic pictures in his mind. Also, he may think it fun to realize that he knows where all the parts of his body are, and that if his arm or hand is placed in a certain position, he can return it to the same position, or place the other in corresponding position, without looking. He is reminded that when he catches a ball thrown from a distance, he does not look at his hand to get it under the ball. He simply watches the ball and by the marvelous

---

* There are some schools that do not teach handwriting as a separate subject. Students will need special teaching in these schools.

**FORWARD SLANT MOST COMFORTABLE FOR MOST
RIGHT-HANDED STUDENTS**

a o d g q c

l b h k f e

i u v w m n p t j y

r s x z

A B C D E F G H I J K L

M N O P Q R S T U V W

X Y Z

Fig. 11

**BACKWARD SLANT MOST COMFORTABLE FOR MOST
LEFT-HANDED STUDENTS**

Fig. 12

mechanism in his brain the message goes to his hand, which is in the right spot when the ball arrives! In the same way he must forget his hand as he writes. Some suggestions for instilling this idea are as follows:

- His pencil is placed on a certain dot. Without looking he draws a line from this dot and then retraces, seeing whether he can estimate both direction and distance so as to stop on the same dot.
- Again he starts and draws a circle or a square, endeavoring to return to the starting point. Sometimes he draws a line, places his pencil below one end and tries without looking to draw another of the same length.
- He writes a word without looking at the paper and may be amused to see how well he is able to form the letters.
- He is told about Helen Keller and shown a specimen of her writing, which could be produced by kinesthetic imagery alone since she had no visual memory pictures stored up in her brain.
- He has his passive hand moved by his teacher to form circles, squares, letters, and must name what he has made, or reproduce it without seeing it.

For all these exercises we prefer that the eyes remain open but gaze out into space, rather than being closed. The intensity that a student may use in keeping his eyes closed may result in rigidity of the whole body. He must understand that although he must execute his ordinary writing with the general supervision of his eyes for direction and margins, it will never be rapid or easy until his hand has been so well trained in forming the letter patterns that he does not need to supervise their shape with his eyes. He should not have to bend over and peep around his fingers to see how a letter is getting along. He should be able to give his attention solely to the thought of what he is composing and let the letters take care of themselves. As long as he has to direct the formation of each letter with his eyes, his hand will move erratically and his knees and whole body will be cramped. His eyes are so used to directing the writing and his hand so dependent upon them, that it will be difficult to get the necessary training for the hand. Therefore, during the early part of his reteaching, his hand is on its own responsibility with little aid from his eyes.

- The teacher selects a letter that the student makes poorly. The letter is examined as to proportion, straight lines, curves, and other features. The teacher makes it on the board. The student draws it with utmost precision. He is warned that this is *drawing*, not *writing*.
- With his eyes upon the blackboard model, and his pencil on a large sheet of unruled paper correctly placed, he directs his hand to form the letter his eyes are seeing, remembering all the special points just discussed, and being very careful not to glance down at his hand a single time.

It is astonishing to each student and a fresh revelation to the teacher to find how smoothly and easily he makes the letter, how the fingers lose their cramp, and how the knees and shoulders relax.

- After a few lines have thus been filled with this letter, the blackboard model is erased. The task is then to command the hand to follow the outline that the student has stored in his mind as a visual picture.

Fig. 13

This process continues daily, estimating distances, tracing, training for form, with a new letter or two added. As soon as the student has practiced two or three letters, they are joined in pairs or in short words. Joining the letters can be the most difficult aspect of writing. Students may often have a problem joining letters like *br, oa, ow, wr, vi,* and *vi*. Practicing these combinations is necessary. For days or even weeks, sometimes for months, the practice periods are entirely spent in writing without looking. An increasingly frequent exercise should be copying from print. This introduces a factor not present when the model is in cursive writing. Sometimes it is necessary to relieve the student of all writing except that done under the supervision of the remedial teacher. Teachers are requested to accept oral examinations, and themes are dictated to parents or classmates, or written on a computer if possible. Writing under normal classroom pressure may undo all that is being gained.

We continue to emphasize that an act is not properly learned as long as it requires visual supervision. A good rower can row just as well in the dark; her eyes merely direct her course, not the dip or pull of the oars. Knitting is not mastered as long as one must watch the needle draw the stitch through. Any really skilled knitter can watch television while doing simple knitting. In the same way the writer's thoughts should not be hampered by attention to the form of the letters.

A large number of halting writers have difficulty in reading and spelling as well. We have seen that poor spelling is often due to making one letter when another was intended; there is insecure linkage between kinesthetic and visual or auditory memory. While laying special stress upon the kinesthetic factor of the above training, we can also be forming associations with visual and auditory records. While the student is copying the letter from the way it looks in her memory, she is sometimes asked to say its name, at other times its sound, just as in the Association drills for spelling. If she is truly a case for remedial spelling she will be given the copying and dictation presented in Chapter 6. These will help reinforce the handwriting training. Student and teacher scrutinize the daily output; they select poorly formed letters for special practice. In addition to the training in lengthened visual and auditory span, the student should be given an opportunity for kinesthetic discrimination. Most of the copying or dictation exercises should be done without looking at the pencil while writing.

There is much controversy over whether students should be taught to write using print or cursive—too much for us to address here. However, the case for cursive is strong.

> There is no reason why cursive writing should not be taught from the beginning to all students. However, in the case of dyslexics, there are several reasons for insisting on cursive. To begin with, in cursive writing there is no question as to where each letter begins—it begins *on* the line. The confusion with forms is not merely a left and right reversal as with *b/d* and *p/q*; it is also an up and down reversal as with *m/w* and *u/n*; hence the uncertainty as to whether a letter begins at the top or the bottom. Second, spelling is fixed more firmly in the mind if the word is formed in a continuous movement rather than in a series of separate strokes with the pencil lifted off the paper between each one. (Diana Hanbury King, *Writing Skills for the Adolescent.* Cambridge, MA: Educators Publishing Service, Inc., 1985, p. 3.)

While cursive handwriting is to be preferred in almost all cases, there are situations in which manuscript must be taught. Many students are in school systems in which cursive handwriting is not introduced until the middle of the third grade. Often students misform letters from an early age, and once the pattern is incorrectly fixed in the motor system, it becomes almost impossible to change. Incorrect manuscript formations make the transition to cursive difficult. Correct lowercase letter formations should be carefully taught and established, preferably by the end of kindergarten. This should not, especially at first, be a paper and pencil task. Instead, use:

- blackboards and whiteboards (there is merit to a vertical surface)
- shaving cream or finger paint
- trays filled with colored sand, lentils, cornmeal, corn, flour, sugar, or similar material.

Varying the surface keeps it interesting for young children.

As with cursive writing, the steps are as follows:

- trace the teacher's model
- copy several times
- form from memory
- write with eyes averted or closed

Unlike cursive formations, no lowercase letter begins on the line. Early practice in judging distances can include such activities as drawing "short grass" and "tall grass" always coming down. Say to students, "We always go down; we never go up."

As much as possible, letters should be made with a single stroke without lifting the pencil from the paper. The "ball and stick" formation of a, b, d, p, q, is particularly undesirable as it is conducive to reversals. Only six letters cannot be made in one movement: i, j, t, f, k, x.

Letters can be practiced in groups:

> tall letters: b d f h k l t
> t and f should be "tall," not "half tall"

> "basement" letters: g j p q y

To avoid reversals, stress:

> g and j go the same way . . . so does y
> make y like u, rather than with two strokes
> make q with a sharp "fishhook" (q) rather than finishing it like g

> "two o'clock" letters that begin like c:

> c d g q

> and a little c: s f

> o is the "midnight letter" and begins on top.

Some students are helped by being told "z begins like 7."

Whichever form is taught, the letters should be large. Small, indistinct letters, requiring little movement of the arm, do not make a kinesthetic impression adequate for definite recall. Narrow-spaced lining on exercise paper and the cramped space for answers in some workbooks exert a negative influence upon good handwriting.

It is by definite intention that we do not recommend one special system of handwriting. The remedial student should learn the same letter forms as those taught to his classmates. However, for some students it may be helpful to make associations between letters that are formed similarly. See the section on handwriting in the Appendix.

There are two practical standards for satisfactory penmanship—legibility and speed. Thus far we have discussed only legibility. Speed must be handled carefully. A hurried feeling produces poor writing and repeatedly breaks down good habits as fast as they are built up. Teachers should not mention speed until concepts of form are well established. As a reward for an excellent paper a student may occasionally be timed while he writes and allowed to calculate his rate of letters per minute. He must realize that increase in this rate is not cause for satisfaction unless he maintains the excellence of form. We believe that results are more desirable if the gain in speed is counted on the basis of the individual's own record rather than by comparison with his peers.

Figure 14 (page 285) shows what can be accomplished by rigorous adherence to writing without looking. The student was an extremely poor speller. His attempts at composition were discouraging indeed. Several weeks of remedial work showed little gain. His knowledge of phonics was fairly reliable, and he had mastered a good many spelling patterns and generalizations so that his oral spelling had improved. But his cramped, strained writing, with letters irregularly placed or reversed, was blocking his progress.

Handwriting reteaching was begun in January and was conducted along the lines already described. For many weeks the student never saw his hands form the letters. His eyes rested on the board or gazed into space. He produced this paper in May. The student looked at his book, read a line, glanced down to place his pencil and then looked away while he wrote the line. Although by the end of the term he occasionally looked while he wrote, he never had his eyes glued to the paper watching the shaping of each letter, and his writing was characterized by a freedom he had never experienced before. The improvement in spelling seemed to justify the experiment, as it has in other cases.

To promote legibility, the student should do the following:

- Anchor each letter exactly on the line
- Slant each letter consistently in the same direction (\\\ ||| ///)
- Use a release stroke (shown here by the arrow) at the end of each word to relax the hands and fingers

class

Bed in Summer.

In winter I get up at night
And dress by yellow candle-light.
In summer, quite the other way,
I have to go to bed by day.

I have to go to bed and see
The birds still hopping on the tree:
Or hear the grown-up people's feet
Still going past me in the street.

And does it not seem hard to you,
When all the sky is clear and blue,
And I should like so much to play,
To have to go to bed by day?

Fig. 14

CASES FOR WHOM RETEACHING IS NOT ADVISABLE

Not all severe cases should be regarded as candidates for reteaching. Any remedial department will need to be on guard against requests from teachers, parents, and students themselves for assistance that would entail long courses of remedial work without adequate return. Many poor writers cannot be regarded as candidates for weeks of practice. For them, handwriting is a tool for expression, but it suffers in appearance and even in legibility because their thoughts move more swiftly than their hands. Cases of this sort challenge our sense of proportion. The criterion must be whether the poor writing is a real handicap to school progress. Poorly formed writing cannot be classified as due to a specific writing disability, as in the case of people who with great effort cannot express themselves in writing because the actual letter forms are not a part of their kinesthetic memories.

Two individual instances may illustrate conditions under which responsibility should not be accepted for mortgaging months of a student's crowded program in formal drill.

MATT

Matt, IQ 157, was a case of general apraxia, probably the result of a slight birth injury, though of this the neurologist did not feel certain. From infancy he was awkward in all his movements, fell easily, dropped objects, was poor in all games. His writing was almost illegible. As a child he did not care, but as a high school student he began to realize the handicap and wanted help.

Careful examination convinced us that months of daily drill would not produce improvement commensurate with the time and effort. Typing lessons were substituted and he was taught (and encouraged) to use a word processor. Matt had no difficulty in locating the letters by the touch method. It is not probable that he will ever attain great speed as an operator, but his typing is much more rapid than writing with a pen and is, of course, perfectly legible.

JASON

Jason, IQ 135, was a typical case of severe handwriting disability. His parents said that he was a left-handed baby whom they shifted. Repeated testing convinced us that as an infant he was probably what he is now, perfectly ambidextrous. When he used his left hand they regarded this as evidence of left-handedness and forced the use of the right, neglecting to note the equally frequent use of the right hand. In high school he showed absolutely equal skill, or lack of it, with both hands in games, shop work, and drawing.

Jason was extremely sensitive, conscientious, and ambitious. He had always been a good oral speller and dictated words to himself as he wrote them so that if the letters could be read the result was not bad. His grasp of subject matter was excellent. He could write very well as long as his eyes carefully supervised each stroke; that is, he could draw each letter correctly with meticulous care. But this did not suffice for high school work. He seemed devoid of kinesthetic patterns. The instant he tried to speed up, his letters became indecipherable scrawls. He was greatly discouraged, and asked his parents to seek our aid.

Here again we felt the odds to be entirely against the boy unless an overwhelmingly disproportionate amount of time could be devoted to kinesthetic training. We advised him to learn to touch-type. Jason's progress was astonishing.

In a few weeks he was able to sit with eyes fixed on copy, or looking out the window in the case of original composition or an examination, and click the letters off faster than his classmates could write. He became the center of admiring attention, and the machine was an instrument for mental and spiritual liberation. Jason is a perfect candidate for a word processor. He can edit instantly with no tedious recopying.

Learning to touch-type is not the solution for every student. But for those for whom it is appropriate, learning a new motor process is a great aid to fluent writing.

In *Writing Skills for the Adolescent,* Diana Hanbury King states:

Teaching, especially of dyslexics, must be multisensory. These days, the word *modality* is in vogue. But, paradoxically, nobody seems to pay much attention to the teaching of handwriting. Rapid, legible, and comfortable handwriting is important for success in high school and college. But more than that, it is almost a prerequisite for teaching reading to the dyslexic. It is the kinesthetic sense, the feeling of the movement, that fixes the letters in one's memory. Writing is needed to reinforce the reading. Maria Montessori noted that young children make attempts at writing before they read—and anybody who has young children can observe the same thing. Too little attention is paid to the teaching of writing in the early grades, and none at all later on. Few teachers seem to know what to do about it, other than asking students to recopy their work, sometimes repeatedly. Yet—and this is a useful statement to make to students—handwriting affects every grade a student receives, for papers are corrected, not by machines, but by tired teachers, often at the end of the day or late at night, and the illegible or messy paper inevitably receives less credit.

Dictionary Technique

CHAPTER OVERVIEW

It is important for all students to learn to use the dictionary. For the weak or unsure speller, the dictionary is an essential tool. Every student should have ready access to one.

In previous editions of this manual, dictionary technique was strongly emphasized, in part because of the limited resources available to obtain information or support in learning to spell and define words. Today, however, there are many tools (computer programs with spellchecking systems, installed dictionaries and thesauruses, and so on) that make needed information more readily available. Yet the dictionary is still a valuable tool. It enables a student to read and pronounce unknown words correctly, using the symbolic representation of sounds.

This chapter will teach and reinforce alphabetizing, use of guide words and pronunciation symbols, and overall efficient use of the dictionary.

Materials Needed

- Dictionary of the appropriate level (elementary, intermediate, or collegiate)

DICTIONARY TECHNIQUE

Many times in the preceding pages we have advised that the student consult a dictionary. One must not assume that, given a dictionary, he or she will know how to use it. It is a complex instrument and its functions must be systematically explained. Teachers should help all remedial students to form the "dictionary habit."

With remedial cases instruction may begin earlier than might be advisable with an average class; it should certainly be more intensive. It is especially important that pleasure, not boredom, be associated with the use of the dictionary.

Many people take it for granted that students will dislike a dictionary. Accustomed to seeing puzzled youngsters fumbling unsuccessfully through its pages, they are incredulous when told that many students turn to it voluntarily and with pleasure.

ALPHABETICAL ARRANGEMENT

It is always necessary for anyone who uses the dictionary to understand alphabetical arrangement. It is obvious that students are not born knowing how words are placed in a dictionary, but it seems to surprise many adults that not all students can master the discovery for themselves.

Working Knowledge of Alphabetical Sequence

Work with the dictionary, even for students receiving individual instruction, should seldom begin earlier than the second grade. By the time students reach that grade, most can say the letters of the alphabet in their proper order. Occasionally one finds a student in a higher grade who cannot do so. For such a student the first step is to learn to say the alphabet in sequential order. However, this ability does not assure a *working knowledge* of alphabetical sequence. Students may immediately grasp the idea of alphabetical arrangement but fumble helplessly when trying to locate a letter in the dictionary. Drill in the relative position of the letters may be necessary.

ACTIVITY 1
Using the Phonics Drill Cards as alphabet cards, spread the cards out on a table in the proper sequence. Call attention to the fact that the middle of the alphabet falls between m and n. Have the student look the letters over carefully and say the alphabet aloud several times as she points to each letter. Using m and n as reference points, have the student (with eyes closed) point in the direction a given letter would be located in the sequence (pointing left or right).

ACTIVITY 2
Using the salmon vowel drill cards, help the student to remember their order in jingle fashion as "a, e, i, o, u, y." Then distribute the consonants and ask, "What shall we put between a and e? Now what shall we put between e and i?" And so on. At first, students begin with a and repeat the letters straight through to the second vowel of the pair in question. Slowly, they will begin to remember a group without beginning at a.

When the student reaches this stage, after the vowels are in place, the teacher can shuffle the consonants and time the student as he places them. The idea is for him to lay down each letter in the correct alphabetical order, trying not to say the alphabet for assistance. He should use the right hand for letters in the right half of the alphabet, and the left hand for those in the left half, thus reinforcing the visual impression with the kinesthetic. Students will be eager to beat their records from day to day.

ACTIVITY 3

After the cards are arranged in alphabetical order and the student's eyes are closed, a letter is removed. When the student opens her eyes, she is asked what letter belongs in the vacant place. Again, she is asked to tell, without looking at the cards, what letter follows f, n, q, or what precedes t, j, l. Teachers should repeatedly remind students to point with the correct hand to the half of the alphabet in which a designated letter appears.

As soon as the student has attained sufficient ease in card placement, the daily exercise should be followed by locating letters in the dictionary.

Many confused spellers share, to some extent, difficulty in remembering the location of letters in the alphabet. Before such students attempt to locate words they should have some training along the lines of the above activities.

Arranging Words in Alphabetical Order

It is not possible or desirable to wait until a student is unerring in locating letters before advancing to the next step. He may never achieve such perfection and, moreover, new elements must constantly be introduced to maintain interest.

Words like those in the following lists are typed, each on a separate card. The teacher gives these cards to the student to arrange alphabetically, sometimes in a horizontal line, sometimes in a vertical column. Familiarity with both directions is necessary to become familiar with the dictionary.

When the student can arrange the words in a list quickly, another word is sometimes given to insert in the line or column between the two words where it belongs alphabetically. The student states clearly why she places this word where she does: *annual* comes after *angry* and before *apart*; *conspire* comes after *conquer* and before *consult*, and so on.

- In the first list students need to consider only the initial letters:
  tub, ant, sail, man, boy, wind, gate, fence, rain, queen, violin, orange
- In the next, the first two letters:
  atlas, admit, about, angry, acorn, arch, amber, awake, apart, almost, axis, aster
- In the next, the first three letters:
  belong, beside, beach, begin, become, bent, berg, behave, bevel, befall, betray, bedeck
- In yet another list, the first four letters:
  consult, congress, conceal, content, condense, converse, conquer, conifer, confess, connect, conjugate

By the time they have worked out several exercises like these, most students realize that the alphabetical arrangement in the dictionary continues beyond the initial letter. Words with the first three letters alike are arranged alphabetically by their fourth letters; those with the first four letters alike are arranged alphabetically by their fifth letters.

Teachers can give more advanced students the same lists, not on cards, to alphabetize.

LOOKING UP WORDS

Spelling Known

Students will need this technique when they meet a word of unknown meaning or pronunciation in reading or when the spelling is well known.

GUIDE WORDS EXPLAINED

The first words to look up should be familiar and should lie before the student typed or written.

The following model lesson deals with words in *Merriam-Webster's Elementary Dictionary*.

> *"Begin* is an interesting word. Let's try to find it. I will help you a bit. It begins with *b*. We know that *b* will be near the beginning of the book. I have found it on page 44. Turn to that page. At the top you will find two words, *bedroom* and *behind*. These are guide words. *Bedroom* is repeated at the top of the first column, and *behind* at the bottom of the second column. There are guide words at the top of every page of the dictionary, and it is important to use them always. I know that *begin* must be on this page, because *beg* comes after *bed* and before *beh* (behind). See, here it is.
>
> "I will show you another word, *sailor*. It is on page 429, between guide words *sail* and *salt*."

ATTENTION FOCUSED ON GUIDE WORDS BY SKELETON DICTIONARY

After this introduction to the dictionary and demonstration of its make-up, a "skeleton dictionary" will be helpful in establishing correct habits. It is prepared by folding three or four sheets of paper and stapling them to make a booklet of six or eight pages about the size of the dictionary page. Each page is marked with numbers and guide words as indicated in Figure 1. There should be one of these booklets for each of perhaps a dozen letters.

Show the student the "skeleton dictionary" open at page 44 and explain that one might call this page a skeleton of page 44 in his real dictionary. Let him compare the two.

Place before him a paper on which the word *begin* is written.

> "The word *begin* belongs on this page. Can you tell me how I know?"

Before he can answer, it will be necessary to tell him that the guide words are signboards that show the first and last words between which all the words on that page are alphabetically arranged, in this case *bedroom* and *behind*.

> "The word must be somewhere on that page. Look in your dictionary. See, there it is."

After this, the student lays aside the dictionary for several days or weeks while he practices locating words in the skeleton dictionary.

With the skeleton dictionary for <u>S</u> open at page 429, let the student explain independently how he can know that the word *sailor* is on that page between the guide words *sail* and *salt*.

Fig. 1

After the student has explained the presence of words on pages in several booklets, the teacher should help him decide in which column to look for the word. *Begin* was on page 44. The *first* word of the second column is *before*, therefore *begin*, which comes alphabetically after *before* (because g comes after f), must be in the second column, because beg comes after bef in the word *before*. To continue, the word *sailor* belongs in the first column because sai comes before sal.

The final step is for the student to find for himself the page and column, thus locating the word. Given a booklet including pages 315 to 340 and a paper on which the word *okra* is written, he decides that the word cannot be on page 339 between the guide words *obscene* and *occurrence*, or on page 340, but must be on page 342, between *oil* and *on*, and in the first column because ok comes before ol, of *old-world*, the first word in the second column. If he now turns to his dictionary he will find that he has reasoned correctly.

Teachers must not assume that a few lessons will suffice. Students will need repeated exercises extending over a long period to insure facility. Teachers should construct drill lists carefully to provide practice in locating all the letters so that the student may begin to have a feeling about approximately where to turn for each letter. It is not necessary, however, to include a, b, c and x, y, z very frequently. Neither group's location will give trouble and, in addition, the second group will seldom be needed. The occasional omission of these letters makes it possible to include letters more often needed and harder to locate (f̲, g̲, h̲, k̲, r̲, s̲, t̲) more frequently.

In teaching the upper-grade student, the approach will be different. He will usually assert that he knows how to look up words. When given an opportunity to prove his prowess, he will usually demonstrate faulty technique, fumbling with alphabetical order, disregarding guide words, searching over the pages at random, or starting at the first page of the initial letter and looking down each column.

The younger student who cannot decipher most of the words on the dictionary page may not really need the skeleton dictionary since the maze of print is sufficient to prevent his discovering the word by chance. For the older student practice with the skeleton dictionary is indispensable to establish correct habits. He may be interested in the guide words, but instead of using them he furtively scans the words up and down the printed page until he happens upon the right one, thus unintentionally evading acquisition of the new technique. With the skeleton dictionary this is impossible, and he cannot help but use the instrument correctly since there are no words in the column.

The dozen or more leaflets are paged and the guide words copied from the latest edition of the Merriam-Webster dictionary.

The student must practice until a swift glance at the guide words becomes so habitual that it will continue when the real dictionary is employed. The teacher must be continually watchful to make sure of this. Speed exercises, to see how many words can be located in five minutes, for example, should be done with the skeleton dictionary until the student becomes competent.

A convenient arrangement of paper is as follows, the teacher filling in the first column, and the student filling in the second and third:

Word	Dictionary Page	Column

Spelling Unknown

Students, even those well advanced in high school, are often incredulous when first told to consult the dictionary for the spelling of a word. "You can't look it up when you don't know how to spell it. You look words up to find what they mean." Unless he can locate such words, the very information the unsure speller needs is not available to him. He may wish to write a word familiar in his own speech, or to look up the meaning of a strange word heard in a lecture or conversation. Few experiences give a greater sense of conquest over his difficulties than does the recognition that he can turn the pages of his dictionary and find such words.

MULTIPLE SPELLINGS

As soon as the student has learned to use the dictionary he can locate not only words in print or writing, but also perfectly-phonetic heard words, that is, those in which only one symbol can be used to represent each sound. However, as his study of the yellow cards proceeds, the realization comes that there are often several ways of spelling the same sound. Not knowing which is correct in the word, he does not know which to look up. Therefore, this piece of dictionary technique depends upon a study of multiple spellings and generalizations of probabilities selected from possibilities; it is closely integrated with Chapter 8.

INTERPRETATION OF PRONUNCIATION

The student must be able to recognize whether the word located in his dictionary is the one he seeks; he must be able both to understand the definition and pronounce the word. We have presented the dictionary symbols for sounds one by one in Chapters 2–5, and the facts scattered through these chapters are assembled with considerable additional information at the end of this book.

THE PROCESS

Having become familiar with a considerable number of yellow cards and generalizations, the student is ready to use his dictionary as an instrument for checking his "intelligent guessing."

One Ambiguity in the Word. The student places words on a \k\ paper. He must attempt \klōk\. He spells it <u>cloak</u> and <u>cloke</u>, and says, "I don't know which is right and must look it up." At this stage he has no way of knowing which is more probable. He writes both, and tries to look them up. He finds <u>cloak</u> but not <u>cloke</u> and has made his first use of the dictionary as a friend in spelling need.

Teachers can select other words from Chapter 8 as various generalizations are studied. For example, \glēm\. The initial and final sounds are unambiguous, \gl\ <u>gl</u> and \m\ <u>m</u>. The \ē\ might be spelled <u>ea</u>, <u>ee</u>, <u>ei</u>, <u>ie</u>, or <u>eme</u>. The most probable spellings are <u>ea</u>, <u>ee</u>, and <u>eme</u>. One after another must be tried.

Homonyms are especially valuable to study since they emphasize the necessity of reading the definition to make sure that the word located is the one wanted at the moment.

More Than One Ambiguity. After considerable practice with comparatively easy words, the teacher can introduce those with more than one ambiguity: \shāz\, <u>chaise</u>. The initial sound might be spelled <u>sh</u> or <u>ch</u>; the \ā\ might be <u>a</u>, <u>ai</u>, or <u>ei</u>. A student who is familiar with the long <u>a</u> generalizations in Chapter 8 should not suggest <u>ea</u> or <u>eigh</u>; the \z\ might be spelled <u>s</u> or <u>z</u>. With these possibilities before him—<u>sh</u>, <u>ch</u>; <u>a</u>, <u>ai</u>, <u>ei</u>; <u>s</u>, <u>z</u>—the student, trying one alternative after another, can find the word.

At the beginning of this work, the teacher pronounces each word as in ordinary conversation, then says it slowly with the syllables evenly stressed, so that all the vowel sounds are distinct. The student repeats the word slowly, writing a dash for each syllable: \lī 'sē əm\, <u>lyceum</u> _____ _____ _____ The possibilities for the doubtful syllables are discussed: <u>li</u> or <u>ly</u>, <u>se</u> or <u>ce</u>, <u>um</u> or <u>om</u>.

As the work progresses the student must try to spell the word as it sounds to her when spoken at ordinary speed, correctly accented. Some unaccented syllable is sure to prove baffling, for she will not hear the sound distinctly enough to form an opinion about it.

By this time students will realize that finding words in the dictionary is just another approach to the possible spellings of Chapter 8. Whether or not a certain syllable presents genuine ambiguities will often depend upon the thoroughness with which the possible spellings and general trends were taught and how well students remember them.

No teacher should assume that she can teach and finish the use of the dictionary on a certain date. As other types of work proceed, there must be occasional practice in dictionary technique. Words required in correcting written papers, as well as the lessons accompanying the study of a particular sound in the generalizations, can be used for practice.

Lists such as those below are miscellaneous. The teacher should introduce unfamiliar words often to universalize skill and develop confidence in attempting any word suggested. How else can a student learn to look up strange words heard for the first time, or, for that matter, words for which he knows the meaning but cannot spell?

Exercises like these have been known to rouse a listless and discouraged speller to enthusiastic interest in this game of deduction. It is encouraging for both teacher and student to observe increasingly good judgment about which spelling of an ambiguous syllable is most probable. Some of the words are especially valuable as training in retention of a long auditory sequence when this is broken by questions about one syllable or another.

congeal	phosphate	pleasant	hydraulic
python	moisture	charade	fathom
proceed	dissimilar	typhoon	hawser
proboscis	abysmal	worthily	centipede
martyrdom	centrifugal	lethargy	mischievous
flamboyant	caldron	conscience	seneschal
orchestra	chrysalis	irrecoverable	stalactite
intermittent	stomach	confederacy	perversity
competence	asphyxiate	disadvantage	hydrophobia
ingenuity	surcingle	competitor	monarchial
accidentally	dictatorial	nighttime	catastrophe
significant	reciprocity	vexatious	appropriation

DERIVATIONS

Many dictionaries intended for the use of secondary school students prominently feature the derivation of words. The language and the root from which a word is derived are given, enabling the student to discover how the familiar word that he is looking up came to have the meaning that it does. For example, <u>nasturtium</u>. This word has an amusing derivation. It comes from two Latin words, *nasus*, "nose" and *tortum*, "twisted." The name was given because of the pungent, biting taste of the juice.

Other dictionaries, however, give meager attention to derivations. Since students often find such word histories interesting, the teacher should be on the alert for words with interesting origins. He should consult dictionaries and books on the history of the language, and books dealing with etymology, in advance. Even elementary students can be interested in such stories.

Some words with interesting histories are escape, salary, sandwich, boycott, forsythia, algebra, cloud, ukulele, khaki, calico, curfew, and hippopotamus.

DEFINITIONS

Definitions are constantly used for both their informational value and in order that the student may assure himself that he has found the word he seeks. However, the concentrated, particular style in which they are expressed often makes them difficult to understand and demands instruction in interpreting them.

Moreover, there are frequently different variations of meaning for a given word. The student must learn to select the definition that best defines the word as used in context. Is *plant* a noun or a verb? Is it used in connection with vegetation, or with manufacturing, or as slang?

In other cases there are separate entries for words of the same spelling and pronunciation but with entirely different meanings, as with *font*. One boy reading about printing located *font* explained as a receptacle used in baptism and exclaimed, "It doesn't make sense." Just above it was *font*, defined as a printer understands it. For the word *cricket* there are entries meaning an insect, a game, and a footstool.

The student must be alert to such possibilities when a definition doesn't seem to fit.

SURPRISING SOUNDS AND LETTER COMBINATIONS

We come to a much more difficult situation now, namely the attempt to find words which contain silent letters, or sounds represented in spelling by utterly erratic combinations of letters.

Some students will have met words containing silent letters, and will have learned to spell a few of them: <u>know</u>, <u>knight</u>, <u>lamb</u>, <u>gnaw</u>. Even so, they may not think to look under the silent letter in their search for a word in the dictionary.

When they have learned to translate indicated pronunciations, silent letters at the end of a word or within a syllable need not cause a great deal of trouble. They can find <u>thumb</u> and <u>comb</u>, <u>benign</u> and <u>diaphragm</u>, <u>column</u> and <u>hymn</u> because they begin sensibly and are then recognizable as the word they are looking for since the pronunciation and definition are satisfactory.

When the initial letter is silent, a student should not be expected to locate the word unless it falls under the heading of certain combinations she has memorized: <u>kn</u> \n\ as in <u>knee</u>; <u>gn</u> as in <u>gnash</u>. It will also be helpful for her to learn that <u>h</u> is silent after <u>g</u> and <u>r</u>, as in <u>ghost</u> and <u>rhinoceros</u>.

Teachers can make the idea of silent letters interesting rather than irksome; students can understand their use in some words by a study of the derivations. One could say that silent letters are the ghosts of departed sounds from earlier in the word's history. Interest and attention influence the memory of even the confused speller.

Still more puzzling than silent letters are combinations which, translated phonetically, do not produce the sound usually attributed to them: <u>quet</u> pronounced \kā\ in <u>croquet</u> \krō-'kā\; <u>lough</u> pronounced \lō\ in <u>furlough</u> \'fər-lō\. In some cases a teacher may help the student find such a word by the indicated pronunciation. For example, there are only two words in which the letter <u>o</u> follows <u>furl</u>: <u>furlong</u> and <u>furlough</u>.

Suppose that in his writing he wishes to use the word \'yät\, <u>yacht</u>, and comes to the teacher saying, "I can't find anything like it in the dictionary. It ought to be spelled <u>y-o-t</u>, but it isn't here." There is really nothing to do but present it in writing or say, "Spell it <u>y-a-c-h-t</u>. I don't think you could possibly find it for yourself. It is a very strange spelling!"

To aid teachers and students in using the symbolic representation of sounds, we present the sound symbols as they appear on the endpapers of the dictionaries we are using. The page of symbols is located at the back of the book for easy reference.

Appendix

Table of Contents

INTRODUCTION

An essential trait of the remedial teacher is resourcefulness. He or she will need to provide enough successful experiences so that the student's attitude toward learning will be enthusiastic. Teachers must present the information in an enjoyable way, providing the appropriate amount of formal practice and reinforcement. They must use their creativity and be sensitive to the needs of the individual student, ready to develop the appropriate exercise at a moment's notice. Nothing prepared by others in advance can be as valuable as material developed by the teacher to meet a student's changing needs.

The information included in this Appendix is provided to assist the teacher in developing lessons; however, it does not need to be followed in order and should not be presented to the student if the drill is not needed. Preparing lessons takes a great deal of time; therefore, we offer some exercises that have been useful in the past. In many ways, students have similar needs, and devices which have been interesting and practical for one student may have value for another. Teachers should regard these exercises as a resource and, as always, modify them as appropriate. Some of the skill pages provided may be reproduced; others are sample ideas or formats, or are for quick reference and information. The word lists included may be in print too small for a student to read; if so, the teacher should enlarge them.

This Appendix also includes various compilations of information that we believe will be helpful for the teacher, including a list of materials, resources, and reference books, as well as quick reference pages of skills covered within the manual lessons.

An important first step in the remedial lesson is assessing a student's needs. To this end, we have included an informal inventory for determining strengths and weaknesses.

THE SPECIFICS OF THE ORTON-GILLINGHAM APPROACH*

1. **INDIVIDUALIZED:** meeting the needs of learners, no two of whom are alike.
2. **MULTIDISCIPLINARY:** drawing on the minds of experts in many different fields.
3. **MULTISENSORY:** combining *sight, hearing,* and *tactile/kinesthetic* pathways in a *thinking brain.*
4. **ALPHABETIC PHONICS:** learning letter sounds to facilitate spelling and reading. This includes learning the *feel* of correctly pronounced sounds.
5. **SYNTHETIC/ANALYTIC:** the process that means putting sounds together to spell words and taking them apart to read.
6. **SYSTEMATIC and LOGICAL:** language is organized and taught in a way that can be understood by intelligent learners.
7. **SEQUENTIAL:** the learning process moves from simple to complex in a gradual, orderly progression.
8. **CUMULATIVE AND INTEGRATED:** the learner moves from known to new material, alternating reading and spelling so that both develop together as skills.
9. **COGNITIVE:** the student is taught to think through language problems rather than to guess at words.
10. **FLUENCY:** drill brings about the automatic response, which enables better comprehension and attention to ideas.
11. **COMMUNICATION IS PARAMOUNT:** the learner is able to convey his or her thoughts to others and receive their ideas better.
12. **EMOTIONALLY SOUND:** the approach grows out of an understanding of how the person is able to learn, and an appreciation of the effort needed to master language.

---

* Adapted from the pamphlet "What is Dyslexia?" published by the Orton Dyslexia Society, 1991, and used with permission.

INFORMAL READING INVENTORY

This inventory will assist you in evaluating your students in terms of their strengths and weaknesses in beginning reading skills.

Name of Student _____ Date _____

TUTOR _____

CAUTION: If your student makes five consecutive errors in any group of questions that follow, move on to the next group. When he or she has failed in the same way in three groups, STOP TESTING. This test, and any other administered to students in remedial reading, must be given with great sensitivity and must minimize any feelings of failure, frustration, and pressure on the part of the student.

1. Does he know his left from right?
Ask these questions only if your student is under 12. List the responses in the appropriate columns at the right.

	<u>Correct</u>	<u>Hesitant</u>	<u>Incorrect</u>
Point to your right eye.			
Point to your left ear.			
Which is your right hand?			
Point to your right ear.			
Point to your left eye.			
Which is your left hand?			

2. How much sight vocabulary does he have?
A measure of the number of words the student can read at sight is made by asking him to read from a list of commonly used English words. A sample is on the Dolch list. Present to the student a set of cards with these words on them. Ask him to make two piles: knowns and unknowns. Have him read to you the pile that he knows. Count those he reads correctly. His sight vocabulary is _____ words.

3. Can he hear initial consonants? Auditory recognition.
Say, "I will say a word to you. Write the sound you hear at the beginning of the word."

Sample: seem (s)

If the student fails to write ten of the sounds correctly, ask him to repeat the sounds to you. Thus you will know whether he hears the sounds correctly even though he is not yet able to write the letters associated with the sounds.

1. daily	7. jam	13. timber
2. gown	8. rabbit	14. walnut
3. sober	9. barber	15. youth
4. marry	10. pile	16. kangaroo
5. fish	11. lazy	17. zero
6. happy	12. naughtily	18. violent

4. Can he hear the final consonant?
Say, "I will say a word for you. Write the sound you hear at the end of the word."

Sample: rap (p)

Follow the instructions for giving Section 3.

1. bird	5. half	9. sedan
2. dialogue	6. topaz	10. fight
3. miss	7. lack	11. rope
4. stream	8. boil	12. soup

5. Can he recognize the consonants and associate the correct sounds with them? Print the consonants on individual cards. Present each card, saying, "These letters have sounds. Can you sound them?"

List the responses in the appropriate column below:

Correct	Incorrect	Hesitant	Comments

6. Can he read the short vowel sounds in words? Print the following words on cards. Present each card to the student. If he sounds it incorrectly, record what sound he produced.

1. lip	3. rag	5. bump	7. sit	9. not
2. jet	4. hot	6. fin	8. scuff	10. match

7. Can he read the long end vowels? Can he blend the sounds? Say, "Read these words as well as you can." Present each word on a separate card.

1. mat	3. let	5. bill	7. robe	9. fun
2. mate	4. theme	6. fine	8. rob	10. fume

8. Does he reverse? Present these words on cards. Say, "Read these to me."

1. pal	6. put	11. saw	16. read
2. no	7. tops	12. tan	17. lap
3. raw	8. meat	13. won	
4. tar	9. never	14. rats	
5. keep	10. even	15. hop	

9. Can he hear consonant combinations? Say, "I will say a word. Write the sound that you hear at the beginning of the word. This sound will be a combination of two or more letters."

Sample: clean (cl)   speak (sp)

Follow the instructions given for section 3.

1. smoke	11. practice	20. snore
2. drive	12. sloop	21. frank
3. thank	13. stripe	22. splendid
4. grow	14. clay	23. shape
5. plaster	15. squat	24. spring
6. glue	16. flower	25. brass
7. skate	17. crank	26. swing
8. play	18. spy	27. block
9. trip	19. scream	28. sparrow
10. stand		

10. Can he recognize consonant combinations? Print the following combinations on separate cards. Present each card to the student, saying, "Can you tell me a word that starts with this sound?" Write the combination in the appropriate column below.

sm, dr, gr, pl, gl, sk, tr, pr, str, cl, fl, cr, scr, sn, fr, spl, spr, br, sw, bl, sp.

<u>Correct</u>   <u>Hesitant</u>   <u>Incorrect</u>

11. Can he read the vowel combinations? Present the following words on cards, saying, "Try to say these words as well as you can even if you have never seen them before."

1. cool	8. avoid	15. harm
2. burn	9. nook	16. meant
3. morn	10. spray	17. term
4. bawl	11. laid	18. joy
5. ice	12. firm	19. howl
6. free	13. loot	20. brew
7. leak	14. maul	21. lie
		22. lay

12. Can the student name the letters of the alphabet in sequence? Record sequence and errors in pronunciation or order.

13. Can he print the alphabet in sequence?

14. Can he write the alphabet in cursive in sequence?

15. Can he name the days of the week in sequence starting with Sunday or Monday? Record sequence and errors in pronunciation or sequence.

16. Can he write (in cursive or print) the days of the week in order?

17. Can he name the months of the year in sequence? Record sequence and errors in either pronunciation or order.

18. Can he write (in cursive or print) the months of the year in sequence?

INFORMAL SPELLING INVENTORY

1. ALPHABET
   a. can name the letters of the alphabet in sequence.

   b. can write the letters of the alphabet in sequence.

   c. can write the letters associated with the single consonant sounds:
   b, d, f, h, k, l, m, n, p, r, s, t ,v, w, z

   d. can write the letters associated with the single short vowels:
   i, e, u, o, a

   e. can spell consonant blends:
   bl, cl, fl, gl, pl, sl, br, cr, dr, fr, gr, pr, tr, sc, sk, sl, sm, sn, sp, st, sw, tw

   f. can spell consonant digraphs:
   ck, sh, ch, th, wh, kn, ph, gh, qu

   g. can spell a long vowel sound when the vowel is at the end of the syllable:
1. fever		5. label
2. acorn		6. humane
3. tiger		7. cradle
4. secret		

   h. can spell a long vowel sound when the word ends in a silent <u>e</u>:
1. life		6. lone
2. five		7. hole
3. came		8. rule
4. dame		9. tube
5. game		10. mine

2. SYLLABLES
   a. can spell single syllable words with a short vowel sound:
1. bat		6. ham
2. bed		7. hut
3. pit		8. rig
4. hot		9. nod
5. set		10. tug

   b. can spell single syllable words containing consonant blends:
1. small	8. prim	15. snow
2. drink	9. sleep	16. fry
3. green	10. string	17. splash
4. plea	11. clean	18. bring
5. glass	12. flag	19. sweep
6. skate	13. cry	20. blank
7. tree	14. scrub	21. spring

c. can spell single syllable words containing consonant digraphs:
1. lock
2. dash
3. chip
4. think
5. whip
6. match
7. phone
8. laugh
9. light
10. queen

d. can spell single syllable words ending in <u>ch</u> or <u>tch</u>:
1. notch
2. latch
3. pinch
4. hitch

e. can spell single syllable words ending in <u>f</u>, <u>l</u>, or <u>s</u>:
1. fluff
2. fell
3. ball
4. mass

f. can spell the soft sounds of <u>c</u> and <u>g</u>:
1. page
2. cinder
3. gin
4. trace
5. gent
6. city

g. can add the suffix -<u>ed</u> to single syllable words with short vowels:
1. butted
2. hopped
3. canned
4. matted

h. can add the suffix -<u>ing</u> to single syllable words with short vowels:
1. butting
2. getting
3. canning
4. matting

i. can add suffixes to words ending in silent <u>e</u>:
1. coming
2. skating
3. driving

3. VOWELS
a. can spell vowel digraphs, ea, ee, oa, ay, ie:
1. feed
2. week
3. boat
4. coal
5. each
6. tail
7. seat
8. piece
9. may
10. fail

b. can spell vowel diphthongs, oi, oy, ou, ow:
1. boil
2. coil
3. boy
4. toy
5. foul
6. out
7. low
8. plow

    c. can spell "r-controlled vowels," ar, er, ir, ur, or:

1. after	6. farm
2. sister	7. card
3. fort	8. hair
4. cord	9. cur
5. burn	10. bird

    d. can spell syllables containing vowel digraphs in which the first vowel is long and the second is silent:

1. please	4. rail
2. scream	5. teach
3. laid	

    e. can add a suffix to a single-syllable word containing more than one vowel:

1. pleasing   2. meaning   3. freeing

4. PLURALS AND MULTISYLLABIC WORDS

    a. can spell compound words:

1. steamship   2. baseball   3. classroom

    b. can spell multisyllabic words:

1. November   2. cobblestone   3. consonants

    c. can spell multisyllabic words to which an ending has been added:

1. collective   2. extension   3. dangerous

    d. can spell plural forms of nouns by adding s:

1. desks   2. pencils   3. flowers

    e. can spell plural forms of nouns by adding es:

1. glasses   2. watches   3. matches

    f.   can spell plural forms of nouns ending in y:

1. days   2. plays   3. boys

    g. can spell possessives by adding 's:

1. teacher's   2. Mary's

5. SIGHT WORDS

    a. can spell the days of the week:
    Monday through Sunday

    b. can spell the months:
    January through December

c. can spell basic sight words important for communication and survival:

1. closed	23. watch your step
2. danger—poison	24. ladies
3. stairs	25. office
4. push	26. danger—cars
5. in	27. this way
6. keep out	28. press
7. out	29. entrance
8. use other exit	30. tickets
9. gentlemen	31. telephone
10. cashier	32. don't walk
11. no trespassing	33. use crosswalk
12. exit	34. do not enter
13. use other door	35. quiet
14. men	36. open
15. pay here	37. caution
16. no admittance	38. deposit money here
17. rest rooms	39. information
18. move to the rear	40. stop
19. women	41. railroad crossing
20. fragile	42. one way
21. private	43. do not disturb
22. toilet	44. pull

d. can spell the Dolch basic sight word list.

A TEST FOR ASSESSING PHONEMIC AWARENESS IN YOUNG CHILDREN

Hallie Kay Yopp

The Yopp-Singer Test of Phoneme Segmentation provides teachers with a new tool for assessing children's phonemic awareness and identifying those children who may experience difficulty in reading and spelling.

Two decades ago few educational researchers and practitioners were familiar with the concept of phonemic awareness. In the last several years, however, phonemic awareness has captured the attention of many individuals in both the research community and elementary classrooms, and this interest is likely to continue for some time. What is this concept that has attracted so much attention? Phonemic awareness, as the term suggests, is the awareness of phonemes, or sounds, in the speech stream. It is the awareness that speech consists of a series of sounds.

Most youngsters enter kindergarten lacking phonemic awareness. Indeed, few are conscious that sentences are made up of individual words, let alone that words can be segmented into phonemes.

By the end of the first grade, however, many (but not all) children have gained this awareness and can manipulate phonemes in their speech. For example, they can break spoken words into their constituent sounds, saying "/d/-/i/-/g/" when presented with *dig;* they can remove a sound from a spoken word, saying "rake" when asked to take the /b/ off the beginning of the word *break;* and they can isolate the sound they hear at the beginning, middle, or end of a word. [Parallel lines surrounding a letter (e.g., /z/) are used to represent the sound rather than the name of the letter. For the ease of the reader, typical spellings of sounds will be used within these lines rather than the symbols used in phonetic transcriptions.]

Research has demonstrated that phonemic awareness is a very important ability. There is substantial evidence that phonemic awareness is strongly related to success in reading and spelling acquisition (Ball & Blachman, 1991; Liberman, Shankweiler, Fischer, & Carter, 1974; Perfetti, Beck, Bell, & Hughes, 1987; Share, Jorm, Maclean, & Matthews, 1984; Treiman & Baron, 1983; Yopp, 1992a). In a review of the research, Stanovich (1986) concluded that phonemic awareness is a more potent predictor of reading achievement than nonverbal intelligence, vocabulary, and listening comprehension, and that it often correlates more highly with reading acquisition than tests of general intelligence or reading readiness. He restated this conclusion recently in the pages of *The Reading Teacher:* "Most importantly, [phonemic awareness tasks] are the best predictors of the ease of early reading acquisition—better than anything else that we know of, including IQ" (Stanovich, 1994, p. 284).

A growing number of studies indicate that phonemic awareness is not simply a strong predictor, but that it is a necessary prerequisite for success in learning to read (Bradley & Bryant, 1983, 1985; Tunmer, Herriman, & Nesdale, 1988; see also Stanovich's 1994 discussion). For instance, Juel and Leavell (1988) determined that children who enter first grade lacking phonemic awareness are unable to induce spelling-sound correspondences from print exposure or to benefit from phonics instruction. Likewise, in her comprehensive survey of the research on learning to read, Adams (1990) concluded that children who fail to acquire phonemic awareness "are severely handicapped in their ability to master print" (p. 412).

The importance of phonemic awareness appears to cut across instructional approaches, as evidenced by the work of Griffith, Klesius, and Kromrey (1992), who found that phonemic awareness is a significant variable in both whole language and traditional classrooms. Few now would argue with the claim that this ability is essential for reading progress.

Given the evidence that phonemic awareness is necessary for success in reading development, many researchers are sounding the call for teachers of young children to include experiences in their curriculum that facilitate the development of phonemic awareness (Griffith & Olson, 1992; Juel, 1988; Lundberg, Frost, & Petersen, 1988; Mattingly, 1984). Particular attention needs to be given to those children lacking this ability. How, then, can teachers determine which students have this critical ability?

Any assessment instrument used to identify those students needing more activities that facilitate phonemic awareness must be both reliable and valid. The purpose of this article is to provide teachers with a tool for assessing phonemic awareness, and to offer evidence of its reliability and validity. The Yopp-Singer Test of Phoneme Segmentation is easy to administer, score, and interpret.

THE INSTRUMENT

The Yopp-Singer Test of Phoneme Segmentation measures a child's ability to separately articulate the sounds of a spoken word in order. For example, given the orally presented word *sat,* the child should respond with three separate sounds: /s/-/a/-/t/. Note that sounds, not letter names, are the appropriate response. Thus, given the four-letter word *fish,* the child should respond with three sounds: /f/-/i/-/sh/ (see the 22-item test). Words were selected for inclusion on the basis of feature analysis and word familiarity. (For a complete discussion of the word list rationale, see Yopp, 1988.) The test is administered individually and requires about 5 to 10 minutes per child.

Children are given the following directions upon administration of the test:

> Today we're going to play a word game. I'm going to say a word and I want you to break the word apart. You are going to tell me each sound in the word in order. For example, if I say "old," you should say "/o/-/l/-/d/" (The administrator says the sounds, not the letters.) Let's try a few words together.

The practice items are *ride, go,* and *man.* The examiner should help the child with each sample item—segmenting the item for the child if necessary and encouraging the child to repeat the segmented sounds. Then the child is given the 22-item test. Feedback is given to the child as he or she progresses through the list. If the child responds correctly, the examiner nods or says, "That's right." If the child gives an incorrect response, he or she is corrected. The examiner provides the appropriate response.

Yopp-Singer Test of Phoneme Segmentation

Student's name _____   Date _____

Score (number correct) _____

Directions: Today we're going to play a word game. I'm going to say a word and I want you to break the word apart. You are going to tell me each sound in the word in order. For example, if I say "old," you should say "/o/-/l/-/d/." (*Administrator: Be sure to say the sounds, not the letters, in the word.*) Let's try a few together.

Practice items: (*Assist the child in segmenting these items as necessary.*)   ride,   go,   man

Test items: (*Circle those items that the student correctly segments; incorrect responses may be recorded on the blank line following the item.*)

1. dog ————————	12. lay ————————
2. keep ————————	13. race ————————
3. fine ————————	14. zoo ————————
4. no ————————	15. three ————————
5. she ————————	16. job ————————
6. wave ————————	17. in ————————
7. grew ————————	18. ice ————————
8. that ————————	19. at ————————
9. red ————————	20. top ————————
10. me ————————	21. by ————————
11. sat ————————	22. do ————————

A child's score is the number of items correctly segmented into all constituent phonemes. No partial credit is given. For instance, if a child says "/c/-/at/" instead of "/c/-/a/-/t/," the response may be noted on the blank line following the item but is considered incorrect for purposes of scoring. Correct responses are only those that involve articulation of each phoneme those that involve articulation of each phoneme in the target word.

A blend contains two or three phonemes and each of these should be articulated separately. Hence, item 7 on the test, *grew*, has three phonemes: /g/-/r/-/ew/. Digraphs, such as /sh/ in item 5, *she*, and /th/ in item 15, *three*, are single phonemes. Item 5, therefore, has two phonemes and item 15 has three phonemes. If a child responds with letter names instead of sounds, the response is coded as incorrect, and the type of error is noted on the test.

Teachers of young children should expect a wide range of performance on this test. A sample of kindergarteners drawn from the public schools in a west coast city in the United States obtained scores ranging from 0 to 22 correct (0% to 100%) during their second semester. The mean (average) score was 11.78, with a standard deviation of 7.66 (Yopp, 1988, see below). Similar findings from a sample of kindergarteners on the east coast of the United States were reported by Spector (1992): the mean score was 11.39 with a standard deviation of 8.18.

Students who obtain high scores (segmenting all or nearly all of the items correctly) may be considered phonemically aware. Students who correctly segment some items are displaying emerging phonemic awareness. Students who are able to segment only a few items or none at all lack appropriate levels of phonemic awareness. Without intervention, those students scoring very low on the test are likely to experience difficulty with reading and spelling.

Teachers' notes on the blank lines of the test will be helpful in understanding each child. Some children may partially segment—perhaps dividing words into chunks larger than phonemes. These children are beginning to have an insight into the nature of speech. Others may simply repeat the stimulus item or provide nonsense responses regardless of the amount of feedback and practice given. They have very little insight into the phonemic basis of their speech. Still others may simply offer letter names.

If the letter names are random (e.g., given *red* the child responds "n-b-d-o"), the teacher learns that the child lacks phonemic awareness but knows some letter names. If the letter names are close approximations to the conventional spelling of the words (e.g., given *red* the child responds "r-a-d"), the teacher knows that either the child has memorized the spellings of some words or that he or she is phonemically aware and has mentally segmented the items, then verbally provided the examiner with the letters corresponding to those sounds—an impressive feat! The examiner should repeat the instructions in this case to make sure the child fully understands the task.

DATA ON THE INSTRUMENT

A number of years ago I undertook a study to compare tests of phonemic awareness that appeared in the literature and to examine the reliability and validity of each (Yopp, 1988). Nearly 100 second-semester kindergarten youngsters drawn from three public elementary schools in a southern California school district that serves children from a lower middle to an upper middle class population were each administered 10 different phonemic awareness tests over a period of several weeks. Children ranged in age from 64 to 80 months with an average age of 70 months, and were predominantly White, with 1% Black, 2% Asian, and 15% with Spanish surnames. All children were fluent English speakers.

Performance on the phonemic awareness tests was compared, the reliability of each test was calculated, and a factor analysis was conducted to determine validity. One of the tests in the battery, the Yopp-Singer Test of Phoneme Segmentation, had a reliability score (Cronbach's alpha) of .95, indicating that it can be appropriately used in the assessment of individuals. Experts in tests and measurement tell us that instruments should have reliability coefficients above .85 (Hills, 1981) or even .90 (Jensen, 1980) if they are to be used to make decisions about individuals.

Analyses also indicated that the Yopp-Singer Test is a valid measure of phonemic awareness. Construct validity was determined through a factor analysis (for details see Yopp, 1988). Predictive validity was determined by collecting data on the reading achievement of the same students each year beginning in kindergarten and concluding when the students were in sixth grade; spelling achievement data were obtained in Grades 2 to 6. Thus, 7 years of longitudinal data are available. (See Yopp, 1992a for details on this study.) A test of nonword decoding was administered in kindergarten. In order to determine reading and spelling achievement in Grades 1 through 6, records of the students' performance on the Comprehensive Test of Basic Skills (CTBS, 1973), a timed, norm-referenced, objectives based test, were obtained. This standardized test, widely used by school districts as part of their regular testing program, includes word attack, vocabulary, comprehension, and spelling subtests in the reading and spelling achievement battery. These tests are described in Table 1.

Table 2 presents the correlations between performance on the Yopp-Singer Test of Phoneme Segmentation administered in kindergarten and all subtests on the reading and spelling achievement battery throughout the grade levels as well as the kindergarten nonword reading measure. Each of the correlations is significant: performance on the Yopp-Singer Test of Phoneme Segmentation has a moderate to strong relationship with performance on the nonword reading test given in kindergarten and with the subtests of the CTBS—word attack, vocabulary, comprehension, and spelling (and the total score)—through Grade 6. Thus, the phonemic awareness test has significant predictive validity.

Because reading and spelling achievement are related to phonemic awareness and to future reading and spelling achievement, these impressive correlations (as high as .78) do not address the question of whether a measure of phonemic awareness truly contributes to the prediction of reading and spelling performance years later, independent of previous reading and spelling achievement. For instance, a significant correlation between phonemic awareness in kindergarten and reading in Grade 1 might be obtained because reading performance in kindergarten and Grade 1 are highly correlated, and reading performance in kindergarten and phonemic awareness in kindergarten are highly correlated.

Thus, the relationship between phonemic awareness in kindergarten and reading in first grade might simply be a byproduct of these other relationships. We want to know whether a measure of phonemic awareness obtained in kinder-

Table 1
Descriptions of reading and spelling tests used to determine predictive validity

Nonword Reading Test
> The nonword reading test was administered for the purpose of determining each child's ability to use sound-symbol correspondences to decode nonwords. Children were assessed on their ability to sound and blend printed nonwords such as *paz* and *kov*. Administered in kindergarten.

CTBS Word Attack Subtest
> The word attack section requires students to identify letters corresponding to the initial or final single consonant, cluster, or digraph sounds or the medial vowels heard in orally presented words. Recognition of sight words is also measured in this subtest. Administered during Grades 1 through 3.

CTBS Vocabulary Subtest*
> The vocabulary section measures children's ability to identify a word associated with an orally presented category or definition, in addition to identifying same-meaning words or unfamiliar words in context.
> Administered during Grades 1 through 6.

CTBS Reading Comprehension Subtest*
> The reading comprehension section is used to measure children's comprehension of both sentences and stories. Children are asked to respond to objective questions after reading each selection.
> Administered during Grades 1 through 6.

CTBS Spelling Subtest
> The spelling section measures children's ability to recognize correctly spelled words. Administered during Grades 2 through 6.

---

* A "total" reading score is generated for each child that combines the vocabulary and comprehension subtests.

Table 2
Correlation of performance on phonemic awareness task administered in Grade K with performance on reading and spelling subtests, Grades K–6

			Subtests			
Grade Level	Nonword	Word Attack	Vocabulary	Comprehension	Total	Spelling
K	.67**					
1		.46**	.66**	.38**	.62**	
2		.62**	.72**	.55**	.67**	.53**
3		.56**	.66**	.62**	.67**	.44**
4			.51**	.62**	.58**	.60**
5			.56**	.57**	.59**	.55**
6			.78**	.66**	.74**	.46**

$* p < .05$ $** p < .01$

garten contributes to the prediction of future reading and spelling achievement above and beyond the contribution that past reading and spelling achievement makes on future achievement in reading and spelling. Does performance on a measure of phonemic awareness offer us any unique insights into future performance in reading and spelling?

In order to rule out the effect of reading and spelling achievement over the years on subsequent reading and spelling performance, partial time-lag correlations were also conducted. These correlations are "partial" in that they partial out, or eliminate, the effects of one variable (in this case, past reading or spelling performance) on another (in this case, later reading or spelling performance); they are "time-lag" in that they examine the relationship between two variables over time (earlier phonemic awareness performance and later reading or spelling achievement). The partial time-lag correlations are presented in Table 3.

Each correlation coefficient indicates the strength of the relationship between performance on the phonemic awareness test in kindergarten and performance on reading and spelling subtests in Grades 1–6 when the previous year's achievement in these areas has been controlled. Thus, the .54 correlation found in Table 3 between phonemic awareness in kindergarten and vocabulary in Grade 5 is the strength of the relationship after fourth-grade vocabulary performance has been accounted for.

Table 3 reveals that most of the correlations remain significant, some as high as .51, .54, and .55. Thus, they reveal that scores on the Yopp-Singer Test of Phoneme Segmentation make a unique contribution to predicting students' reading and spelling achievement above and beyond their previous achievement in these areas.

The power of a 5- to 10-minute, 22-item test administered in kindergarten to predict students' performance in reading and spelling achievement years later, even after controlling for previous reading and spelling achievement, is

---

Table 3
Partial time-lag correlation of performance on phonemic awareness task administered in Grade K with performance on reading and spelling subtests, Grades 1–6, controlling for performance on reading and spelling subtests administered the previous year

	Subtests				
Grade Level	Word Attack	Vocabulary	Comprehension	Total	Spelling
1	.33**	.55**	.08	.43**	
2	.51**	.36**	.43**	.32**	
3	.20	.19	.43**	.33**	.11
4		−.05	.38**	.10	.43**
5		.54**	.18	.36*	.26
		.51**	.45**	.47**	−.05

$* p < .05$ $** p < .01$

quite surprising. In his review of the research on phonemic awareness, Stanovich (1994) noted the strong relationship between performance on a number of simple, short phonemic awareness tasks and reading acquisition and suggests that the power of such simple tasks to predict reading acquisition is one of the reasons for the tremendous research energy currently devoted to this line of inquiry.

IMPLICATIONS

What do these findings mean for teachers? They mean that we now have a tool—one that is both valid and reliable as well as simple and quick to administer—that can be used to determine a child's phonemic awareness, and we have the knowledge that performance on this measure is significantly related to a child's achievement in reading and spelling for years to come.

What can we do with this information? We can identify children quite early who are likely to experience difficulty in reading and spelling and give them appropriate instructional support. Fortunately, a growing body of evidence indicates that training of phonemic awareness is possible and that it can result in significant gains in subsequent reading and spelling achievement (Ball & Blachman, 1991; Bradley & Bryant, 1983; Cunningham, 1990; Lie, 1991; Lundberg et al., 1988). Thus, a child need not be labeled "phonemically unaware" and therefore inevitably a "poor" reader. Phonemic awareness is an ability that teachers and reading/language arts specialists can develop in many students.

Some researchers have argued that systematic training in phonemic awareness should be part of every youngster's education before the onset of formal reading instruction (Mattingly, 1984; Tunmer et al., 1988). The need for this, of course, depends upon the abilities of the individual children in the classroom. Further, in many classrooms the onset of formal reading will be difficult to identify—there is no onset of "formal" instruction and reading is not differentiated from prereading.

A growing number of teachers hold an emergent literacy perspective, viewing literacy as an evolving process that begins during infancy and they provide a wealth of valuable literacy experiences for children very early on. Certainly these experiences should not be withheld until children become phonemically aware!

However, it is important for teachers and other practitioners to appreciate that children will likely make little sense of the alphabetic principle without phonemic awareness, and so phonemic awareness should be developed as part of the larger literacy program for many children. Fortunately, phonemic awareness activities can be readily incorporated into preschool, kindergarten, and early primary grade classrooms. Recent articles in *The Reading Teacher* (Griffith & Olson, 1992; Yopp, 1992b) have provided suggestions for helping young children focus on the sounds of language through stories, songs, and games. A few suggestions will be highlighted here.

Griffith and Olson (1992) and I (Yopp, 1995) suggest that one simple means to draw children's attention to the sound structure of language is through the use of read-aloud books. Many children's books emphasize speech sounds through rhyme, alliteration, assonance, phoneme substitution, or segmentation and offer play with language as a dominant feature. For instance, P. Cameron's

"I Can't," Said the Ant (1961) makes use of a simple rhyme scheme, Seuss's *Dr. Seuss's ABC* (1963) uses alliteration as each letter of the alphabet is introduced, and his *There's a Wocket in My Pocket* (1974) incorporates initial phoneme substitution to create a household of humorous nonsense creatures.

I have suggested (Yopp, 1995) that such books can be read and reread, their language can be enjoyed and explored in class discussions, predictions that focus on language can be encouraged, and additional verses or alternate versions of the texts can be created using the language patterns provided. (See Yopp, 1995, for an annotated bibliography of books to develop phonemic awareness.)

A guessing game that I have used successfully both with groups of children and in individualized settings is "What am I thinking of?" (Yopp, 1992b). This game encourages children to blend orally spoken sounds together. The teacher tells the children a category and then speaks in a segmented fashion the sounds of a particular item in that category. For instance, given the category "article of clothing," the teacher might say the following three sounds: "/h/-/a/-/t/." Children's attempts to blend the sounds together to say "hat" are applauded and the game continues. Eventually, children may become the leaders and take turns providing their peers with segmented words for blending.

Categories may be selected to relate to curriculum areas under investigation (e.g., "I'm thinking of one of the types of sea animals we have been learning about—it is a /c/-/r/-/a/-/b/") or as an extension of integrated literacy experiences. When teaching about bears and their habitats, teachers may encourage children to write about bears, listen to stories about bears, view films about bears, create art projects involving bears, and learn poems and songs about bears. After singing the song, "The bear went over the mountain," children may play the guessing game to hypothesize the kinds of things seen by the bear on his outing (*A Treasury of Literature*, 1995)—"he saw a /t/-/r/-/ee/."

Common children's songs can be easily altered to emphasize the sounds of language. For instance, the initial sounds of words can be substituted. Instead of "merrily, merrily, merrily, merrily: in "Row, Row, Row Your Boat," children can suggest other sounds to insert in the initial position—"jerrily, jerrily, jerrily, jerrily" or "terrily, terrily, terrily, terrily." Young children often find such manipulations of sounds amusing and are likely to be heard singing nonsensical lyrics on the playground.

Concrete objects may help children attend to the sounds in speech. Elkonin boxes have been used in Reading Recovery to help low achieving readers focus on the sounds in words (Clay, 1985). A series of connected boxes are drawn across a page. The number of boxes corresponds to the number of sounds in a target word. The word *chick*, for example, is represented by three boxes. As the teacher slowly says the word, he or she models moving an object such as a chip into each box (from left to right) as each sound is articulated. The child eventually takes over the process of articulating the word and moving the objects into place.

Ultimately, the moving of chips into the boxes is replaced by the writing of letters in the boxes. (In the case of *chick* two letters are written in the first box because two letters spell the first sound: *ch*. Likewise, two letters are written in the third and final box: *ck*.) This activity is purposeful in the larger context of literacy acquisition when used to support children as they attempt to record thoughts or communicate in writing. (For a similar activity to facilitate phonemic awareness and support invented spelling, see Cunningham & Cunningham, 1992.)

Note that these activities fit into a meaning-based framework. Phonemic awareness should not be addressed as an abstract isolated skill to be acquired through drill type activities. It can be a natural, functional part of literacy experiences throughout the day.

USE OF THE TEST

The Yopp-Singer Test of Phoneme Segmentation was designed for use with English speaking kindergarteners. It may be used as a general assessment tool in order for teachers to learn more about their students and so develop suitable experiences; or it may be used selectively as teachers observe individual children experiencing difficulty with literacy-related tasks. Certainly, it need not be administered to the child who is already reading. Independent reading implies the existence of phonemic awareness. Further, phonemic awareness is not an end to itself—rather, it is one aspect of literacy development.

First-grade teachers, too, may wish to administer the test to students at the beginning of the school year in order to determine the phonemic awareness needs of the children in the classroom. Reading/language arts specialists or clinicians who work with children experiencing difficulty in literacy acquisition may also wish to assess their students' phonemic awareness as part of a larger diagnostic survey. And, although there are currently no data regarding the use of this particular test with older populations, we know that often older nonreaders lack phonemic awareness.

This instrument may be helpful to teachers of older individuals, including adult emerging readers, as they begin to build a profile of the strengths and needs of the individuals with whom they work. If phonemic awareness is poor, then it is appropriate to include activities that support its development in the larger picture of literacy experiences.

Should students who are limited in English proficiency be given this test? There are no data on using this test with an EL (English learner) population. Further, the issue is problematic since not only is there a potential problem with understanding task directions and familiarity with vocabulary (recall that the items on the test were selected, in part, on the basis of word familiarity), but there is also the possibility that performance on the test could be influenced by the fact that some speech sounds that exist in the English language may not exist in a student's dominant language.

Research does indicate that phonemic awareness is a critical variable in languages that have an alphabetic orthography (i.e., ones that map speech at the level of the phoneme rather than larger units). Therefore, the ideas presented in this article apply to children learning to read in an alphabetic script. The next step for educational researchers, therefore, is to develop reliable, valid assessment tools in other alphabetic languages to help teachers working with populations of children who are reading in languages other than English.

CONCLUSION

One of many insights that individuals must gain along the path to literacy is phonemic awareness. Research has shown that phonemic awareness is a more potent predictor of success in reading than IQ or measures of vocabulary and listening comprehension, and that if it is lacking, emergent readers are unlikely to gain mastery over print. However, teachers can provide activities that facilitate the acquisition of phonemic awareness. With an assessment device readily available, practitioners can quickly identify those children who may benefit most from phonemic awareness activities and reduce the role that one factor—phonemic awareness—plays in inhibiting their success in reading and spelling.

Previously a kindergarten and first-grade teacher, Yopp now teaches courses in reading and language arts education in the Department of Elementary and Bilingual Education at California State University, Fullerton, CA 92634, USA.

References

Adams, M.J. (1990). *Beginning to read: Thinking and learning about print.* Cambridge, MA: MIT Press.

Ball, E.W., & Blachman, B.A. (1991). Does phoneme segmentation training in kindergarten make a difference in early word recognition and developmental spelling? *Reading Research Quarterly, 26,* 49–66.

Bradley, L., & Bryant, P. (1983). Categorizing sounds and learning to read: A causal connection. *Nature, 301,* 419–421.

Bradley, L., & Bryant, P. (1985). *Rhyme and reason in reading and spelling.* Ann Arbor, MI: University of Michigan Press.

Cameron, P. (1961). *"I can't," said the ant.* New York: Coward-McCann.

Clay, M.M. (1985). *The early detection of reading difficulties* (3rd ed.). Portsmouth, NH: Heinemann.

Cunningham, A.E. (1990). Explicit versus implicit instruction in phonemic awareness. *Journal of Experimental Child Psychology, 50,* 429–444.

Cunningham, P.E., & Cunningham, J.W. (1992). Making Words: Enhancing the invented spelling–decoding connection. *The Reading Teacher, 46,* 106–115.

Griffith, P.L., Klesius, J.P., & Kromrey, J.D. (1992). The effect of phonemic awareness on the literacy development of first grade children in a traditional or a whole language classroom. *Journal of Research in Childhood Education, 6,* 86–92.

Griffith, P.L., & Olson, M.W. (1992). Phonemic awareness helps beginning readers break the code. *The Reading Teacher, 45,* 516–523.

Hills, J.R. (1981). *Measurement and evaluation in the classroom* (2nd ed.). Columbus, OH: Charles E. Merrill.

Jensen, A.R. (1980). *Bias in mental testing.* New York: Free Press.

Juel, C. (1988). Learning to read and write: A longitudinal study of 54 children from first through fourth grades. *Journal of Educational Psychology, 80,* 437–447.

Juel, C., & Leavell, J.A. (1988). Retention and nonretention of at-risk readers in first grade and their subsequent reading achievement. *Journal of Learning Disabilities, 21,* 571–580.

Liberman, I.Y., Shankweiler, D., Fischer, F.W., & Carter, B. (1974). Explicit syllable and phoneme segmentation in the young child. *Journal of Experimental Child Psychology, 18,* 201–212.

Lie, A. (1991). Effects of a training program for stimulating skills in word analysis in first-grade children. *Reading Research Quarterly, 23,* 263–284.

Lundberg, I., Frost, J., & Petersen, O. (1988). Effects of an extensive program for stimulating phonological awareness in preschool children. *Reading Research Quarterly, 23,* 263–285.

Mattingly, I.G. (1984). Reading, linguistic awareness, and language acquisition. In J. Downing & R. Valtin (Eds.), *Language awareness and learning to read* (pp. 9–25). New York: Springer-Verlag.

Perfetti, C., Beck, I., Bell L., & Hughes, C. (1987). Phonemic knowledge and learning to read are reciprocal: A longitudinal study of first grade children. *Merrill-Palmer Quarterly, 33,* 283–319.

Seuss, Dr. (1963). *Dr. Seuss's ABC.* New York: Random House.

Seuss, Dr. (1974). *There's a wocket in my pocket.* New York: Random House.

Share, D., Jorm, A., Maclean, R., & Matthews, R. (1984). Sources of individual differences in reading acquisition. *Journal of Educational Psychology, 76,* 1309–1324.

Spector, J.E. (1992). Predicting progress in beginning reading: Dynamic assessment of phonemic awareness. *Journal of Educational Psychology, 84,* 353–363.

Stanovich, K.E. (1986). Matthew effects in reading: Some consequences of individual differences in the acquisition of literacy. *Reading Research Quarterly, 21,* 360–407.

Stanovich, K.E. (1994). Romance and reason. *The Reading Teacher, 47,* 280–291.

A treasury of literature. (1995). Orlando, FL: Harcourt Brace.

Treiman, R., & Baron, J. (1983). Phonemic-analysis training helps children benefit from spelling-sound rules. *Memory and Cognition, 11,* 382–389.

Tunmer, W., Herriman, M., & Nesdale, A. (1988). Metalinguistic abilities and beginning reading. *Reading Research Quarterly, 23,* 134–158.

Yopp, H.K. (1988). The validity and reliability of phonemic awareness tests. *Reading Research Quarterly, 23,* 159–177.

Yopp, H.K. (1992a). A longitudinal study of the relationships between phonemic awareness and reading and spelling achievement. Paper presented at the annual meeting of the American Educational Research Association, San Francisco, CA, USA.

Yopp, H.K. (1992b). Developing phonemic awareness in young children. *The Reading Teacher, 45,* 696–703.

Yopp, H.K. (1995). Read-aloud books for developing phonemic awareness: An annotated bibliography. *The Reading Teacher, 48,* 538–542.

PHONOGRAMS AND KEY WORDS

Vowel Key Words
(Salmon Phonics Drill Cards)

Letter	Key Word	Card Number
a	apple	1a
a	baby	1b
a	fall	1c
a	father	1d
e	eddy	2a
e	eject	2b
i	itchy	3a
i	spider	3b
o	octopus	4a
o	pony	4b
o	lion	4c
u	upper	5a
u	music	5b
u	push	5c
y	gym	6a
y	cyclone	6b
y	candy	6c
a-e	ape	7
ai	sail	8
au	August	9
aw	saw	10
ay	play	11
e-e	eve	12
ea	steak	13a
ea	eat	13b
ea	bread	13c
ee	feed	14
ei	ceiling	15a
ei	vein	15b
eigh	eight	16
eu	feud	17
ew	pew	18a
ew	grew	18b
ey	valley	19
i-e	pine	20
ie	piece	21a
ie	pie	21b
igh	light	22
o-e	home	23
oa	boat	24
oe	toe	25
oi	boil	26
oo	food	27a

Letter	Key Word	Card Number
oo	book	27b
ou	ouch	28a
ou	soup	28b
ow	snow	29a
ow	plow	29b
oy	toy	30
u-e	mule	31a
u-e	ruler	31b
ue	rescue	32
y-e	type	33
ar	car	34
er	her	35
ir	bird	36
or	horn	37a
or	doctor	37b
ur	burn	38

PHONOGRAMS AND KEY WORDS

Consonant Key Words
(White Phonics Drill Cards)

Letter	Key Word	Card Number
b	boy	1
c	cat	2
d	dog	3
f	fish	4
g	goat	5
h	hat	6
j	jam	7
k	kite	8
l	lamp	9
m	man	10
n	nut	11
p	pan	12
qu	queen	13
r	rat	14
s	snake	15a
s	nose	15b
t	top	16
v	van	17
w	(Words not memorized. To be read when card is presented.)	18
x	box	19a
x	exam	19b
y	yoyo	20
z	zebra	21
ch	chin	22a
ch	Christmas	22b
ch	chute	22c
ck	clock	23
ph	phone	24
sh	ship	25
tch	catch	26
th	this	27a
th	thumb	27b
wh	whistle	28
cl, cr, ca ce, ci, co cu, cy, gl gr, ga, ge gi, go, gu, gy	(Words not memorized. To be read when card is presented.)	29–44
ed	scolded	45a
ed	sailed	45b
ed	jumped	45c

Letter	Key Word	Card Number
sion	expansion	46a
sion	mission	46b
sion	television	46c
tion	attention	47a
tion	station	47b
ble, dle, fle gle, kle, tle	(Words not memorized. To be read when card is presented.)	48
ang, ing, ong ung, ink, onk unk	(Words not memorized. To be read when card is presented.)	49
ild, old ind, ost	Words not memorized. To be read when card is presented.)	50

PHONOGRAM CHECKLIST

Use one checklist per student.

KEY: Not introduced   NI
Introduced   I
Mastered   M
Needs review   R

CONSONANTS

One sound

_____ b
_____ d
_____ f
_____ h
_____ j
_____ k
_____ l
_____ m

Two sounds

_____ n
_____ p
_____ r
_____ t
_____ v
_____ w
_____ y
_____ z

_____ c
_____ g
_____ x
_____ s

DIGRAPHS

_____ sh
_____ wh
_____ ph
_____ qu
_____ ck

_____ th
_____ ch

Trigraph

_____ tch

VOWELS

Single

_____ a
_____ e
_____ i
_____ o
_____ u
_____ y

Vowel-Consonant-E

_____ a-e
_____ e-e
_____ i-e
_____ o-e
_____ u-e
_____ y-e

Vowel-R Combinations

_____ er
_____ ir
_____ ur
_____ ar
_____ or

Digraphs and Diphthongs

_____ ai
_____ ay
_____ au
_____ aw

_____ oa
_____ oe
_____ oo
_____ ou
_____ ow

_____ ea
_____ ee
_____ ei
_____ eu
_____ ew
_____ ey
_____ eigh

_____ ie
_____ igh

_____ ue

_____ oi
_____ oy

OTHER

tion	ed (\ed\)	ild	ble	ang
sion	ed (\t\)	old	dle	ing
	ed (\d\)	ost	fle	ong
		ind	gle	ung
			kle	ink
			tle	onk
				unk

SUGGESTED ORDER OF INTRODUCTION OF CONCEPTS

Can also be used as a checklist for skills presented or mastered.

Name _____

I. Group I Letters

    1. vowel and consonant concept   _____

    2. syllable concept   _____

    3. 1st syllable division pattern   _____

    4. c-v-c syllables   _____

II. Group II letters

    1. digraph concept   _____

    2. 1st spelling pattern   _____

    3. 1st vowel generalization   _____

    4. 2nd vowel generalization   _____

    5. consonant blends   _____

    6. closed syllables   _____

    7. jumbled syllables   _____

    8. compound words   _____

    9. 2nd syllable division pattern   _____

    10. concept of accent   _____

    11. spelling pattern 2   _____

        a. prefix   _____

        b. suffix   _____

II. Group II letters

    12. open syllables   _____

    13. spelling pattern 3   _____

    14. syllable division pattern 3   _____

    15. syllable division pattern 4   _____

    16. syllable division pattern 5   _____

(continued)   Name _____

  III. Group III Letters

     1. c-le syllable   _____

     2. ild, old, ind, ost words   _____

     3. syllable division pattern 6   _____

     4. syllable division pattern 7   _____

     5. syllable division pattern 8   _____

     6. spelling pattern 4   _____

     7. spelling pattern 5   _____

     8. syllable division pattern 9   _____

     9. syllable division pattern 10   _____

Continue teaching spelling and syllable division patterns in sequence.

PROGRAM OF A DAILY LESSON*

(Approximately 45–60 minutes)

The teacher should use each lesson plan as a diagnostic tool for planning future lessons.

I. The basic drill with the necessary phonograms covering all three associations.

    a. Teacher shows drill card, student:

        says letter name—"writes" letter(s) on roughboard,

        says key word,

        says sound.

II. Teacher pronounces sound—student says letter name(s) that make the sound and "writes" letter(s) on roughboard.

III. Teacher says sound, student says letter name(s) and student writes letter names on paper (in cursive).

IV. Reading Drill

    a. Teacher spells words with appropriate drill cards and student blends letters into words.

    b. Presents Jewel Case cards and student reads them.

    c. Combines Jewel Case cards in appropriate phrases and sentences—student reads.

    d. Oral reading in context.

V. Review previously learned patterns and teach appropriate vowel syllable or spelling pattern.

    a. Review pattern—have student repeat it.

    b. Have student restate it in his or her own words.

    c. Have student read words that apply (and do not apply) and explain why they do.

    d. Provide practice from appropriate texts.

VI. Spelling Drill

    a. Place the appropriate drill cards on the desk, pronounce a word slowly and very distinctly, and have student pick out a drill card (letter name) for each sound until the word is spelled.

    b. Then have her read it back (good self-correction).

---

* Pine Ridge School Tutor Training Manual.

c. Follow S.O.S. technique to spell words that cover the phonograms, syllable type, spelling patterns, and syllable division patterns learned at that point.

d. S.O.S. (a vertical spelling list of single words)

1. Teacher dictates words, over-pronouncing (carefully spacing syllables).
2. Student repeats word—make *sure* she says it correctly.
3. Student spells word out loud—names letter names.
4. Student writes word naming each letter out loud as she spells.
5. Student reads word back.

e. Horizontal spelling (spelling of phrases, sentences, and paragraphs).

1. Start with a phrase, say the whole phrase carefully, and have student repeat it until he says it correctly (trains auditory memory).
2. He spells each word—S.O.S.—and rereads whole phrase.
3. *Gradually* work up to sentences and paragraphs.

VII. Additional Components of a Gillingham Lesson

a. Handwriting drill for handwriting (not spelling) practice.

b. Sight word drill (especially Dolch lists).

c. Auditory and/or visual sequential memory training exercises.

d. Oral reading:

1. Pick a more challenging book than the Gillingham work or strictly linguistically controlled materials that are at student's grade level.
2. *Preview* material, looking for every word he cannot read because he has not been taught the necessary phonograms, rules, and syllable patterns (if too many, choose another story).
3. Write each unknown word on a separate index card.
4. Teach this word by sight before student reads story.
5. Leave it on the desk and show it to him when he gets to it in the story.
6. Have him read each passage silently before orally.
7. Have him question you about words before he reads orally.
8. If he forgets it, tell him what it is and go on—*no guessing*.
9. Have him read every word he legitimately can.
10. Ask comprehension questions orally after reading.

e. Silent Reading

1. Technique for sight words same as for oral reading.
2. Ask verbal or written questions after the reading.

ACTIVITIES FOR AUDITORY TRAINING AND SOUND-SYMBOL ASSOCIATION

Appendices 1–27 from the Seventh Edition of the Gillingham Manual

1. In responding to the yellow cards the student may know which phonogram represents a particular sound, yet still not readily discriminate these sounds in a word.

The following exercise can be employed in various applications through all phonetic spelling:

The teacher reads a prepared list of words, and the student tells her what the first sound in each is; she repeats the list, and he tells the last sound; then, perhaps most important of all, he gives the vowel sound in each. In each case he then names the letter that spells this sound. The teacher can keep a graph of correct answers.

As work advances this exercise can be carried even further. Words such as <u>flash</u>, <u>print</u>, <u>brand</u> can be read by the teacher. The student tells what letters he hears before the vowel sound; again down the list, what he hears after the vowel, and then what vowel he hears. This exercise can fit special defects of the student's pronunciation, even though part of the word involves phonograms not yet taught. "What do you hear before the vowel in <u>play</u>?" If the student says "\p\" the teacher asks, "Do you *pay* with a ball?" Thus he is more likely to notice the \l\.

2. Teachers can select from the following two lists of words and sentences for a student inclined to confuse the sounds \sh\ and \ch\. At first these words can be used only for discrimination exercises, the teacher reading and the student recognizing and spelling <u>sh</u> or <u>ch</u>. Later the teacher can ask the student to read them himself.

shy	chop	sham	sheer	chain
shut	chapter	sherbet	shag	she
ship	dash	shred	chase	shift
children	channel	shore	chamber	chest
champion	checkers	shone	show	charity
shun	short	much	shoe	shoal
cheap	fresh	shelf	sheep	shave
shed	shrill	chief	chime	shin
shrunk	choice	shame	chide	shatter
China	check	lurch	shady	chafe
shell	wish	chaste	charter	chuck
chicken	chant	shrank	sheen	shine
chance	shot	lunch	shoddy	sharp
shrug	choke	shelter	chalk	chess
shall	cash	child	fish	charge

shrub	shovel	shale	churn	such
shop	shriek	shown	chick	chubby
cheat	shoot	champ	chart	shiver
shrink	shrimp	chatter	hush	cherry
dish	should	shook	shove	shark
chip	cheer	shelf	chair	shirt
cheek	shack	shake	shod	share
shrine	shrewd	shower	church	shirk
smash	choose	chime	chew	which
change	shade	thrush	shear	charcoal
chirp	bench	sheet	charm	shank
shorn	chapel	cheese	shield	rich

You can buy cheap shells at the store.
I want some fresh cheese.
The chair has a good shape.
The little chicken shivered in the cold.
Wash the dishes.
I like mush very much.
The child chose to sharpen the red chalk.
Catch the mice with cheese.
Set the chair in the corner.

Put the sheets into the chest.
The French people raise many sheep.
The charcoal fire burned on the shore.
Stitch the shirt with fine stitches.
Share the cheese with each other.
The ship sank in the channel.
You have a choice of shade or shelter.
The shower came while they were at church.

3. The teacher can read the following poem for the student to spell the first sound in the \hw\ and \w\ words. Later the student himself can read the poem, and much later he can write it as a dictation exercise.

Whether the weather be cold
Or whether the weather be hot,
Whether the weather be dry
Or whether the weather be not,
We must weather the weather
Whatever the weather,
Whether we like it
Or not.

4. Some students do not readily detect rhymes (matching sounds). To help them to do this is a useful phonics lesson.

- Cards may be prepared with words such as Dan, den, din, don, dun. The teacher says "Nan." The student finds and reads the rhyming word: "Dan." There could be many more words in the lists.
- The teacher types several cards, each with a group of words similar to those below. As she shows them one by one, the student selects and reads the word that rhymes with the underscored one at the top.

<u>pig</u>	<u>get</u>	<u>nod</u>	<u>mad</u>	<u>cut</u>	<u>sob</u>
rod	dot	fig	pup	gap	dim
gas	fun	pod	bad	but	mob
fig	net	bud	top	sad	tug
<u>wit</u>	<u>Ned</u>	<u>not</u>	<u>bat</u>	<u>hip</u>	
fit	fed	cot	hat	bag	
hen	did	rut	cut	hid	
pat	fog	cup	fan	dip	

5. As one listens to the speech of children—or adults—one can often detect confusions. These may lead to blurred understanding in reading or to faulty spelling. The ingenious teacher must devise just the right exercise to meet the immediate need. Some of these confusions are more common than others. Any of the vowel sounds may cause trouble, but \e\ and \i\ are the most likely. Here are two suggestions:

- The teacher reads a list of words like the following, one by one, each with two pronunciations, e.g., "I write with a pen—pin," "The fish swims with his fins—fens." The student is to choose and write the correct word with S.O.S.
- The teacher types the two words and places them before the student, who must use one in a sentence, speaking it distinctly.

fin	bid	den	win	it	kid
rid	rim	net	hid	him	pet
dip	dim	fix	big	did	set
wet	fit	Ned	hen	hip	dig
ten	tip	in	beg	peg	pin
web	bit	set	sip	six	red
pit	vex	met	hem	fig	led
fed	lid	let	wit	bed	mid
men	lip	bib	pen	rip	rib
wig	tin	jig	sin	mix	den

6. Sometimes "tongue gymnastics" seem to assist in rapid association of symbol with sound. Here are two.

- Groups of words such as the following are typed on cards. The student is to turn a card over and immediately, without study, read the words, which contain *all* the short vowel sounds.

bag	pump	flask	print	skin
beg	fifth	black	cup	plant
big	blend	crisp	mend	grand
twelfth	risk	lent	hem	web
split	hen	rob	led	
bran	drag	slat	slab	
grip	brim	skip	trim	
den	drift	that	pet	

- A particular student may have a greater tendency to displace certain letters than others, and teachers must devise exercises to give him the practice he needs. Several of our teachers have found l to be especially likely to change its position—for example, <u>felt</u> is often read <u>flet</u>. The following lists are useful in correcting this tendency. They can be retyped randomly for general practice in placing the l, or they can be presented to be read in pairs as they are here to contrast the two possibilities sharply.

flet	selp	culd	feld	polt	gald	palm	puls
felt	slep	clud	fled	plot	glad	plam	plus
calp	culp	salp	seld	malt	plug	bled	flat
clap	clup	slap	sled	mlat	pulg	beld	falt

7. The function of the final <u>e</u> is often clearer if the form without the final <u>e</u> is a real word. In most of the words that follow this is true. In a few it is not.

The lists can serve for exercises in auditory discrimination or for practice in rapid reading. They can also be used for dictation.

He <u>ate</u> lunch <u>at</u> noon.
We <u>can</u> see a <u>cane</u> in the man's hand.
The cat was sleeping with his <u>mate</u> on the <u>mat</u>.
I cannot <u>dine</u> in this <u>din</u>.
He fed the <u>cub</u> a <u>cube</u> of sugar.
I saw a <u>dime</u> in the <u>dim</u> light.
The <u>tube</u> of toothpaste has fallen into the bath<u>tub</u>.
He <u>cut</u> his hand on the <u>cute</u> little saw.
How could he <u>hope</u> to <u>hop</u> so far?

ban	cut	gap	mat	pop	tub
bane	cute	gape	mate	pope	tube
tun	bid	dim	hid	mop	rid
tune	bide	dime	hide	mope	ride
rip	win	cap	dot	hug	not
ripe	wine	cape	dote	huge	note
sit	cod	fat	mad	pat	tin
site	code	fate	made	pate	tine
glad	grim	quit	spin	spit	strip
glade	grime	quite	spine	spite	stripe

snip	dam	hat	met	rat
snipe	dame	hate	mete	rate
van	can	din	hop	nap
vane	cane	dine	hope	nape
rob	slid	dun	lop	pan
robe	slide	dune	lope	pane
cop	fin	man	pin	tot
cope	fine	mane	pine	tote
Sam	at	fad	slat	tap
same	ate	fade	slate	tape

8. Teachers and students wrote the sentences that follow. They can be used just as the separate drill words are, to see how many a student can read without a mistake. Longer words can be introduced as taught.

Ann went up the hill.	A big rat ran up the hill.
Ned did not hit Sam.	Nan had a big nut.
The pet bit the man.	A rat bit the man's leg.
I will not hit Ben.	Jill ran up to the man.
Ned must stop and rest.	I shall get a big bat.
I am glad.	I shall not let him get the nest.
Nat sat on a keg.	A man shot a pig.
A man had a bag.	Tom's hand hit the peg.
Ann had a red hat.	Fill the pan with nuts.

9. \kyü\ and \kw\, spelled respectively cu and qu, are really entirely different sounds and many students never have any difficulty with them. It would be foolish to create confusion by using a routine drill if not needed. On the other hand, the following list is exceedingly helpful for students who need more repetition.

The teacher pronounces a word. The student names or writes the first two letters, cu or qu.

cute	cupola	quotation	cure
quartet	cubic	curate	curious
cubical	quiet	cubit	cupidity
quill	cue	quirk	quite
cube	Quebec	culinary	cuticle
cucumber	quack	quintuplet	quixotic
quaint	cumulus	Cuba	cumulative
quake	quart	Cupid	quote
quiver	quit	curio	curiosity
quintuple	quinsy	curable	quarter
quaver	quick	quest	queen
quince	quilt	quiz	qualify
qualitative	cuneiform	qualification	curriculum
quantity	quantitative	quiescent	quoit

10. Words that contain both sounds of c or of g respectively make for valuable drill.

c		g	
codicil	circus	geography	graphology
pacific	coincide	gamboge	gigantic
success	crucible	gage	egregious
recalcitrant	secrecy	glycogen	negligence
calcite	reconcile	gorgeous	regurgitate
cancel	crucifix	gouge	suggest
cicada	bicycle	grange	ginseng
occident	concert	garbage	gorget
vaccinate	clemency		

11. The following game is most suitable after most of the phonograms have been introduced, although teachers may adapt it to any stage of the word.

Words containing the phonograms for the day's drill, such as <u>noise</u>, <u>play</u>, <u>steam</u>, <u>seed</u>, <u>plow</u>, <u>scream</u>, <u>down</u>, <u>gray</u>, <u>boil</u>, <u>sweep</u>, <u>bean</u>, <u>brown</u>, are typed on separate cards. Teacher gives sounds in miscellaneous order, saying, "Give me a word that contains this sound."

12. Words may be selected from the following for practice in reading -<u>ed</u>.

-<u>ed</u> \ed\

started	waited	delighted	landed	sounded	trusted
wanted	jolted	scolded	folded	intended	grunted
mounted	coasted	clouded	crowded	needed	

-<u>ed</u> \d\

seemed	lived	pulled	opened	closed
raised	seized	enjoyed	supposed	happened
bloomed	grabbed	returned	snowed	smelled
				smiled

-<u>ed</u> \t\

slipped	chased	marched	talked	looked
jumped	fished	reached	poked	picked
placed	lashed	remarked	waked	soaked

13. Some teachers have converted the game of "tic-tac-toe" into a phonics game, the point being to put phonograms with the same sound in a row.

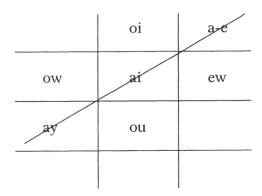

14. Words ending in <u>a</u>, <u>i</u>, <u>e</u>, or <u>u</u> are for the most part foreign words taken into English without alteration in spelling. In most cases the final vowel retains its foreign sound, as this list shows.

Final a

\ə\

cornea	Latin
corona	L.
comma	L.
Diana	L.
diploma	L.
farina	L.
flora	L.
hepatica	L.
insomnia	L.
petunia	L.
tarantula	L.
formula	L.
gladiola	L.
delta	Greek
dilemma	Gr.
drama	Gr.
panorama	Gr.
gondola	Italian
lava	It.
tarantella	It.
Madonna	It.
magenta	It.
cafeteria	Am. Spanish
flotilla	Spanish
llama	Sp.
puma	Sp.
copra	Hindi
pagoda	Portuguese
rutabaga	Swiss dialect

Final u

\yü\

emu	Probably from Portuguese
impromptu	Fr. from L.
jehu	Heb.
menu	Fr.
parvenu	Fr. from L.

\ü\

fichu	Fr.
ecru	Fr. from L.
Hindu	Hin.
jujitsu	Japanese
igloo	Eskimo
Manchu	Manchu
coypu	Sp.
ormolu	Fr. from L.
Vishnu	Sanskrit
virtu	It.
leu	Romanian

Final i

\ī\

Magi	Gr.
Delphi	Gr.
rabbi	Hebrew
Haggai	Heb.
Levi	Heb.
Gemini	L.
alibi	L.
alumni	L.

\ē\

Delhi	Hin.
frangipani	It.
macaroni	It.
spaghetti	It.
osmanli	Turkish
banditti	It.
broccoli	It.
confetti	It.
effendi	Tur. from Gr.
kiwi	Maori
penni	Finnish
parchisi	Hin.
mifi	Arabic
salmagundi	French
Tahiti	Polynesian
wadi, wady	Arabic
wapiti	Algonquin
chili	Sp. from Nahuatl
safari	Swahili

\ī\ or \i\

alkali	Ar.
lapis lazuli	Ar.
Naomi	Heb.

\ē\

ski	Norwegian
litchi	Chinese
Loki	Old Norse
peccavi	L.
jinni	Ar.
ravioli	It.
timpani	It.
Wahabi	Ar.

Final e

\ē\

recipe	L.
simile	L.
apostrophe	L. from Gr.
anemone	L. from Gr.
facsimile	L.
aborigine	L.
extempore	L.
acme	Gr.
epitome	L. from Gr.
catastrophe	Gr.
Arachne	Gr.
Penelope	Gr.
Persephone	Gr.
Daphne	Gr.

French

\ā\

glacé
habitué
moiré
piqué
resumé
répoussé
abbé
appliqué
attaché
blasé
café
consommé

Spanish and Portuguese

\ē\, \ā\, \i\

vigilante
infante
padre
tamale
alcade
adobe

15. The words in the following list all end in <u>i</u> followed by a consonant sound. The spelling is either <u>i-e</u> or <u>i</u>-consonant. In reading, the student would expect to pronounce the <u>i-e</u> words with \ ī \, instead of which the <u>i</u> sounds \ i \ or \ ē \. Those words in which it sounds \ ē \ are nearly all from the French or from some other language through the French. There should be miscellaneous reading exercises to establish familiarity with these exceptions to the ordinary vowel-consonant-<u>e</u>, usage, to which <u>i</u> presents more exceptions than any other vowel.

Sometimes in a miscellaneous spelling exercise words that the student has not studied should be dictated from this list. The student who has been trained to think about such matters should recognize that the final \ iv \ will be spelled <u>ive</u>; final \ id \, \ ip \, \ im \, <u>id</u>, <u>ip</u>, <u>im</u>; but that if he hears \ il \, \ in \, \ is \, \ it \, or \ ēl \, \ ēn \, \ ēs \, he cannot tell what the spelling will be. The \ i \ may be spelled <u>i</u> as in <u>margin</u>, or <u>i-e</u> as in <u>engine</u>; the \ ē \ may be <u>e-e</u> as in <u>benzene</u>, or <u>ea</u> as in <u>glean</u>, or <u>ee</u> as in <u>between</u>, or <u>i-e</u> as in <u>machine</u>. He should say, "I don't know—I must consult the dictionary."

\ iv \ <u>ive</u>

active
motive
restive
objective
primitive
retentive
descriptive
destructive
reflective
figurative
suggestive
restorative
executive
decorative
infinitive
retributive
representative
captive
diminutive
collective
festive
native
passive
responsive
defensive
expensive
inclusive
abusive
impressive
explosive
persuasive

\ iv \ <u>ive</u> (*cont.*)

aggressive
intrusive
extensive
pervasive
depressive
regressive
impulsive
seclusive
effusive
massive
adhesive
vindictive
conservative
imaginative
defective
elusive
possessive
evasive
selective

\ id, ip, im \ <u>id</u>, etc.

splendid
candid
rigid
frigid
forbid
stolid
stupid

\ id, ip, im \ <u>id</u>, etc. (*cont.*)

squalid
rancid
florid
torrid
horrid
tepid
timid
torpid
turbid
rabid
morbid
valid
viscid
vivid
vapid
turnip
pilgrim
verbatim
victim

\ il \ <u>ile</u> or '<u>il</u>

fragile
agile
docile
reptile
domicile
mercantile
prehensile
ductile

\ il \ <u>ile</u> or '<u>il</u> (*cont.*)

tranquil
civil
cavil
pupil

\ in \ <u>ine</u>, <u>in</u>

ermine
masculine
famine
doctrine
genuine
examine
determine
discipline
margin
dolphin
pepsin
muffin
terrapin
toxin
pumpkin

\ is \ <u>ice</u>, <u>ise</u>, <u>is</u>

chalice
justice
malice
service
office

\is\ ice, ise, is (cont.)	\it\ ite, it	\ēn, ēs, ēl\ i-e	\ēn, ēs, ēl\ i-e (cont.)
	respite	machine	
notice	opposite	ravine	guillotine
crevice	infinite	marine	gabardine
precipice	favorite	magazine	grenadine
practice	granite	quarantine	tangerine
promise	exquisite	sardine	praline
mortise	explicit	nicotine	routine
tennis	exhibit	Vaseline	pristine
thesis	pulpit	limousine	Listerine
parenthesis	prohibit	gasoline	caprice
paralysis	permit	Ovaltine	police
trellis		dentine	valise
emphasis		nectarine	automobile
Paris		morphine	castile

16. The following sentences give practice in copying or dictation involving specified phonograms. They are only examples. Handle other phonograms similarly.

Involving knowledge of ck, ch, tch:

I will chase him.
Jack romps too much.
Bess can chase the chick.
She will not catch it.
Bill chats at lunch.

Use of ea and ee:

See the peach.
Can Tom reach it?
The bee will buzz.
The queen wore green.
He will sneeze in that breeze.
He will sweep the street.

The teacher may have to give several words in the following to the student to copy if the passage is used for dictation:

Sunset

The sun set.
It was dark over land and sea.
Then the moon rose.
A silver light shone over all.

The following, supplying drill on \aủ\ spelled ow and ou, was written for a Honolulu child who had had a great deal of training in phonics. Teachers can often enhance the value of the work by writing paragraphs embodying local color.

Welcome Home

Tom Dow lived in Honolulu. Mr. Dow was coming home. Tom went to meet his father. He rode downtown in the big, brown car.

At the dock he jumped out of the car with a shout. His father waved to him from the deck. When his father reached the dock, Tom put a lei around his neck.

A lei, \lā\, is a wreath of flowers. In Hawaii, departing and returning travelers are decorated with leis.

17. Proverbs and weather rhymes interest most students and are usually expressed in simple words. They are also good for dictation.

Better late than never
Better never late.

He does much who does a little well.

Many hands make light work.

Horses will do more for a whistle than they will for a whip.

What is the use in running when you are not on the right road?

A dripping June keeps all in tune.

March winds and April showers
Bring forth May flowers.

18. Short, simple poems are good material for dictation. We have found the following satisfactory:

The Purple Cow
I never saw a purple cow
I never hope to see one.
But this I will say anyhow
I'd rather see than be one.
—Gelett Burgess

Rain
The rain is raining all round,
It falls on field and tree,
It rains on the umbrellas here,
And on the ships at sea.
—R.L. Stevenson

Autumn Fires
In the other gardens
And all up the vale,
From the autumn bonfires
See the smoke trail!

Pleasant summer over
And all the summer flowers,
The red fire blazes,
The grey smoke towers.

Sing a song of seasons!
Something bright in all!
Flowers in the summer!
Fires in the fall!
—R.L. Stevenson

Children's poetry books contain many other suitable poems.

19. The next selection is an adaptation from Henry van Dyke, *Fisherman's Luck* (Charles Scribner's Sons, 1931), pp. 199–209, by permission of the publishers.

Who Owns The Mountains?

One afternoon Dr. Henry van Dyke and his little boy took a long walk through the woods. They were watching for birds and listening to birds' songs.

At last they came out on an open hillside. They could look across a wide valley with beautiful mountains on the other side. The boy said, "Father, who owns the mountains?"

Dr. van Dyke told him of a number of lumber companies that owned parts of them.

The boy thought for a moment and then said, "I don't see what difference that makes. Everybody can look at them."

His father answered, "You are right. You and I are very rich. We own the mountains, but we can never sell them, and we don't want to."

20. The following gives practice in applying Spelling Pattern 1.

A Sad Mishap

Jack Bagg went to the store to buy a bag of candy.

When he was walking home the wind blew off his hat. He ran after it and the candy fell on the street. Jack found his hat, but a big dog found the candy and ate it.

Jack was very cross.

21. The slanting lines in the following exercises indicate suggested stopping places. Exercises without such lines are to be broken according to the needs of a particular student. In no. 23 we show the stopping places that seemed desirable for the fifth grade student for whom it was written. When the same exercise was used with seventh and eighth grade students, each sentence, with one possible exception, was considered a unit. It may be necessary to make a break after the word *figures* in the next to the last paragraph.

A Pleasant Walk

There had been rain for several days. / When the rain stopped \ and it was bright and sunny, / Mother and I went for a walk. /

For some distance the road went through a beautiful forest. / We heard and saw many birds. /

Beyond the forest was pasture land / where herds of cattle were grazing. / We heard a dog bark / and beyond a turn in the road / discovered a farmhouse. / The dog was chained / but her puppies ran toward us / wagging their stubby tails. / We wanted to stay and play with them, / but it was late and we had to go home.

22. The next exercise was written by an experienced remedial teacher.

An Unwelcome Gift

The heir to the throne received a weird shield, of great weight, from a foreign chief. It was decorated with a frieze in low relief, and was a cleverly conceived and executed piece of work.

The prince was not deceived by the gift. He could not believe that their fierce neighbor had become friendly. Surely he would not voluntarily forfeit the prize so lately won from the reigning monarch.

23. The teacher knew that the boy for whom "A Narrow Escape" was written had been over this trail. Of course he was interested in the incident.

A Narrow Escape

The trail we were following / ran along a hillside, / on one side a steep descent, / on the other a sharp rise. /

Suddenly we heard the sound / of horses' hoofs approaching rapidly. / We knew what it meant. / The horses that had been in the pasture / were coming in for the night. / Quick action was necessary. / We must get off the trail. / The down slope seemed more possible. / We scrambled as best we could / to a fallen tree trunk. / Still we were very near the trail. /

When he spied us, / two crouching figures, / up went the first horse's head and tail / and he was off at a gallop. / Of course all the other horses followed. /

Riding the last horse was the man / who was driving the herd home. / He waved his hand and called out, / "A narrow escape!"

A Surprise on a Montana Prairie

We had driven many miles across the rolling prairie without seeing a building of any kind. Indeed, we had seen no sign of human life except occasionally a shepherd with a huge flock of sheep.

Imagine our surprise when by the roadside we spied a tiny wooden building surmounted by a cross. "That's a church for the shepherds," said our driver.

When we had driven a mile or two, the driver pointed to a covered wagon on a low hill. "That's a shepherd's summer home," he said.

Presently there passed us a dingy little car driven by a kind-faced man. Our driver bowed most respectfully. "The shepherds' priest," said he, "as good a man as ever lived."

24. This exercise not only serves to emphasize a new word, but shows that in some cases the same word can be used as a proper as well as a common noun.

Palisades

Long ago there was a palisade across Manhattan Island. It was built to keep out the Indians. The street near the palisade was called Wall Street. The palisade is gone, but the street is still there.

Some Indians built palisades around their villages. De Soto found such a palisaded town in Alabama.

When white people first settled in the West they built palisades around their forts. When there was danger of an Indian attack all the settlers went to the fort inside the palisade.

Sometimes a line of high cliffs is called a palisade, such as the Palisades along the Hudson.

25. The following narrative took the place of an independent composition, which the student could not have written. By this means he was able to experience the joy of writing familiar ideas just studied in the classroom:

Marco Polo

Marco Polo lived in Venice. It was fun to live there. The streets were of water and people went about in gondolas.

Marco's uncle was a merchant. His ships brought spices from the Indies.

The year that Marco was born his father and uncle started on a trip to the East. They did not get back to Venice until Marco was fifteen years old. They had been to far-away Cathay or China.

Two years later Marco, his father and his uncle started for Cathay again. It took them three years to reach Kublai Khan's palace. Marco said, "The palace is so vast and so beautiful that no one could make anything finer."

The Khan thought Marco Polo was very clever. He sent Marco on important trips. Marco served the Khan for seventeen years.

At last the Polos wanted to go home, but the Khan did not want them to leave him. Just at that time a Chinese princess was to be sent to Persia to marry the king. She was to go by boat. Marco Polo knew the water route better than anybody else, so the Khan let the Polos go with the princess.

The trip took more than two years. They left the princess in Persia and went on to Venice. They had been gone for twenty-six years.

26. An eighth grade student dictated the next composition to his teacher. This boy had not learned to read until he was in the fourth grade, and, as is usual under such circumstances, spelling continued to be difficult enough to constitute a serious handicap. He had never written a composition except of the most meager proportions.

His interest was caught by the suggestion that he develop his topic to make it clear and entertaining to his readers.

"I never tried to make a composition interesting. I don't know why."

He agreed that this might have been because spelling and writing had always been so difficult for him that he had tried to write as little as possible.

The boy was interested in his subject, but had no idea how to tell about the experience interestingly. His answers to leading questions showed that the flatness of his first attempt was not due to poverty of ideas. The second attempt, worked out very thoughtfully, gave clear pictures of the expedition. It seems probable that if this boy had had practice in dictating during the earlier grades, he might have been expressing his thoughts fluently before he reached the eighth grade.

Only a small portion of the composition is given below:

A Visit to a Vermont Quarry

My father, my mother and I were touring Vermont and New Hampshire this summer, and we decided that we would stop and see the marble quarry at Proctor, Vermont.

In the town we saw the company's exhibit of all their different types and colors of marble. There were specimens made into fireplaces, floors and walls. They had some samples of marble from Alaska. There were some specimens which contained fossils.

In a near-by building was the company's shop for repairing their machinery and engines.

The quarry is about twelve miles from Proctor. When we got there we were told to put on extra coats. In the office we signed a piece of paper so that the company would not be held responsible if anyone was hurt.

From this point the boy described the descent into the quarry and what the party saw. Several words occurred which he was unable to spell. Before the paragraphs were dictated back to him a number of words were learned. Others were simply given him to copy.

27. The following words (compiled by Sally B. Childs) do not conform to the principle taught in Chapter 3, that g is usually soft before e, i, or y.

The first group consists of words so common that even a young student may encounter them and demand indignantly why that g is not soft.

g says \ g\ instead of \ j\.

geese	begin
get	anger
gift	finger
Gilbert	hunger
gild	linger
girdle	longer
girl	stronger
give	

The second group contains less common words.

gear	gingham
Gettysburg	gird
geyser	girder
Gibson	girt
giddy	girth
Gideon	gizzard
gig	beget
gill	nugget
gilt	

Then there is a third group consisting of monosyllables ending in g when adding suffixes such as -ed, -er, -ing, -y, to keep the \g\ sound hard:

bag, beg, big, bog, bug.

Student Name: _____ Date: _____

BAR GRAPH FOR WORD RECOGNITION
ACTIVITY RECORD SHEET

Number of Words Read Correctly
(Teacher may number words individually or in groups of five or ten.)

Day - Date - Lesson
(Teacher may record progress daily, by date, or by given lesson.)

WRONG - RIGHT TEST

WORDS WRITTEN BY TEACHER	CORRECT	CORRECTED BY STUDENT	REASON

LETTER FORMATION CHART

Alphabet organized according to letter formation for the right-handed student.

For letter formation in the first group, start at the X and swing up to the dot and then go back down.

a g o d g c

b h k f l e

t i j p r u s w

m n y v z x

th ch sh

Digraphs

LETTER FORMATION CHART

Alphabet organized according to letter formation for the left-handed student.

For letter formation in the first group, start at the <u>X</u> and swing up to the <u>dot</u> and then go back down.

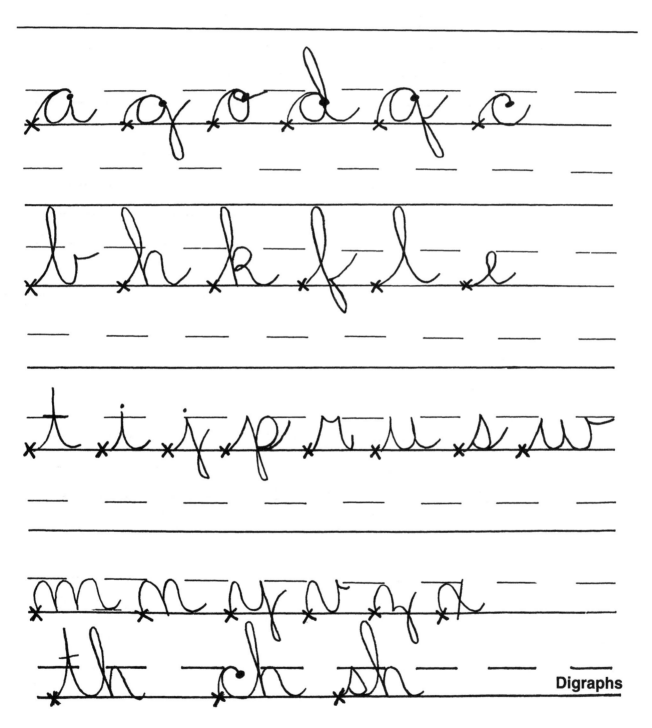

Digraphs

THE FIRST SEVEN YEARS OF THE GILLINGHAM READING PROGRAM—AN EVALUATION*

The Gillingham Preventive Program has been in operation at the Francis W. Parker School for seven years. During that time, there have been fifty students selected and trained by the Gillingham method. The size of the first grade has been consistently thirty. The numbers in the Gillingham groups have varied from five to nine. With the exception of two cases, all children have left the program at the end of the fourth grade as independent readers, capable of keeping up in their reading with the regular group. In one instance, a boy read adequately while working in the small group with the special teacher. However, there was no carry-over into the classroom. The boy has since changed to a school where the class is smaller and reports indicate that he is enjoying success. The other child is a girl who repeated the fourth grade. The fifth year of the Gillingham method has given her a better foundation.

Thus the two who were not fully successful nonetheless benefited to some extent by the training. For the remaining ninety-six percent, the program was eminently successful, as demonstrated by teachers' judgments of their academic work and the test scores that follow. This success becomes particularly important when one remembers that these children would presumably have been serious casualties in a regular reading program.

Following Miss Gillingham's advice, we do not consider achievement test results valid for the Gillingham classes until the end of the fourth grade. At this time the children are usually sufficiently trained to take the Metropolitan Intermediate Achievement Test. We have taken an average of the scores in the Gillingham group and compared it with the class average. As indicated on the following pages, the two sets of scores fall close to each other. Group I is the present seventh grade, the first group to complete the program. Group II, the present sixth grade, is the second group to complete the program. Test scores for both spring and fall testing have been used.

In our opinion, the results of the seven years' work have been successful.

---

*A discussion of the program at Francis W. Parker School as presented at the Gillingham Institute January 26, 1957. (Special thanks to Margaret Rawson for supplying this data.)

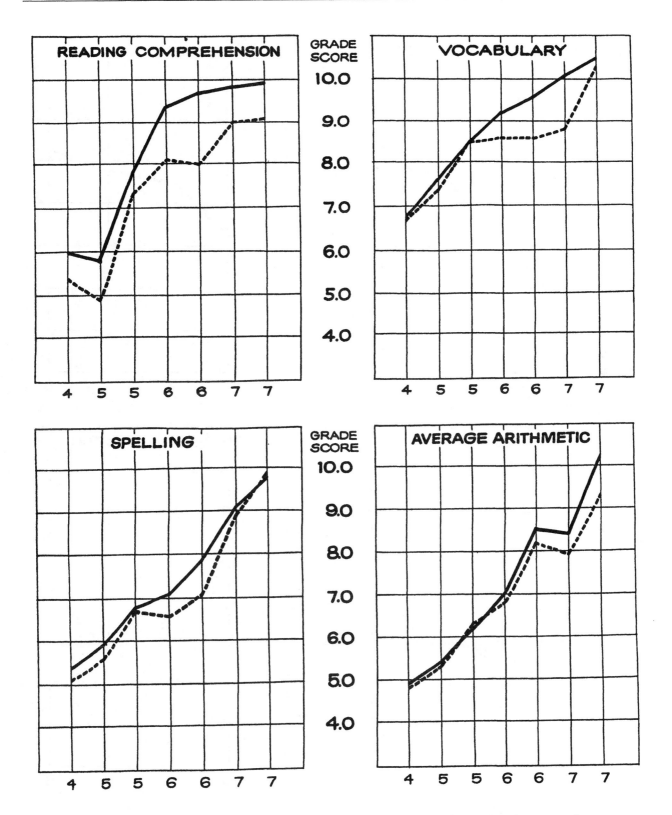

Metropolitan Achievement Test Results
GROUP I (SEVENTH GRADE 1956–7)

CLASS AVERAGE ——
GILLINGHAM AVERAGE – – –

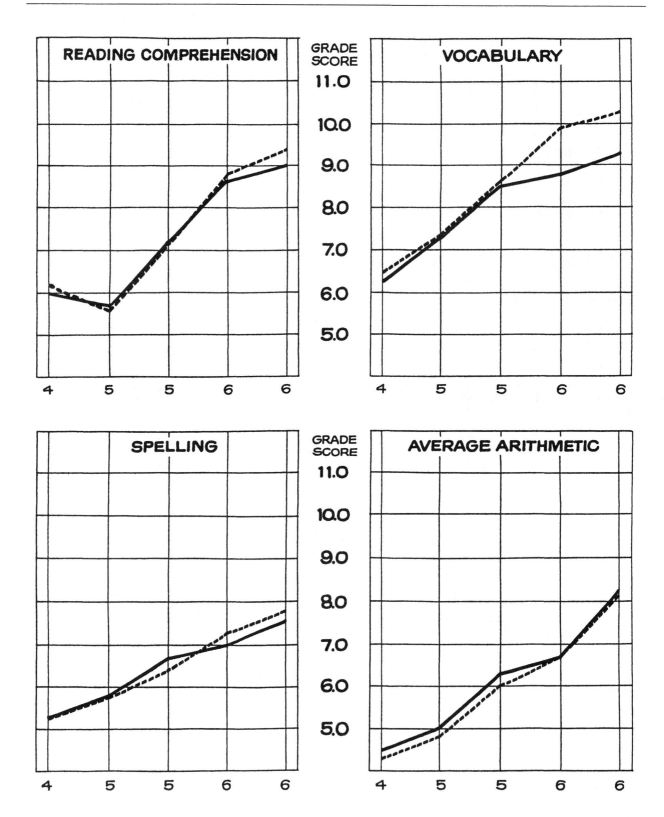

Metropolitan Achievement Test Results
GROUP II (SIXTH GRADE 1956–7)

CLASS AVERAGE ——
GILLINGHAM AVERAGE – – –

SUGGESTED BOOKS AND ARTICLES LIST
On the Nature of the Dyslexic Learner

Adams, Marilyn Jager. 1991. *Beginning to Read.* Cambridge, MA: MIT Press.

Barkley, Russell A. 1990. *Attention-Deficit Hyperactivity Disorder: A Handbook for Diagnosis and Treatment.* New York: Guilford Press.

Benton, Arthur L. 1975. "Developmental Dyslexia: Neurological Aspects." In *Advances in Neurology,* in Walter J. Friedlander, (ed.). *Current Reviews of Higher Nervous System Dysfunction.* New York: Raven Press.

Benton, Arthur L. and David Pearl (eds.). 1978. *Dyslexia: An Appraisal of Current Knowledge.* New York: Oxford University Press.

Chall, Jeanne. 1996. *Learning to Read: The Great Debate.* 3rd ed. Fort Worth, TX: Harcourt Brace.

Chall, Jeanne. 1983. *Stages of Reading Development.* New York: McGraw-Hill.

Clark, Diana Brewster. 1988. *Dyslexia: Theory and Practice of Remedial Instruction.* Parkton, MD: York Press.

Clarke, Louise. 1973. *Can't Read, Can't Write, Can't Talk Too Good Either.* New York: Penguin Books.

Cordoni, Barbara. 1987. *Living with a Learning Disability.* Carbondale: Southern Illinois University Press.

Critchley, MacDonald and Eileen Critchley. 1978. *Dyslexia Defined.* London: William Heinemann Medical Books.

Duane, Drake and David B. Gray (eds.). 1991. *The Reading Brain: The Biological Basis of Dyslexia.* Parkton, MD: York Press.

Duane, Drake and Margaret Rawson (eds.). 1975. *Reading, Perception, and Language.* Parkton, MD: York Press.

Duane, Drake and Paula D. Rome (eds.). 1977. *Developmental Dyslexia.* New York: Insight Publishing.

Ellis, Andrew W. 1984. *Reading, Writing and Dyslexia: A Cognitive Analysis.* London: Lawrence Erlbaum Associates.

Farnham-Diggory, Sylvia. 1978. *Learning Disabilities: A Psychological Perspective.* Cambridge, MA: Harvard University Press.

Gaddes and Edgell. 1994. *Learning Disabilities and Brain Function.* New York: Springer-Verlag.

Galaburda, Albert (ed.). 1993. *Dyslexia and Development.* Cambridge, MA: Harvard University Press.

Gardner, Howard. 1983. *Frames of Mind.* New York: Basic Books.

Gardner, Howard. 1976. *The Shattered Mind.* New York: Knopf.

Note: This bibliography has been compiled by the Academy of Orton-Gillingham Practioners and Educators. The Curriculum Committee of the Academy tries to revise and update such sources each year. Books published before 1984 are considered classics in the field and may only be available through a library system.

Geschwind, Norman. 1982. "Why Orton was right." *Annals of Dyslexia* 32:13–30.

Geschwind, Norman and Albert M. Galaburda (eds.). 1984. *Cerebral Dominance: The Biological Foundations.* Cambridge, MA: Harvard University Press.

Goldberg, Herman, et al. 1983. *Dyslexia: Interdisciplinary Approaches to Learning Disabilities.* New York: Grune and Stratton.

Hampshire, Susan. 1982. *Susan's Story.* New York: St. Martin's Press.

Healy, Jane. 1994. *Your Child's Growing Mind.* New York: Doubleday Books.

Intimacy with Language. 1987. Baltimore: Orton Dyslexia Society.

Johnson, Doris and Jane Blalock. 1986. *Young Adults with Learning Disabilities— Clinical Studies.* New York: Grune and Stratton.

Kalmi, Alan and Hugh Catts. 1989. *Reading Disabilities: A Developmental Language Perspective.* Boston: Little, Brown and Co.

Kavenaugh, James F. (ed.). 1991. *The Language Continuum from Infancy to Literacy.* Parkton, MD: York Press.

Kavenaugh, James and Tom J. Truss, Jr. (eds.). 1988. *Learning Disabilities: Proceedings of the National Conference.* Parkton, MD: York Press.

Language and Literacy. Baltimore: Orton Dyslexia Society.

Levine, Melvin. 1990. *Keeping A Head in School.* Cambridge, MA: Educators Publishing Service, Inc.

Levine, Melvin. 1987. *Developmental Variation and Learning Disorders.* Cambridge, MA: Educators Publishing Service, Inc.

Levine, Melvin, et al. 1980. *A Pediatric Approach to Learning Disorders.* New York: John Wiley & Sons.

Masland, Richard and Molly Masland (eds.). 1988. *Preschool Prevention of Reading Disorders.* Parkton, MD: York Press.

Mathews, Mitford. 1966. *Teaching to Read, Historically Considered.* Chicago: University of Chicago Press.

McCracken, Mary. 1986. *Turnabout Children.* Boston: Little, Brown and Co.

Miles, T.R. 1983. *Dyslexia: The Pattern of Difficulties.* Springfield, IL: Charles C. Thomas.

Orton, Samuel Torrey. 1937. *Reading, Writing, and Speech Problems in Children.* New York: W.W. Norton.

Pavlides, George Th. and T.R. Miles. 1981. *Dyslexia Research and its Application to Education.* New York: John Wiley & Sons.

Pennington, Bruce F., et al. 1991. "Evidence for major gene transmission of developmental dyslexia." *Journal of the American Medical Association* 266:1527–1534.

Rawson, Margaret. 1995. *Dyslexia over the Lifespan: A Fifty-five-Year Longitudinal Study.* Cambridge, MA: Educators Publishing Service, Inc.

Rawson, Margaret. 1992. *Many Faces of Dyslexia.* Baltimore: Orton Dyslexia Society.

Roswell, Florence, and Gladys Natchez. 1977. *Reading Disabilities: A Humane Approach.* New York: Basic Books.

Rudel, Rita. 1981. "Residual effects of childhood reading disabilities." *Bulletin of the Orton Society,* 31:89–102.

Simpson, Eileen. 1979. *Reversals.* Boston: Houghton-Mifflin.

Smith, Shelly, William Kimberling, Bruce Pennington, and Herbert Lubs. 1983. "Specific reading disability: Identification of an inherited form through linkage analysis." *Science,* 219:1345–1347.

Snowling, Margaret. 1987. *Dyslexia: A Cognitive Developmental Perspective.* Basil Blackwell, Inc.

Stanovich, Keith. 1986. "Mathew effects in reading: some consequences of individual difference in the acquisition of literacy." *Reading Research Quarterly,* Fall:360–406.

Thomas, Michael. 1989. *Developmental Dyslexia: Its Nature, Assessment and Remediation.* 2nd ed. London: Edward Arnold.

Vellutino, Frank. 1979. *Dyslexia: Theory and Research.* Cambridge, MA: MIT Press.

Vellutino, Frank. 1987. "Dyslexia." *Scientific American* 256:34–41.

Wender, Paul. 1987. *The Hyperactive Child, Adolescent, and Adult.* New York: Oxford University Press.

Williams, Joanna. "Educational treatments for dyslexia at the elementary and secondary levels." In *Proceedings of the Orton Dyslexia Society Symposium: Dyslexia and Evolving Education Patterns.* Baltimore: The Orton Dyslexia Society.

Witelson, Sandra F. "Developmental dyslexia: Two right hemispheres and none left." *Science* 195:309–311.

History and Structure of the English Language

Balmuth, Miriam. 1982. *Roots of Phonics—A Historical Introduction.* New York: McGraw-Hill.

Brady, Susan and Donald P. Shankweiler. 1991. *Phonological Processes in Literacy.* Hillsdale, NJ: Lawrence Erlbaum Associates.

Brown, Roger. 1983. *Words and Things.* New York: Free Press of Glencoe. Springfield, IL: Charles C. Thomas.

Bryson, Bill. 1990. *Mother Tongue: English and How it Got That Way.* New York: Avon Books.

Francis, Nelson: 1958. *The Structure of American English.* New York: Free Press of Glencoe.

Intimacy with Language. 1987. Baltimore: Orton Dyslexia Society.

Jespersen, Otto. 1982. *Growth and Structure of the English Language.* Chicago: University of Chicago Press.

Kavenaugh, James F. (ed.). 1991. *The Language Continuum from Infancy to Literacy.* Parkton, MD: York Press.

Lieberman, Philip. 1984. *The Biology and Evolution of Language.* Cambridge, MA: Harvard University Press.

Mathews, Mitford. 1966. *Teaching to Read, Historically Considered.* Chicago: University of Chicago Press.

McCrum, Cran, and Robert MacNeil. 1993. *The Story of English.* New York: Penguin.

Palermo, David. 1978. *Psychology of Language.* Grandview, IL: Scott, Foresman and Co.

Pinker, Stephen. 1994. *The Language Instinct.* New York: William Morrow and Co.

Potter, Simeon. 1959. *Our Language.* New York: Pelican Books A 227.

The Orton-Gillingham Approach

Ansara, Alice. 1966. *A Guide to the Teaching of Reading for Teachers of the Disadvantaged.* Cambridge, MA: Educators Publishing Service, Inc.

Childs, Sally (ed.). 1968. *Education and Specific Language Disability: The Papers of Anna Gillingham, MA: 1919–1963.* Orton Dyslexia Society.

Clark, Diana Brewster. 1988. *Dyslexia: Theory and Practice of Remedial Instruction.* Parkton, MD: York Press.

Cole, Edwin. 1942. "The Neurological Aspects of Defects in Speech and Reading." *New England Journal of Medicine,* 226:977.

Cox, Aylette. 1974. *Structures and Techniques: Remedial Language Training for Use with Alphabetic Phonics.* Cambridge, MA: Educators Publishing Service, Inc.

Duane, Drake and Paula D. Rome. (eds.). 1977. "Developmental Dyslexia." New York: Insight Publishing. Reprinted from *Psychiatric Annals,* 7 (Sept., 1977).

Enfield, Mary Lee and Victoria Green. 1988. *Project Read Guides.* Bloomington, MN: Language Circle.

Gallagher, Roswell. *Can't Spell, Can't Read.* Baltimore: Orton Dyslexia Society.

Healy, Jane. 1994. *Your Child's Growing Mind.* New York: Doubleday Books.

Henry, Marcia. 1988. "Beyond phonics: Integrated coding and spelling instruction based on word origin and structure." *Annals of Dyslexia,* 38: 259–275.

Hornsby, Beve, PhD. 1984. *Overcoming Dyslexia.* New York: Arco Publishing, Inc.

Intimacy with Language. 1987. Baltimore: Orton Dyslexia Society.

Jansky, Jeannette and Katrina deHirsch. 1972. *Preventing Reading Failure—Prediction, Diagnosis, Intervention.* New York: Harper and Row.

Kavenaugh, James F. (ed.). 1991. *The Language Continuum from Infancy to Literacy.* Parkton, MD: York Press.

King, Diana Hanbury. 1987. *Cursive Writing Skills.* Cambridge, MA: Educators Publishing Service, Inc.

King, Diana Hanbury. 1986. *Keyboarding Skills.* Cambridge, MA: Educators Publishing Service, Inc.

Orton, June Lyday. 1964. *A Guide to Teaching Phonics.* Cambridge, MA: Educators Publishing Service, Inc.

Orton, Samuel Torrey. 1937. *Reading, Writing, and Speech Problems in Children.* New York: W.W. Norton.

Rawson, Margaret. 1995. *Dyslexia over the Lifespan: A Fifty-five-Year Longitudinal Study.* Cambridge: Educators Publishing Service, Inc.

Rawson, Margaret. 1992. *Many Faces of Dyslexia.* Baltimore: Orton Dyslexia Society.

Rome, Paula and Jean Osman. 1977. "Procedures for helping the dyslexic child: Remediation." In Duane, D. and P. Rome. *The Dyslexic Child.* New York: Insight Publishing Co., 29–41.

Slingerland, Beth. *A Multisensory Approach to Language Arts for Specific Language Disability Children.* Cambridge, MA: Educators Publishing Service, Inc.

Whitehead, Dorothy. 1995. *Dyslexia: Unlocking the Power of Print.* Portland, OR: Dorothy Whitehead.

Wilson, Barbara. 1988. *Wilson Reading System.* Millbury, MA: Wilson Language Training.

Assessment

Barkley, Russell A. 1990. *Attention-Deficit Hyperactivity Disorder: A Handbook for Diagnosis and Treatment.* New York: Guilford Press.

Duane, Drake. 1977. "The dyslexic child: Diagnostic implications." In Duane, D. and P. Rome. *The Dyslexic Child.* New York: Insight Publishing Co. 29–41.

Grimm and Skowronek. 1993. *Language Acquisition Problems and Reading Disorders, Aspects of Diagnosis and Interaction.* Hawthorne, New York: Walter D. Degruyter, Inc.

Jansky, Jeannette and Katrina deHirsch. 1972. *Preventing Reading Failure—Prediction, Diagnosis, Intervention.* New York: Harper and Row.

Lezak, Murial. 1983. *Neuropsychological Assessment.* New York: Oxford University Press.

Lyon, G. Reid. (ed.). 1994. *Frames of Reference for the Assessment of Learning Disabilities.* Baltimore: Paul H. Brookes Publishing Co.

Lyon, G. Reid. (et al., ed.) 1993. *Better Understanding of Learning Disabilities.* Baltimore: Paul H. Brookes Publishing Co.

Miles, T.R. 1983. *Dyslexia: The Pattern of Difficulties.* Springfield, IL: Charles C. Thomas.

Pavlidis, George Th. and T.R. Miles. 1981. *Dyslexia Research and its Application to Education.* New York: John Wiley & Sons.

Pennington, Bruce. 1991. *Diagnosing Learning Disabilities.* New York: Guilford Press.

Wren, Carol T. (ed.). 1983. *Language Learning Disabilities: Diagnosis and Remediation.* Rockville, MD: Aspen Systems Corp.

Practical Experience

Clarke, Louise. 1973. *Can't Read, Can't Write, Can't Talk Too Good Either.* New York: Penguin.

deHirsch, Katrina. 1977. "Interactions between educational therapist and child." *Bulletin of the Orton Society* 27:88–101.

Foss, Jean. 1986. "The tutor-student instructional interaction." *Annals of Dyslexia,* 36:15–27.

Hampshire, Susan. 1982. *Susan's Story.* New York: St. Martin's Press.

McCracken, Mary. 1986. *Turnabout Children.* Boston: Little, Brown and Co.

Osman, Betty. 1982. *No One to Play With: The Social Side of Learning Disabilities.* New York: Random House.

Simpson, Eileen. 1979. *Reversals.* Boston: Houghton-Mifflin.

General Learning Disabilities

Barkley, Russell A. 1990. *Attention-Deficit Hyperactivity Disorder: A Handbook for Diagnosis and Treatment.* New York: Guilford Press.

Bryant, Peter and Lynette Bradley. 1985. *Children's Reading Problems: Psychology and Education.* New York: Basil Blackwell, Inc.

deHirsch, Katrina. 1977. "Interactions between educational therapist and child." *Bulletin of the Orton Dyslexia Society,* 27:88–101.

Myklebust, Helmer. 1973. *Development and Disorders of Written Language,* vol. II. New York: Grune and Stratton.

Myklebust, Helmer. *Progress in Learning Disabilities.* New York: Grune and Stratton.

Osman, Betty. 1982. *No One to Play With: The Social Side of Learning Disabilities.* New York: Random House.

Roswell, Florence, and Gladys Natchez. 1977. *Reading Disabilities: A Humane Approach.* New York: Basic Books.

Smith, Lynn. 1982. "Learning disabled students." *The College Student with a Disability: A Faculty Handbook.* Washington: U.S. Government Printing Office.

Stevens, Suzanne H. 1984. *Classroom Success for the Learning Disabled.* Winston-Salem, NC: John F. Blair.

Vail, Priscilla. 1991. *Common Ground: Whole Language and Phonics Working Together.* Rosemont, NJ: Modern Learning Press.

Vail, Priscilla. 1987. *Smart Kids with School Problems.* New York: E.P. Dutton.

Wender, Paul. 1987. *The Hyperactive Child, Adolescent, and Adult.* New York: Oxford University Press.

West, Thomas. 1991. *In the Mind's Eye.* Buffalo, NY: Prometheus Books.

Wren, Carol T. (ed.). 1983. *Language Learning Disabilities: Diagnosis and Remediation.* Rockville, MD: Aspen Systems Corp.

Glossary

accent: stress or emphasis on one or more syllables in a word. The accented syllable is spoken louder or in a higher pitch than the other syllable(s).

acquired dyslexia or alexia: refers to impairment of reading and related language skills due to some type of brain damage experienced by those who have learned to read and write normally.

affix: a letter or group of letters added to the beginning (prefix) or end (suffix) of a base word or root. The resulting word may differ in meaning or may have its function as a part of speech changed.

affricate: a speech sound that starts with a stop followed immediately by a slow release characteristic of a fricative, e.g., the sounds that end the words *badge* and *inch* are voiced and unvoiced affricates, respectively.

alphabetic principle: applicable to a writing system whose symbols (graphemes) represent the speech sounds (phonemes) which comprise the spoken words of the language. English is among the languages to which the principle applies: the twenty-six letters of its orthography, singly and in combination, represent the sounds that make up English speech.

analytic-synthetic principle: refers to the relationship between spelling and reading in the coding process. One analyzes (breaks apart) spoken words into individual sounds for spelling. One synthesizes (blends together) discrete sounds to form words for reading.

aphasia: impairment or loss of the ability to use or understand spoken language due to brain damage.

assessment: ongoing evaluation which may compare self to self, or self to others, in relation to learned behaviors.

auditory discrimination: assuming normal hearing acuity, the ability to hear likenesses and differences in phonemes or words.

automaticity: automatic and correct responses to linguistic stimuli without conscious effort.

base word: a word to which affixes may be added to create related words.

This Glossary has been adapted from one compiled by the Academy of Orton-Gillingham Practioners and Educators. The Curriculum Committee of the Academy tries to revise and update such sources each year.

blending: fusing the segmented speech sounds represented by contiguous graphemes into a sound continuum.

breve: the curved diacritical mark above a vowel letter indicating a short sound.

capital letters: uppercase letters of cursive or manuscript, as opposed to lower-case letters.

closed syllable: a syllable containing a single vowel letter, ending in one or more consonants. The vowel letter in this syllable typically represents a short vowel sound. This does not apply when an <u>r</u> follows the vowel letter. (See **r-controlled syllable.**)

comprehension (reading): understanding the meaning of a written expression.

consonant: a letter of the alphabet whose sound is usually blocked or influenced by the lips, tongue, teeth, or other articulators. All the letters of the alphabet represent consonant sounds except the vowel letters, frequently <u>y</u>, and <u>w</u> when combined with a vowel.

consonant blend: two or three adjacent consonant letters that flow smoothly together, e.g., <u>bl</u>-, -<u>nd</u>, <u>str</u>-. They may appear at the initial or final position of the word.

consonant digraph: two adjacent consonant letters in the same syllable used to represent one of the primary phonemes of English, such as <u>ch</u>, <u>th</u>, and <u>sh</u>.

consonant-le syllable: a final syllable conforming to the pattern consonant-le as in <u>can/dle</u> and <u>ri/fle</u>.

continuant: a speech sound in which the airstream continues without complete interruption through the mouth as with the vowel and some consonant sounds in English.

criterion reference testing: a test created by a teacher to test the student's knowledge of what has been taught.

cursive writing: joined, rounded handwriting; handwriting with the slanted strokes of successive characters joined and the angles rounded. Words are written as single units without raising the pencil.

decoding: a process of recognizing unfamiliar written words by sequentially segmenting the sounds represented by the letters of the word and then by blending the sounds into a meaningful word or into syllables which are then combined into words.

diacritical mark: a distinguishing mark added to a grapheme to indicate a specific pronunciation. These marks are especially helpful in clarifying the correct speech sounds represented by letters such as vowels which can represent more than one speech sound.

dictation: oral presentation of syllables, words, phrases, or sentences for the student to write down. Dictation is crucial in developing phonic spelling skills and in lengthening the student's auditory span.

digraph: two adjacent letters representing a single speech sound. **Consonant digraphs** are two adjacent consonant letters representing a single consonant sound, e.g., <u>sh</u> or <u>th</u>. **Vowel digraphs** are two adjacent letters representing a single or blended vowel sound, e.g., <u>ee</u> or <u>oo</u>. (See also **diphthong.**)

diphthong: a phoneme that begins with a vowel sound and, by change of tongue position, glides into another vowel sound, e.g., <u>ou</u> as in <u>ouch</u> and <u>oy</u> as in <u>boy</u>. In teaching dyslexic students, the term <u>diphthong</u> is modified to include specified **vowel digraphs** as well as true diphthongs.

diphthong syllable: a syllable with typically two adjacent vowel letters, e.g., <u>oi</u> in <u>oil</u>, <u>ay</u> in <u>play</u>, <u>ow</u> in <u>show</u>, which represent a dipthong sound.

direct instruction: an instructional approach in which the teacher informs the student of the *what, why, and how* of a learning session. Instruction is structured, modular, and sequential (simple to the complex and concrete to the abstract). It stresses practice and mastery, and provides a high level of success experiences and positive feedback to the student.

dyscalculia: difficulty in learning to calculate or to remember easily and to work accurately with number facts.

dysgraphia: difficulty in learning the physical act of writing.

dysorthography: difficulty in learning to spell.

dyslexia: can be summarized as difficulty in the use and processing of arbitrary linguistic/symbolic codes. This is an aspect of a language continuum which includes spoken language, written language, and language comprehension.

encoding: in spelling, a process by which students segment sounds of a word, translate each phoneme into its corresponding letter, and then spell the word. Encoding requires predictable sound-symbol correspondences and phonic generalizations (spelling rules).

fricative: a consonant speech sound made by constricting but not stopping the airstream, resulting in a hiss or friction; sometimes called *spirants*.

Gillingham linkages: the associations used in instructing dyslexic students to connect visual, auditory, and tactile-kinesthetic senses. These multisensory linkages for language learning, essential for the dyslexic learner, are the core of the Orton-Gillingham Approach.

glide: a sound produced with little or no obstruction of the airstream; it is always preceded or followed by a vowel. In producing a glide, articulators make a transition from one position to another, as in the initial sound in *yes*.

grapheme: a single letter or letter combination that represents a phoneme.

IEP: Individualized Educational Program. Required under federal law for any student in special education; an educational program, based upon multidisciplinary assessment, deemed appropriate for meeting the individual needs of the student. An IEP is developed by school representatives and provides parents and professionals an opportunity to review and discuss the program before its approval.

key word: a word which illustrates a sound/symbol relationship and serves as a key to "unlock" the student's memory of that sound. Key words are also used for prefixes and roots, e.g., **ex,** exit, out; or **port,** portable, carry.

kinesthetic memory: a remembered pattern of voluntary movement; an integrated pattern of activity which the student can recall after repeated practice and training.

kinesthetic perception: sensory experience derived from muscles, tendons, and joints which is stimulated by body movements and tensions. It is often applied to the student's feeling of letter shapes while moving parts of the body through space without relying on visual guidance.

language: a complex and dynamic system of conventional symbols that is used in various modes for thought and communication. Contemporary views of human language hold that (a) language evolves within specific historical, social, and cultural contexts; (b) language, as rule-governed behavior, is described by at least five parameters—phonologic, morphologic, syntactic, semantic, and pragmatic; (c) language learning and use are determined by the interaction of biological, cognitive, psychosocial, and environmental factors; and (d) effective use of language for communication requires a broad understanding of human interaction, including such associated factors as nonverbal cues, motivation, and sociocultural roles.

liquid: sounds like /r/ and /l/ in which there is some obstruction of the airstream in the mouth but not sufficient to cause any real constriction or friction.

long-term memory: involves the encoding, storage, and retrieval of sensory information. It lasts over a long period of time and has great storage capacity. See also **short-term memory, auditory memory,** and **visual memory.**

long vowel: vocalic sounds which are the same as the names of the letters used or the alphabet used to represent these sounds. The letter y̲, when used as a vowel, may also represent the long vowel sound of the vowels i̲ or e̲. Several paired vowel letters typically also represent long vowel sounds.

macron: a straight line diacritical mark above a vowel letter indicating a long sound.

manuscript writing: a type of handwriting similar to print-script; letters are typically independent units unconnected within each word.

mnemonic: pertaining to the memory.

monosyllable: a single syllable.

morpheme: the smallest unit of meaning in a word, including prefixes, root words, and suffixes. It can be free-form, able to stand alone as a word (as in *pin*) or bound (as in the *s*, which is not a word, in *pins*).

morphology: the study of the structure of words; the component of grammar which includes the rules of word formation including derivation, inflection, and compounding.

multisensory: the use of visual, auditory, and kinesthetic-tactile pathways to reinforce learning in the brain.

nasal: a speech sound produced with an open passage permitting air to go through the nose as well as the mouth so that the nasal cavity acts as a resonator, e.g., m̲, n̲.

non-phonetic words: those words whose spelling or pronunciation does not conform to the usual letter-sound correspondences of English and cannot be correctly read or spelled by their application or by use of other phonetic generalizations, e.g., s̲a̲i̲d̲ or w̲a̲s̲.

observation: in Orton-Gillingham, observation refers to direct monitoring and assessment by one instructor of one student therapist who is teaching a dyslexic student, for a minimum of one hour for each observation plus time for feedback and questions.

open syllable: a syllable which ends with a single vowel letter. The final vowel letter in an accented open syllable will represent a **long vowel** sound. The vowel letter in the final position in an unaccented syllable will usually have the **schwa** sound.

orthography: the total writing system of a spoken language. The term also refers to the established spelling rules of a written language.

perception: a process involving the reception, selection, differentiation, and integration of sensory stimuli. The teacher of dyslexics must teach the student to attend actively and consciously to aspects of the perception process until it becomes automatic.

phoneme: smallest unit of speech that serves to distinguish one utterance from another in a language or dialect (as in the /b/ of *bat* and /m/ of *mat*). English is made up of 44 or 45 phonemes (depending on dialect).

phonetics: the study of speech sounds, how they are produced (articulatory phonetics), how they are perceived (auditory phonetics), and what their physical properties are (acoustic phonetics).

phonemic segmentation: the process of sequentially isolating the speech sounds that comprise a spoken word or syllable.

phonics: a teaching approach that gives attention to letter-sound correspondences in the teaching of reading and spelling. Phonics is a teaching approach and should not be confused with **phonetics.**

phonogram: a term often used in Orton-Gillingham teaching in lieu of **grapheme.**

phonology: the sound system of a language; the part of a grammar which includes the inventory of sounds and rules for their combination and pronunciation; the study of the sound systems of all languages.

plosive: a speech sound that is made by stopping the airstream and then suddenly releasing it from the mouth, so-called because it "explodes" with its release.

practicum: a course of study and guided practice used specifically for instructing prospective teachers and clinicians. It involves supervised practical application of theories that practitioners have been learning, taught one on one.

pragmatics: the study of how context influences the interpretation of meaning.

prefix: a letter or group of letters added to the beginning of a base word or root, e.g., untie, immoral. See **affix.**

prosody: the study of the stress and intonation patterns which convey meaning in spoken language.

r-controlled syllable: a syllable which contains a vowel followed by an r. The r is said to "control" the vowel sound, i.e., to produce its own special vowel sound which is neither long nor short, e.g., her, bird, doctor, hair, surf.

reading: a complex process in which a reader brings **graphic, phonological, orthographic, semantic,** and **syntactic** knowledge to bear on written and printed material in order to understand the meaning the writer is trying to convey through the written words.

regular words: words whose spelling or pronunication can be correctly produced by applying the knowledge of sound/symbol correspondences and relevant spelling patterns.

root: the basic element of a word to which a **prefix** or **suffix** may be **affix**ed; sometimes called a base word or a stem, e.g., re<u>make</u>, dis<u>tract</u>, pre<u>vent</u>. It may or may not be a full English word.

schwa: the vowel sound in an unstressed syllable, e.g., the first sound in <u>ago</u>. It approximates /u/ and can be represented by any vowel and some diphthongs. It is represented in most dictionaries by the inverted <u>e</u> (ə).

semantics: the study of the linguistic meaning of words and sentences.

short-term memory: memory that lasts only briefly, has rapid input and output, and is limited in capacity. In the area of language, short-term memory functions to store and process language-related information temporarily. Some part of this information may go on to storage in long-term memory; if not, it is lost.

short vowel: a vocalic sound. The common vowel letters in the alphabet each represent at least two sounds. In **phonics** programs, these are called **short** and **long** vowel sounds. The short sound typically is found in an **accented closed syllable,** e.g., the <u>a</u> in <u>apple</u>, the <u>e</u> in <u>eddy</u>, the <u>i</u> in <u>itchy</u>, the <u>o</u> in <u>octopus</u>, and the <u>u</u> in <u>upper</u>.

silent <u>e</u>: In most English words ending with the letter <u>e</u>, the <u>e</u> represents no sound itself. It may function as a diacritical mark letter which alerts the reader to something special about another letter in the word. For example, the <u>e</u> in the silent-<u>e</u> syllable signals that the vowel in the word is long, as in the word <u>gate</u>. When it follows <u>c</u> and <u>g</u>, it signals that these consonants represent the "soft sounds," as in <u>ice</u> and <u>age</u>. A silent <u>e</u> regularly follows <u>v</u> in the final position, e.g., <u>have</u> and <u>nerve</u>.

S.O.S. (Simultaneous Oral and written Spelling): a technique for establishing visual-auditory-kinesthetic associations to create a linkage of sound with letter form and to impress letter sequence.

spelling: the conversion of the separate speech sounds of words or syllables into their letter names (oral spelling) or into their corresponding **graphemes** (written spelling).

standardized achievement test: provides measures for an individual which can be compared to the performances (norms) of a larger group using techniques of statistical inference.

stop: a sound in which the airstream is briefly but completely stopped in the oral cavity. Voiceless stops are /p/, /t/, /k/ and voiced are /b/, /d/, /g/.

strephosymbolia: "twisted symbols"; a term invented by Dr. Orton to describe sensory confusion (reversals, mirror-writing, etc.).

syllable: a word or part of a word that has, as its core, a single vowel sound. There are different kinds of syllables; knowledge of them can help students learn to spell and read.

syllable division: the process of breaking multisyllabic words into separate syllables in order to decode and encode.

syllable types: in the Orton-Gillingham approach, there are six types of syllables. Identifying the kind of syllable provides the clue to determine the sound which the vowel letter in the syllable represents. The six types of syllables are closed, open, vowel-consonant-silent <u>e</u>, r-controlled, consonant-le, and diphthong/vowel digraph. Some Orton-Gillingham teachers divide the last into two separate syllables: diphthong and vowel digraph syllables.

syntax: the rules of sentence formation.

therapeutic environment: refers to the total learning environment to be established by the clinician or teacher, in accordance with established psychological or clinical protocols, which fosters healing and promotes cognitive, emotional, and social growth.

visual memory: involves the encoding, storage, and retrieval of visually presented information.

visual discrimination: assuming normal visual acuity, the ability to distinguish slight differences in visual stimuli, especially in letters and words that have graphic similarities.

visualization: a teaching technique to increase reading comprehension by teaching readers to form images or pictures in their minds to help retain the important points of a passage.

voiced sounds: speech sounds which involve the vibration of the vocal cords during the production.

voiceless sounds: a consonant sound made without vibrating the vocal cords. The unvoiced consonant sounds often have **voiced** equivalents, that is, the mouth position is the same for both, e.g., /p/ (unvoiced) and /b/ (voiced).

vowel: letters of the alphabet whose sounds are **voiced, open,** and unobstructed. In English the vowel letters are <u>a</u>, <u>e</u>, <u>i</u>, <u>o</u>, <u>u</u>, and sometimes <u>y</u>. Each vowel letter has a short and long sound. The <u>w</u> also functions as a vowel in combination with a vowel letter, as in <u>aw</u> (<u>saw</u>), <u>ew</u> (<u>grew</u>), and <u>ow</u> (<u>snow</u>). Vowels pair up to form **diphthongs** (<u>oi</u> in <u>coin</u>, <u>oy</u> in <u>toy</u>, <u>ou</u> in <u>out</u>) and vowel teams (see **vowel digraph**) or vowel pairs, e.g., <u>ee</u> in <u>feed</u>, <u>oa</u> in <u>boat</u>.

vowel digraph (vowel team, vowel pair): two adjacent vowel letters in a single syllable which represent a single long sound, such as <u>ea</u> in <u>eat</u>, <u>ue</u> in <u>argue</u>, <u>oa</u> in <u>boat</u>.

Index

Letters to Sounds (*continued*)

p	/p/	pan	33
ph	/f/	phone	68, 189
	Word lists		68, 190
qu	/kw/	queen	69
	Word list		69
r	/r/	rat	42
s	/s/	snake	43, 70, 190–191
	/z/	nose	70, 194
	Word lists		43, 70, 192–193
	See Spelling Patterns #1, #6		45, 130, 145
sh	/sh/	ship	43, 201
	Word lists		43, 201
	See Spelling Pattern #6		145
sion	/chən/	expansion	84, 188
	/shən/	mission	84, 201, 203
	/zhən/	television	84, 207
	Word lists		84, 202, 206, 207, 208
t	/t/	top	31, 33, 38, 39, 200
	/t/	tot	200
	Word list		200
tch	/ch/	catch	83, 188
	Word lists		83, 188
th	/th/	this	43, 83
	/th/	thumb	83
	Word lists		43, 83
tial	/shəl/	martial	202
tion	/chən/	attention	84, 188
	/shən/	station	84, 201, 202
	Word lists		84, 202, 205
u	/ə/	upper	43, 72, 112
	/yü/	mule	49
	/yü/	music	72, 262
	/ü/	rule	49, 256
	/ü/	ruby	256
	Word lists		43, 257, 259, 261, 264–266
	Ratio chart		262
ue	/yü/	rescue	93, 262
	/yü/	mule	262
	/ü/	true	88, 256
	Word lists		88, 93, 257, 259, 261, 264–267
	Ratio chart		262
ur	/ər/	burn	82, 221
	Word lists		82, 223
us	/əs/	circus	213
v	/v/	van	44
	Word list		44

M

N

O

P

W

PRONUNCIATION SYMBOLS

ə .... banana, collide, abut

ˈə, ˌə .... humdrum, abut

ə .... immediately preceding \l\, \n\, \m\, \ŋ\, as in battle, mitten, eaten, and sometimes open \ˈō-pᵊn\, lock and key \-ᵊŋ-\; immediately following \l\, \m\, \r\, as often in French table, prisme, titre

ər .... further, merger, bird

ˈər-⎫
       ⎬ .... as in two different pronunciations
ˈə-r ⎭   of hurry \ˈhər-ē, ˈhə-rē\

a .... mat, map, mad, gag, snap, patch

ā .... day, lade, date, aorta, drape, cape

ä .... bother, cot, and, with most American speakers, father, cart

à .... father as pronounced by speakers who do not rhyme it with *bother*; French patte

aù .... now, loud, out

b .... baby, rib

ch .... chin, nature \ˈnā-chər\ (actually, this sound is \t\ + \sh\)

d .... did, adder

e .... bet, bed, peck

ˈē, ˌē .... beat, nosebleed, evenly, easy

ē .... easy, mealy

f .... fifty, cuff

g .... go, big, gift

h .... hat, ahead

hw .... whale as pronounced by those who do not have the same pronunciation for both *whale* and *wail*

i .... tip, banish, active

ī .... site, side, buy, tripe (actually, this sound is \ä\ + \i\, or \à\ + \i\)

j .... job, gem, edge, join, judge (actually, this sound is \d\ + \zh\)

k .... kin, cook, ache

ḵ .... German ich, Buch; one pronunciation of loch

l .... lily, pool

m .... murmur, dim, nymph

n .... no, own

ⁿ .... indicates that a preceding vowel or diphthong is pronounced with the nasal passages open, as in French *un bon vin blanc* \œⁿ -bōⁿ -vaⁿ -bläⁿ\

ŋ .... sing \ˈsiŋ\, singer \ˈsiŋ-ər\, finger \ˈfiŋ-gər\, ink \ˈiŋk\

ō .... bone, know, beau

ȯ .... saw, all, gnaw, caught

œ .... French boeuf, German Hölle

Œ .... French feu, German Höhle

ȯi .... coin, destroy

p .... pepper, lip

r .... red, car, rarity

s .... source, less

sh .... as in shy, mission, machine, special (actually, this is a single sound, not two); with a hyphen between, two sounds as in *grasshopper* \ˈgras₁hä-pər\

t .... tie, attack, late, later, latter

th .... as in thin, ether (actually, this is a single sound, not two); with a hyphen between, two sounds as in *knighthood* \ˈnīt-₁hùd\

th̲ .... then, either, this (actually, this is a single sound, not two)

ü .... rule, youth, union \ˈyün-yən\, few \ˈfyü\

ù .... pull, wood, book, curable \ˈkyùr-ə-bəl\, fury \ˈfyù(ə)r-ē\

ue .... German füllen, hübsch

ūē .... French rue, German fühlen

v .... vivid, give

w .... we, away

y .... yard, young, cue \ˈkyü\, mute \ˈmyüt\, union \ˈyün-yən\

ʸ .... indicates that during the articulation of the sound represented by the preceding character the front of the tongue has substantially the position it has for the articulation of the first sound of *yard*, as in French *digne* \dēnʸ\

z .... zone, raise

zh .... as in vision, azure \ˈa-zhər\ (actually, this is a single sound, not two); with a hyphen between, two sounds as in *hogshead* \ˈhȯgz-₁hed, ˈhägz-\

\ .... slant line used in pairs to mark the beginning and end of a transcription: \ˈpen\

ˈ .... mark preceding a syllable with primary (strongest) stress: \ˈpen-mən-₁ship\

ˌ .... mark preceding a syllable with secondary (medium) stress: \ˈpen-mən-₁ship\

- .... mark of syllable division

( ) .... indicate that what is symbolized between is present in some utterances but not in others: *factory* \ˈfak-t(ə-)rē\

÷ .... indicates that many regard as unacceptable the pronunciation variant immediately following: *cupola* \ˈkyü-pə-lə, ÷-lō\

The system of indicating pronunciation is used by permission. From Merriam-Webster's Collegiate® Dictionary, Tenth Edition ©1996 by Merriam-Webster Inc.

DATE DUE

AUG - - 2016